HOW **RUSSIA** SHAPED

THE **MODERN WORLD**

HOW **RUSSIA** SHAPED

THE **MODERN WORLD**

From Art to Anti-Semitism,

Ballet to Bolshevism

Steven G. Marks

PRINCETON UNIVERSITY PRESS

PRINCETON AND OXFORD

7-23-2003
LAN
+29.95

Library of Congress Cataloging-in-Publication Data

Marks, Steven G. (Steven Gary), 1958–

How Russia shaped the modern world : from art to anti-semitism, ballet to bolshevism / Steven G. Marks

p. cm.

Includes bibliographical references and index.

ISBN 0-691-09684-8 (alk. paper)

1. Russia—Civilization—1801–1917. 2. Soviet Union—Civilization. 3. Civilization, Modern—Russian influences. I. Title.

DK32 .M274 2003

947'.07—dc21   2002016908

British Library Cataloging-in-Publication Data is available

This book has been composed in Sabon typeface
Printed on acid-free paper. ∞

www.pupress.princeton.edu

Printed in the United States of America

10 9 8 7 6 5 4 3 2 1

TO **ELISA**

AND **JULIA**

CONTENTS

ILLUSTRATIONS

ACKNOWLEDGMENTS

IF THIS BOOK has any merits, they are in no small measure due to the people I relied on for help in writing it.

For advice, assistance, and encouragement, I thank Joe Arbena, Stephanie Barczewski, William C. Brumfield, Paul Curry, Steven Grosby, Alan Grubb, Patricia Herlihy, Tom Kuehn, the late Bruce Lincoln, David Nicholas, Alan Schaffer, and Dietmar Wulff.

I am very grateful to the many scholars and friends who read parts of the manuscript in their areas of expertise and saved me from many errors: Paul Anderson, Mark Bassin, James Burns, Jonathan Daly, Cesare G. De Michelis, Joseph Frank, John Fuegi, Abbott Gleason, Roger Grant, Michael Hagemeister, Gordon Horwitz, Lance Howard, John D. Klier, Donald McKale, James Miller, Edwin Moise, Carmi Neiger, Michael Silvestri, John Stephan, Melissa Stockdale, and William Mills Todd III.

I am deeply indebted to Caryl Emerson, Aviel Roshwald, and Richard Stites for reading the entire manuscript and offering vital suggestions to improve the text and correct misinterpretations.

My editor, Brigitta van Rheinberg, deserves special thanks for her enthusiastic endorsement of the book and the insightful advice that guided its revision. Lauren Lepow's expert copyediting put the finishing touches to the text.

It is a pleasure to acknowledge several individuals for their particular contributions to the book. My former department chair, Roger Grant, created an ideal working environment. Alan Grubb took the photographs. Jens Holley and the staff at the Clemson University Interlibrary Loan Office delivered hundreds of sources from the libraries of the world, which enabled me to write the book within sight of the lush woods outside my window. My sister, Phyllis Mentser, gave me a computer. My former professor, the late André de Saint-Rat, whom I greatly miss, shared his collection of Russian avant-garde art with me over the twenty-five years of our friendship.

Most important, I thank my wife, Cindy, who tolerated my preoccupation with the book and bent over backward to make sure that I finished it.

HOW **RUSSIA** SHAPED

THE **MODERN WORLD**

PROLOGUE

IN 1985, Mikhail Gorbachev became Communist Party boss of the Soviet Union. Intent on revitalizing the economically stagnating superpower, he introduced unprecedented liberalizing reforms that, among other things, curtailed the powers of the KGB and the central state planning agency. But the treatments he administered to his debilitated patient were as harmful as the disease. He could not arrest the political and economic unraveling that ensued, and by 1992 Communist Russia and its empire had expired.

It was just over seven decades earlier that the Soviet Union's predecessor state had collapsed. Like the USSR, imperial Russia was considered one of the great European military powers. But if ossification was the challenge Gorbachev initially faced, Tsar Nicholas II had to contend with a society that was changing so fast he could not keep pace. Russia was an impoverished, rural nation undergoing industrialization and urbanization at the same time that its political system remained rigidly autocratic. The tsar and his court were reactionary and unimaginative in their responses to the challenges of the times. Modern war proved fatal to them. Amid military defeat and popular uprisings, imperial Russia came crashing down in the revolution of February 1917.

The plight of Russia in these two eras eventually gave rise to the impression that it was an anachronistic monolith incapable of thriving in a world dominated by European and American technology and democratic ideals. This may well seem true if we consider Russia's material condition or the many ordeals suffered by its citizenry. Yet both the tsarist empire and the Soviet Union exerted a significant impact on the world between the 1880s and the 1980s through the power of political and cultural ideas generated there.

It was Russia that gave birth to the basic methodologies of modern terrorism as well as a venomous new form of anti-Semitism that proved to have potent effect in post–World War I Germany and elsewhere. Russian thought had a formative influence on Gandhism in India, the African American civil rights struggle, and contemporary environmental movements. Russia was the setting for remarkable innovations in art, literature, ballet, and theater that transformed the cultural life of the entire world. And its communist regime provided techniques of dictatorship on which Hitler, Mussolini, and many Third World leaders drew.

How could a nation so troubled that it imploded twice in less than a hundred years produce ideas that swayed much of the globe? It was precisely because of its seeming divergence from the path followed by England, France, or America that it did. The image of Russia as a collectivist, agrarian society, the autocratic policies of its governments, and the radicalism of its intelligentsia all suggested that here was a culture far removed from Western ideals. These were the perceptions outsiders held of the country, but Russian thinkers also offered compelling critiques of what we call Western modernity, with its representative government, capitalist economics, and primacy of the consumer-oriented middle class in an urban-industrial society. Many of the world's angry and alienated intellectuals blamed oppression, poverty, and the ills of earthly existence on the all-powerful but deeply resented West. For them, Russia became the symbol of resistance to Western civilization itself.

These sentiments arose in reaction to the effects of the Western program of modernization. For better or worse, by the late nineteenth century, liberalism, capitalism, and imperialism were tearing world societies away from their traditional moorings. The wrenching social disruptions accompanying industrialization and urbanization resulted in existential shock and disorientation for some segments of the population, inside as well as outside the West. In southern and eastern Europe, as in the Third World, integration into the global economy uprooted old agrarian patterns of life. From the Gilded Age on, the small-town, rural United States was forged into a nation of big cities and big business. In western Europe, too, socioeconomic developments were jarring, further compounded by the devastation of World War I. "Modern man," wrote Martin Buber, had "lost the feeling of being at home in the world."[1]

Buber's statement cannot be applied to the supporters of the process, but in those times of unprecedented change, some who benefited materially from modernization felt spiritually disquieted by it. Between them and the people it marginalized, the number of disaffected people grew. Many were looking to cast off the liberal-capitalist Western system and found hope in extremist politics and irrationalist philosophies. Vocal and rebellious countercultures emerged in Europe, America, and Japan seeking to undermine the dominant ideologies and governments. Africans and Asians, chafing under the subjugation of colonial rule, sought new political and economic models as they stepped up the struggle for independence. Writers and artists, disillusioned with the materialism and rationalism of progress-bedazzled capitalist society, conveyed their discontent through the experiments of the Modernist movement— a paradoxical name for what were antimodern cultural rebels. All were attracted to the novel intellectual currents radiating out of Russia and offering alternatives to Western power and values.

These currents had originated in the first half of the nineteenth century, but grew stronger as Russia became one of the first non-Western nations to undertake a conscious effort at state-led industrialization. Intent on stimulating industrial growth in order to maintain military parity with France and England, the tsarist government had launched Russia on a course of unrelenting social transformation. Beginning in the 1860s, serfdom was abolished, and this overwhelmingly rural, early "developing nation" experienced industrial booms and stock market busts, a communications revolution with the expansion of railroads and print media, and the formation of urban slums crowded with peasant migrants seeking work in factories and shops. Many Russian observers sensed that these changes had come or would come too abruptly and were far more alien and destructive than they had been in western Europe, where industrialization had occurred more gradually and spontaneously, despite severe negative side effects. The escalating problems that came in the wake of tsarist modernization, combined with the regime's determination to maintain its monopoly on political power, stimulated the Russian intelligentsia to conceive radical solutions to the country's woes.

The nature of those solutions reflected the estrangement of the intelligentsia from both the government and the larger society. The intelligentsia was isolated from the tsar's autocratic regime with its corrupt and repressive bureaucracy, but equally distant from the Russian peasant masses in their primitive rural villages. Owing to their Europeanized upbringing and education, the members of the intelligentsia lamented (and sometimes romanticized) Russia's shortcomings. They committed themselves to the country's renovation, but being excluded from full participation within the political system, many of them rejected existing authority, sought refuge in the realm of ideas, and took solace in revolutionary and utopian schemes. Their frustrations, anguish, and, in some cases, messianic hopes were channeled into distinctive ideas about culture, politics, and economics that magnetized similarly uprooted, alienated, anti-Western individuals all around the world from the 1880s into the 1980s.

Although Russia's intellectual elite was part of a broad European culture, there was a perception of tsarist Russian and Soviet thought as Eastern and exotic, which made it especially appealing beyond the empire's borders. This was a strain of "Orientalism" that was embraced as an antidote to modern civilization. Some European and American intellectuals imagined Asia—which, they believed, included Russia—to be the source of wisdom and renewal. For them the "Russian soul" betokened a higher form of truth. Well before the communist revolution of 1917, Russian society and culture had acquired special status as a spiritual haven in the minds of many foreigners. In its desperate poverty and blissful ignorance of the bickering of parliamentary politics, Russia seemed all the more saintly and removed from the crassness and corruption of the capitalist West. Third World intellectuals, reacting to their own countries' traumas in the throes of modernization or imperialism, were similarly attracted to Russian culture and ideology. They, too, perceived Russia, despite a thin European veneer, as being non-Western, and thus close in spirit to their own experiences.

Although the Russian intelligentsia's ideas were often utopian, they acted as beacons for many modern thinkers, artists, and political extremists as they sought a better world than the one that existed. Russia was not the only such beacon, but the most influential of Russia's thinkers spread their nation's unique intellectual legacy globally and played an integral part in the antimodern and anti-Western forces that have had a constant presence in the last hundred years. This book was written as an attempt to reveal this little-appreciated dimension of modern history.

Readers should take note of the book's limitations and specific objectives. This is a synthesis intended for a broad readership and is structured with that audience in mind. Each chapter begins with an introduction to the Russian figures or movements at issue and continues with an examination of their international reception in both the West and the non-Western world. I make no pretense of breaking new ground on every topic. In some cases my interpretations are original and differ from established views, while in others they conform with them. As a result, the work relies on primary and secondary sources in varying measures. For topics that might be controversial or little known, I have made more extensive reference to original sources and where necessary added brief historiographical commentary.

Additionally, I have not attempted to be comprehensive in coverage. I make little or no mention, for instance, of writer Maxim Gorky, filmmaker Sergei Eisenstein, philosopher Nicolas Berdyaev, and many others. My reasoning was that these figures had a more limited impact than the ones I do treat, but in any case in a one-volume book I could not include everyone who was relevant. I also do not deal here with Russian scientists. No full assessment of Russia's intellectual history can be complete without reference to them, but they do not belong in a book whose purpose is to illuminate the Russian influence on anti-Western, antimodern trends in recent history.

In developing this theme, I do not wish to denigrate the enormous role played by American and western European ideas in the world or imperial Russia's receptivity to European thought. But in order to highlight the cultural movement in the other direction, from Russia outward, I have had to differentiate Russian from European ideas and to emphasize the unique qualities of the former. No one should assume, however, that I believe Russian intellectual life developed in anything but a close and symbiotic relationship with that of the West.

A few words are also necessary about my approach to the problem of tracing intellectual or cultural influence. I have striven to avoid examples of coincidental similarity in ideas or cultural creations, and to restrict myself to claims of influence for which there is adequate evidence. I am not arguing, furthermore, that Russian thinkers were always the causal or sole determining factors in other intellectual movements. My point is that the Russians *shaped* ideas, sometimes fundamentally and sometimes less so, but in either case sufficiently that drawing attention to the process sheds new light on critical aspects of twentieth-century history. For as will become apparent, Russian thought has had a profound effect on the course of modern history.

Organizing Revolution:

The Russian Terrorists

ANARCHISM was the first Russian intellectual movement to have a significant international impact. Its glorious promises for society's future electrified followers around the world, and the organizational and killing methods developed by its Russian revolutionary adherents to fight the tsarist regime marked the birth of modern terrorism.

Anarchism was a branch of socialism that arose in mid-nineteenth-century France and England as a combined legacy of the Enlightenment belief in the perfectibility of humankind and the Romantic fervor for noble savages and stormy rebelliousness. It stood against the European state, whose powers had grown tremendously in recent decades, and against bourgeois industrialism, the ills of which were often, in the beginning, more apparent than the benefits.[1]

Given the overbearing power of the tsarist state and the sudden encroachments of capitalism, Russia's intellectuals were naturally receptive to European ideas like anarchism, and in fact Russians became the acknowledged leaders of the international anarchist movement as it developed after the 1860s. These radicals transformed anarchist thought from a philosophy dreamed up by a few eccentric western Europeans into a strategy of revolutionary action. Their anarchism was a form of underground political warfare that battled to destroy the existing political-economic system and prepare the ground for a new egalitarian era in human existence.

The methods they devised were imitated and adapted around the world, making Russian revolutionary practice a global phenomenon well before the appearance of Bolshevism.

"The passion for destruction"

The most internationally prominent Russian revolutionary was the anarchist leader and rival of Karl Marx, Mikhail Bakunin (1814–1876), who should be regarded as one of the fathers of modern terrorism, as he was known at the turn of the nineteenth century.[2] As a young man, this wealthy nobleman had renounced his elevated status and devoted his life to the cause of revolution. From the 1840s to the 1870s, when not detained in the dungeons of eastern Europe, Bakunin exhorted zealously radical audiences to action in France, the Germanies, Italy, Poland, and Switzerland. He threw himself into their uprisings, often fighting on the barricades himself in Breslau (1848), Prague (1848), Dresden (1849), Chemnitz (1849), Lyons (1871), and Bologna (1874).

Or that was the image he cultivated. The reality was somewhat different. An unscrupulous egotist, Bakunin wanted to be considered the sole leader of world revolution and fantasized wildly about his revolutionary activity. This "Romantic dilettante" egged on the street fighters and was quick to preach revolutionary violence, but flitting from revolt to revolt, he fired only a few shots at best.[3] He was more a radical celebrity than an active participant. And his theoretical tracts were illogical, clichéd, and semicoherent. Full of "fire and imagination, violence and poetry," their mood was more important than their philosophical content, which was far inferior to the prodigious work of his nemesis Marx.[4]

Bakunin and most Russian anarchists were atheists. Yet Russian revolutionary ideas were infused with spiritual yearning and secular ideological substitutes for religiosity. It is not surprising that these elements should have remained so strong, given the emphases of contemporaneous European Romanticism and the centrality of Orthodox Christianity in Russian culture. Religious messianism was transferred to the revolutionary movement, a process Bakunin embodied. Philosophy was for him a substitute for religion, and never in his career did he refrain from speaking of the Absolute or from using quasi-mystical language. His whole life was a search for inner harmony and what he supposed to be the lost unity of mankind. He was convinced that his own existence was part of a cosmic plan, that he was destined to remake the earth along the lines of the Kingdom of Heaven.

Like many of his intelligentsia contemporaries, Bakunin believed that Russia would be the salvation of the world. Russia to him was the guiding star for all mankind: "In Moscow from a sea of blood and flame the constellation of the revolution will rise, high and beautiful, and will become the guiding star for the good of all liber-

1. Mikhail Bakunin. From Bakunin, *God and the State* (New York, 1970).

ated mankind."[5] Portraying himself as a barbarian from the savage East fighting for the liberation of humanity, he preached Russia's radical mission in Europe, where the number of proselytes grew steadily larger: in the age of Romantic-inspired exoticism and Orientalism, his appeal was enormous.

Bakunin's messianism was centered on the peasantry. Like many of his Russian intelligentsia contemporaries, Bakunin worshiped the peasant masses as the vessels of the Absolute. Having absorbed European Romantic notions of the noble savage and the rebellious spirit, he was convinced that in Russia and elsewhere they were ripe for revolt against contemporary civilization. He also saw bloodthirsty bandits as subconscious revolutionaries and assumed that urban riffraff and economically threatened craftsmen would play a large role in the coming revolution. They would all be led by the déclassé intellectuals of preindustrial nations, who were, unlike their comfortable Western counterparts, "unwashed" and full of revolutionary vigor.

Bakunin's call for violent peasant uprising was a far cry from Marxism, which by and large focused on the urban working class and expected that the revolution would come first in the advanced industrial regions of Europe. Bakunin had a prophetic understanding that the great revolutions of the modern era would come from the lower depths of what we would call underdeveloped, but proto-capitalist societies. His emphases on the revolutionary spontaneity of peasants and the urban rabble gained him a large following in the agrarian southern periphery of western Europe as well as throughout Latin America.

Everywhere, though, the non-Marxist left was attracted to Bakunin's attacks on government in defense of freedom. In his apocalyptic anarchist vision, once the destruction of the modern state took place, paradise would appear on the ruins, "a new heaven and a new earth, a young and magnificent world in which all our present discords will resolve themselves. . . . Let us . . . trust the eternal Spirit which destroys and annihilates only because it is the unfathomable and eternally creative source of all life. The passion for destruction is a creative passion, too."[6] With these expectations he declared war against all centralized governments, whether de-

mocracies or monarchies. And he vilified Marx's concept of a dictatorship of the proletariat "because it concentrates the strength of
society in the state, . . . whereas my principle is the abolition of
the state, which has perpetually enslaved, exploited, and depraved
mankind under the pretext of making it moral and civilized."[7]

Curiously, Bakunin, whose fame as an anarchist rests on his
struggle to shield the freedom of the individual from the depredations of big government, was a closet authoritarian. Bakunin talked
extensively about "absolute liberty" and the rejection of all authority, but this meant all authority except the one he wanted to create.
At the same time that he wrote *Statism and Anarchy*, an unfinished
work on the philosophy of liberty, he was writing private letters
arguing for the necessity of a dictatorship to organize the future
anarchist communal society.

How do we reconcile the apparent contradictions in Bakunin,
the defense of individualism and liberty on the one hand and the
belief in the necessity of dictatorship on the other? By "freedom"
Bakunin meant not what Western liberals understood it to be—the
condition resulting from legal limits that curtailed the intrusiveness
of government—but rather something akin to spiritual freedom
and universal wholeness. This was a mystical notion derived from
both Russian Orthodox metaphysics and the Romantic-era assumption that all men partook of the Absolute. It required not the
preservation of individualism but rather its *total dissolution* in a
collective form of unity that would free humankind from the suffering brought on by the selfish competitiveness of the capitalist bourgeoisie. In his vision, human liberation would come about only
after a revolutionary elite seized power through its secret organization and established a dictatorship to force people to accept a new
egalitarian social order.

He developed these conspiratorial notions in the second phase
of his career. For his participation in the 1848 revolutions, he spent
more than ten years in captivity in Saxony, Austria, and, finally,
Russia. But in 1861 he escaped from Siberian exile, crossed the
United States, and returned to Europe. Living as a fugitive in Switzerland, he came into contact with young Russian radicals, among
them Sergei Nechaev, with whom between 1869 and 1871 he devel-

oped behavioral guidelines for the professional revolutionary cell. These had a major impact on modern politics, by providing rudimentary principles for the world's first organized terrorist movements.

Nechaev was born in 1847, the son of a house-painter.[8] He cultivated a resentment of cultured society in his provincial town and was inspired by Bakunin's writings to enter the growing Russian radical movement. He became a fanatical ascetic, living on bread and milk and sleeping on the bare floor. He developed conspiratorial ideas drawing on Russian and French revolutionary sources, including the theories of the Russian Jacobin, Pyotr Tkachëv. On a visit to Switzerland, Nechaev conned Bakunin into believing that he was the head of a revolutionary organization with hundreds of members. To impress Nechaev, Bakunin boasted of leading the World Revolutionary Alliance, which despite Bakunin's intimations had at the time exactly two members—Bakunin and Nechaev.

Nechaev returned to Russia as an agent of this "organization" with instructions to form a Moscow branch. There he encountered a student named Ivanov who expressed doubts about Nechaev's credentials. To exact the total obedience he expected of the other

2. Sergei Nechaev. From *Katorga i ssylka*, no. 14 (1925).

members he had recruited, Nechaev induced them to collaborate in Ivanov's murder, falsely claiming he was a police spy. The deed was done in November 1869, and the body was dumped into an ice-covered pond, the whole episode forming the basis for Dostoevsky's antirevolutionary novel, *Devils*. All of the perpetrators were caught but Nechaev, who escaped back to Switzerland. In 1872, he was arrested there and deported back to Russia, where ten years later he died of scurvy in prison.

In tandem with Bakunin, Nechaev has left a mark on history through the fruit of their collaboration, the "Catechism of a Revolutionary." The Catechism was written by the two of them in Geneva in the summer of 1869. It consists of twenty-six commands on revolutionary organization, behavior, and commitment. According to its commands, members of the conspiracy are grouped in cells and are to carry out assigned tasks obediently. An adherent must sacrifice traditional morality, family ties, and, if need be, his own life for the revolution. "He is not a revolutionary if he feels compassion for something in this world." He assumes a normal existence to conceal his true identity, but he must be dedicated to the total destruction of corrupt, civilized society. "Day and night he should have only a single thought, a single aim: pitiless destruction."[9]

Although some of these elements were evident in earlier nineteenth-century Russian, French, and Italian revolutionary thought, the Catechism marked a step toward the systematization of revolutionary conspiracy. Together, Bakunin and Nechaev established the terrorists' creed and suggested the organizational means to kill in the name of a cause. Partly stimulated by Bakunin and Nechaev, terrorism was given its specific modern forms as a portion of the next generation of Russian radicals became converts to revolutionary conspiracy.

If Bakunin and Nechaev provided the ultra-radicals with the Catechism, Nikolai Chernyshevsky's novel, *What Is to Be Done?*, written in 1863, served as their Bible.[10] Chernyshevsky (1828–1889) was the son of a parish priest in Saratov on the Volga River and a graduate of a theological seminary. Attracted to socialism, he ended his theological studies and moved to St. Petersburg, where by the late 1850s he had become a prominent literary critic and revolutionary publicist. He was arrested in 1862 for his connection to radical organizations and spent seven years at hard labor and thirteen additional years in exile in Siberia, all of which lent him the aura of a martyr. In the words of the terrorist Nikolai Ishutin, "there have been three great men in the world: Jesus Christ, Paul the Apostle, and Chernyshevsky."[11]

While he saw himself primarily as a social and literary critic, he also earned his reputation from *What Is to Be Done?*, written while he was incarcerated. The novel featured heroes Vera Pavlovna and Rakhmetov, who came to be seen as prototypes of the new man and new woman. Although recent scholarship shows that Rakhmetov was intended as a minor, negative character, through him the book unintentionally provided a model of a disciplined, fanatical revolutionary. Rakhmetov sleeps on a bed of nails and renounces relations with women. He disdains good manners and male dominance as products of an artificial civilization. Many readers thought Rakhmetov peculiar, as the author meant him to appear, but some extremists admired him as the ideal revolutionary, who lives in a commune, is morally perfect, and offers devotion not to God but to science, equality, and socialism. More central to the novel was the female protagonist, Vera Pavlovna, who escapes her oppressive life by means of a fictitious marriage, then establishes a sewing co-op and becomes a political activist. She is a Nihilist who stands for wiping the slate of culture and politics clean and is dedicated to working for social improvement, but she also has room for personal fulfillment through love.

The effect was the opposite of what Chernyshevsky expected from a book that ridiculed utopianism. *What Is to Be Done?* had a dramatic impact on the Russian intelligentsia. Whether they called themselves Nihilists, Populists (Narodniki—from *narod*, Russian for "the people"), anarchists, or Marxists, succeeding generations of radical youth attempted to conform with their perceptions of Chernyshevsky's characters. A newspaper in 1864 described female Nihilists: "Most [of them] . . . dress in impossibly filthy fashion, rarely wash their hands, . . . always cut their hair, and sometimes even shave it off. . . . They read [materialist philosophers] exclusively, . . . live either alone or in [communes], and talk most of all about the exploitation of labor . . . [and] the silliness of marriage and family."[12]

Because of the impression it made on countless numbers of young Russians, it has been asserted that *What Is to be Done?* was the single most influential nineteenth-century Russian novel.[13] But its impact was not felt in Russia alone. It appeared in most European languages and was first translated into English in 1886 by the American anarchist Benjamin Tucker. It was kept alive in the United States and England by Jewish immigrants, many of whom were sympathetic to the revolutionary movement and some of whom accepted the book as sacred scripture. Two famous American radicals of Russian-Jewish origin, Emma Goldman and Alexander Berkman, were reared on it. Berkman assumed the name Rakhmetov when he stabbed the antiunion steel magnate Henry Clay Frick in Pittsburgh during the 1892 Homestead strike.[14] Those radicals in America, Europe, and elsewhere who affected Russian intelligentsia style were in part patterning themselves after the characters in Chernyshevsky's novel. That group includes subsequent female revolutionaries of the world, who emulated prototypes from the Russian radical movements.[15]

The writings of Chernyshevsky might have attracted less international attention if not for the concrete actions of Russian revolutionaries. As a result of growing impatience with ineffectual propaganda efforts to incite mass revolt, a segment of the Russian intelligentsia began to advocate terrorism. Assassinations and attacks had taken place in the late 1870s, including some spectacular but unsuccessful attempts on the life of Tsar Alexander II, but they were carried out by individuals operating as a minority faction within the main Populist party, Land and Freedom, many of whose members opposed terrorism. Neither that revolutionary group nor any of the others of the day was tightly run. But that began to change with the formation of the People's Will.

The People's Will (Narodnaia Volia) was the first professional terrorist-revolutionary organization of any size in Russia. It was formed in 1879 after some members of Land and Freedom became aware that assassination required rather sophisticated preparation.

Experience convinced them that tighter organization was necessary to enable them to make a more concerted fight against the government, which had cracked down in response to the spate of recent terrorist acts.

"Sheer Nechaev" was the way Vera Figner described the People's Will.[16] It was a militant, centralized, underground organization, the prototype of virtually all subsequent terrorist groups in the world. The party consisted of roughly twenty members at the apex of the pyramidal organization in an executive committee or "military organization" that soon came to be led by Andrei Zheliabov, and at most three to four hundred rank-and-file members. The executive committee was designed to be highly secretive, invisible, and inacessible to the membership so as to prevent police infiltration. Members were supposed to be divided into cells and to be kept ignorant of the workings of the party outside of those cells—only the executive committee was aware of the activities of all of its component parts. Special sections were established for the military, the provinces, the intelligentsia, and youth. In practice, the organization maintained neither secrecy nor a clearly defined cell structure, and the professionalization to which it aspired remained lacking. But the ideal was an inspiration to future revolutionaries.

The People's Will was more successful at experimenting with killing devices, advancing the methods of political murder through new bombing technologies. Technical experts in its ranks, such as Nikolai Kibalchich—son of a priest, former engineering student, and early theoretician of jet propulsion—quickly adopted the recent discoveries of Alfred Nobel for their own ends. Nobel had spent much of his youth in Russia and, for commercial purposes unconnected to his distaste for the Russian autocracy, developed nitroglycerine and dynamite. The People's Will was the first terrorist organization to deploy such weapons.[17] This was the fruit of modernization and the government's sponsorship of technological training—sometimes a dangerous proposition in repressive regimes.

Armed with its new "high-tech" weaponry, the People's Will issued a death sentence against Tsar Alexander II. The party's first attempts to carry out the sentence failed: they involved elaborate but mistimed preparations for mining the railroad tracks over which the tsar's train would travel from his summer palace in the Crimea back to the capital. The hunt for the "crowned game" finally succeeded on March 1, 1881, when Nikolai Rysakov and Ignat Hryniewicki lobbed handheld bombs at the emperor as the royal carriage passed over the Catherine Quay in the heart of St. Petersburg.[18] This tiny party with a handful of active members for a short time paralyzed one of the most powerful states in the world. But the assassination of the tsar backfired, as it initiated a period of reaction and an expanded police state during the reigns of Alexander III and Nicholas II.

Although the government crushed the People's Will, its legacy survived in Russia. For one, Lenin's Bolshevik Party drew on some of the organizational innovations of the People's Will.[19] To an even greater extent, so did the Socialist Revolutionary Party, which was responsible for numerous terrorist attacks in the first decade of the twentieth century. The SR Party was founded by People's Will survivors and divided into a mass organization and a terrorist organization, the former semiopen, the latter underground. Here the division of responsibilities was even more precisely delineated than in the People's Will. The SRs, as they were known, achieved a complete separation of functions, with the job of committing political murder left to professional assassins in the terrorist wing. But these "combatants" were difficult for the party leadership to manage, and their head, the infamous Evno Azev, was exposed in 1909 as a secret-police agent. Some were criminals who conveniently wrapped their activities in the cloak of revolution, and for many of the hit men, terror became a craft disconnected from political or moral concerns.[20]

The "Russian Method" Abroad

Russian revolutionary radicalism from Bakunin to the SR Party was the main origination point for world terrorism as well as various strains of anarchism in the late nineteenth and early twentieth centuries. This is not to say that it was the *cause* of terrorist activity abroad, but that the Russians inspired the adoption of new organizational forms and new methodologies of terrorism. What were the lines of transmission between Russian anarcho-terrorism and the world? The exploits of Bakunin, the People's Will, and their Socialist Revolutionary successors after 1902 were made known globally by means of Russian exiles, newspaper accounts, and popular books.

Firsthand knowledge of the Russian revolutionary movement spread with the thousands of people leaving Russia for abroad. Active revolutionaries fleeing from the law, members of the intelligentsia seeking political refuge, Jewish emigrants, and aristocrats on tour all spread word of Russian developments to the European continent, England, and the United States.[21] And also to Japan, its proximity to the penal colony of Siberia making it a common destination for radicals escaping exile. Russian Populists passed through Japan from the 1870s on, eventually establishing a colony in Nagasaki. Numerous revolutionary conspirators landed there, among them the assassin Grigory Gershuni and the future leader of independent Poland, Jozef Pilsudski. Those who sojourned in Japan helped to stimulate a contingent of Japanese radicals to opt for political violence.[22]

Newspapers spread the word farther afield. Numerous depictions of Russian terrorist attempts in the 1880s appeared in the *Illustrated London News* and elsewhere. The spectacular successes of the SRs, including the assassinations of the government ministers in charge of the hated secret police, D. S. Sipiagin and V. K. von Plehve, in 1902 and 1904, respectively, gained worldwide newspaper coverage.[23] French anarchist publications began to give instructions on bomb making along with editorial approbation.[24] Spanish terrorists responded to newspaper reports on the SR assassinations of 1904 with their own murder campaign.[25] In China, radical papers "told and retold" the story of the assassination of Alexander II for years.[26]

In India there was endless treatment in the English press, semiofficial Anglo-Indian newspapers, and Indian nationalist publications, each with a different reason for justifying Russian terrorism. The British press was anti-Russian because of the rivalry between

England and Russia for control of Central Asia, and it praised the Populists and SRs as heroes fighting for a just cause against a tyrannical autocracy. Little did English journalists in India comprehend the lessons they were helping to teach: the nationalist press gave what it called the "Russian method" extensive attention and began to urge its application against the tyranny of the Raj. Beyond this, the newspaper accounts prepared the ground for widespread sympathy on the part of Indians toward anti-Western ideas emanating from Russia.[27]

Books were the main medium for the spread of knowledge about Russian terrorism. The violence of the Russian Populists spawned a whole subgenre of literature, which expressed the fascination and fear of the public and also publicized terrorist techniques and organizational configurations. The first Russian writer to enjoy an international reputation was Ivan Turgenev (1818–1883), who lived in Europe much of his life and became intimate with Flaubert and other European cultural figures. Turgenev's novels—among them *Fathers and Sons* (1862) and *Virgin Soil* (1877)—were among the earliest literary treatments of the Russian left intelligentsia and were well known abroad.

The revolutionaries themselves wrote some of the books, like the analysis of the intelligentsia written by Lev Tikhomirov, a founder of the People's Will who had recanted and joined the ranks of anti-Semitic monarchists. His volume *La Russie politique et sociale* was published in Paris in 1886 to great acclaim and helped form the French image of the Russian radical movement.[28] The most widely read and influential work by a revolutionary, though, was Stepniak's *Underground Russia*, a hagiography of the People's Will first published in Italian in 1882, then in English in 1883, and thereafter in the major European languages and Japanese. Stepniak (pseudonym of Sergei Kravchinsky), as the son of a military doctor and graduate of an artillery academy, was slated to become an officer in the tsar's army. His revolutionary credentials were impeccable. In 1876, at the age of twenty-four, he joined a Bosnian uprising against the Turks and on the basis of his experiences wrote a manual of guerrilla warfare. In 1877 he joined Italian Bakuninists in a revolutionary uprising near Naples. A year later in St. Petersburg, he stabbed to death General Nikolai Mezentsev, the chief of the Russian secret police. After that Stepniak escaped abroad and settled in London, where he publicized the cause of Russian dissent by cofounding an organization to promote sympathy for the Russian "freedom fighters." He wrote a novel about the revolutionaries, *Career of a Nihilist* (1889), contributed to the English press, and earned celebrity as a socialist socialite. He was hit by a train and died in 1895.[29]

From the 1880s on, publishers in the West and Asia followed Stepniak's lead. *Underground Russia* was one of the first Russian books to appear in translation in Japan, for instance, where it was a best-seller. Newspapers there gave full coverage to the activities of the Russian Populists, and between 1881 and 1883 alone sixty-five books dealing with Russian Nihilists were published in Japan; given the small size of the reading public, this indicates very strong interest in a society fascinated with Russia as a supposedly kindred nation that both emulated and resisted Westernization. Many of the Japanese books on the subject had a local twist, mistakenly equating Nihilism with the Buddhist or Taoist concepts of "nothingness." Others were sensationalized in the manner of a modern Gothic romance. Sophia Perovskaya and the terrorist Vera Zasulich were especially big heroes, dolled up to look aristocratic in illustrations for such titles as Tajima Shoji's *Stories from Europe about Women with a Purpose in Life* (!) or Somada Sakutaro's *Strange News from Russia about the Criminal Case of a Heroine.*[30]

In China the huge popularity of Russian terrorists was reflected in the productions of cheap popular fiction and nonfiction. Chinese fiction canonized Sophia Perovskaya, and an entire section of *Fiction Monthly* was for a time dedicated to stories of Russian radicals. Most Chinese books on Russia dealt with this topic, as in Japan, with little knowledge of the subject and with a Buddhist slant. One Chinese author had his Russian revolutionary character speak the following: "Nihilists, Nihilists! I love you, I worship you. Your undertakings are brilliant and glorious. You never fail to startle heaven and earth with your ability to kill those emperors (the damned bastards), to rescue the multitudes of your suffering brothers and sisters. The comrades of your party are diverse indeed—

beautiful women in disguise, young boys, and the most unusual stalwart men—but all are Bodhisattva redeemers."[31] Chinese works on the topic were romanticized, escapist fantasies infused with a fascination for Western technology that was to become an obsession for Third World elites later in the century: all the revolutionaries were scientists, and all of them used the latest technological gadgetry to rescue damsels in distress as much as to fight the autocracy.

This popular literature inspired some individual revolutionaries and helped to prepare public opinion to accept the attitude that violence could produce positive political change in China as well as remain morally pure—as it was supposed to have done among Russian revolutionaries. Even as late as the 1920s and 1930s, similar characters and themes appeared in China, most prominently in the works of the radical author Ba Jin, a pseudonym derived from a contraction of the names of the two revolutionaries he admired most, *Ba*kunin and Kropot*kin*. His immensely popular novels about Russian Populist terrorists provided young radical idealists in China with role models.[32]

In English and French, too, the terrorist theme was popular in fiction at the turn of the century, directly or indirectly referring to the example introduced by Russians. In France anarchist doctrine was known as much through fictional representation as through philosophical writings.[33] Russian radicals appeared in late-nineteenth-century French novels such as Émile Zola's *Germinal*, in which the terrorist is the Russian Souvarine, or in the work of Alphonse Daudet, the most widely read French author of the day. Daudet's most popular character was the comical Tartarin de Tarascon, the Provençal Don Quixote, Sancho Panza, and Schweik combined in one. In *Tartarin in the Alps* (1885), a satire on tourism to Switzerland, spice and suspense are provided when a female member of a group of murderous Russian Nihilists in exile seduces the bumbling southern French hero.

In English-speaking nations the sentiment was summed up by a reviewer for the October 1881 issue of the *Atlantic*: "Nihilism is so terrible and tremendous a fact in these days" that any novel on it will be found "breathless and melodramatic."[34] Books now forgotten featuring Russian revolutionary adventures included *Condemned as a Nihilist: A Story of Escape from Siberia* (1893) by George Alfred Henty, a popular and jingoistic British children's book writer; the American Kathleen O'Meara's *Narka the Nihilist* (1888); and Oscar Wilde's immature play, *Vera; or, The Nihilist* (1881), anachronistically set in 1800 Moscow, where a young tsar falls in love with the terrorist heroine. More enduring has been Arthur Conan Doyle's "The Adventure of the Golden Pince-Nez," in which Sherlock Holmes solves a mystery involving murderous, chain-smoking, but still tragically gallant Russian "reformers-revolutionists-Nihilists."[35]

All of these minor works have been overshadowed by such international anarchist classics as Henry James's *The Princess Casamassima* (1886) and Joseph Conrad's *The Secret Agent* (1907) and *Under Western Eyes* (1911). *The Princess Casamassima* is a tragic novel centered on the character Hyacinth, in whom ascetic revolutionary commitment and plebeian resentments conflict with love and refined taste. James based this psychological and political study on Turgenev's *Virgin Soil*, and, like its model, the book features a Nechaevist revolutionary circle although the terrorists are English, French, and German and no Russians appear in the work.[36] More directly concerned with the problems presented by terrorism and Russia in the contemporary world was Conrad, who, as the son of a Polish nationalist exiled by the tsarist government for his political views, despised Russians. *The Secret Agent* is a riveting tale—coincidentally close to reality—of tsarist Russian secret police encouraging an agent provocateur to commit an anarchist bombing in order to induce the British police to fight Russian anarchists. *Under Western Eyes* is a study of Russian terrorists in which Conrad expresses his disdain for the Russian autocracy and revolutionaries alike.

Newspapers and novels thus informed the world about the extremist actions of Russian Populist radicals. At the same time, in Mediterranean western Europe, mass movements that were partly shaped by Bakuninism created an atmosphere conducive to the global embrace of violent political techniques originating in Russia.

In Italy and Spain, Bakunin seemed to speak to local conditions, and a devoted following that lasted several generations emerged there. What was true of Russia also applied to these two developing nations of the West: as contact with the outside world increased, a sense of deprivation and frustration grew in the face of oppressive taxation, overcrowded urban slums, the stubborn persistence of mass poverty, and the threat posed by modern industrial production to traditional artisans. In northern Europe, the impact of Russian anarchism was largely restricted to intellectuals. In the south, Russian influence was more pervasive as social and political systems were more retrograde, and native radicalism was antitechnological and anarchic by inclination.

Italian conditions reminded Bakunin of Russia with its large peasantry, and his views seemed compatible with native revolutionary traditions associated with Mazzini, Garibaldi, and the secret societies.[37] A devoted Bakuninist following emerged in Italy, first in Naples, then in the Romagna, both regions long known for their political violence. In the early 1870s Bakunin's contacts with Italian anarchists were organized by young students and admirers such as Errico Malatesta (1853–1932), important in radical politics until his death; Andrea Costa (1851–1910), who became the moderate leader of parliamentary Italian socialism after his revolutionary youth; and Carlo Cafiero (1846–1892), who gave up his wealth in support of Bakunin.

Bakuninist anarchism became an important rejectionist force in Italian politics from the 1870s into the 1920s. Although uprisings inspired by Bakunin's ideas between 1874 and 1877 failed for lack of organization, he was the first to offer a left-wing alternative to republicanism in Italy, which satisfied very few at the time because of the compromise its leaders had made with Italy's elites and its resulting weak social program. Bakuninism was the first socialist movement in Italy, the first of many subversive movements to fight against the national government, and the first to introduce the idea of social revolution—as opposed to narrow political revolution. Well after the 1890s, when Marxism was on the rise, Bakuninism retained strong support throughout central and northern Italy. It played an integral role in the antimilitarist campaigns during World

War I and remained strong in the radical syndicalist unions. In 1914, 1919, and 1920, anarchist shock troops were active in strikes, demonstrations, and revolutionary agitation. Mussolini's father was a lifelong devotee of Bakunin and raised his son in a family atmosphere accepting of revolutionary extremism; what better example of the way Bakuninism encouraged the violent mood among Italian radicals, helped to lay the groundwork for antiauthoritarian and antiliberal revolutionary movements, and undermined stability in general?

With his influence in Italy consolidated by the early 1870s and growing among émigré Russian and European radicals, Bakunin was prepared to convert Spain.[38] Here he achieved his greatest success (much of it posthumous), with the creation of an extensive and long-lasting anarchist movement. Under the auspices of the International Alliance of Social Democracy—Bakunin's secret society within the Socialist International, one of the means by which he hoped to wrest control of the movement from Marx—Giuseppe Fanelli was sent to Spain in 1868 to form the Federación Regional Española, the Spanish section of the First International. Fanelli (1829–1877) was a former architect and engineer from Italy who had forsaken his profession to become a revolutionary and agent of Bakunin. He spoke no Spanish but received a warm welcome and, along with a French disciple, Elie Reclus (1827–1904), had great success in setting up a Bakuninist movement that would be a major force in Spanish politics for sixty years.

The situation in Spain was in some ways similar to that of Italy and Russia—a developing European country ever conscious of northwestern Europe's power and prosperity, a sharp contrast to its own poverty and tumult in the midst of the disruptive transition to a modern urban industrial economy. Fanelli and Reclus brought word of Bakuninism to people already familiar with French utopian socialism, eager to rebel against the traditional powers of church and state, and receptive to Bakunin's pronouncements that provincial autonomy would be the essential precondition for a future anarchist Spain. The Bakuninists emphasized the primacy of the local unit, federalism, autonomy, and decentralization; they therefore struck home in the Spanish regions, especially in Catalonia, which was perpetually at odds with the central government.

These issues were of concern mostly to the intelligentsia of the country, but the backing Spanish Bakuninism gained among the masses had largely to do with local factors, especially when exacerbated by encroaching modernization. In feudal, latifundist Andalusia, where the anarchist word was spread by itinerant "missionaries," it had concrete political application for peasants, rural laborers, and artisans, whose livelihoods seemed threatened by capitalism in the form of mechanization, new market relations, and the liberalization of property, employment, and tax laws. Anarchism gave them an outlet for their gripes against the large-scale capitalist grain producers and the centralized, seemingly rapacious Bourbon state. In Barcelona, meanwhile, Bakuninist anarchism also grew strong, but for reasons that stemmed from circumstances unique to this industrial Catalonian port city: the numerous immigrants streaming in from the south were strongly attracted to it, as were small-enterprise workers who felt threatened by big business. The overcrowding of proletarian neighborhoods, the presence of large numbers of Italian immigrants, and the brutality of police and factory owners all helped to generate further support.

By the end of the nineteenth century, the movement had fragmented into terrorist and labor-union wings. Although there was some overlap between them, to a large extent this, too, reflected regional divisions. The Andalusian agrarian anarchists tended to be the more violent and ready to adopt terrorism; the more industrialized northeast was inclined toward the militant industrial strike of the syndicalists, whose movement had some of its own roots in anarchism.

Syndicalism was born in France in the early twentieth century but was quickly exported around the world.[39] It was a form of belligerent trade unionism that fought against the central state and the reformism of mainstream socialism. Tellingly, it was also known as anarcho-syndicalism. Its French theoreticians were Georges Sorel (1847–1922), who warned against Bakuninism but nevertheless reflected his influence, and Émile Pouget (1860–1931), who was an anarchist outright. Many other leaders of the movement, such as Fernand Pelloutier (1867–1901) and Paul Delesalle (1870–1948), had also come out of French anarchism but critiqued it for its indifference to labor organization. What they imparted to the syndicalist trade unions from Bakuninism was its spirit of revolutionary activism and hostility toward moderation, capitalism, and the democratic system—which explains why anarchism and syndicalism were also breeding grounds for French protofascism. In Spain, too, anarcho-syndicalists played a violent role in trade unions and politics, from 1917 well into the 1930s. During the Spanish Civil War of 1936–1939 they controlled large sections of the country and attempted experiments in rural and urban collectivization before the Francoist victory wiped them out.

Politically significant as they were at home in the early twentieth century, Italian and Spanish followers of Bakunin were equally important as emigrants lugging his ideas around the world. Italian anarchist "missionaries" of revolution were to be found wherever there were large Italian communities. In Argentina, Brazil, Egypt, England, France, Switzerland, Tunisia, the United States, and elsewhere, Italian immigrants introduced the notions of Bakunin in pure form or alloyed with other ideas. For their part, Spanish as well as Italian and Portuguese anarchists spread syndicalist ideas to Latin America. Anarcho-syndicalist strikes and violence were common in Argentina and Brazil from 1900 to the mid-1930s, in Cuba into the 1920s, and in Mexico until the movement was crushed after World War I. Introduced by Spanish, Portuguese, and Italian emigrants who saw themselves as followers of Bakunin, it was stridently anticapitalist and anticommunist at the same time. Of course, these ideas coexisted with other radical opinions. They colored some of the patterns in the kaleidoscopic revolutionary movements active in these societies. Nonetheless, for an entire era anarcho-syndicalism was the chief form of labor protest for workers whose peasant backgrounds had not fully receded, and this speaks to the international diffusion of Bakuninism and the relevance of Russian extremist ideas for developing nations even at this early date.[40]

If syndicalism was a crossbreed of radical Russian and non-Russian origins, political terrorism was purebred, and from Spain to

India and Japan to New Jersey, it became known as the "Russian method." Beginning in the late nineteenth century, systematic terrorist movements proliferated around the world. Each fought for a different cause, but their mind-sets were almost identical, as were their techniques, which could be mastered and applied regardless of ideological affiliation. Almost all in one way or another took guidance from Russia's vast pantheon of terrorists and revolutionaries, however remote their specific goals may have been from those of the Russian intelligentsia.[41] The Populist revolutionaries contributed the methods that typified political murder in the twentieth century: deadly innovations in explosives; reliance on the mass media for publicity; the belief that a few bold violent acts would provoke a wider popular revolution; and clandestine, centralized organizational principles.

The turn of the nineteenth century coincided with a rash of anarchist bombings and assassinations in western Europe and the United States (more on which in the next chapter). But these murders committed by lone operators cannot be considered systematic terrorism of the Russian Populist variety. The Russian method proliferated not so much in the West as in politically oppressed eastern Europe, the seething ethnic regions of the Ottoman Empire, the British colony of India, and rapidly changing Japan. In some of these places, conditions were similar to those in Russia at the time: newly industrializing yet rife with ambivalence, if not hostility, toward Westernization. In others, these issues were bound up with nationalism; indeed, some of the early-twentieth-century imitators of Russian terrorism were the first of many national liberation movements for which the formulations of Russian Populism seemed relevant and effective. Whatever the precise reasons, in Poland and Serbia, Armenia and Macedonia, India and Japan, Russian terrorism exerted a magnetic pull on the politically enraged.

Russian Populism and the Russian method radiated out to the eastern European and Caucasian borderlands of the Russian Empire, at first as part of the ethnic-nationalist struggle against tsarist rule, then against neighboring oppressors. In Poland, perpetually bucking under Russian rule, radicals inclined toward the People's Will once it came onto the scene. It was a Polish member of the party, Hryniewicki, who threw the bomb that killed Alexander II. Jozef Pilsudski (1867–1935), later nationalist dictator of independent Poland, and Tomasz Arciszewski (1877–1955), future Polish legislator and statesman, emerged as socialist terrorists between 1881 and 1905 as, in Pilsudski's words, "hatred for the Russian regime grew within [us] from year to year."[42] Implicated in the same plot to assassinate Tsar Alexander III as Lenin's brother, Pilsudski was exiled to eastern Siberia for five years after 1887. After his release in 1892 he played a major role in the Polish Socialist Party (PPS), which stood for full independence from Russia and was organized in cells and fighting groups, following the example of the People's Will. The PPS can be seen as a revival of earlier insurgencies against Russian dominion, but it also shared in the legacy and spirit of the multiethnic Russian terrorist movement.[43]

The same is true of terrorism in Turkish Armenia, where the radical Dashnak Party (or Armenian Revolutionary Federation) of the 1890s had close organizational and personal ties to Russian Armenia, and whose weapons were supplied by the underground in Tblisi, capital of Russian Georgia. Partly inspired by the example of the Greeks and Bulgarians who had used force to gain independence from Turkey, the party was founded in 1890 with the prominent participation of two former members of the People's Will, Christopher Mikaelian and Simon Zavarian. The Dashnaks were organized into terrorist cells along the lines of the People's Will. The purpose was to fight the Ottoman regime, which had tolerated or itself carried out massacres of hundreds of thousands of Armenians in a series of incidents dating back to 1860. In the first two decades of the twentieth century, its members moved constantly throughout the Ottoman Empire, the Transcaucasus, Russia, Persia, Europe, and the United States, often conspiring with terrorists of other nationalities and sharing Russian-derived revolutionary ideas and techniques with them wherever the message was welcome.[44]

The Armenian terrorists of the Dashnak Party had close ties to Macedonian revolutionaries, whose movement was active for nearly five decades. Macedonia, a centuries-old ethnic and political tangle, has a convoluted history reflected in the complexity of the Internal Macedonian Revolutionary Movement (IMRO). IMRO's roots go back to 1893–1894 with the founding of various revolutionary organizations in Macedonia proper, and in Bulgaria by Macedonian exiles under the sponsorship of the Bulgarian and Russian governments. These closely related, although often rival, organizations arose as a reaction to Turkish persecution; they were in competition with Serbian guerrilla units fighting in Macedonia on behalf of Serbian interests. The Bulgaro-Macedonian groups eventually unified under the name IMRO, whose goal was to achieve Macedonian independence from, at various times, Turkey, Bulgaria, Greece, or Yugoslavia.

Like so many other movements over the century to be touched by Russian radicalism, this, too, was an organization of educated intellectuals in an agrarian society founded to fight against a repressive state. The means by which Russian influences were transmitted varied: through a former member of the Russian Socialist Revolutionary party who had joined IMRO, and through two of its leaders, Boris Sarafov and Giorche Petrov, who held meetings with the Dashnaks and took lessons in bomb making from these Armenian students of the Russians. But beyond these personal links, all of the IMRO terrorists absorbed the mood of their Russian counterparts by reading the novels of Chernyshevsky, Stepniak, or Turgenev and the philosophical works of the Russian Populists. Among many others, this was true of Gotse Delchev, the founder of IMRO who died in a Turkish ambush in 1903, and Svetoslav Merdzhanov, who read these authors and then sought contact with Russian radicals in Geneva.

IMRO was divided into fighting cells, *chetas*, sometimes called armed committees, with the leadership asserting—if often not achieving—strict centralized control over members, including the right to have them shot for transgressions. The organizational pattern was reminiscent of old Balkan outlaw gangs and partly modeled on the Italian Carbonari, but borrowings from the Russian revolutionary movement are evident in IMRO statutes. Relying on the publicity its terrorism brought it, it recruited assassins and raised funds in the slums of Skopje and Sofia. Finally crushed by the Bulgarian police in 1934, IMRO was clearly a child of the Balkans, but nourished by the Russian terrorist tradition.[45]

If Macedonian extremists terrorized the Balkans, Serbian terrorists shook the entire world. Here, too, in a land with a long tradition of political violence conducted by clans and secret societies, the Russian method reinvigorated old ways of fighting ethnic enemies and waging dynastic feuds. Serbian ultranationalists—among them Gavrilo Princip of Young Bosnia—fed on Russian conspiratorial-revolutionary literature by Bakunin, Chernyshevsky, and Dostoevsky, glorified Russian revolutionaries of old, followed the dictates of the "Catechism of a Revolutionary," organized themselves after the People's Will, and made contact with SRs in Europe. They were intoxicated with the success of violence in the 1905 Russian revolution, as their fathers had been with the Pan-Slav saber rattling of Dostoevsky's Balkan journalism. Ironically, Serb nationalists, who adopted Russian left-wing terrorist techniques, operated with the connivance of the imperial Russian government. From the 1870s on, the Russian tsars had taken Serbia under their wing as they sought geopolitical advantage against the expansionist Habsburg empire. Russia's encouragement of Serbia through its guarantee of assistance against Austria "unsettled the unbalanced minds" of Serb youths ready to assassinate Austrian Archduke Franz Ferdinand at Sarajevo in 1914.[46] The Serbs and Montenegrins seriously believed that they were a force of 160 million, so certain were they of the support of their Russian brethren. Serb terrorism in Sarajevo exemplifies the potency of nationalism, revolutionary conspiracy, and terrorism combined. This is a convergence that would surface time and again in the years ahead, with no small contribution from Russian quarters.[47]

Poles, Armenians, Macedonians, and Serbs formed the earliest organized terrorist movements outside Russia to serve the cause of national liberation—a logical development considering these people's proximity to and familiarity with Russian affairs. Less obvious connections but just as important ones existed linking Russia with India and Japan.

The political and economic transformation of Japan in the late nineteenth century was accompanied by anger and dismay over disrupted traditional hierarchies and ways of life. Change undermined the preeminence of the old warrior class, some members of which fought back by turning to radical rejectionist politics. In Japan, terrorism was partly the result of an effort to revive the samurai fighting tradition, but it also borrowed consciously from the Russian method. Populist exiles taught in Japanese universities and inspired some leftist revolts before the turn of the century. But for the most part Japanese terrorism was the domain of the nationalists, who adopted Russian techniques even though their hostility to the socialist left wing in Japan grew as the latter became more strident in the wake of the Russian Revolution. That notwithstanding, there was always overlap in the joint hostility of the radical right and left toward the West.

Not all of the paramilitary and terrorist groups that flourished in Japan in the first decades of the twentieth century had a Russian connection. But the most powerful and influential one did. The godfather of Japanese organized crime and founder of an early right-extremist and gangster association, the Genyosha, was Toyama Mitsuru (1855–1944). In 1901, he and his protégé, Uchida Ryohei (1874–1937), established the ultra-nationalist Amur River Society (Kokoryukai, also known as the Black Dragons). Uchida had been a student in St. Petersburg, knew Russian, and was in contact with Russian revolutionaries in Nagasaki, whose violent politics he admired. Although his society's aim was to encourage Japanese domination of Manchuria and the entire Far East, in 1917 he called for an anti-Western alliance of Japan, Russia, and China, which he considered superior Asian civilizations. The assassination of moderate politicians was also a specialty of the organization, whose leaders were disillusioned with the existing parliamentary order and opposed the government's domestic authority just as much as they urged its military expansion abroad.[48]

The impact of Russian terrorism at the time was perhaps nowhere as deep as in India, where both pro-British and Indian nationalist newspapers publicized Russian affairs and sympathized

with the terrorists' fight against autocracy. An armed militant wing
of the Indian nationalist movement lauded Russian terrorists, corresponded with them, and imitated them. Although ideologically
closer to Italian nationalism, anti-British Indian extremists took
over the entire inventory of Russian terrorist methodology. Among
the figures in this wing of the movement at the turn of the century
were Bal Gangadhar Tilak (1856–1920), Har Dayal (1884–1939),
Aurobindo Ghose (1872–1950), and Vinayak Savarkar (1883–
1966). Despite their different organizational affiliations, regional
bases, and philosophical leanings, each stood for armed resistance
on behalf of *swaraj* (home rule) and generally opposed Western
civilization. Tilak—Brahmin, Sanskrit scholar, journalist, anti-
Western Hindu nationalist—urged Indians to adopt "Russian
methods of agitation in fighting with their rulers."[49]

They did just that after 1905, forming secret societies on the
model of the Russian SR organization in the belief that this was the
only way to fight the despotism of the British, whom the Indians
perceived as more tyrannical than the Russian government. The nationalist Marathi paper, *Kal*, praised the SR assassination of the
arch-reactionary Russian minister of the interior, von Plehve, whom
it compared favorably with Lord Curzon, viceroy of India. British
intelligence reports indicate a concern about the ties between Indian
and Russian revolutionaries,[50] and police raids on Indian terrorists
uncovered extensive materials on Russian terrorist activities, organization, and philosophies. One such pamphlet in the possession of
Savarkar's brother Ganesh when he was arrested in 1908 was titled
How the Russians Organize a Revolution. Russian terrorists also
taught the Indians the financial and propaganda benefits of robbing
banks and bomb-making principles: Hem Chandra Das and P. M.
Bapat traveled to Paris in 1907 specifically to learn about explosives
from Russian revolutionary exiles. They brought back to India a
manual on bombs, given them by Nikolai Safransky of the SR Party,
which was reproduced around the country.[51]

The main center of terrorist activity in India was Bengal. Bengali
terrorists considered themselves the disciples of Nechaev and Bakunin and expected that terrorism would set off mass revolt. In
1908 a bombing campaign began in the region, encouraged by the

1905 Russian revolution; it continued sporadically over the next ten years. As late as 1931, the memory of the Populist war against tsardom remained inspirational. In that year, two teenage girls assassinated a British district magistrate in eastern Bengal; according to a police agent, "the object of sending two girls to murder Mr. Stevens was to set up an Indian record of female heroism to emulate that of some Russian girl in the time of the Tsar. This would encourage other girls in Bengal to become terrorists."[52]

After independence the Indian heirs of Nechaevist methodology claimed their most famous victim, Mahatma Gandhi. Vinayak Savarkar, the dominant personality among Indian terrorists in the first half of the twentieth century, had become leader of an anti-Muslim Hindu nationalist party. He was idolized by Gandhi's assassins, and they visited him just before murdering the man who resisted the violence in India by espousing Tolstoyan pacifism.[53]

The Indian example shows us that Russian-style terrorism would have the best chance of gaining a foothold in agitated, largely agrarian nations similar to Russia where radicals had little or no hope of working within the system and nothing to lose. One nation that might have been expected to look toward Russia was Ireland, but the Fenian movement that arose against English rule developed a homegrown variety of terrorism. The cell structure of the Irish Republican Brotherhood did owe something to the Russians, but it is clear that traditional Irish gangs were far more the prototypes. Irish terrorists admired their Russian counterparts, whom they read about in the European press of the 1870s and 1880s, and took lessons on homemade dynamite from Russian experts in America, but they preferred to plan for armed insurrection and never warmed to the People's Will strategy of assassinating leading officials. The Irish, with a long-standing tradition of political violence of their own, paid little attention to the new modes of terrorist action emanating from Russia. This, of course, changed with the advent of the Provisional Irish Republican Army, which broke with Irish traditions and conformed to universal terrorist standards in the 1970s.[54]

After the 1917 Bolshevik revolution, the attention of the world was focused on communism, and the anarchist movement withered. Once the last bastion of anarchism was defeated in the Spanish Civil War of the 1930s, it seemed to have died, only to be revived by the New Left in the 1960s. A minority of its adherents turned to violence, forming revolutionary parties or terrorist cells. And one conduit of Russian terrorist ideas was again literature: the mass-consumed work of the contemporary French *philosophe* and Nobel laureate, Albert Camus.

Camus wrote three major, popular books dealing with Russian terrorism: *The Just* (1950), an original play; *The Possessed* (1959), a dramatic adaptation of Dostoevsky's novel of that name (more accurately translated as *Devils*); and *The Rebel* (1951), a book-length philosophical essay with sections on Bakunin, Nechaev, and Russian Populist terrorism.[55] Camus's writings on the subject are penetrating psychological studies of the problem of revolutionary violence—the terrorist mentality, its hesitations and motivations, the moral relativism and the subordination of human feelings to a higher good, the willingness to die for the cause. Camus praises revolutionary murder if it is for a justified, specific cause rather than for an abstract ideal, and if it is carried out after deep moral searching, with great reluctance, within carefully controlled limits, and with self-sacrifice. For instance, in *The Just*, the hero is Ivan Kaliaev, the SR assassin of Grand Duke Sergei in 1905. Kaliaev delays throwing his bomb at Sergei to avoid killing innocent children-bystanders, bringing on himself the scorn of his fellow terrorists. Only when his royal target is alone does he finally carry out his assignment.

But Camus was himself troubled by the murderous inclinations of rebels and publicly condemned the violence of the far left and the far right. Indeed, over this issue he and the French existentialist philosopher Jean-Paul Sartre broke off relations—Sartre being a lifelong apologist for Bakunin-like revolt, which he saw as having a regenerative effect on humanity. Camus critiqued Bakunin and Nechaev for their advocacy of indiscriminate murder, their thirst for power, and their tendency toward authoritarianism, all characteristics he depicts in both *The Rebel* and *The Possessed*. By contrast, he had a more positive—and idealistic—view of the People's

Will and the Socialist Revolutionaries, whom he presumed to have been acting only with restraint and the noblest of motives.

Camus was not the only icon of the New Left in the 1960s to popularize ideas deriving from Bakunin and the Russian Populist-terrorists, whom radical intellectuals knew either directly or from familiarity with the internecine disputes within European socialism a century earlier. Leftists turned to Bakuninism because of their growing disillusionment with the repressive bureaucratic regimes of the Soviet bloc, and because Bakunin's theories seemed more applicable than classic Marxism to contemporary revolutionary conditions. In such works as *One-Dimensional Man* (1964) and *An Essay on Liberation* (1969), the Freudian-Marxist Herbert Marcuse (1898–1979) expanded Bakunin's conception of the revolutionary alliance of déclassé intellectuals and criminals to encompass all outsiders opposed to Western industrial society—rebellious students, dropouts, oppressed minorities in the slums of the United States, the Third World masses, and Third World dictators. Marcuse does not discuss Bakunin in his published writings, but his ideas and terminology of the 1960s suggest a strong influence. The same is true of Frantz Fanon (1925–1961), a Martinique-born, French-trained psychiatrist and the author of a classic of the Third World revolution, *The Wretched of the Earth* (1961). Fanon's call for spontaneous insurrection by the Algerian and African peasantry, whom he glorifies in the fashion of a Russian Populist, owes its essence to Bakunin. Writing in connection with the Algerian revolution, but intending his ideas for application anywhere imperialism and oppression existed, Fanon, like Sartre, espoused the liberating and redemptive effects of violence.[56] His writings were especially popular among Arab intellectuals and ideologists of the Iranian Islamic revolution of the 1970s like Ali Shariʿati, who rejected Marxism and urged a return to his country's religious roots to combat "Westoxication."[57]

In Latin America, too, underneath the veneer of Marxism-Leninism or Maoism, a vestigial Bakuninism was apparent—not surprisingly, considering the spread of anarcho-syndicalist ideas earlier in the century and some of the similarities between Russia and this region. It was on the cultural fringe of Europe; underdeveloped but modernizing; starkly divided into rich and poor; and riven by a vast gulf between the Europeanized elite and the native Indian peasantry. Régis Debray (1940–), the French apologist for Fidel Castro and associate of Che Guevara (1928–1967) in his failed Bolivian insurgency, was a widely read theoretician of radical violence. In Debray's *Revolution in the Revolution?* (1967), a manual for Latin American *guerrilleros*, some observers have noticed undertones of Bakunin and Nechaev alongside Lenin, Mao, Ho, Castro, and Guevara. As for Guevara, although not an advocate of urban terrorism, his life of fighting, disdain for Soviet bureaucratism, and belief in the revolutionary potential of underdeveloped nations echoed the spirit of Russian anarchism. Indeed, he relished East-bloc criticism of him as a "new Bakunin."[58] Whether consciously or unconsciously, this modern Hispanic rebel who was one of the main sources of the New Left cult of the guerrilla, passed on Bakuninist ideals to revolutionaries of Latin America and the world.[59]

While Marcuse, Fanon, Debray, and Guevara to different degrees suggest the Bakunin-Nechaev legacy, it was more explicit among other Western radicals of the 1960s, who rediscovered Bakunin's rhetoric and found that it matched their own rebellious mood. In May 1968 during the student riots in Paris, Bakuninist aphorisms like "The passion to destroy is a creative passion" were scrawled on the walls of the Sorbonne. German terrorists regarded the Catechism as scripture, and the Bewegung 2. Juni (June 2nd Movement) published the works of Bakunin.[60] In Italy, the Red Brigades, an organization responsible for thousands of terrorist incidents between 1969 and 1980 resulting in hundreds of dead and wounded, consciously applied Bakuninist and Nechaevist tactics and recruited disaffected intellectuals, students, and petty criminals to assault the central government.[61] In the United States, the Black Panthers published the "Catechism of a Revolutionary," and Eldridge Cleaver in the early days of his revolt patterned himself after its revolutionary persona. In *Soul on Ice*, he writes that he "fell in love" with the Catechism: "I took the Catechism for my bible and . . . I began consciously incorporating these principles into my daily life, to employ tactics of ruthlessness in my dealings with everyone with whom I came into contact. And I began to look at white America through those new eyes."[62]

Outside the Western world, too, a new phase of political violence emerged. International terrorism from the 1960s into the early twenty-first century continued the tradition of its turn-of-the-century forebears. Modern-day terrorist groups have become more sophisticated, are better financed, have the logistical support of established governments, and are far more deadly than the revolutionary pioneers throwing primitive homemade bombs. But in order to survive underground, terrorists must follow the organizational patterns first established by the Russians (without necessarily being aware of their provenance). This was the case with the Italian Red Brigades and is also true of Hamas, the Islamic-fundamentalist, Palestinian terrorist group first active in the 1990s, which has a highly centralized cell structure and is divided into open political and secret operations sections.[63] The cell structure of Osama bin Laden's al-Qaeda organization has complicated efforts by Western governments to uproot and destroy it in the wake of the September 11, 2001, attacks on New York and Washington.[64] In the words of a former colonel attached to the GRU, the Main Intelligence Directorate of the Soviet army, which oversaw East-bloc terrorist training camps during the Cold War, "the methods and ideology of training terrorists . . . have remained substantially unchanged [over the century]."[65]

The nineteenth-century practitioners and theoreticians of Russian radicalism were the first to formulate the terrorist practices that have been in use ever since. It is important to note, however, that very different strains of Russian anarchism and Populism coexisted with terrorism. One of those strains, which also had a far-reaching influence, is associated with the name Peter Kropotkin.

CHAPTER 2

Kropotkin's Anti-Darwinian Anarchism

BAKUNINISM was not the only form of revolutionary anarchism coming from Russia. Bakunin's successor as world anarchist leader was Peter Kropotkin (1842–1921). Scion of an ancient princely family, Kropotkin trained as a geographer and naturalist, became a revolutionary conspirator, then settled down in English exile as anarchism's sage. Little is known about him today, but as a progenitor of modern environmentalism and back-to-the-land movements, he deserves to be regarded as one of the most influential social thinkers of the modern era.

"A man with the soul of that beautiful white Christ"

Prince Kropotkin was born into a rich family that traced its ancestry back to the rulers of medieval Russia. He received a military education in the elite Corps of Pages but, like many young educated noblemen, grew discontented with the tsarist regime and forswore entry into both the government and the glittering social life of the court. To the dismay of his family, he chose to enter service with a Cossack regiment in Russia's Wild East, Siberia, where he explored unknown regions, observed nature and the local peasantry, and wrote prize-winning geographical studies. Out of philosophical conviction he left the army for the University of St. Petersburg and became a prominent member of the Imperial Russian Geographical Society, his reputation secured by his research on Siberia.

Kropotkin's moral repugnance at the state of affairs in Russia made him sympathetic to anarchism. In 1872 he joined the conspiratorial Chaikovsky Circle but was arrested in 1874. He spent two years imprisoned in a Russian fortress, his sentence cut short by a dramatic escape engineered by fellow revolutionaries. This was only the first episode in his life to establish his worldwide reputation. He made his way from Russia to Switzerland, where he founded one of the most important radical publications of the late nineteenth century, *Le Révolté*, which, later, in France, became *Les Temps nouveaux*. He was expelled to France in 1881, where he was soon arrested on trumped-up charges and sentenced to five years in prison. He became an international cause célèbre, was released after three years, and found refuge in England from 1886 until his return to Russia after the 1917 revolution.

At the turn of the century he was at the height of his fame, promoted by worldwide publications that expressed in a readable style and a reasonable tone ideas people around the world were eager to take in. His biological and historical survey of cooperationism, *Mutual Aid: A Factor of Evolution*, was serialized between 1890 and 1896 in the popular middle-class magazine *Nineteenth Century*. His vivid account of his revolutionary exploits in *Memoirs of a Revolutionist* first appeared in 1898–1899 in the *Atlantic Monthly* but was reissued as a book and—reflecting his wide audience—translated into Bulgarian, Chinese, Czech, Danish, Dutch, Esperanto, French, German, Hindustani, Italian, Japanese, Norwegian, Polish, Russian, Spanish, Swedish, and Yiddish. His political pamphlets and philosophical tracts were issued in all these and other languages as well. He also gave lectures in Britain, France, and the United States, the last on two tours in 1897–1898 and 1901.

His reputation soared. In England, he was likened to a divinity. George Bernard Shaw wrote of him that he was "amiable to the point of saintliness, and with his full red beard and lovable expression might have been a shepherd from the Delectable Mountains"; Oscar Wilde wrote that his was one of the "most perfect lives I have come across in my experience. . . . [He is] a man with a soul of that beautiful white Christ which seems coming out of Russia."[1]

What is it that explains this religious imagery? This period of history was an age of intense spiritual searching, especially for

3. Peter Kropotkin. From William E. Walling, *Russia's Message* (New York, 1908).

those who had rejected traditional religion and sought to fill the void it left with something that corresponded to their sensibilities: anticapitalist, repelled by bourgeois convention, full of hope for the new era they expected to be ushered in with the turn of the century. These are the ingredients that blended together to create the protest against modern life that we call the Modernist movement; they aroused the new taste for Russian culture as well as for the European avant-garde as a whole. All of these ingredients were present in Kropotkin too.

The paradox is that Kropotkin rejected spiritualism and dedicated himself to establishing a scientific foundation for anarchism.[2] He did so by challenging the Western understanding of competitive, conflictual relations between and within species as put forth by Thomas Malthus and Charles Darwin. Their concept of the "struggle for existence" had been applied to human societies by the social Darwinist publicist Herbert Spencer. The writings of these men formed the basis for the justification of all manner of policies and ideas repugnant to Kropotkin and most other Russian socialists—be they imperialist racism, big-power militarism, laissez-faire economics, or expanded state control over the uncivilized and unruly lower classes.

Kropotkin's objections to these prevailing assumptions of British biology and its application to economics and politics derived first and foremost from his observations of the Russian environment. Siberia was Kropotkin's Galapagos.[3] But Siberia presented a very different setting from the tropical islands Darwin studied. Kropotkin found in Siberia not competition or a struggle for existence within species but the opposite—cooperation as an instinctual strategy for survival. His study of wolves, for instance, showed that they did not kill one another in the search for scarce sources of food but, rather, roamed in cooperative packs. For him, nature is not a struggle for existence between individuals but a struggle between individuals and the environment. The fittest are not the strongest but those who have learned how to live cooperatively, what he called the practice of mutual aid. "The war of each against all is not *the* law of nature," he proclaimed.[4]

Likewise did Kropotkin reject Malthus's proposition that competition between human beings was inevitable given their insatiable reproductive desires, ineluctable population growth, and the earth's limited resources. Kropotkin argued that limited productivity of the soil was not the obstacle to solving the problems of hun-

ger and overpopulation; rather, it was wasteful agricultural practices and a system that threw people off the land and into cities.
Restore them to the land, introduce intensive market-gardening
and greenhouse techniques, and they will produce more than
enough to feed themselves and still have time to work at their occu-
pations and—the point of it all—enjoy life.[5]

Although he was stirred as all anarchists were by the vision of
the early French socialists such as Charles Fourier, Kropotkin's utopian solution also relied on the Russian peasant commune as prototype of the ideal form for the future organization of humanity. In
the Populist view, the peasant commune stood as a bulwark in Russia against the ravages of capitalism: communes combined craft
production and farm work to protect the peasants from the division of labor; they guaranteed sufficient land and bread to sustain
all their residents, in contrast to the shocking poverty of industrial
cities; and they exemplified successful cooperative existence without modern dislocation.

Once he arrived in Europe, Kropotkin's search for like communal forms drew him to an idealization of medieval towns. These,
too, were worthy examples of cooperationism, with craft production controlled by guilds and the division of society into local par-
ishes. Indeed, Kropotkin saw the end of the Middle Ages as a tragedy for humanity: in the modern era the malevolent alliance of
centralizing, absolutist state and capitalist bourgeoisie destroyed
what was in his mind the blissful communitarianism of European
towns. He dreamed of restoring mankind's psychological integrity,
true freedom, and peaceful social interaction, all of which he supposed existed in medieval cities and the Russian peasant commune.

Kropotkin worked out a blueprint for this future ethical society
in his most widely read works, *The Conquest of Bread* (1892),
Fields, Factories, and Workshops (1899), and the entry on anarchism in the famous eleventh edition of *The Encyclopaedia Britan-
nica*. He proposed a decentralized system of economics and a corresponding approach to primary and secondary education.
Regional communities of individuals would produce and consume
their own agricultural products and manufactured goods. This
would encourage the conservation of resources as people produced

only what was needed locally. It would do away with the competitive free-market system. It would eliminate many of the functions of national governments. As in the Russian peasant commune, each person would be involved in both agricultural and small-scale industrial or handicraft work. Hands-on "integral education" that combined academic and vocational schools and taught children to be "manual workers" as well as "brain workers" would close the division of labor for good.[6] These arrangements would result in the highest quality manufactures and food, relieve monotony on the job, and lead to full production. Ultimately, "one half of the working day would remain [free] to everyone for the pursuit of art, science, or any hobby he or she might prefer."[7] Once all individuals were fully satisfied with work, life, and each other, their humanity and totality restored, social conflict would come to an end.

Kropotkin announced as his slogan "To every man according to his needs," and labeled his program "anarchist communist" because of the stress on cooperative organization in the future.[8] This should be distinguished from Marxist communism, which incurred the rhetorical wrath of Kropotkin, anarchist enemy of the state. He disparaged the contemporary Marxist radical as "a centralizer, a state partisan, a Jacobin to the core."[9] If, according to Kropotkin, natural evolution entails mutual aid rather than conflict, then the Marxist propositions regarding class struggle and the dialectic were conceptually flawed. For him, the modern state was an institutionalized form of violence that had forced people to repress their cooperative instinct. Hence the goal should be to free humanity from interference by the state, not to sanctify its growth as Marxists were doing.

Despite the similarities between Kropotkin's ideas and Bakunin's on this issue, Kropotkin's anarchism was fundamentally different from Bakunin's. For Kropotkin resisted the principle that the ends justified the means. Kropotkin was consistently critical of other socialists who valued their ideology above the fate of individual human beings—a charge that he leveled time and again, after the Bolshevik revolution of 1917, against Lenin, whom he accused of "perpetrating horrors, . . . ruining the country, . . . annihilating human lives."[10] Not only was "mindless" political violence immoral; by the 1890s Kropotkin was arguing that it was ineffective in bringing on the revolution: "A structure based on centuries of history cannot be destroyed with a few kilos of explosives," he wrote.[11]

The "noblest human idea": Kropotkin's International Reception

Kropotkin's moral standpoint clearly accounted for the ready acceptance of his philosophy in various parts of the world. But unintentionally, Kropotkin also helped to inspire the rash of violent anarchist murders that terrified the West at the turn of the nineteenth century, acts not of organized terrorist organizations so much as the work of lone individuals. From 1890 to 1914, assassinated heads of state included President Carnot of France (1894), Prime Minister Canovas del Castillo of Spain (1897), Empress Elizabeth of Austria (1898), King Umberto of Italy (1900), and President McKinley of the United States (1901). Between 1904 and 1906 three attempts were made on the life of Spanish King Alfonso XIII, but prior to that, solo anarchists had launched public bombings in Spain, among the bloodiest in 1892 in Barcelona, at the Liceo Theater and then the Corpus Christi procession. France, too, between 1892 and 1894 experienced a heavy spate of violence—including bombings, acid throwing, and shootings—in the Paris stock exchange, the Chamber of Deputies, restaurants, cafés, and factories.

Through his writings, Kropotkin bears some, although by no means all, of the responsibility for encouraging these violent acts. He gave a green light to revolutionary violence with his promotion of the slippery concept of "propaganda by the deed." This term first gained currency in Bakuninist circles of France and Italy and referred to the process of awakening the lower classes through illegal revolutionary acts; Kropotkin developed the concept further and made it synonymous with his own name. He argued that any illegal demonstration, incitement, act of insurgency, or property damage by anarchists would have a useful propaganda effect on the masses. The problem was that "propaganda by the deed" was twisted by others to mean political murder. Thus Kropotkin may not have incited any specific acts of terrorism, but he did provide some of the theoretical justification for them.[12]

Kropotkin regretted that his intellectual discourse stoked the fiery revolutionary passions of a deranged fringe within the anarchist movement. For it set his reputation among the defenders of the established order as a dangerous extremist at a time when terrorism was making its first appearance and the Western bourgeoisie feared a (nonexistent) international anarchist conspiracy. *The Spectator*, a mouthpiece of Tory conservatism, judged his writings to be "a matter for the pathologist of disease."[13] The American reaction was especially hostile. In 1884 the *New York Herald* editorialized that Kropotkin deserved to die the "death of a dog."[14] After the assassination of President McKinley by a mentally unbalanced Polish anarchist, Kropotkin, who had just been visiting the United States, was widely blamed for planning the deed, and he was one of the targets of the government when, in 1903, it banned all anarchists from entering the country.

But this image of Kropotkin is a distorted one if, as some contemporaries did, we stop at the encouragement he unintentionally gave to a few assassins. Kropotkin's influence only began there; it traveled far and wide in other directions as he encouraged Western avant-garde writers and artists in their bohemian rejection of social and cultural conventions. Anarchism was the "radical chic" of the 1890s, appealing for its attacks on the philistine bourgeoisie, the state, and modernity. It was enticing as an ideology associated with Russia, whose cultural figures were increasingly at the height of intellectual fashion.

French, Italian, and Spanish writers and artists were steeped in Kropotkin's thought, which they usually tied in with their own radical and revolutionary traditions. Although it cannot be clearly separated from either the very different arch-individualism of Nietzsche and Max Stirner or the sans-culottes anarchism of Proudhon, Kropotkin's propaganda-of-the-deed concept provided a rationale for revolt that much of the avant-garde sought after. "Good literature is an eminent form of propaganda by the deed," proclaimed the French Symbolist writer Pierre Quillard, who also hailed poetry's "destructive power."[15] Most of the Symbolist writers and Post-Impressionist artists were apolitical, but anarchism suited their mood of individual autonomy, spontaneity, intuitiveness, and anti-rationalism in opposition to the "objectivity" of the naturalist school. Anarchism meshed with the Symbolist rejection of controlled rhyme for free verse and natural rhythm in poetry.

Beyond helping (along with many other thinkers) to set the mood for a whole generation, Kropotkin had an impact on many individual cultural figures. Most solidly in his camp were the French Neo-Impressionist painters Camille Pissarro and Paul Signac, both admirers of Kropotkin for his specific views and for his general rejection of bourgeois social and aesthetic rules. Of the two, Pissarro was the more politically involved in anarchist circles, and he connected himself to Kropotkin's political philosophy, although he did not see the need to make his art conform to Kropotkin's call for social-realist painting: "All arts are anarchist," wrote Pissarro, "when they are beautiful and good."[16] Signac's pointillism was a more consciously anarchist aesthetic, the goal of which was to achieve a harmony between nature and individual autonomy. His painting *In the Times of Harmony* (1896), a glimpse of leisurely labor and bucolic serenity, was a conscious representation of Kropotkin's vision of the future as detailed in his book *The Conquest of Bread* (1892). All of these followers of Kropotkin—indeed, almost the entire avant-garde—yearned not just for political revolution but for social transformation and the very renovation of mankind.[17]

A large part of this influence, like the simultaneous bombing craze, was unintended by Kropotkin, who did not think much of his own cultural legacy in France—he considered it individualistic and elitist, insufficiently collectivist, revolutionary, or dedicated to the people.[18] More to his taste was an even larger following in England, the United States, and elsewhere that is known variously as the "simple-life" or "back-to-the-land" movement, an early wing of the counterculture dedicated to re-creating the uncomplicated, pristine existence allegedly lost with the urbanization of society.

Center stage in the growing simple-life movement was taken by the Arts and Crafts revival. The person responsible more than any other for this was William Morris (1834–1896), British poet, social reformer, decorator, and craftsman. Morris applied the concepts of the Gothic enthusiast John Ruskin in his famous wallpaper, book, furniture, glass, and fabric designs, as well as devotion to historic preservationism. His aesthetic philosophy, which displaced the fine arts with handicrafts, led him to socialism. This, he believed, provided an answer to the problem of the division of labor by reuniting artistry and craftsmanship and restoring the medieval communal guilds to social prominence. His revolutionary ideas on artistic style and education affected much of Europe and the United States; it has been kept alive throughout the Western world to this day as an established component of educational curricula, but also as a desideratum for Western intellectuals in rebellion against middle-class society.

Morris encouraged Kropotkin's attraction to the Middle Ages, just as Kropotkin inspired Morris: given the prominence of Kropotkin in English socialism at this time, his influence on Morris should not be surprising. Although Morris was more willing to wait a while for the withering away of the state, his libertarianism and interest in decentralized federations of communes, as well as the basic anarchist thrust of his economic and political views, owe a great deal to Kropotkin. Each planted the seed of the other's influence wherever they made an impact.[19] And that joint impact was extensive. Morris's role in all this is well known; Kropotkin's has been largely forgotten, but it was often just as crucial.

The Arts and Crafts movement was related to anarchist socialism and was part of a broader radical mind-set in Europe and America that rejected modern urban industrial life; if it did not succeed at replacing that, at the very least it revitalized architectural and furniture design. In the United States, the leading promoter of the arts and crafts was Gustav Stickley (1858–1942), a Wisconsin-born furniture maker who was converted to the counterculture on a trip to England. He returned home determined to fight against the related evils of inequality, urbanization, and standardized patterns in furniture design. His strategy was to strengthen the position of handicrafts and subsistence farming within the industrial economy, to propagate the Arts and Crafts style, and to advocate a return to the simple life—all straight out of Kropotkin and Morris. Stickley became the most important progenitor of the Mission style in furniture—characterized by a natural, utilitarian design, what Stickley called "honest" and "democratic." And he promoted the suburban bungalow with its rustic materials and simple lines of design as a retreat from the body-and-soul-polluting city into a rusticated, aesthetic environment. He introduced the arts and crafts to a wide audience when in 1901 he founded a monthly magazine, *The Craftsman*. This joined other like magazines founded at the time—*House Beautiful*, *House and Garden*, *Ladies Home Journal*, and *American Homes and Gardens*—in featuring bungalows, home furnishings, gardening, and American Indian lore as reflective of the high value placed on rural life, wilderness, intensive farming, craftsmanship, and outdoor recreation, all in contrast to the noxiousness of the city. *The Craftsman* and these other magazines were popular at a time when the frontier had vanished and rural life was being challenged by a dynamic, rapidly urbanizing society. It was assumed that the restoration of human "wholeness" would be achieved by a return to the land, even if "land" meant only the backyard.

The Craftsman published discussions by Kropotkin, Morris, Ruskin, and Tolstoy.[20] One of Stickley's contemporaries described *The Craftsman* as a "journal advocating the influence of beautiful home surroundings as factors of the highest importance in the right development of civic and national life, and the mental and physical healthfulness that comes from the habit of spending at least a portion of each day in useful labor out of doors."[21] A comparison with the words of Kropotkin makes his compatibility with these sentiments apparent: it is an emotional "necessity for each healthy man and woman to spend a part of their lives in manual work in free air," and "simply to enjoy life . . . [by spending] their time in play and sports, after having given a few hours every day to find their daily food."[22]

The irony is that Kropotkin's radical ideas partially account for the ancestry of certain features of the modern American suburban landscape. To be sure, Stickley's furniture works and the bungalow

were transformed from back-to-the-land alternatives to the city
into mainstream middle-class accoutrements, the work of stronger
forces in America: commercialization, real estate development, and
mass production. But their partial origins in Kropotkin's radicalism are revealing. It is the genius of American (and English) commercial cultures that they can capitalize on the aesthetics of revolt
and turn a profit from the assault on modernity.

Exemplifying this process were the creation of garden cities and
the related birth of modern urban planning. Both owed a great deal
to Kropotkin's elaboration of Russian Populism, with its hopes of
remaking the world along the lines of the Russian peasant-village
commune. The major proponents of these ideas, Sir Ebenezer Howard (1850–1928), Sir Raymond Unwin (1863–1940), Sir Patrick
Geddes (1854–1932), and Lewis Mumford (1895–1990), were all
decentralist planners dedicated to the realization of Kropotkin's
program for the transformation of society as outlined in *Fields,
Factories, and Workshops.*

The originator of this effort was the "elder statesman of a worldwide planning movement," Ebenezer Howard.[23] As a young man
in the 1870s, Howard had been a pioneer in Nebraska and stenog-
rapher in Chicago, but he returned home to England, where he
breathed in the communitarian, back-to-the-land, brotherhood-of-
humanity spirit that was in the air in the late nineteenth century,
and became a teacher of Esperanto and a follower of Kropotkin
and earlier English utopian socialists. Under their inspiration,
Howard developed the blueprints for garden cities, which he introduced in his 1898 book, *To-morrow: A Peaceful Path to Real Reform* (later reissued as *Garden Cities of Tomorrow*). Here and in
his subsequent town-development activities he attempted to find
alternatives to what he saw as the poisonous, overcrowded cities
of his day. His solution was to establish moderate-size communities
of no more than thirty thousand inhabitants each, located in the
countryside and surrounded by a rural greenbelt of parks, farms,
and woods, with homes surrounded by gardens, communal ownership of land, and small-scale cooperatively owned cottage industries to provide goods and services. This was a setting that would

not only clean up urban blight but would encourage direct democracy, eliminate the necessity of central government, and, in joining town and country, lay the basis for a new civilization.

Howard's plans were eventually implemented in tandem with those of Patrick Geddes.[24] This Scottish polymath was an eccentric, rambling mumbler obsessed with drawing up categories of knowledge on tiny scraps of paper; associate of Darwin; sociologist; biologist; professor at Edinburgh, London, and Bombay; founder of student hostels in France; adviser to the Indian Raj; and designer of the Hebrew University in Jerusalem. He was also one of the founders of the regional planning profession. A friend and admirer of Kropotkin, he sought to ease social tensions through humanistic urban design that took cognizance of the environment and the individual. These are basic notions today but were radical at the turn of the century; through Geddes's many writings and energetic activities, he turned Kropotkin's ideas into common currency.

Under the influence of Kropotkin and Geddes, and working as Howard's principal lieutenant, Raymond Unwin was responsible for translating his mentors' ideas into reality by designing the first English garden city in 1903–1904 at Letchworth, followed by Hampstead Garden near London and several other sites. Unwin's garden communities—with their tastefully designed homes built in pseudohistorical styles facing medieval-inspired village commons and surrounded with greenbelts—flourished, as they were co-opted by the urban middle class and evolved into far-from-radical suburban real estate developments.[25] The same deviation from the original philosophy behind garden cities is apparent in the United States. There, towns founded in the garden-city spirit after World War I on Long Island, in Radburn (New Jersey), and elsewhere, rapidly became white-collar residential suburbs.

This was despite the effort of Lewis Mumford. Mumford was a college dropout who became an intellectual force in America as a social philosopher, professor, and founder of the Regional Planning Association of America. As a self-designated disciple of Kropotkin, Howard, and Geddes, he criticized American urban, industrial civilization and yearned for its radical transformation and a return to the simple life. He wanted not to do away with the cities but to make them more humane by distributing their population to garden cities spread around the country. By this means it would be possible to revivify the nonurban regions of the nation and provide the environment in which people might achieve their full potential both as individuals and as members of a community. At the same time it would be possible to preserve older villages, enhance social harmony in larger cities, protect regional environments, and place man and nature in balance.[26] Thanks to Mumford's labors, joined with those of Geddes, Howard, and Unwin, the notion of replacing urban blight with planned open spaces and greenbelts became commonplace throughout the West. Through all of them, something of Kropotkin and his Russian Populist anarchism lived on, however much in mutated or attenuated form.[27]

In still other ways, Kropotkin's ideas were propagated throughout the non-European world, where they also produced distinct hybrids of social thought to satisfy local needs and tastes. The radical intelligentsias of Asia shared an interest in Russian affairs, an attachment to Kropotkin's communitarianism, and a revulsion at the implications of social Darwinism. Young, elite intellectuals of Japan, China, Vietnam, and India were all struggling with issues of national identity in the face of overbearing white European power. Direct Western political control, foreign economic domination, and/or cultural intrusion, when joined with the weakness of native central governments and the perpetuation of rigid local social hierarchies, sparked nationalist indignation. The resentment was stoked by extremist ideas introduced, ironically, through contact with the West. Radical movements in these countries came to incline toward Russian-generated anarchism, presaging and preparing the ground for the later Third World appropriation of the message of Russian communism. Before 1917, just like the advocates of the simple life and the arts and crafts in rapidly urbanizing and industrializing Europe and America, many Asian intellectuals reacted against Western-derived modernization, an understandable sentiment in countries where it seemed even more alien, appeared more suddenly, and was more disruptive of traditional socioeconomic patterns—and where its arrival was sometimes accompanied by hostile foreign soldiers.

Chinese anarchism serves as an illustrative example of these trends.[28] In China, anarchism was one of the fruits of the Chinese encounter with Europeans and Westernization. It budded as an intellectual movement at a time of crisis and flux in the late nineteenth century, when Chinese intellectuals in their search for meaning were attracted to utopian ideologies. The decline in the legitimacy of the Qing dynasty and the collapse of the antiforeign Boxer movement of 1899–1901 brought anarchism into full flower. But the anarchists of China aimed not just to respond to the disgrace of political defeats at the hands of foreigners but also to foster spiritual and social unity—again this craving for wholeness—and to forge a new civilization.

Although French anarchist writings also had a persistent appeal, Chinese anarchism was largely under the spell of Kropotkin. The ground had been well prepared for the reception of Russian radicalism. Russian politics received a great deal of attention in China, where several nationalist newspapers—among them the Shanghai *Russian Affairs Alarm*, later called *Alarming Bell Daily News*—were founded for the sole purpose of publicizing the evils of Russian imperialism in Manchuria. In attacking the Russian autocracy, these papers brought to light arguments that would be adapted for use against the corrupt Chinese government. And Chinese hostility to capitalism for its associations with Western imperialism opened the door to the antiurban, anarchist emphases of Russian Populism. By 1907, Kropotkin's and Bakunin's writings were well known among the disaffected, Westernized, upper-class opponents within the anti-Manchu movement, whose intellectuals admired the Russian revolutionaries for advocating the violent negation of the traditional state and society. For Chinese anarchists, Kropotkin's *Mutual Aid* appealed because of its scientific rebuttal of Darwinism, which had been used to proclaim the superiority of whites and justify European imperialism. Kropotkin's views on decentralized associations and farming methods echoed the goals of neo-Confucianists; indeed, his ideas seemed to mesh with Confucius on the whole (at the same time Kropotkin also inspired those who wanted to rid China of its Confucian heritage). And, for many Chinese intellectuals in this rural country, the Marxist emphasis on the working class was senseless; Kropotkin's ideas justified the radicals' preoccupation with the peasantry. Even Li Dazhao (1888–1927), one of the founders of Chinese communism and its early ideologist, used Kropotkin's mutual aid concept to detach the Marxist class-struggle theory from its restrictive socioeconomic base in the industrial proletariat: as he saw it, the people were not divided by class but had a common will expressed through cooperationism.

Kropotkin was the premier thinker to inspire Chinese anarchism, but his ideological seed was disseminated far and wide along the entire range of the nascent Chinese intelligentsia. Its anarchist members introduced European radical literature, including Marxism, to their country. Their anti-Manchu agitation played a role in precipitating the revolution of 1911. They were the first to set up trade unions in China and the first to think of rural revolution. By 1930, Chinese anarchism was largely supplanted by either Guomindang radical nationalism or communism, but anarchism had paved the way for these revolutionary movements.

Throughout the world, Kropotkin's ideas lay dormant after the Russian Revolution, only to be reawakened in the West in the 1950s. In 1917 Kropotkin returned to Russia, full of hopes for the socialist renovation of mankind, but disappointed by the violence and dictatorial centralism of Lenin. When he died, his funeral march on February 13, 1921, was the occasion for the last mass demonstration against Bolshevism. After that, anarchism seemed to have been put to rest with its leader: the new socialist autocrats of Russia crushed the movement at home, and anarchism suffered a quick decline abroad. Marxism-Leninism seemed to outmuscle it with the apparent triumphs of the Soviet system, winning the adoration of the world's radical leftists.

But a number of thinkers kept the flame of Kropotkin's anarchism alive for the post–World War II New Left, all of them political and economic decentralizers under the spell of Kropotkin, whose vision they considered the "noblest human idea."[29] Perhaps the one who has remained closest to pure Kropotkinism is the British anarchist Colin Ward (1924–), who in numerous books and periodicals appearing from the 1940s to the 1980s outlined cooperative ownership of industry, local advocacy planning for citizen control of development, community groups, tenants' associations, squatters' rights, and an end to big government. Ward's thought, which was premised on Kropotkin's concept of mutual aid, inspired alternative lifestyles throughout western Europe and America.[30]

Relatedly, Kropotkin was one of the most significant of the various intellectual forebears of the contemporary ecological movement. His visions of democracy as local politics and economics as local trade; his arguments that human intervention in the environment should respect nature and advance the cause of egalitarian cooperativism; and his related encouragement of resource conservation and intensive husbandry all contributed to the pulp of ideas recycled through the generations to form the philosophical fiber of ecoradicalism.[31]

Ecological activism could not have emerged as it did without having been cross-fertilized by the work of biologists whose research empirically sustained the cooperationist theories at the heart of Kropotkin's science of anarchism. Crucial in the development of the academic field of ecology was Warder Clyde Allee (1885–1955), who became a professor of zoology at the University of Chicago in 1921 and remained there into the 1950s. Allee was an opponent of World War I and an associate of the Chicago reformer (and Kropotkin admirer) Jane Addams. He was influenced at the time by pacifists' rejection of Darwinism as the ideology of the German military. In the contexts of both international tensions and Progressivism, he became familiar with Kropotkin's work, which was being republished on both sides of the ocean by antiwar groups; he devoted his professional life to finding empirical evidence that would sustain the hypotheses of Kropotkin and other cooperationist biologists.

Allee applied what he called "naturalist ethics" to politics for the purpose of saving mankind. Through his research over the years he claimed to have found evidence to oppose warfare and support a social system centered not on the family but on the cooperative association of individuals. This pattern of behavior, he believed, was common at an unconscious, physiological level among all animals, even the most primitive single-celled organisms. At first wary of the findings of genetics and evolution as deterministic, Allee adapted to them in the 1930s by arguing that animal populations as well as individuals are selected for in evolution according to the extent of their mutual-aid tendencies. Transmitted in evolution, cooperation served the purpose of reducing social tensions and maintaining the social equilibrium essential for the survival of species.[32]

A large body of research in anthropology, zoology, and biology continues to point toward cooperation and mutual aid rather than conflict and exploitation as dynamic factors in the Darwinian struggle for existence. As a team of leading British and Austrian evolutionary biologists wrote in 1995, "[Kropotkin's] arguments have succeeded far beyond what [he] could ever have foreseen."[33]

The spirit of Kropotkin-inspired cooperationist biology permeated twentieth-century environmentalism. The wellspring of Kropotkin's decades-long influence in German ecological circles was an anarchist-socialist philosopher and the first German "Green," Gustav Landauer (1870–1919), who motivated a portion of the many disaffected, educated intellectual young to retreat from the tense and frenetic city into rural communes. Drawing heavily on Kropotkin's *Mutual Aid*, Landauer (before his brutal murder by German soldiers) meditated on the formation of cooperative communities as a means of achieving spiritual regeneration, a common yearning in the troubled post–World War I German Republic. A garden-city movement emerged in Weimar Germany in connection with these and related English Kropotkinite ideas. As filtered through Martin Buber, a follower of the German Jew Landauer, they also became one of several philosophical influences on the early Israeli kibbutzim.[34]

The later heir to these sentiments was the Green Party, which became a political force in the 1970s and 1980s. Emerging out of the German protest movement of the preceding two decades, the Greens were agitated about new issues such as nuclear disarmament, but Kropotkinism also provided one of their vital sources of ideological energy. This was the intellectual fuel for the Green movement's concepts of "fundamental opposition" to bourgeois

industrial society and its call for *Basisdemokratie*, or direct, participatory, local, activist politics. Kropotkin, too, fed their longings to
alter existing social arrangements and bring about harmony between all living creatures and the environment, to decentralize politics and economics for the preservation of nature's diversity, and
to fashion a sustainable and egalitarian economy.[35]

Closely linked to the German Green movement was American
radical environmentalism, whose most prominent theorist, Murray
Bookchin (1921–), was also the leading anarchist of the post–
World War II era. Bookchin called Kropotkin an "eco-anarchist"
and updated his philosophy for a new generation of activists committed to saving the planet. Bookchin imbibed Kropotkin's interconnected beliefs in nature as a source of ethics, in biological inter-
dependence and the lack of hierarchy and stratification in the
animal world, in mutual aid, in the virtues of restraining rampant
individualism, in industrial decentralization, in deurbanization,
and in organic agriculture. Virtually the whole of Kropotkin's
worldview was taken over by Bookchin, who elaborated an "ecology of freedom" that called for the economic predominance of
small-scale industrial enterprises, alternative technologies, and intensive farms producing goods and crops suited to and marketed
within the various "bioregions" of the nation. This arrangement
would be more environmentally and locally sensitive than existing
agrobusiness and industry, and it would support a society organized into decentralized, self-sufficient democratic communities.
Bookchin's ecological utopia is a 1960s remake of Kropotkin's an-
archo-communism and fed the small-is-beautiful, limited-growth,
sustainable-development, and ecofeminist views of fringe and
mainstream environmentalism that have grown to be a visible out-
crop of Western politics and attitudes ever since.[36]

What an unusual mix of things Kropotkin was. Prince and Populist. Romantic arcadian and positivist scientist. Revolutionary conspirator and cooperationist-ethicist. Individualist and collectivist.
Ideologue and anti-ideologue. Extremist and gradualist. Nostalgic
for an idyllic past and expectant of social bliss in the future. Modern and antimodern. The mix reflected his breadth and complexity

as a thinker, and his dual Russian and European intellectual ances-try. Kropotkin's anarchism came partly out of a long-standing western European radical philosophical tradition emphasizing antiauthoritarianism, rationalism, and moral self-mastery as the constituent elements of human perfectibility and social progress. But it was also deeply rooted in his native Russian soil. Extolling the individualism and social equality that shriveled in the shadows of the rigid tsarist autocracy and the factories and tenements of suddenly industrial cities, Kropotkin joined his Populist contempo-raries in positing the Russian peasant commune as the cure-all for the ailments of modern society.

The power of Kropotkin's thought comes from the fusion of these intellectual traditions. His prescription for social change, which included a large dose of Russian folk medicine, gained wide acceptance in Western and non-Western circles eager to experi-ment with alternatives to established European liberal remedies. In this way Kropotkin joined Bakunin, Dostoevsky, Tolstoy, and the Russian avant-garde in altering the cultural genes of the twenti-eth century.

CHAPTER **3**

Dostoevsky's Messianic Irrationalism

IN INDUSTRIALIZING, urbanizing, nineteenth-century western Europe, religion was increasingly challenged by a brash faith in social progress, science, and reason. This worldview, represented in the arts by literary naturalism and painterly realism, called forth a series of intellectual reactions that by the end of the century crystallized into the early Modernist movement. Despite its many forms and internal contradictions, Modernism was united in revolt against philosophical rationalism, scientific positivism, capitalist economics, parliamentary politics, and bourgeois individualism. As heirs of Romanticism, the Modernists trumpeted the virtues of "authentic" living, exploration of the irrational forces at play in human nature, and a renewed spirituality. As the aftershocks of World War I undermined the European political and economic system, their message came into its own and Modernism rose to dominate Western culture.

Alongside Schopenhauer, Kierkegaard, Nietzsche, and Bergson, the Russian writers Dostoevsky and Tolstoy stood as patriarchs of Modernist culture. Established as literary giants in Russia during the 1860s and 1870s, a period of whirlwind socioeconomic change, they made their mark by pondering man's fate and shattering the mold of the novelistic genre. So innovative were their works that the American critic George Steiner considered them to be responsible for one of three great turning points in all of European literature, the other two being Athenian drama and Shakespeare.[1] In the 1880s, a "Russian invasion" of Western literature began, with Dostoevsky and Tolstoy in its forefront.[2]

As sensitive witnesses to the upheaval brought to Russia by the rapidity of its modernizing thrust, Dostoevsky and Tolstoy were far more conscious of a break with the past than were contemporary western Europeans, for whom the process was somewhat more gradual. The two authors responded to this new situation and captured this new mood in their writings. They were among the first to grapple with questions that would remain at the center of worldwide intellectual discourse from the late nineteenth century on.

For the time being we leave Tolstoy to concentrate on Dostoevsky and trace his remarkable influence on the crosscurrents of Modernist literature, theology, psychology, and philosophy. He was unmistakably one of the seminal figures of the modern era throughout the world, because "the anxiety and doubts that flood his works are our anxieties and doubts."[3]

Life of a Russian "saint . . . prophet . . . genius"

Dostoevsky was born in Moscow in 1821 and came of age in St. Petersburg.[4] One of the great chroniclers of the modern metropolis, he grew up in poverty, unlike the rich plantation aristocrats Bakunin, Kropotkin, and Tolstoy. The major turning point in his life took place in 1849, when the government arrested him as a member of a utopian-socialist discussion circle. He and several others were condemned to death, but in fact a mock execution was planned to impress the prisoners with the mercy of almighty Tsar Nicholas I. At the very last moment, as the firing squad was preparing to shoot, an imperial decree was read out granting a reprieve to the condemned. The incident profoundly shook Dostoevsky, who felt he had been resurrected. For the rest of his life he tried to recapture this spiritual ecstasy in his fiction.

His imprisonment left a lifelong imprint on him. Here he first became aware of the divide that separated the common people of Russia and the Westernized elite. The perversions of the upper-class inmates repelled him, and he began to develop sympathy toward the crude peasant convicts for their Christian devotion. In the view of his biographer, Joseph Frank, epileptic illness and the strains of imprisonment led Dostoevsky to undergo a kind of religious conversion to faith in the Russian people.

After four years of hard labor and six additional years of exile, Dostoevsky returned to St. Petersburg in 1859, where his fame as a writer began to grow. But in 1867, to escape gambling debts, he and his wife fled to western Europe. His experiences there confirmed to him the antithesis between Russia and the West he had first glimpsed in prison. Disgusted with the European bourgeoisie's worship of money, convinced of the evil of separating oneself from

4. Fyodor Dostoevsky. From V. S. Nechaeva, *Fedor Mikhailovich Dostoevskii v portretakh, illiustratsiiakh, dokumentakh* (Moscow, 1972).

one's native soil, and desperately homesick, he left for St. Petersburg in 1871.

In the last decade and a half of his life he established himself as one of the major Russian authors. He issued a one-man, far-right periodical called *The Diary of a Writer*, which brought him popularity and fame. But it is his short stories and novels that account for his enduring reputation, above all *Notes from Underground* (1864) and the four murder novels, *Crime and Punishment* (1866), *The Idiot* (1868), *Devils* (a.k.a. *The Possessed*) (1872), and *Brothers Karamazov* (1880). He died in 1881. At his funeral, thirty thousand people accompanied the coffin, fifteen choirs sang, and seventy-two delegations laid wreaths. In his last months he had been spoken of as "our saint . . . our prophet . . . more than a genius";[5] little could the crowd of mourners have imagined that much of the world would soon come to see him in this very light.

Dostoevsky's fiction encapsulates the convulsive dynamism and instability of his own life and the rapidly changing world he lived in. It was the modern metropolis—in his case St. Petersburg—seething with squalor and despair, that accounted for much of his own experience and the style and orientation of his writing. Like the European Romantics, Bakunin, Kropotkin, Tolstoy, and multitudes of other radical cultural critics, Dostoevsky bemoaned the destruction of the traditional community by industrial capitalism and its replacement by cities inhabited by lone individuals without strong personal bonds. Like Dickens and Balzac, both of whom he greatly admired, he devoted himself to depicting the old way of "life which is in a state of decomposition" and the "life forming anew, on novel foundations."[6] His novels throb with the misery, loneliness, alcoholism, whoremongering, and criminal abominations of its destitute inhabitants, delirious with nightmares and hallucinations and mental breakdowns.

Along with subject matter, the Dostoevskian style and technique were also derived from this setting. In the words of the Soviet cultural commissar Anatoly Lunacharsky, Dostoevsky's works were "the painful but necessary voice of the confusion of his times."[7] His sensitivity to the teeming Russian metropolis partly accounts for what the Russian scholar Mikhail Bakhtin argued was the most

distinctive feature of Dostoevsky's writing, his dialogism or po-
lyphony. According to Bakhtin, Dostoevsky, like no previous author, gave his characters full play, allowing them to speak and often
leaving their clashing viewpoints unresolved as in real life. His
characters' ideas seemed almost independent of their creator's, "as
if the character were not an object of authorial discourse, but
rather a fully valid, autonomous carrier of his own individual
word." Dostoevsky "creates not voiceless slaves . . . , but *free* people, capable of standing *alongside* their creator, capable of not
agreeing with him and even of rebelling against him." Bakhtin's
thesis has been disputed by scholars who argue that Dostoevsky's
fiction did intend to convince readers of the author's point of view.
Nonetheless, many who accept this criticism would agree with Bakhtin that what emerged from the novels is a *"plurality of independent and unmerged voices and consciousnesses, a genuine polyph-
ony of fully valid voices."*[8] And this proliferation of voices in Dostoevsky's dialogue, while not a completely original innovation, was
a masterly advance in the art of novel writing.

The heroes of Dostoevsky's writings scream out in the torment
of urban life, their humanity overshadowed, sometimes crushed by
the heartlessness of St. Petersburg, whose starkly rational conception and architectural design reproduced in stone and iron the imperial bureaucracy's power over the populace. This, too, was the
breeding ground for Russian radicals, a distinct social grouping
that in Dostoevsky's mind mirrored the city's unbending, inhuman
devotion to rational principle. For these die-hard materialists,
human beings were just a chemical process, creatures lacking any
true moral or spiritual faculty. Although echoing the views of European Romantic conservatives, Dostoevsky's attack was more strident than any previous critiques.[9] For him the intelligentsia's ultra-
rationalism produced a cold, unloving kind of devotion to
humanity that often concealed an abhorrence of humans as individuals. Russian intellectuals in his fiction are personalities whose
basic human feelings and moral sense are frozen. The disturbing
consequence of this Western-born dehumanization was violence
and the potential for political tyranny.

These themes were at the heart of Dostoevsky's major works. The protagonist of *Crime and Punishment*, Raskolnikov, kills an old crone pawnbroker to prove the validity of his theory that a few self-designated great men—himself and Napoleon included—are above the law and may transgress ethical boundaries to refresh society and save mankind. In *Devils*, inspired by the Nechaev affair, Dostoevsky depicts the destructiveness of revolutionary intellectuals lusting for power. And in "The Grand Inquisitor," a chapter of *Brothers Karamazov* that is considered one of the masterpieces of world literature, he predicts the emergence of future tyrannies. Socialism, according to Dostoevsky, offered humanity a guarantee of false religious faith, bread, and social harmony in return for their giving up the burden of freedom. A socialist dictator could rule despotically, but as long as he took care of the submissive people's most basic survival needs, "mankind will run after . . . [him] like a flock of sheep, grateful and obedient."[10] Like children, humanity will obediently accept the repression that comes with living under an absolute authority because of the economic certainty and psychic protection offered by it. This, Dostoevsky felt, was the great allure and danger presented by the left wing in Europe and in Russia.

So compelling were the cynical arguments of the Grand Inquisitor that many people came to see them as Dostoevsky's position. In fact, his writings were an effort to fight against them, and nowhere in his stories are they associated with positive connotations. In opposition to the Grand Inquisitor and the radical worldview, Dostoevsky advances a trinity of coequal philosophical tenets: individual freedom; Orthodox Christianity; and Russian nationalism.

These three facets of Dostoevsky's belief form an indivisible whole. All presuppose the complexity of human psychology, contrary to the simplistic radical understanding of the psyche as an emanation of environmental and/or chemical forces. Dostoevsky's focus on the individual's consciousness and the irrational forces within it established him as one of the seminal figures in the history of nineteenth- and twentieth-century thought. His understanding of human psychological complexity (along with his attempt to analyze the mental effects of urban life) propelled him to devise new

literary techniques that revolutionized fiction writing. His polyphonic technique accented the amorphousness of personality and
unveiled the mental processes of his stories' characters. He did not
eliminate the role of the narrator or delve into his characters' subconscious inner monologue to the same extent as did stream-of-
consciousness literature. But he certainly foreshadowed it.[11] And
his powerful, original literary discourses on the depths of the
human mind helped to prepare the world for the reception of
Freudianism.

Dostoevsky's view of human psychology and the literary techniques he devised to capture its elusive qualities reflected the philosophical divide between him and the radicals. The adherents of
utilitarianism/positivism saw man as "nothing more than a kind of
piano key or an organ stop; . . . so that everything he's done has
not been in accordance with his own desire, but in and of itself,
according to the laws of nature."[12] Dostoevsky, by contrast, rejected the image of man as a chemical process or machine operating
according to the ironclad laws of nature: he believed in free will
and was convinced that simply existing was not enough for man.
As the embittered, neurotic, reclusive antihero of *Notes from Underground* proclaimed: "What do I care about the laws of nature
and arithmetic when for some reason I dislike all these laws and I
dislike the fact that two times two makes four? Of course, I won't
break through that wall with my head if I really don't have the
strength to do so, nor will I reconcile myself to it, just because I'm
faced with such a stone wall and lack the strength."[13] These words
sputtered by the narrator of a story that is a founding manifesto of
Existentialism are a slap in the face of rationalism.

But for Dostoevsky this assertion of one's "own stupid will," in
the words of the underground man, was also dangerous.[14] When
they exercise it, many of his central characters discover the pitfalls:
individual license, evil, self-destruction, and death. The underground man himself is an abject hero rather than a positive one.
Yet without free will there is no chance that human beings will
choose to do good. By denying free will, in Dostoevsky's opinion,
scientists and radicals had eliminated morality from their

worldview, and that was a disaster. At a time of chaos and social crisis, universal ethical standards were more necessary than ever.

With human freedom at the heart of his opposing argument, Dostoevsky would seem to many intellectuals in the decades after his death to be a defender of Western individualism. But he was often misinterpreted. Freedom for Dostoevsky was not a juridical or constitutional problem, as in the West, but an inner, spiritual one, as suggested earlier in the century by Russia's Slavophile Romantics; he understood individualism not as a display of unbridled liberty but as the condition of living ethically according to Christian precepts. He equates true freedom with a Christlike spirituality that overcomes modern man's fractured and wounded personality through love, brotherhood, and community. These conditions were not to be found in the West, according to him, but in Orthodox Russia.

And Dostoevsky was on a one-man crusade on behalf of that cause. His work was "pierced with the rays" of Russian religiosity.[15] Despite his alarm at contemporary life, he was an optimist whose fiction held open to man the possibility of salvation. Redemption was possible for transgressors—including murderers—through faith, repentance, suffering, and acceptance of the authentic or "living life." Imbued with the loving, ethical spirit of the New Testament, in awe of God's work on earth, the "living life" is the attainment of Dostoevskian freedom. It means simple, Christian living, or, as Raskolnikov, the murderer in *Crime and Punishment*, was counseled, "[giving] yourself up to life directly, without [rational theorizing]." When finally "life replaced logic" for Raskolnikov, his resurrection could begin.[16]

Dostoevsky's conception of God's creation identifies the earth with the Russian landscape—"the boundless steppe, flooded with sunshine."[17] Here Russia and religion are conjoined to form messianic nationalism, the third facet of Dostoevsky's trinity of beliefs. Writing at a time when Russia was grappling with its national identity in the face of the dominance of Western military, economic, and cultural power, Dostoevsky, in contemplation of these problems, approached the chauvinistic position that Russia alone represented religious and political truth.

He inflated the Slavophile sense of Russian uniqueness into a strident and hostile anti-Western credo—despite his intellectual engagement with European philosophy and literature. Brotherhood and community have disappeared in the West, where rationalism and the false idol of progress have made man "bloodthirsty in a nastier, more repulsive way than before."[18] In Russia, the Catholic Poles, the Jews, and the radical intelligentsia acted as the uprooted agents of Westernization, and he excoriated them mercilessly in his journalism and fiction. There are no positive characters representing European ideas in his fiction; all those who do so are doomed and spell doom for Russia.

While Europe was in decay, Russia was predestined for greatness. For the Orthodox Russian people were representatives of the universal truth of Christianity. "God will save Russia as He has saved her many times. Salvation will come from the people, from their faith and meekness."[19] Like Tolstoy, Dostoevsky saw the Russian peasants as untouched by Western civilization and the embodiment of his ideals of spirituality. Even if they were occasionally drunken and cruel, their essence was pure, preserved in their religiosity and in the unity of the rural commune.

Dostoevsky was convinced that Russia would save Europe. "The Russian nation is an extraordinary phenomenon in the history of all mankind," he wrote, that "may hold the power to bring a new light to the world."[20] This conviction took on an apocalyptic quality in the 1870s as he lauded the virtues of a Pan-Slavic war against Europe. Only with Russian military victory would true Christianity survive. So fanatically certain was he that Russia was the earthly embodiment of the Kingdom of God that, like Bakunin, Nechaev, and the other radicals he so despised, he advocated violence in the service of a higher good, in this case the Orthodox Russian messianic mission, the salvation of mankind.

Dostoevsky's worldview does not fit neatly into any ideological category. Just as it is often hard to tell the radical left and right apart, so Dostoevsky overlapped with the Populist intelligentsia, despite their many differences. He loathed Western capitalism, parliamentarism, cities, and the bourgeoisie as much as they did. He revered the peasant masses, albeit for their religiosity rather than their revolutionary potential. He longed for the simplicity, harmony, and wholeness of the preindustrial world and for the restoration of community. Like many of the Populists, he held a deep-seated belief in Russia as the carrier of universal Truth, and remained a utopian until his death.

Of course, fundamental differences separated Dostoevsky and the left. He derided their notion that subversion of political and social institutions was enough to ameliorate human existence: his profound conviction was that only inner spiritual and moral renewal would work. This was not a minor quibble but goes to the heart of his rejection of the radical intelligentsia. Their vision did away with the divine; his was God-centered. For these reasons he (as well as Tolstoy) contemplated the mysteries of psychology and spirituality.

These preoccupations, in tandem with his unswaying hostility to Westernization, helped to undermine the nineteenth-century worldview and give rise to Modernist culture. Thus he was an inspiration to the growing multitudes of "men at odds with themselves and their times."[21]

"Shakespeare of the lunatic asylum": The Western Reception of Dostoevsky

Dostoevsky's reputation in Europe as a spirit alien to the West, which in the most general sense accounts for his popularity in the world, was shaped in France. The French frigidity toward Russia that followed Napoleon's defeat in 1812 gave way to Russophilia after the humiliation of the Franco-Prussian War in 1871. France now looked to Russia as a counterbalance to unified Germany. As their military and economic relationship grew more intimate, the French passion for Russian culture heated up.

The first Russian novelist to impress the French was Ivan Turgenev, who lived much of his life in France. French naturalism was in ascendance at the time and was receptive to Turgenev's lyrical realism. But naturalism was on the wane by the 1880s, for the same reasons that Impressionism in painting, the final stage of realism, gave way to Post-Impressionism. Cultural innovators were tired of the naturalists' excessive documentation of exterior reality; they wanted literature to do more than skim the surface of human experience.

Piquing the French fascination with Russian culture and, indeed, molding the opinions of all Europeans toward Russia was Viscount Eugène Melchior de Vogüé (1848–1910). Having been wounded in the Franco-Prussian War, he devoted himself to reinvigorating France at the expense of Germany. In 1876 he became secretary of the French embassy in St. Petersburg. There he married into an aristocratic family, learned Russian, and became an expert on the country and its writers. From this vantage point he established himself as a bridge between the two cultures.

De Vogüé's articles on Russia of the 1870s were brought together in *Le Roman russe* (1886), a major event in the literary history of the nineteenth century and rapidly translated into English. Here he depicts Russian culture as closer to Hindu or Buddhist than to European civilization. He wants to see the Russian people as Asians: "Many a Moscow student or peasant from certain provinces might, except for his light complexion, easily pass in a street of Lahore or Benares for a native of the valley of the Ganges." His treatment of Dostoevsky follows suit: "with Dostoevsky, that true Scythian, who will revolutionize all our previous habits of thought, we now enter into the heart of Moscow, with its giant cathedral of St. Basil, like a Chinese pagoda as to form and decoration, and built by Tartar architects, but dedicated to the worship of the Christian's God"; with Dostoevsky we are "looking into a different world than ours."[22] What a recommendation to all those seeking alternatives to the existing order!

As a Catholic conservative, de Vogüé promoted the moralizing and religiosity of Russian writers against the scientific determinism and coldly clinical dissection of human behavior practiced by the Zola school of naturalist writers. As he put it, "the influence of the great Russian writers will be wholesome for our exhausted art" of the novel, which dealt only with the "slime of the earth." Russian novels, by contrast, put the soul and emotions back in man, and he recommended them as a way for French youth to find "the spiritual nourishment that our own imaginative literature no longer provides them."[23]

At first, Dostoevsky did not go over very well in France. He seemed unbalanced, illogical, and indigestible. If *Crime and Punishment*, first translated into French in 1884, had any early success, it was as a horror story. According to a critic for *La Nouvelle Revue* in 1885, it was "a highly curious and amusing novel" that not gentlemen but "the ladies would rather read."[24] Even de Vogüé, who did so much to introduce Dostoevsky to France, had his doubts about this "Shakespeare of the lunatic asylum."[25] But Dostoevsky appealed to a younger generation, and even at the start there were those who were fascinated by him. "His monstrous, extravagant world grips you and holds you fast," was the judgment of one.[26] "I worship Dostoevsky," novelist Marcel Proust, another explorer of the human soul, once told a friend.[27]

Dostoevsky was soon all the rage, owing to the growing absorption in individual psychology and the irrational, joined by a desire for moral, ethical, and religious renewal. In this the new literary generation from the turn of the century to the First World War was at one with de Vogüé against French realism: Russian literature "gave us the strength to roll away the stone from the sepulchre" of naturalism.[28] Writers such as Georges Bernanos (1888–1948), Paul Claudel (1868–1955), André Gide (1869–1951), and Charles-Louis Philippe (1874–1909) were enthused about Dostoevsky and Tolstoy as un-French and non-Western alternatives to the naturalists and positivists. Here as soon elsewhere, the two Russian greats helped to destroy the traditional form of the novel. Together with their themes of religion, the soul, and the mystery of human nature, they taught new French writers techniques and themes that let them push Zola aside. The best example was Gide, who became one of the central figures in the Modernist movement for his fiction that captured the mercurial, ambiguous nature of humankind. This theme was an assimilation of the lessons of Dostoevsky.

With so many prominent writers taken with the Slavic soul, Dostoevsky was bound to provoke a reaction. French nationalist conservatives were dismayed by the foreign threat to the purity of French culture. This sentiment was behind the 1892 charge made by Maurice Barrès (he later changed his tune about Dostoevsky) on the literature of the day as writing served up with the unsavory Russian flavors of "caviar and smoked sprats."[29] But conservative ranks were divided—de Vogüé, after all, was one of them—and in any case they could not have stopped literary innovation coming from Russia any more than they can keep Hollywood movies out of France today.

Above all, it was already an international phenomenon. De Vogüé introduced Dostoevsky and Tolstoy to a large audience on the Continent, where *Le Roman russe* was read widely either in French or translated into the local languages. His book enhanced the popularity of the two Russian authors in eastern Europe and established their reputation in Italy, Spain, Portugal, and Latin America. In Germany and Scandinavia, late-nineteenth-century writers were also infected, and it was in Holland that the first full-length Western biography of Dostoevsky was published, in 1889. Everywhere now, writers were discovering Dostoevsky and the Russian spirit.

Perhaps everywhere but in England and America, that is, where it took longer for the Dostoevsky fever to take hold than it did in Europe. A host of factors account for the chilly reception given Dostoevsky in these two countries. America had its own spiritual writing in Ralph Waldo Emerson, Nathaniel Hawthorne, Herman Melville, and the like, and so had less need to look for it abroad. In any case, Protestantism in the United States sanctioned the materialism of business, which further reduced the size of Dostoevsky's potential audience. And the social conflicts brought on by political tensions, military defeats, and industrialization were simply not as extensive as in Europe, let alone Russia. The writer W. D. Howells explained why it was difficult for Americans to fathom the Dostoevsky mood: "Our novelists . . . concern themselves with the more smiling aspects of life, which are the more American; . . . [and, unlike Dostoevsky], very few American novelists have been led out to be shot, or finally exiled to the rigors of a winter in Duluth."[30]

For England, the foremost capitalist and industrial country, Dostoevsky's concerns were also more distant than on the Continent.

Some authors, however, did warm to Dostoevsky early on. Robert Louis Stevenson, who had read the French translation of *Crime and Punishment* in 1884, wrote to a friend when the first English version was produced in 1886: "*Raskolnikoff* is easily the best book I have read in 10 years. . . . Many find it dull: Henry James could not finish it: all I can say is, it nearly finished me. It was like having an illness."[31] Stevenson wrote "Markheim" (1885), about the murder of an antique dealer, a short story with suspense and theme modeled directly on *Crime and Punishment*. His attraction can be explained by his own interest in psychological ambiguity, personality doubles, crime, and moral analysis. With his Modernist's sense of loneliness in the modern metropolis and use of inner monologue as a fictional device, he recognized in Dostoevsky a kindred spirit. The flamboyant aesthete Oscar Wilde also praised Dostoevsky in reviews of the mid-1880s, favoring his "interesting and curious psychological studies" over "the obscene brood of pseudo-realists which roosts in the [great sewer] of France."[32]

But most Anglo-American critics before the twentieth century disliked Dostoevsky for his morbidity or apparent lack of style and, in their ignorance, often accused him of being a Nihilist himself. At best he was seen as a photographer of a kind of fantastical Russia. Among those who disapproved of him (and Tolstoy) were Henry James and, a few years later, Joseph Conrad. James derided their works as "baggy monsters" and "fluid puddings" with a "strong, rank quality." To the Polish-born Russophobe Conrad, *Brothers Karamazov* seemed "like some fierce mouthings of prehistoric ages."[33] By Conrad's time, though, circumstances had changed and he was the exception. Largely because of Pan-European developments—Freudianism and World War I—England dropped its resistance to Dostoevsky and Russian culture.

Europeans discovered Dostoevsky at the same time that they were probing the inner workings of the mind. It was not so much, as some have claimed, that he was far ahead of contemporary psychology in his exploration of irrational states of mind and the interpretation of dreams; rather, he presented them in his writing in exceptionally compelling and original terms. Indeed, his works were cited by European psychological and medical journals—for example, the *Berliner klinische Wochenschrift* in 1914—as an essential source for the study of psychiatry and especially of criminal pathology. The famous Italian-Jewish physician Cesare Lombroso (1836–1909) referred to Dostoevsky in his pioneering work on the inherited nature of criminality, as did other European criminologists and jurists. Of course, many contemporary psychologists saw Dostoevsky's novels as emanations of a sick mind, even of sexual depravity, and worth studying for that reason too.[34]

Among those who held that point of view was Sigmund Freud (1856–1939), who was fascinated with Dostoevsky. Russia overall had a strong presence in Freud's life and work. His ancestors had come to Austria from the Jewish Pale of tsarist Russia, and he remained in contact with relatives there. Some of his more renowned patients were Russians. He was an avid reader of Russian literature, kept abreast of Russian politics, and investigated Russian anti-Semitism, radicalism, and mysticism. A cultural and scientific revolutionary himself, he was initially enthused about the Russian Revolution's potential for liberating humanity from the oppressions of the superego, but Stalinism in the USSR contributed to his growing disillusionment with humanity. With this background he developed a view of Russians as neurotic, melancholic, and sexually repressive—hence inclined to ascetic mysticism, chauvinism, fanaticism, violence, and other "compromise[s] with morality."[35] These stereotyped images of Russian national character shaped his theories regarding psychological ambivalence and the swings in personality from the authoritarian/repressive to the orgiastic.

Dostoevsky's fictional characters also yielded plenty of these traits, and Freud used them as "proofs" of his conjectures. His 1928 essay "Dostoevsky and Parricide" was an analysis of the psychology of both *Brothers Karamazov* and its author. As several recent studies have shown, the essay reveals the flawed leaps of faith Freud made in his psychoanalysis.[36] His assessment of Dostoevsky is that he was a sadomasochist with repressed homosexuality and a possible past as a rapist. Dostoevsky's gambling addiction and epilepsy, he asserts, were neuroses stemming from the Russian writer's castration fears, Oedipus complex, and desire to both sub-

mit to and murder his father. Parricide was the central incident of
Brothers Karamazov, and Freud associated it, along with much else
in Dostoevsky's novels, with the author, as if it were an expression
of his psyche. The specialists now know enough about Dostoevsky's medical condition to decisively repudiate Freud on the matter; for them his article calls into question the validity of his psychoanalytic method, which often cited evidence culled from literature
and mythology. But Freud himself said that he was carrying on the
work of the poets and philosophers who had come before him in
uncovering the subconscious and the irrational. Among them was
Dostoevsky, whose star rose even higher with the ascent of psychoanalysis.

England finally caught Dostoevsky fever around 1912. Exposure
to the psychology vogue accounted for some of it, but Dostoevsky
was by then a part of the world's cultural repertoire and impossible
to ignore. Dramatizations of his novels were becoming numerous
on stages across Europe; in the coming decades there would be
hundreds of theatrical versions, scores of film interpretations, and
a handful of operas set to librettos based on Dostoevsky's fiction.
Constance Garnett began to produce the elegant translations of
Dostoevsky's collected works still in print today. World War I with
its disintegrating effects also generated a mood receptive to the
Russian message.

It was during the war that the British avant-garde became delirious over Dostoevsky, starting with the 1916 publication of J. Middleton Murry's *Fyodor Dostoevsky*. With his wife, the story-writer
Katherine Mansfield, Murry (1889–1957) had done much to introduce the Russian author Anton Chekhov to the English stage; now
he promoted a Modernist mystical interpretation of Dostoevsky to
a receptive intellectual set. In reading the work of this "tormented
soul," we "pass through a fire of spiritual experiences such as one
hundred years could not have kindled." For Murry, Dostoevsky
was more than a novelist. Novelists merely represent life; Dostoevsky puts forth a "vision of eternity" and discovers the "inmost essence of the truth of life." He is a "miracle" who initiates "a new
epoch" and brings to all mankind "a new form and a new con-

sciousness." Dostoevsky's writings were "the trumpet-note of a new word . . . [and] the revelation of a great secret.[37] Murry himself was one of the self-anointed high priests mediating between their mysteries and the laity.

The novelist D. H. Lawrence (1885–1930) reacted violently to Murry's twaddle: "Both [Dostoevsky and Murry] stink in my nostrils," he wrote.[38] Despite his antimodern passions and admiration of Tolstoy, Lawrence called Dostoevsky a "rat, slithering along in hate" who could "nicely stick his head between the feet of Christ, and waggle his behind in the air." With his particular erotic obsessions, the author of *Lady Chatterley's Lover* was put off by Dostoevsky's lack of interest in sensuality: "The whole point of Dostoevsky lies in the fact . . . that the individual ego . . . shall be infinite, God-like, and absolved from all relation." After all, Lawrence argued, people are not "fallen angels, they are merely people."[39]

There was actually a lot of common ground between the two novelists in their detestation of modern civilization and rationalism, and Lawrence later expressed a more favorable impression of Dostoevsky. In any case, his negative criticism did not represent the majority position among authors, most of whom had become Dostoevsky enthusiasts and worshiped the Russian soul. One who differed with Lawrence was Virginia Woolf (1882–1941), a leader of the Bloomsbury group of intellectuals and famed for her literary experiments in writing psychologically subjective novels dominated by the subconscious-exposing soliloquy. She esteemed Dostoevsky's works, which she reviewed as soon as Constance Garnett issued the translations. The gist of Woolf's commentary highlighted "the unlikeness between ourselves and the Russians."[40] An English novelist "reproduce[s] all the external appearances . . . but very rarely, and only for an instant, penetrate[s] to the tumult of thought which rages within his own mind. But the whole fabric of a book by Dostoevsky is made out of such material."[41] In her own stream-of-consciousness writing, she sought the same mystical terrain of the psyche Dostoevsky had explored: in him, "it is the soul that matters, its passion, its tumult, its astonishing medley of beauty and vileness. . . . the elements of the soul are seen, not separately . . . as our slower English minds conceive them, but streaked, involved, inextricably confused, a new panorama of the human mind is revealed."[42]

Woolf, Murry, and their associates were neo-Romantics enchanted with Dostoevsky as much out of pessimism about Western society as out of a desire to adapt his literary techniques. These were undercurrents rippling through all of Modernism, and they are conspicuous in two of the greatest writers of the movement, Irish expatriate James Joyce (1882–1941) and American expatriate T. S. Eliot (1888–1965). The temperaments and literary inclinations of both opened the door to Dostoevsky's influence.

Eliot, *the* Modernist English-language poet, steeped himself in Dostoevsky while studying in Paris. He confirmed his affinity for the Russian in the metaphysical, psychological, polyphonic poems "The Love Song of J. Alfred Prufrock" (1915) and *The Waste Land* (1922). Both of these pathbreaking works make subtle allusions to Dostoevsky's fiction, especially, as Eliot described it, its "continuation of the quotidian experience of the brain into seldom explored extremities of torture."[43] Eliot would eventually abandon what he saw as Dostoevsky's violent rebelliousness and revelation of the inner psyche; but in his early, most renowned poems, these qualities are omnipresent: nightmarishness, madness and split personality, confusion of reality and fantasy—all amid a bleak urban setting clearly invoking Dostoevsky's St. Petersburg. Eliot endows Prufrock with spiritual resemblances to Raskolnikov and makes symbolic reference to *Crime and Punishment*. Yet the regeneration that is at the heart of the latter is pointedly lacking in Eliot's poetry of this period, a mark of its author's Modernist hopelessness in the wake of the First World War.

Joyce, too, regarded Dostoevsky as one of the greatest of all novelists and consciously assimilated elements of *Crime and Punishment* in *Ulysses* (1922), among the other literary, linguistic, and symbolic references embedded there. Both novels are set in the modern city, one St. Petersburg, the other Dublin. Like most Modernist writings, both were psychological-metaphysical dramas. A young male intellectual in each struggles with God. Defiance of him leads to guilt, and both authors urge submission to a God-

ordered world and end their works with affirmation. George Orwell's interpretation of *Ulysses* pinpoints the thematic similarities:
"What Joyce is saying is, 'Here is life without God. Just look at
it.' "[44]

If Joyce gave a nod to Dostoevskian themes, he bowed to the
Russian author's technique. He saw himself as continuing Dostoevsky's attempt to shatter the Victorian novel, and he stated that Dostoevsky helped him to achieve a revolution in literature. He considered him his predecessor in Modernism, "the man more than any
other who has created modern prose, and intensified it to its pres-
ent-day pitch." He attributed to Dostoevsky the attention he gave
to "the subterranean forces, those hidden tides [of the mind] which
govern everything." In this sense especially, he and Eliot took over
where Dostoevsky left off, making consciousness the central arena
of action in their writing.[45] It is noteworthy in this regard that the
term "stream-of-consciousness," eventually attached to Joyce, was
originally coined in 1918 by the American critic Charles Gray
Shaw as a description of Dostoevsky.[46]

Through Joyce, Eliot, and others, Dostoevsky's influence radiated through modern English-speaking cultures. But his political
and philosophical—as opposed to literary—influence in Britain
was minimal: disaffection here, despite World War I, was not as
widespread as elsewhere. It was a different story in Germany,
where the Dostoevsky fever reached epidemic proportions.

The introduction of factories and the ideology of economic liberalism suddenly jerked nineteenth-century Germany out of its agrarian and guild-based economic torpor. Politically what had been a
medieval jumble of petty principalities was unified through the iron
and blood of three wars into a nation led by the Prussian monarchy.
But progress came at the cost of the fragmentation of traditional
bonds and resultant social disorientation. In reaction to these transformations, German cultural figures throughout the century were
more rejectionist and escapist than their French, English, or American counterparts. Modernist discontent and metaphysical flight
came readily to a nation whose native soil was Romanticism. And
Russia seemed to offer what was missing from a secularized, mechanized, and materialistic Germany: a spiritual and social message

that promised the restoration of individualism and community alike. It is in this light that the German reception of Dostoevsky must be understood.

Dostoevsky was a huge phenomenon, soaring in popularity between 1900 and the late 1930s.[47] He was more widely read in Germany than any other foreign author—and Tolstoy was not far behind him. In 1920–1922 alone, 400,000 copies of Dostoevsky's books were sold. Most tellingly, by 1934, 800 secondary works had been published on Dostoevsky, making him one of the most widely addressed topics in the country, second only to Goethe! According to novelist Heinrich Mann, Russian literature—above all Dostoevsky—was an intellectual revolution for Germans; every word was absorbed as the teaching of a great master. In the estimation of historian Fritz Stern, no other writer save Friedrich Nietzsche had as great an impact on German thought as Dostoevsky in the period before and after World War I.[48] Like Nietzsche's, his influence cut across all sectors of German opinion, obscuring neat divisions between left and right, reactionary and progressive.

At first the reaction to him was not much different from what occurred elsewhere. Far ahead of England and France, Germany saw almost all of Dostoevsky translated by 1890. Various German naturalist writers, especially in Berlin, were impressed by his depiction of the urban milieu and of people in all their complexity. And Nietzsche saw him as "the only psychologist . . . from whom I had something to learn."[49] It was to Dostoevsky's *The Idiot* that Nietzsche also owed an understanding of Jesus that shaped his critique of Christianity. But most of the critics were hostile, preferring Turgenev or Tolstoy over Dostoevsky, who they felt mucked about in the "cesspools of mankind." One reviewer found reading him to be psychological torture, after which one wants to "creep on all fours. . . . in Gothic humility."[50]

By the end of the century, however, the cultural vanguard's despairing mood and boredom with bourgeois society led to a search for the authentic life and the rejuvenation of humanity. The German establishment under Kaiser Wilhelm II may have been Russophobic enough to plan for war, but a large segment of the intelligentsia idolized Russia. Russia promised all that Germany was not; it was exotic, primitive, vital, deeply religious and soulful rather than orderly and repressed. The image of Russia came partly through Dostoevsky, who seemed to hold the key to deciphering the secrets of the Slavic East and offered holistic solutions to the disharmony of Western man. This was the ecstatic message of the first German biography of Dostoevsky, written in 1899. Few of the scholarly works published before the end of World War II were any more objective: for some, his epilepsy proved he had demonic, mystical powers; others equated him with Christ or Thor. One biographer attributed to him the ultimate Germanic fantasy: "He died like Beethoven in the sacred uproar of the elements, in a storm."[51]

This was a veritable cult of Russia and of Dostoevsky in the making, and it became a mass phenomenon owing to the efforts of Arthur Moeller van den Bruck (1876–1925), the man who coined the expression "Third Reich." Moeller was responsible for the Piper Press's decision to publish the collected works of Dostoevsky in German, which became a huge commercial success and provided the biblio-infrastructure behind Dostoevsky's blitzkrieg on Germany. Although he visited Russia in 1912, he learned all he knew about the country from his mentor Dmitry Merezhkovsky, the St. Petersburg mystical writer under whose tutelage he read and venerated Dostoevsky as a visionary. With Merezhkovsky's assistance, Moeller edited the series and wrote introductions to the twenty-two volumes of the first edition, which appeared between 1907 and 1919.

In his essays he promoted Dostoevsky as a new guide for humanity dissatisfied with modern liberalism, Christianity—indeed, all of Western civilization: Dostoevsky "knew Europe and the West and recognized liberalism . . . as the bearer of selfishness and individualism, as the spreader of the all-too-Russian nihilism, and the bringer of the totally un-Russian industrialism, capitalism, and materialism."[52] His Dostoevsky is the "expression of Russian madness, of the tragedy in Slavdom, the incarnation of all its mystical internalizations and hectic tension." Through him one partakes of the blessedness of the Russian soul, that "dark yearning after intuition and knowledge" and the wisdom of the Russian peasants, "born heralds of faith."[53] Russians are the "most religious of all people in Europe," a "mystical people" who, as the original Aryans, can bring the Germans closer to their ancestral religion.[54] Dostoevsky is the incarnation of Russia, and that is the source of coming salvation: "If some day evening comes to Western humanity and the German is at rest, only a Slavic mother could again bear Buddha or Jesus out of the Eastern world."[55] Moeller made Dostoevsky into a symbol of an imagined Oriental prophecy and an ally in his hate-filled campaign against modernity. His widely read tracts helped to encourage Germans before and after World War I to unquestioningly accept their leaders' representation of the West as their mortal enemy.

The mythic aspects of Moeller's Dostoevsky were present as well in the avant-garde literary movement known as Expressionism.[56] Active from 1905 into the late 1920s, Expressionist writers threw out aesthetic rules and experimented to achieve shock effect. Theirs was an expression of angst within a militarized, commercialized German society, a revolt against the bourgeois world, and a quest for psychological and spiritual truth. Along with Nietzsche, Dostoevsky was a philosophical and literary deity for Ernst Barlach, Gottfried Benn, Maximilian Harden, Georg Heym, and Franz Werfel, among many other Expressionist authors.

Like Moeller, the Expressionists accepted Dostoevsky as a ravager of the Western literary canon, a painter of the dark recesses of the soul, a poet of the chaos of modernity. Adversary of the classical heritage and American mechanization, he was the Slavic spirit of Asia, vitalist and primitive, Devil and God. They equated him with Christ as a prophet of universal brotherhood at the same time that those with apocalyptic hopes for a purifying war justified their bellicosity with reference to Dostoevsky's saber-rattling *Diary of a Writer*. Stylistically the writers emulated his intensity and his method of "looking through" external reality. Thematically, some of them misread *Crime and Punishment* as a parallel to the Nietzschean superman, while others stressed the renunciation of material comfort for spiritual happiness.

The carnage of trench warfare and the humiliating Versailles peace intensified the tendencies associated with Moeller and the Expressionists and broadened the appeal of Dostoevsky across the intellectual horizon. Sketching out the opposition between a phoenix-like Germany and the doomed West became a cultural cottage industry that owed some of its capital to Dostoevsky. That was the message coming from *The Decline of the West* by Oswald Spengler (1880–1936), a best-seller in the defeated Germany of 1918. This lengthy work explains the German predicament in deceptively scholarly language. It announced the coming end of individualism, humanism, intellectual freedom, and philosophical skepticism, all associated with the fading, "I"-centered West. Russia, on the other hand, was a rising "we"-centered Asiatic power, whose glory lay in the future. The major source for his views of Russia was Dostoevsky, the prophet of "apocalyptic revolt" against the West for whom he professed his limitless adoration. "To Dostoevsky's Christianity," he predicted, "the next thousand years will belong."[57]

In the polarized atmosphere of Weimar Germany, Dostoevsky appealed to extremists. Both the far left and the far right claimed him as their own, and he fed the already strong sentiments throughout the nation that undermined support for the parliamentary regime. Communists and other radical social critics valued him for exposing the ills of capitalist society, seeing him as a fellow Marxist in Christian guise. On the other side, the Nazis reacted more positively to Dostoevsky than to other foreign writers. Nazi critics lauded his mystical nationalism and animosity toward the West. Typical was Richard Kappen's 1936 study, *The Idea of the Volk in Dostoevsky*, which claimed him as a protofascist anti-Semite and advocate of war between the races.[58]

At the same time, Dostoevsky also figured in the works of some of the great German authors of imaginative literature, Hermann Hesse (1877–1962), Franz Kafka (1883–1924), and Thomas Mann (1875–1955). They, too, saw Russia as one of the sources of an irrationalism that stood against the spirit of the West.

Hesse was one with the Expressionists in interpreting Dostoevsky as a harbinger of a new, non-Western civilization. Simultaneously criminal and holy, Dostoevsky to him prefigured the new man who would emerge in the coming age of chaos. But unlike the Ex pressionists, Hesse was wary of all this, a subtle but vital distinction that Weimar Germans tended to miss. He voiced his fears in his book *In Sight of Chaos* (1920), in which Dostoevsky figures prominently. He laments the preference for Dostoevsky over Goethe or even Nietzsche among young Germans and warns that the Asiatic ideal of the Karamazovs was beginning "to devour the spirit of Europe."[59] Perhaps the confusion over where Hesse stood is understandable, for he also hailed Dostoevsky as an Eastern visionary who pointed the way to universal harmony, true spirituality, and the ethical integrity absent in Europe. Dostoevsky confirmed for him his long-standing expectation that salvation would come through non-Western religion and philosophy, and encouraged the exploration of the unconscious forces of the soul that he undertook in his novels *Demian* (1919) and *Steppenwolf* (1927), among others.

Thomas Mann was equally absorbed with the inner, irrational self and adapted aspects of Dostoevskian themes to interpret the subconscious. He, too, was discontented with Western civilization and, during World War I, wrote sympathetically of Dostoevsky's prediction that a great war would spell the end of bourgeois society. In his essay *Reflections of an Nonpolitical Man* (1918), he defended German values against those of the West and attributed to Dostoevsky his own cry for Germany to rebel.[60] This work helped make Dostoevsky acceptable to German archconservativism, but not long after its publication Mann became more accepting of Western civilization and German democracy. Thereafter, it was Dostoevsky "within limits": he continued to esteem Dostoevsky's depiction of the "dark side of man" and the "grotesque, apocalyptic realm of suffering," but he embraced Freud's view that Dostoevsky's sick, maybe criminal, mind was the source of his accomplishments, and that he was more a "great sinner than a great artist."[61] He no longer agreed with Dostoevsky's perception of the black-and-white difference between Germany and the West; his 1947 novel *Doctor Faustus* suggests Mann's change of heart regarding the orientation of German politics in his time. The visit of the gentlemanly Devil to the hero, Adrian Leverkühn, is a parodic borrowing from an episode in *Brothers Karamazov*, and the novel opposes Dostoevskian religious zeal and anti-Westernism with a moral humanism based on reason and moderate piety.[62]

Kafka had thematic links with his contemporaries Mann, Hesse, and the Expressionists. The self-obsessed Jewish writer from Prague was similarly fascinated with Russia and counted Dostoevsky, in his words, as one of his artistic "blood relatives."[63] Dostoevsky's stylistic and philosophical imprints are apparent in "The Judgment" (1913), *The Trial* (written 1914–1915, published 1925), and "Metamorphosis" (1915), haunting allegories involving "underground" men in the modern metropolis, dreams, oedipal situations, explorations of the subconscious, and existential isolation and guilt. Kafka constantly engaged in dialogue with Dostoevsky, but in the final analysis, Kafka repudiated him. Dostoevsky's characters can achieve salvation; Kafka's are crushed, alienated, and disconnected from life, untouched by universal justice. Here the absurd takes primacy over life, and with that assessment, Kafka anticipates the twentieth-century Existentialist perspective and its shifting interpretation of Dostoevsky.[64]

Existentialism originated in Germany after World War I and was transplanted from there to France. Taken as a group, Existentialist thinkers deplored the dehumanization of man in modern industrial society and repudiated Western rationalism. Although in this sense they may seem no different from their subjectivist, psychologizing predecessors, the interwar time of troubles gave their body of thought a distinctive, traumatized character.

Amid mounting political and economic turmoil, the faith of these intellectuals in the future was almost obliterated, and their frustrations with Western philosophical tradition heightened. They were concerned more than ever with man's existence in the world and the universe—whence the label Existentialist—and sought new avenues to overcoming human suffering and isolation. The central issue for them was one of moral values, shattered in the calamities of modern Europe. Whether they believed in God or not, the Existentialists' hopes for the renewal of humanity lay with individual consciousness: each person had the free will—and the responsibility—necessary to shape his own essence and, through that, to collectively affect the destiny of the world. The individual's realization of the implications of his freedom was a terrible burden and one of the sources of his ontological anxiety, but only by taking action, by making tangible ethical choices in the here and now, could man overcome his predicaments.

Existentialism harked back to Dostoevsky, Nietzsche, and the Danish philosopher Søren Kierkegaard. Among its German originators in the 1920s, Karl Jaspers (1883–1969), the psychiatrist turned philosopher, viewed Dostoevsky and Nietzsche as its forerunners, although he differed with others in critiquing the Russian novelist's dialogism as an untenable representation of consciousness.[65] Dostoevsky's impact on the other father of Existentialism, Martin Heidegger (1889–1976), is "hard to overestimate," notes one scholar.[66] Heidegger subscribed to Moeller's irrationalist brand of politics (and for a time hailed the rise of Hitler). That befitted someone who considered Dostoevsky the greatest critic of European civilization and kept the Russian's portrait on his desk. Reading Dostoevsky had induced Heidegger to break with the Catholic Church and seek authentic existence in a primitive Christianity and the mystical self-liberation of Being—a vital step on the road to his Existentialism.

The crisis atmosphere of Weimar Germany that gave rise to Existentialism had its counterpart in France after the First World War. Here the anguish at the war's death toll and physical destruction—compounded by political polarization in the Third Republic, economic depression, and finally the ravages of fascism—shook what remained of the optimistic faith in progress and reason that had once defined French culture. Existentialist tendencies came to dominate the intellectual scene; Dostoevsky's relevance grew stronger in tandem.

The French Existentialists were attracted not to Dostoevsky's Russian Orthodoxy but to his treatment of individualism, revolt, freedom, life, and death. They neutralized Dostoevsky's religion-based optimism, saw the Absurd where he saw God, and favored his chaotic, freedom-seeking, self-creating rebels and underground men.[67] Partly under the inspiration of Dostoevsky, the Existentialists tended to express their ideas in fiction; as a literary movement as much as a philosophical school, they were widely read outside of academic circles.

Jean-Paul Sartre (1905–1980) sought an exit from man's dilemma, and his reading of Dostoevsky gave him one of the keys. This philosopher, novelist, playwright, essayist, and political activist was raised bilingual in Alsace and was equally at home in French and in German culture. A student of Heidegger's before World War II, Sartre made arcane German Existentialism comprehensible in his philosophical works and fiction, and eventually tried to reconcile it with psychoanalysis and Marxism. Like most of his intellectual contemporaries, he hated capitalist society. He moved politically from a vague anarchism and anti-Nazism to eventual advocacy of Soviet communism, then Third World rebellion. Sartre explained his outlook with reference to Dostoevsky:

> The Existentialist . . . thinks it very distressing that God does not exist, because all possibility of finding values in a heaven of ideas disappears along with Him; there can no longer be an *a priori* Good, since there is no infinite and perfect consciousness to think it. . . . Dostoevsky said, "If God didn't exist, everything would be possible." That is the very starting point of existentialism. Indeed, everything is permissible if God does not exist, and as a result man is forlorn, because neither within him nor without does he find anything to cling to.[68]

That forlorn state—Sartre called it nausea—emanated from man's twin anxieties over holding responsibility for determining his own essence and over the limits to his aspirations. Alone in the universe, man was "condemned to be free," his being shaped not by God or nature but by his own actions alone.

Clearly, Sartre differs from Dostoevsky on the metaphysical and ideological basics, but echoes of Dostoevsky resound throughout his Existentialist fiction. Sartre believed that it was possible to overcome the ontologically induced nausea: through choice, commitment, and engagement, man could try to force his own destiny and create his own world. This was an expression of Sartre's faith in human consciousness as independent of the physical universe, his repudiation of environmental determinism, and his tie to Dostoevsky. Out of a similar impulse, Sartre lauded Dostoevsky for showing that the will to freedom, however painful, was crucial insofar as each individual, in the process of creating himself, would affect the destiny of all humanity.[69]

If Sartre caught echoes of Dostoevsky, Albert Camus (1913–1960) heard the voice itself: he considered not Marx but Dostoevsky to be the prophet of the twentieth century, and he hung his portrait, with Tolstoy's, in his study.[70] Reared in French Algeria, an athletic boy suddenly struck with tuberculosis, Camus pondered the nearness of death and the absurdity of existence. Like Sartre, he won fame as a writer serving the French Resistance, and the two names have been linked ever since. But their respective interpretations of Dostoevsky make their differences of opinion and temperament apparent.

Camus relied on Dostoevsky to refine his understanding of man's existence. The central proposition for Camus was the notion of the absurd, the cosmic letdown that occurred when a sense of God's nonexistence jarred the human conviction in order, meaning, and justice in the universe. In his essays *The Myth of Sisyphus* (1943) and *The Rebel* (1951), Camus presents Dostoevsky as an "existentialist novelist" who "propounds the absurd problem." Dostoevsky's characters fill the vacuum left by the absence of God with moral values of their own making, going so far as to sanctify murder in the cases of Ivan Karamazov and Rodion Raskolnikov. Or self-murder: Kirillov in *Devils* commits suicide to show the world that man can control the destiny he once thought was in the hands of God. Camus rejects Christianity and so brushes aside Dostoevsky's faith in God and immortality as the answer to the problem. Yet he joins Dostoevsky in defending life in the face of the absurd. Camus urges man to rebel against the absurd and assert his freedom and personality. He recognizes that the rebel, like Dostoevsky's underground man, is never at peace. He knows that, like Raskolnikov, he can overstep the bounds of human solidarity to commit acts of violence or self-destruction. But the point of rebellion is not to gain unlimited freedom and the right to murder, but to thumb one's nose at the absurd and, despite it, to "live and create, in the very midst of the desert."[71] This is the response of a self-proclaimed pagan, conditioned both by his impression of the

Mediterranean joie de vivre and by the Dostoevskian celebration of the "living life."

Camus's answers to the absurd set him apart from Sartre, who publicly broke with him after the publication of *The Rebel*. Sartre replaced universal moral values with commitment, which would lead him to equate the Communist Party with morality and accept political violence against the West or the bourgeoisie as an appropriate means of stopping oppression. He downgraded the individual man as the supreme ethical value in favor of abstract humanity. Camus, by contrast, without acknowledging God-given rules of ethical conduct, spurned Sartre's exhortation to establish one's own moral code; this, after all, was what had brought on murder and evil in Dostoevsky. In the same vein, informed by Dostoevsky's Grand Inquisitor, Camus condemned Marxism-Leninism-Stalinism and all rigid ideological commitment as dangerous substitutes for morality and absolutist threats to freedom. In the process of making this argument, he incurred the wrath of Sartre.

With his focus on life and man as the supreme value, Camus remained truer to the spirit of Dostoevsky than did Sartre. Not that one should overlook Camus's differences from Dostoevsky. Denying the validity of Christianity, Camus located the basis of ethics in human reason. He misunderstood Dostoevsky's Russian Orthodox view of freedom and individualism. And he overlooked Dostoevsky's political extremism. But a give-and-take with Dostoevsky runs through the entire corpus of Camus's writings. Indeed, the last work published in his lifetime, *The Fall* (1956), with its tonal and thematic allusions to *Notes from Underground* and the Grand Inquisitor, perpetuates the Dostoevskian tradition.[72] In the words of Camus, "Today he continues to help us live and hope."[73]

Lost in America

Existentialism was a philosophy of crisis that emerged in Germany and France in the years surrounding the Second World War. Initially seen in America as a sign of European decline and decadence, it flourished in the United States only in the disturbed atmosphere of the Vietnam War era. The same can be said of the American reception of Dostoevsky. Before the 1960s, although there were some exceptions, the Dostoevsky aura was strongest among Jewish, Southern, and black authors—all to varying degrees "outsiders" who felt close to Russian literature.

Like readers elsewhere, Americans read Dostoevsky for his breathtaking melodrama, penetration of the soul, and insights into criminality. But American Modernists never took to him the way their European counterparts did.[74] Early ones like Sherwood Anderson and Theodore Dreiser admired his artistry and anticapitalism but were largely oblivious to his Russian Orthodox and irrationalist worldview. Much the same was true of the Lost Generation, the disenchanted literary greats of the post–World War I years. If there was any stylistic and thematic overlay of Dostoevsky in the work of F. Scott Fitzgerald and Ernest Hemingway, it was very thin. Fitzgerald's portrayals of the psychological and moral malaise of the decadent Roaring Twenties owed a little more to Dostoevsky than did Hemingway's masculine novels set in exotic lands but far from Russia physically and philosophically. Turgenev, Tolstoy, and Dostoevsky had been important to Hemingway when he started out as a writer, but he moved farther and farther away from them as he developed his terse literary style. A notable exception was Modernist playwright Eugene O'Neill, who said that Dostoevsky's novels had roused his desire to become a writer and inspired the emotional tone of his dramatic works.[75]

The Lost Generation's lukewarm interest in Dostoevsky is a function of the distance between American and European Modernisms. However much American writers were shaken by the war and the Great Depression, however much they struggled with alienation or the psychic and social effects of mass production and commercialism, however much they witnessed the passing of the old ways—their dread at the modern was mixed with excitement at the energy of the new. Modernization proceeded with far less upset here, and the war had not been fought on American soil. Those who left for European exile soon returned; few went so far in removing themselves body and soul from the United States as T. S.

Eliot did. Their works were ambivalent toward Western civilization or American democracy, but few questioned the fundamentals. Even if they did borrow freely from European Modernism, they resisted the slavish imitation of it, for they had great hopes in America and contrasted themselves favorably to Europe's defeated and demoralized intellectuals. They sought, like their nineteenth-century literary forebears, to produce an original, distinctly American literature that would capture the multiple, vital realities of their nation. In his Nobel Prize acceptance speech, Sinclair Lewis—who disliked Dostoevsky—called on writers to give to "an America that is as strange as Russia and as complex as China, a literature worthy of her vastness."[76] With this task before them, American Modernists would find Dostoevsky to be of limited use.

Dostoevsky had a greater presence, on the other hand, in the works of American Jewish authors such as Saul Bellow (1915–).[77] Bellow expressed a "dissent from Modernism."[78] Writing in the shadows of the Holocaust and the atom bomb, the "organization man" and mass consumerism, he was aware of the fragility of civilization and the powerlessness of the individual. Yet he worked past Modernist despair to affirm life, decency, and civilization through characters who moved to the political-philosophical center rather than to the fringes.

Nonetheless, in doing so he remained deeply involved with Dostoevsky as author and philosopher. Bellow's father had read him Dostoevsky and Tolstoy in Yiddish, and his early books *Dangling Man* (1944) and *The Victim* (1947) have been called the gloomy works of a "Chicago Dostoevskian."[79] With Dostoevsky, Bellow pondered questions of existence, moralism, and the metropolis, contrasting the simultaneous spiritual impoverishment and material abundance of Western society. His antiheroes, too, stood for freedom and autonomy against rational society. But if at first he was most attracted to the underground man, he soon pulled himself out of the hole, critiqued Modernism for the inadequacy of its negativist answers, and evolved a far less bleak picture of humanity—at the same time reiterating Dostoevsky-like warnings about intelligentsia dogmatism in works such as *Mr. Sammler's Planet* (1970).

Bellow used Dostoevsky in qualified affirmation of Western civilization, his attitudes corresponding to the liberal intellectual creed of the late 1940s and 1950s outlined by Arthur Schlesinger, Jr., in his influential manifesto *The Vital Center: The Politics of Freedom* (1949). Here Schlesinger makes a plea for a revitalized American left liberalism that shuns communism and extremism. He quotes Dostoevsky's descriptions of reprehensible, bloodthirsty radicals in *Devils* to tar Stalinism as an unacceptable form of leftism.[80] But these voices of moderation were soon to be shouted down by the angry men of the 1950s and 1960s. What Bellow had rejected as "the waste-land attitude" of Modernism, these writers, labeled "Post-Modernists," embraced.

The forerunner of American Post-Modernism was Henry Miller (1891–1980), who spent the 1930s in Paris, after most of the Lost Generation had gone home. His autobiographical, experimental, surreal novels—for years banned in the United States as obscene—blended Nietzsche, Taoism, and individualist anarchism to justify breaking down all limitations on human sexual, emotional, and intellectual impulses. His return to the States in 1940 occasioned a hateful rebuke of American civilization as an "air-conditioned nightmare," a phrase he used as the title of a 1945 novel. In the 1920s, Miller had been close to Russian émigrés in New York, and it was then that he began to assimilate Dostoevsky. "Even in the suburb of Brooklyn, by the time I had come of age, one could be stirred by the repercussions of that Slavic ferment. . . . Was it not Spengler who said that Dostoevsky's Russia would eventually triumph? Did he not predict that from this ripe soil a new religion would spring?" The promise of that religion, which he likened to Buddhism, attracted him as it did so many other disillusioned intellectuals around the world. Dostoevsky, whose portrait was for Miller a religious icon, showed him the way to spiritualism and fed his psychic hunger for exotic alternatives to modern Western culture. His dark view of the city as crucible of that culture's existence was also affected by Dostoevsky: "American life, from the gangster level to the intellectual level, has paradoxically tremendous affinities with Dostoevsky's multilateral everyday life. What better proving grounds can one ask for than metropolitan New York, in whose conglomerate soil every wanton, ignoble, crack-brained idea flourishes like a weed?"[81] In this frame of mind, Miller has the narrator of *Tropic of Cancer* (1934) speak with the violent intensity of the underground man and likewise reject other men and their ideologies. Yet he does so without the self-doubt and inner struggle of Dostoevsky's prototype; for Miller, far from the authentic Dostoevsky, was a carnal individualist and occultist who would easily accommodate himself to California and his eventual role as swami to the beatniks and hippies.

Miller's writings anticipated the function Dostoevsky would fulfill in Post-Modern novels of the 1960s and 1970s. Whereas in Bellow the absurd is close to the surface but still contained by the author's essential optimism and stylistic realism, in these books the optimism breaks down and the absurd breaks through. Both Norman Mailer (1923–) and Kurt Vonnegut (1922–) at different periods of their lives seem to have identified themselves with Dostoevsky. In Mailer's novel *An American Dream* (1965), *Crime and Punishment* and the Grand Inquisitor are revisited. Mailer rolls Raskolnikov and Ivan Karamazov into one in the protagonist, Stephen Rojack, who murders his wife, Deborah, allies himself with the Devil as a possible victor over God, and finds love with the nightclub tart Cherry, patterned after Sonya, the prostitute-savior of Raskolnikov. But how much more pessimistic and amoral than most Dostoevskian novels this book is: the crime is treated as a justifiable struggle against the evil represented by the victim; Rojack is let off by police interrogators; and in the psychological ordeal that nonetheless follows the murder, Rojack fails to find redemption—Cherry dies, and he is suffocated by a diseased, decayed modern America whose "totalitarian" establishment and plastic conformity Mailer elsewhere rails against like the underground man.[82]

Vonnegut's pessimistic adaptation of Dostoevsky is analogous. His comic science fiction is a form of subversion aimed against the self-destructiveness of technological man and the artificiality of civilization. Critical of science, unbridled capitalism, selfish individualism, and authoritarianism, Vonnegut was receptive to Dostoevsky, but from the perspective of someone who survived the Dresden firebombing as an American POW and agonized over the nuclear arms race. In several of his works he mocked the optimism and naïveté of the angelic Alyosha Karamazov. In *Slaughterhouse Five* (1969), Vonnegut expressed the apocalyptic despair he and his contemporaries felt: "Everything there was to know about life was in *The Brothers Karamazov*, by Feodor Dostoevsky. 'But that isn't *enough* any more.' "[83] The Post-Modernists thus reexperienced the Modernists' discontent, but without their whisper of hope.

Dostoevskian motifs had also long been a regular staple in the literary diet of Southern and black novelists, whose unease with American culture paralleled the European Modernist disillusionment with Western civilization. They were, in the words of Carson McCullers, one of the great Southern woman writers, "the progeny of the Russian realists"; for they recognized the similarities between Russian circumstances and their own.[84]

The eldest son was William Faulkner (1897–1962), whose fiction captured the breakup of the old order of the South in the aftermath of the Civil War, the decline of the planter aristocracy, the introduction of Yankee industry, and the crumbling of a society under sudden assault by antitraditional forces. Faulkner, to be sure, was ambivalent toward the myths of the old South and did not seek the restoration of the immoral, archaic world of the slave plantations, but he was equally contemptuous of the new rationalized economy that threatened the Southern agrarian heritage. Outside of America what he deplored was called Westernization, and his novels reflected Southern society's disorientation, similar to modernizing Russia's and defeated Germany's—which helped account for Dostoevsky's appearance in the one and reception in the other. In Faulkner it produced a tension-filled existential outlook and a writing style to match that earned him from some critics the sobriquet "Dostoevsky of the South."

Both Faulkner and Dostoevsky lived in a transitional age and suffered from the sight of a world seemingly dying and going to hell. Their fiction has in common a dramatic intensity and experimentation in the representation of consciousness; passionate, suffering, violent, out-of-synch characters; a denunciation of the moral emptiness of the new men of modern society; an attraction to folk Christianity; a sense of human ambiguity, self-contradiction, and the illusoriness of freedom. In many of his novels, above all *Sanctuary* (1931), thematic references to Dostoevsky are clear; but in the final analysis Faulkner was more of a fatalist, pessimist, and secularist. He turned to Dostoevsky more for his art than for his philosophy, which explains his comments: "He is one who has not only influenced me a lot, but that I have got a great deal of pleasure out of reading, and I still read him every year or so. As a craftsman, as well as his insight into people, his capacity for compassion, he was one of the ones that any writer wants to match."[85]

The bond with Dostoevsky is even closer among other Southern writers, Carson McCullers (1917–1967), Flannery O'Connor (1925–1964), and Walker Percy (1916–1990). From their vantage point in a South still agonizing over its loss in the Civil War, they had imbibed an assumption of fallen man and original sin, which gave them a darker view of the world than that reflected in much of American fiction. All three confessed to being obsessed with Dostoevsky, who came closest to their haunted vision of people as physically, spiritually, and emotionally crippled. Dostoevsky guided them in the depiction of a world filled with violence, dreams, hallucinations, and conflicting good and evil. O'Connor, who also had an abiding interest in Russian Orthodox thought, associated the automobile, symbol of American civilization, with false freedom and the negation of Christianity—reminiscent of the antitheses Dostoevsky established.[86] This American "highway culture" was one of Percy's targets too, partial answer to the question he posed at the start of his writing career: "If D[ostoevsky] were alive, who would he attack?" Percy said that his Catholic, philosophical novels were written in a spirit of "conscious kinship" with Dostoevsky; for he and the other Southern writers of his generation all felt "at odds with modernity."[87]

If in Southern writing the North is the equivalent of the West for Russians or Germans or Asians, the equivalent of the West for black writers was white culture, and their relationship to it had parallels with Russia's relationship to Europe that they did not fail to see. Both Russians and African Americans were people who had been brought into the shadow of Western/white civilization but remained on its edges. Both had an unsettled mix of resentful and envious feelings toward the West/whites that impelled their respective intelligentsias to discover and champion their own unique national or ethnic virtues, what Dostoevsky did in *The House of the Dead*, and W.E.B. Du Bois in *The Souls of Black Folk* (1903).[88] Du Bois was not aware of Dostoevsky or the soulful reputation of the Russian folk at this point (he was to make his pilgrimage to Russia later), but the writers of the 1920s Harlem Renaissance were. Its poet laureate, Langston Hughes, writes of "the vogue for things Russian";[89] its manifesto, Alain Locke's *The New Negro* (1925) quotes short-story writer Jean Toomer: "Georgia opened me. . . . There one finds soil, soil in the sense that the Russians know it,— the soil every art and literature that is to live must be embedded in."[90] And the leading African American novelists of the twentieth century assimilated Dostoevsky as all the world's Modernists did.

The fiction of Richard Wright (1908–1960) and Ralph Ellison (1914–1994) echoed the Dostoevskian themes of ethnic messianism, discontent with the West, individualism versus the community, and revolt as an act of self-definition and freedom. After a period of affiliation with American communism and admiration of Maxim Gorky's Socialist Realist literature, in the 1940s Wright broke with the Marxists and switched literary allegiance to Dostoevsky, for him "the greatest novelist."[91] Dostoevsky informed Wright's understanding of "the psychological state of modern man" and, with his Russian ambivalence toward Europe, affirmed Wright's view of America: "Whenever I thought of the essential bleakness of black life in America, I knew that Negroes had never been allowed to catch the full spirit of Western civilization, that they lived somehow in it but not of it."[92]

The philosophical and structural links to Dostoevsky are exemplified in Wright's *Native Son* (1940), *The Man Who Lived Underground* (1944), and *The Outsider* (1953). In the first of these works, Bigger Thomas is a murderous black Raskolnikov; Fred Daniels, the protagonist of the 1944 novella, flees injustice to the city sewer system only to emerge with a Dostoevskian sense of responsibility for all humans; in *The Outsider*, Cross Damon figures

as another Raskolnikov, and other characters as well as dialogue
and scenes are borrowed directly from *Crime and Punishment*. But
in these novels of black protest and rage, Wright's heroes deviate
from Dostoevsky's. Dostoevsky refutes nihilistic self-assertion, and
his characters' consciences lead them to repentance and deliver-
ance. By contrast, Wright's characters trade off their ethical sense
for the freedom to do as they please or commit acts of violence,
both means of gaining self-identity in a racist society. His killers
self-destruct as in Dostoevsky, but they die convinced that murder
was right and that they were the innocent victims—the perverse
logic of the oppressed. Fred Daniels, the only character who rejects
this viewpoint for confession, love, and humanity, is killed by policemen who represent the system that produced the moral nihilism
in the other characters. Such is Wright's bleak reworking of Dostoevsky in the light of American race relations.

Ellison's fiction entails a similar kind of "extrapolation" from
Dostoevsky, as Joseph Frank has shown. The author of *Invisible
Man* (1947) called Dostoevsky one of his artistic "ancestors," and
the connections between this spellbinding American masterpiece
and *Notes from Underground* are many. Both are first-person con-
fessionals whose narrators explode against humiliation and flee underground seeking refuge from the repugnant, Europeanized culture imposed upon them. Ellison equated Dostoevsky's negative
attitudes toward the materialism, socialism, and utilitarianism of
the Westernized Russian intelligentsia with his own rejection of
both black assimilation to white American culture and the Afri-
canism that he saw as the photographic negative of white racism.
Dostoevsky's *House of the Dead* played a vital role in the making
of Ellison's worldview. In the Russia of its day, this work that Ellison described as a "profound study of the humanity of Russian
criminals" had contributed to the breakdown of the Russian elite's
disdain for the native peasants. For Ellison, according to Frank, it
"provided . . . a powerful precedent for entering into a positive
relation with the Negro folk culture he had imbibed from the cra-
dle." Dostoevsky thus "helped Ellison to find his own way," much
as he did the other modern American writers in their disquietude.[93]

"Spiritual sustenance": Dostoevsky and the Non-Western World

Dostoevsky also helped Arabic, Japanese, and Latin American fiction writers to find their own ways in the age of Westernization. Dostoevsky's questions regarding Russia vis-à-vis Europe were the same ones asked in all modernizing nations, by all intellectuals confronted with the powerful forces of change in the nineteenth and twentieth centuries. The ambivalence of the entire world toward modernity was encapsulated in Dostoevsky's work and reflected in the global fascination with him. He prefigures much of the Russian impact in the twentieth-century Third World with his anti-Westernism, his nationalism, and his messianic hopes.

The Mexican poet and essayist Octavio Paz has testified that Dostoevsky was as feverishly read in the non-Western world as in Europe. The broad range of his ideas inflamed other Latin American writers and many more unknown students. The Mexican José Revueltas (1914–1976); the half-Russian Cuban Alejo Carpentier (1904–1980); the Colombian Gabriel García Márquez (1927–); the Brazilian Jorge Amado (1912–2001); and the Argentine Roberto Arlt (1900–1942)—all spoke of Dostoevsky as a literary mentor. So important was the Russian novel in Latin America that the Argentine novelist Jorge Luis Borges (1899–1986) felt compelled to assert his independence of it by critiquing its imitators and insisting that he could not read *Brothers Karamazov* through to the end.[94] But Latin America was unique in the non-Western world insofar as it had had a long time to figure out its relationship with Europe; so its writers took to Dostoevsky's soulfulness, psychologizing, and fantasy far more than they did to his anti-Western rantings.

The Middle East was in the different position of having to digest Western-based cultural and economic models rather suddenly in the late nineteenth century, as the stability of the Ottoman Empire eroded. There Dostoevsky and other Russian novelists provided an alternative, non-Western self-image. Russian schools and organizations serving native Greek Orthodox Christians taught Dostoevsky and Tolstoy to the Arab world. They introduced that world to the distinctions between Russian and Western ideas and contributed to the creation of an Arab intelligentsia, which saw its own experience portrayed in Russian literature and looked to Russia for support of its nationalist aspirations. In Lebanon, Palestine, and Syria, even small-town schools sponsored by the Russian Palestine Society had extensive collections of Russian literature. Students coming out of the Russian-operated Teachers Higher College in Nazareth started to produce Arabic translations of Russian fiction in the late nineteenth and early twentieth centuries—readers' interests being stimulated by the Russo-Japanese War, the 1905 revolution, and, after 1917, the rise of communism. Among these Orthodox students was the Lebanese literary critic, playwright, essayist, and short-story writer Mikhail Naimy (1889–1988). Educated in Lebanon, Palestine, Russia, and America, for a time a lawyer and journalist in New York, Naimy was notable for helping to introduce the techniques of modern literature into Arabic prose. In his stories he adapted Dostoevsky's style and themes as he strove to emulate, in his words, "the lofty humanity of the most powerful, profound, complete, and penetrating of all Russian writers."[95]

The case of Egypt is paradigmatic. The earliest Egyptian novelists, in the 1890s, were inspired by French and English fiction, but by the mid-1920s they found "spiritual sustenance," as one of them put it, in Russian writing—Dostoevsky, Tolstoy, Turgenev, Chekhov, and others—available in European translations previously but now increasingly in Arabic.[96] One of the key literary figures of the day, Ibrahim ʿAbd al-Qadir al-Mazini (1890–1949), wrote with nationalist pride of his desire to establish a distinctively Egyptian novel separate from the Western fictional prototype, in imitation of the Russians. Along with this sentiment, echoes of Dostoevsky's antiradicalism and antirationalism were sounded in Egyptian prose fiction of the 1920s. Two of the fathers of the modern Arabic novel, Mahmud Taimur (1894–1973) and Yahya Haqqi (1905–1992), among many others, were profoundly influenced by Dostoevsky (and Tolstoy): the broad scope of their novels, set in Egypt but going well beyond the mere depiction of local color; their penetration of the subsurface psyche; their religious intensity; their rejection of modern, urban industrialized society; their portrayal of rebellious youth losing their souls as they abandoned tradition and the "people" for the Western lifestyle—all these are prominent features in Taimur and Haqqi partly taken over from the Russians. For Taimur, modern Arabic writers and readers were attracted to modern Russian literature because they identified its outlook with their own, and that was perceived as very different from the outlook of the West.[97]

Perceptions were similar in Japan, where literati have revered Dostoevsky for over a century.[98] Here, too, Russian Orthodox seminaries taught the Russian language, and noted converts translated and publicized Russian literature, which was foremost among the foreign literary influences in Japan at the turn of this modernizing century. First to catch on were the adventures of the Populist revolutionaries, then Turgenev, Tolstoy, and Dostoevsky, and later Chekhov and Gorky, all of whom had an extensive stylistic impact on Japanese fiction.

Why? Because Russian literature taught the art of social and psychological inquiry, and in particular dealt with the familiar problem of making the transition from a traditional to a new way of life. The Slavophile-nationalist versus modernizing-Westernizer aspects of Russian literature had close parallels in Japan. Japanese writers felt at home with Dostoevsky and Tolstoy, in whom some perceived a Buddhist message that they felt they could comprehend better than Europeans or even Russians. A young generation of writers in the 1880s and 1890s bore the standard of the Russian novel in a revolt against the rigidities and superficialities of their predecessors. But Russian fever peaked between 1910 and the early 1930s, an era of fascination with Western antimaterialist thought thanks to the dominant industrializing trends of state and society—again a parallel with late-nineteenth-century Russia, whose cultural production spoke to the Japanese intelligentsia. Only the intensified militarism and repression of the next decade brought the fever down, but its long-term effects could not be altered.

In this period, interest in Dostoevsky was widespread. He was introduced in the late 1880s, and Uchida Roan's 1892 translation of *Crime and Punishment* from the English version "stirred a whole generation of writers," in the assessment of Donald Keene.[99] Over the next twenty years, all of Dostoevsky's works would be translated. As elsewhere, some read him as a detective-story writer, but others recognized his spiritual depth. The first modern Japanese novel, Futabatei Shimei's *Ukigumo* (Drifting clouds), written in 1886–1889, is a portrayal of newly Westernizing Japan. Based on Russian realist models, it is thematically closest to Turgenev, but the psychological torment of its hero is Dostoevskian. Futabatei (1864–1909) died on his way home from Russia, where he had been St. Petersburg correspondent for the newspaper *Asahi Shimbun*.

For later writers, Dostoevsky was a guide in the expression of Modernist angst at the decay of the old society and the painful birth of the new, understandably the theme common to them all. The naturalist fiction of Shimazaki Toson (1872–1943) was influenced by Dostoevsky's ethical individualism and descriptions of man's inner world to show the suffering induced by social transformation. The pessimistic, Existentialist poetry of Hagiwara Sakutaro (1886–1942) displayed a bleak view of modern man partially derived from his one-sided reading of Dostoevsky. Akutagawa Ryunosuke (1892–1927), one of the greatest Japanese writers, also dwelled on Dostoevsky's treatment of human ambivalence and evil. And Kobayashi Hideo (1902–1983), the father of modern Japanese literary criticism, promoted Dostoevsky as the model for Japanese writing. Kobayashi was critical of modern Tokyo, which he saw under the effect of Dostoevsky's gloomy vision of St. Petersburg: "I do not easily recognize within myself or in the world around me people whose feet are planted firmly on the ground, or who have the features of social beings. I can more easily recognize the face of that abstraction called the city person, who might have been born anywhere, than a Tokyoite born in the city of Tokyo." The Japanese saw Dostoevsky, to use Kobayashi's words, as the supreme chronicler of urban man's "lost home" and interpreter of the "bewildering reality" of modern times.[100]

Before and after World War II the popularity of Russian literary classics was enhanced by film adaptations, which started to appear in Japan as early as 1914. The most famous were the work of the Dostoevskyphile director and screenwriter Kurosawa Akira (1910–1998), who in the late 1950s stated that in his youth he and his friends "spent many hours discussing Tolstoy, Turgenev, Dostoevsky . . . especially Dostoevsky. I loved him very much, and my attraction to him remains to this day. He has been an enormous influence on me." And this not just in his 1951 film *The Idiot*, but in general in the dialogic exploration of his characters' emotions and opinions, in his sense of human paradox, his Christian impulse, and the universality of his themes. Through his many films "in the manner of Dostoevsky," as he put it, Kurosawa interpreted the fate of postwar Japan, which was still coming to terms with Westernization.[101]

The reception of Dostoevsky and Russian literature in other non-Western lands varied in intensity. In China it followed the same trajectory as in Japan. It was by far the most popular foreign literature, and it encouraged the destruction of Chinese literary conventions as well as offering moral guidance during a time of political flux. Ba Jin (1904–), one of the most popular of modern Chinese novelists, expressed a common sentiment: "I liked [Dostoevsky, Tolstoy, and other Russian writers] tremendously because the conditions of life in Russia closely resembled those of the Chinese people at that period. The character, the aspirations, and tastes of the Russians were somewhat similar to ours."[102] I have found only minimal evidence of interest in Dostoevsky in India, where, as we will see, Tolstoy monopolized the transmittal of Russian culture. And in sub-Saharan Africa, I was unable to discover any connection— not surprising perhaps in a continent whose belletristic production did not appear until much later than elsewhere.

But wherever Dostoevsky did hold sway, he helped to provide an alternative to modes of thought associated with Westernization. Dostoevsky and his Russian confreres developed an early, persuasive critique of this phenomenon that fulfilled a vital psychological function for non-Western intellectuals agitated over the cultural, political, and social upheavals of modernity. At the same time, paradoxically, Russian literary models had the effect of breaking down long-term resistance to Westernization, as it brought non-Western cultural norms into alignment with what would soon be the European Modernist mainstream.

Dostoevsky has often been lumped together with Einstein as one of the theoreticians of the disintegrating worldview of twentieth-century humanity. In truth, he did not have the influence on Einstein that some scholars have claimed, and both men, contrary to popular misconceptions, believed in the existence of a stable universe.[103] Yet both Einstein and Dostoevsky reconfigured that universe and thereby helped to reshape the modern outlook. That Dostoevsky did so in Russian and Orthodox Christian terms and in response to Russian circumstances did not prevent his ideas from being exported and voraciously consumed. Dostoevsky's literary representations of modern man's struggle with psychological ambiguity, madness, rebelliousness, and shockingly sudden Westernization produced a following among thinkers of many different stripes far into the twentieth century—however much they read his problems as their own and, accordingly, misinterpreted and altered his viewpoint.

Dostoevsky acted as a leaven to modern culture, but in different places the bread rose in different ways. Like Kropotkin and Bakunin, Dostoevsky appealed to communitarians and individualists alike, and especially to those who tried to square the circle and reconcile these two strains. In places like England and America, Dostoevsky added mere spice to Modernism, but to a small extent there and a great extent elsewhere he frequently gave encouragement to a utopian and unbalanced anti-Westernism. In the Arabic world, East Asia, and Weimar Germany, Dostoevsky contributed to a native self-consciousness that defined itself in opposition to the West. In France, Germany, and elsewhere in Europe, he fed into the celebration of self, the cult of inwardness, and the "philosophy of life" that formed the different sides of the reaction against the allegedly staid, repressed, and materialistic bourgeoisie. German philosopher Theodor Adorno called this cultural reaction the "jargon of authenticity" and pinned on its rejection of reason, law, science, and cities—the joint legacies of the Enlightenment, nineteenth-century liberalism, and industrial capitalism—the twenti-eth-century readiness to accept authoritarian political ideologies.[104] This may not have been Dostoevsky's intent, but it was a logical consequence of many of his ideas.

The foreign reception of Dostoevsky was both cause and effect of the turn to Russia that was bound up with the Modernist quest for the "authentic" and mystical, exotic, or Eastern truth. That was even more evident with Tolstoy, whose distinctive blend of spirituality and anarchism accounts for an international influence that changed the course of the twentieth century.

Tolstoy and the Nonviolent Imperative

IVAN TURGENEV called Tolstoy Russia's "genius and crank" for his cantankerous rejection of standard social behavior and for writing books that ranked among the greatest works in the history of world literature.[1] Recognized today primarily for breaking new ground in the art of fiction writing with novels like *War and Peace* (1869) and *Anna Karenina* (1877), he also had a wide-ranging impact on politics and ideas that is less well known. One of the fathers of the modern counterculture, Tolstoy inspired the occult, pacifist, vegetarian, and sexual-liberation crusades in the decades before and after World War I. And he provided a large part of the philosophical groundwork underneath the concept of peaceful nonresistance associated with Mahatma Gandhi in India and the civil rights struggle in the United States. These movements left indelible marks on the political life of the world in the twentieth century.

Count Lev Tolstoy was born into an ancient and wealthy aristocratic family in 1828 at Yasnaya Polyana, a family estate located 120 miles south of Moscow.[2] In 1847, upon coming into his considerable inheritance of 3,000 acres and 330 serfs, he left the university where he was studying. After a short career as an army officer in the Caucasus and in the Crimean War, he settled in St. Petersburg. From there he traveled to Europe for the first time in 1857 and once more in 1860–1861. By the late 1850s he had achieved literary prominence, but, unattracted to the dissipated lifestyle of the court aristocracy and intent on resisting his attraction to gambling and brothels, he returned to his estate. In 1862 he married eighteen-year-old Sophia Behrs; they eventually had thirteen children. For the next half century, he largely remained at Yasnaya Polyana; with its country-gentry manor house set amid fields, forests, and peasant huts, this archaic environment would provide the setting for his religious, rural utopianism.

A central theme of Tolstoy's literature and philosophy was that true happiness lay in family life; orphaned at the age of nine, he yearned for domestic warmth and love. Despite many good years of marriage and parenthood, family did not turn out to be the cure for the psychospiritual torment that Tolstoy perpetually suffered. In the mid-1870s, he underwent an existential crisis. "I feel that I am perishing—that I am living and dying, that I love life and fear death—how can I be saved?"[3] were the reflections that sparked thoughts of suicide and his famous "conversion" of 1878, when he renounced any further questioning of his religious belief.

Since adolescence Tolstoy had been consumed with the extremes of either debauchery or achieving godly self-perfection through perpetual prayer and repentance. In the years following his conversion, he gave up hunting, meat, smoking, dentists, and alcohol. He tried (but failed) to abstain from sex. He praised poverty, wore homespun peasant clothing, and took up manual labor—splitting wood, fetching water, plowing the field, threshing grain, making shoes—all the while retaining his wealth. He made two pilgrimages to a monastery dressed as a holy beggar with peasant coat and staff.

As Tolstoy altered his behaviors, he and his wife became increasingly estranged and toward the end of his life engaged in a war of mutual torment. He became more attached to his devoted disciple, Vladimir Chertkov (1854–1936), who arranged to publish abroad those of Tolstoy's works that had been censored at home. Chertkov struggled with Countess Tolstaya over access to her husband. She went into hysterics and had nervous breakdowns. Referring to her and his sons, Tolstoy said that he was living among "insane people."[4] He finally sought to escape from his family altogether by becoming a monk; in November 1910 he fled Yasnaya Polyana but

caught pneumonia en route and died of heart failure at Astapovo
railway station.

Tolstoy's father had preserved Yasnaya Polyana as an eigh-
teenth-century serf estate ruled by the absolute authority of the
master. Growing up in this environment, Tolstoy never fully shed
its legacy. Despite his egalitarianism, the best he could do for a
bastard son by a married peasant woman was to make him a ser-
vant to his legitimate children. Tolstoy inherited the rural Moscow
gentry's hostility toward all that St. Petersburg stood for—bureaucracy, Westernization, modern urban culture. Yet he saw himself
as nothing but an upper-class parasite who, to his great regret, had
once beaten his peasants and entered into numerous premarital

5. Lev Tolstoy.
From William E.
Walling, *Russia's
Message* (New
York, 1908).

sexual liaisons with serf girls, maidservants, Gypsies, and prostitutes. Like so many other members of the educated, aristocratic intelligentsia, he repudiated the position of his class and, out of mixed feelings of guilt and compassion, idolized the simple folk. Not only did he dress like them; his fiction dwelled on peasants, Chechens, Cossacks, Gypsies, and Tatars as authentic, natural people, the opposites of the modern, rational, inauthentic, Westernized men who were ruining the world.

Tolstoy's entire body of writing reeks of contempt for Western capitalism, materialism, parliamentary democracy, law, and constitutionalism. And he flatly denied that technological progress benefited humanity. For Russia, the adoption of these features of an "alien civilization"[5] meant poverty and death: the adulterous Anna Karenina and her lover are linked with St. Petersburg, Italy, European scientism—all with strong non-Russian associations. She commits suicide under the wheels of a train, the premier symbol of modernization in the nineteenth century. For revival of a natural existence, individuals must emulate the peasants, "who are less intellectually corrupted and still adhere to a vague concept of the idea of a Christian faith, will finally understand where the means of salvation lie and be the first to make use of it."[6]

Adopting aspects of the peasant lifestyle for himself and advocating it for others became Tolstoy's mission in his postconversion years, his answer to the problems of the world as well as to his own psychospiritual torment. He argued for the abolition of private land ownership, money, and rationalized commercial farming as sins. They should be replaced by barter and the small-scale operations that characterized the Russian communes, which would "show to other peoples the way to a free and happy life lying outside of industrial and capitalistic exploitation and enslavement: this is the historical task of the Russian people."[7] "Bread labor"—that is, subsistence farming—was the central component of the lifestyle that he preached. Strongly influenced by the contemporary American radical Henry George, Russian Populism, and a Siberian peasant writer named Timofei Bondarev, Tolstoy conceived of bread labor as a biblical commandment and the precondition for human equality.[8]

His veneration of the peasant was partly rooted in his early attachment to Russian Orthodoxy. But his relationship with the established church was as conflict-ridden as were his family ties. Following his belief that all men were vessels of the divine, he rejected the clergy and the divinity of Jesus. For his blasphemous attacks on the church in *Resurrection* (1899) and his support of the Dukhobors, a pacifist, anarchistic, Orthodox sect persecuted by the state, the government arranged to have him excommunicated as a heretic in 1901.

Tolstoy's thought had an ecumenical spirit that took him beyond Russian and even Christian theology. He assumed that the Russian peasants in their communes embodied a spiritual truth that the rest of the world might learn from. But he did not believe that "revelation [was] confined to the Christian Church alone."[9] He studied Muslim and Jewish theology, and developed a passion for Hinduism, Buddhism, and other Asian religions, elements of which he integrated into his own thought. Holding that "all men are recognized as being sons of God" and that all humanity should be the beneficiary of the law of love,[10] he repudiated the moral superiority of Christian Europe and lamented its conquests of the American Indians, the Hindus, the Zulus, and the Chinese.

Despite his religious tolerance, he was no liberal. Under the inspiration of the French Catholic reactionary Joseph de Maistre (1754–1821), German pessimistic philosopher Arthur Schopenhauer (1788–1860), Asian religions, Eastern Orthodoxy, and the Russian peasant worldview, he assumed that, since God was in everything, human autonomy was an illusion: "Free will is nothing other than. . . . God within us, working through us."[11] For Tolstoy, as for Dostoevsky, true freedom comes to a man only when he merges with God. Far from the Western definition of individual freedom, it "does not consist in being able to act spontaneously, independently of the course of life and of the influence of existing causes, but it means that by recognizing and professing [divine truth, one can] become a free and joyful participant in the eternal and infinite work performed by God or by the life of the world."[12] Upon perceiving this unity and harmony within the cosmos, Tolstoy wrote of being transfixed with love: "What incomparable amazing joy—and I am experiencing it—*to love* everyone, everything, to feel this love in oneself."[13]

By love, though, Tolstoy meant fulfillment of Jesus' teachings, not physical or romantic love, which he disparaged more and more as time went on. Despite Tolstoy's literary treatment of human sexual drives—a mark of Modernism pointedly absent in Dostoevsky—his later writings pleaded for sexual abstinence. Sex as the root of all evil is the message of *The Kreutzer Sonata* (1889). In this intemperate novel, Tolstoy through the misogynistic hero Pozdnyshev suggests that the institution of marriage is a legalized form of prostitution whose sole function is to guarantee copulation and enslave men through their addiction to sex. To curb this evil, total abstinence may be desirable, even at the expense of further human procreation. The behavior of rabbits, pigs, Parisians, and monkeys should not be the ideal! Sex he saw as animalistic violence that hinders the achievement of spiritual love and the individual's unity with God and mankind.

Tolstoy's metaphysical understanding of love was bound up with his belief in the necessity of forsaking our individual personalities and merging with God. Our purpose as human beings is to conquer evil by following the Golden Rule and leading the ethical existence called for in the Gospels, that is, "act[ing] lovingly towards others, as he would that others should act towards him."[14] Adherence to the Golden Rule included "love for those who abuse us, for the enemy," and refusing to use force to resist his evil.[15] In Tolstoy's eyes, loving one's enemy, coupled with nonresistance, would put an end to physical violence and tyranny in the world.

Once he accepted love for one's enemy and nonresistance as Absolute Law, Tolstoy insisted on applying these principles on earth—for instance, rejecting the death penalty and war. He also opposed the use of force in defense of human life, even if it meant refusing to harm a robber who is about to kill a baby. Was that baby in the end really worth more than the robber? We cannot know God's will, except that it is not to kill. If the commandments are contravened in the name of justice, Tolstoy argues, then they are just bland suggestions. But in fact they are God's law, and *any* act of violence, however it is justified, is a violation of that law.[16]

Tolstoy's idea of passive resistance did not, however, entail quietism. Rather than advocating submission to evil, he felt that we must *act* to oppose it, if need be through civil disobedience. His entire corpus of writings is a lifelong tirade against the multiple forms of injustice, inequality, patriotism, war, and tyranny. He opposed the Russo-Turkish War and Pan-Slav aggression in the Balkans as vocally as Dostoevsky promoted them.[17] He called for people to refuse to pay taxes, join the army, participate in courts and elections, or work for private-property interests. He campaigned against alcohol, drug, and tobacco use. He organized famine relief for the Volga region in 1891–1892. In the late 1890s he and his followers gave international publicity to the Russian government's persecution of the Dukhobor sect for refusing to serve in the army, and he footed the bill for the migration of more than seven thousand of them to western Canada. And since the law of love and doctrine of nonviolence embraced not just humans but all sentient beings, according to Tolstoy, he swore off the killing of animals and became a strict vegetarian. He was one of the leading international advocates of vegetarianism, and his writings on the subject helped to enhance the credibility of a cause that was just getting underway in Western countercultural circles.

Tolstoy's law of love led him to repudiate the whole notion of the state, which he saw as existing to commit acts of violence against its own citizens and others. He could not reconcile warfare or state executions of political prisoners with the commandment not to kill. Thousands of times over, he felt, governments committed murder and violated the most basic of religious principles. If Dostoevsky can be placed—somewhat awkwardly—in the conservative, pro-autocracy camp, Tolstoy was far more sympathetic to the Russian radical cause. In *Resurrection*, the revolutionaries on the whole are the positive characters, full of morality, self-sacrifice, integrity, and love of the people.[18] In his day, Tolstoy was seen as a revolutionary for his attacks on both church and state; as Tsar Alexander III thundered: "This ignominious Tolstoy must be stopped. He is nothing but a nihilist and a non-believer."[19]

But Tolstoy was equally repulsed by the violence of the revolutionaries. With their cynical, unchristian belief that the ends justify the means, they, too, were led astray to commit murder and would, he feared, fail to renounce violence once in power. "Is there not a difference between the killing that a revolutionist does and that which a policeman does? There is as much difference as between cat-shit and dog-shit. But I don't like the smell of either one or the other."[20] As an anarchist, he stood for the abolition of *all* governments and opposed *all* ideologies that hinted at the use of force.

Tolstoy's vision of the kingdom of God on earth was a transmogrification of his perspectives on Yasnaya Polyana and Russia. Where else would ideas like his have come about but in an oppressed land whose traditional ways of life seemed threatened by modernization? Russian conditions bred in him the view that all governmental power and all property were selfish and evil. His Christian anarchism represented another strain of the rejectionist Russian thought that was attracting a global following at the turn of the nineteenth century. Through his fictional and theological portrayals of the peasant, Tolstoy contributed to the international image of the Russian soul as the antipode of the rationalizing, industrializing, exploiting West. And his individual-denying individualism, which he had in common with much of the Russian intelligentsia, suggested to anyone who wanted to see in his writings a philosophy of either universal unity/collectivism or individual freedom, or their reconciliation.

The International Reception: Tolstoy as Artist and Prophet

By the 1890s Tolstoy had become an international figure. In Britain and the United States, more than twenty-five editions of works by him came out in the space of just several years in the 1880s and 1890s, followed by many more thereafter. Among the major early translators was Aylmer Maude, a carpet salesman for a Scottish firm in Moscow who abandoned the business world when he met Tolstoy, and devoted himself to promoting his cause.[21] The Anglo-American audience was large, but the continental European response was even more enthusiastic. In Germany between the 1880s and 1920s, at least six hundred translations, books, and articles related to Tolstoy were published, placing him third after Goethe and Dostoevsky as the most topical subject in the country.[22] Tolstoy took France, too, "by storm." Every major Parisian publishing house came out with its own edition of his works. His popularity was not restricted to intellectuals, as a critic attested in 1896: "Our ladies of fashion affect a taste for Tolstoy's novels. They leave an odd volume lying about their drawing room, with a book-mark; and the servants whisper: 'madame is reading Russian!'. . . Oh! how they delight in the marvellous chapters in which Tolstoy dissects for them fibre by fibre the sufferings of a betrayed husband, and explains to them his impotent rage. . . . These chapters are read and re-read, and got by heart."[23] And in eastern Europe, the example of Bulgaria illustrates his popularity. So great was the demand that in 1900 four Bulgarian presses existed solely to publish Tolstoy literature, and there were entire bookstores that sold nothing else.[24]

Nor was the enthusiasm confined to Europe. In India, English versions of Tolstoy were available as early as the 1870s. By the 1920s, one could find translations in Bengali, Gujarati, Hindi, Malayalam, Marathi, Punjabi, Tamil, and Urdu.[25] In Japan, all of Tolstoy was available from the 1880s on; his religious works sold in the tens of thousands of copies. He was by far the most frequently translated foreign writer in Japan in the nineteenth and twentieth centuries. When his daughter lectured in Japan in 1929, even small-town auditoriums were jammed, and girls wept over her reminiscences of her father.[26] By the early years of the new century, Tolstoy was also well known in China, Turkey, Lebanon, and Egypt, and had a fundamental impact on the literary languages in all these nations.[27]

Throughout the countries of Eurasia and America, Tolstoy's name, stories, and ideas were spread not just through publications but also through stage productions of his plays and novels, and later the movies—to give one of many examples, the 1927 Hollywood film *Love* was an adaptation of *Anna Karenina* starring Greta Garbo. Beyond that, educated travelers from around the world visited Yasnaya Polyana, and during his lifetime Tolstoy received around six thousand letters from foreigners of every continent, seeking his advice or informing him of their own activities. With some he entered into extensive correspondence.

Tolstoy was one of the first international mass-media celebrities, a role he relished, curiously enough, and one that befitted a man who helped usher in the modern world even as he struggled against it. His image and his voice circled the globe thanks to photography, film, phonographs, and popular illustrated magazines. The first color photograph in Russia was of Tolstoy. His wife compiled a photo biography of him, and her rival Chertkov made postcards of his master in old age; both of them fought for control of the many films Tolstoy allowed to be made of himself.[28] His final escape from home and his death were international media events filmed almost in their entirety and foreshadowing the paparazzi frenzies of today.

Tolstoy is remembered now mainly as an artist, and for good reason. His highly structured novels are hardly the "fluid puddings" Henry James deemed them to be.[29] In contrast to Dostoevsky, who brings his characters to life through their dialogue, Tolstoy subordinates dialogue to tightly controlled authorial narration, allowing his characters little "independence." What is striking is less what the characters themselves say, as in Dostoevsky, but what Tolstoy says of them. Dostoevsky's approach requires but minimal attention to physical features; in Tolstoy, it is the subtle descriptions of external movements of the human body that express mood and states of mind. So effectively does he present these intertwined psychological and physical sensations that readers often feel they are "perceiving reality unmediatedly, experiencing his characters' emotions without any barriers."[30] Chernyshevsky, the radical literary critic, named Tolstoy's development of his characters' psychological states the "inner monologue," a concept later adopted by Konstantin Stanislavsky in the Russian theater.[31]

It is a technique that has been compared to cinema with its camera-like view of the action and ability to unveil a character's psychological makeup through "visual" effect. A film strives to bring a viewer into the scene and into the psyches of its characters; so does a Tolstoy story, by means of the narration that proceeds as if the subject were a new, never-before-experienced phenomenon.

Russian literary critic Victor Shklovsky (who did not accept Tolstoy's Christian-moral purpose but nonetheless admired his literary innovations) called Tolstoy's approach "making strange" or "defamiliarization" (*ostranenie*), a technique later applied in Modernist art and theater. This meant not obscuring the subject matter but describing it as if perceiving it for the first time. Tolstoy's method of viewing things "out of their normal context" makes the reader feel almost as if he is entering the minds of the characters.[32] As Tolstoy wrote in *What Is Art?* (1898), his task was to "infect" his audience by "simply and clearly . . . transmit[ting], without any superfluities, the feeling [he] the artist has experienced [or evoked within himself] and wishes to transmit."[33]

Tolstoy's narrative technique reflected his philosophical outlook. He felt that he was both capturing the empirical world on paper and transcending it, achieving a higher level of consciousness tantamount to divine omniscience. Perhaps it was arrogant of him to assume that he could comprehend absolute truth. But because of that assumption, he cannot be said to represent, as some scholars argue, the culmination of the nineteenth-century realist literary tradition. Rather, he helped to initiate the Modernist movement in literature, which sought to move beyond the surface reality of human behavior and the material world. Thus a great number of modern writers felt compelled to respond to him, to imitate or fulfill or fight against his technique and themes and style.

The first thing that probably comes to mind when the typical educated reader thinks about Tolstoy is the bulkiness of his novels. His contemporaries, too, reacted to this epic scale, and not always favorably. Henry James disparaged his prolixity as "a monster harnessed to his great subject—all human life!—as an elephant might be harnessed, for purposes of traction, not to a carriage, but to a coach-house."[34] Proust's put-down of Tolstoy referred to the same creature: his works were like "the droppings of an elephant."[35] Yet for other writers, the drawn-out, epic quality of Tolstoy's novels was admirable and sanctioned their own widely imitated attempts in this direction. Thomas Mann, the greatest twentieth-century German novelist, admired Tolstoy's "Homeric, primal strength," "epic monumentality," "immense creative patience," and sober psychological analysis that was sensitive to the smallest detail. Although biting irony distinguishes his literary tone from Tolstoy's, Mann acknowledged that it was "my dream somehow to imitate" *War and Peace* in *Buddenbrooks* (1901), the magisterial novel that established his reputation in German and world literature.[36]

Like Mann, other writers were also in awe of Tolstoy's treatment of human psychology. In France he was seen as a delicate and melancholy writer who went beyond the surface regions of personality to probe its internal nature. For Paul Bourget, Paul Margueritte, Roger Martin du Gard, Édouard Rod, and Romain Rolland—that is, leading representatives of the fin-de-siècle and World War I generations of French writers—Tolstoy was "le grand Maître."[37] His compassion for humanity, his lack of artificiality, his microscopic and frank depiction of individual emotions, shorn of superfluous details, are what appealed to them and contributed to their abandonment of naturalism.[38]

English and German fiction of the time was also moving in this direction partly under the tutelage of Tolstoy, who taught iconoclastic writers in these languages how to smash old conventions. Caught up in the dynamism of Berlin and eager to break free from the past, German naturalism of the 1880s and 1890s was a literature in revolt against the old guard, and it waved the banner of the "non-Western" writers Ibsen, Dostoevsky, and Tolstoy. The preeminent figure in the movement was Gerhart Hauptmann (1862–1946), who wrote, "My literary roots go down to Tolstoy; I would never deny that."[39]

In English-language fiction, the ultimate legacy of the Tolstoyan literary technique was the stream-of-consciousness writing of James Joyce and Virginia Woolf. Joyce regarded Tolstoy so highly that after hearing of the death of a critic who had once written negatively of Tolstoy, he cheered the news and wished for the critic's eternal damnation. To Joyce, Tolstoy was "a magnificent writer. . . . head and shoulders over the others." His masterpiece, *Ulysses* (1914–1921), represented the coming of age of Tolstoy's inner-monologue technique; Joyce's reading of Tolstoy was one stage in the development of his own approach to rendering the subconscious processes of fictional characters.[40] For her part, Woolf, who wrote a great deal of criticism on Tolstoy, measured herself by Tolstoy's aesthetic standard—far more so than did Joyce. Tolstoy to her was "the greatest of novelists," whose writing makes us "feel that we have been set on a mountaintop and had a telescope put in our hands."[41]

Thus Tolstoy occupied a fundamental position in the evolution of Modernist literature. His novels were "less . . . a literary genre than . . . a mode of understanding." In this respect he played a vital role in the attempt to use language to capture authentic existence and the immediacy of life—perhaps *the* key feature of literary innovation in the twentieth century throughout the world.[42]

Yet for Tolstoy's literary legatees there was a disconnect between his writing and his thinking, as exemplified by Ernest Hemingway's attitude toward him. According to Hemingway, he "had never read of war as it was except in Tolstoy."[43] *Green Hills of Africa* (1935) owes something to Tolstoy's evocation of the environment of the Caucasus and Crimea; *For Whom the Bell Tolls* (1940) contrasted peasant wisdom and moralism with American mores in the Tolstoyan manner. But Hemingway would skip over Tolstoy's philosophy when he came to it: "I love *War and Peace* for the wonderful, penetrating and true descriptions of war and of people but I have never believed in the great Count's . . . ponderous and Messianic thinking."[44] Hemingway's Tolstoy was a writer, not a thinker.

But as a thinker Tolstoy did have a very large following. In his day many people in Europe and the rest of the world were seeking alternatives to Western perceptions of reality and established modes of spirituality. They ate up Tolstoy's nostrums for the ills of modern civilization, "smacking of the Russian soil"[45] and widely advertised through best-selling books and the nascent mass media.

The Prophet in Europe

Tolstoy's contemporaries often read him as a religious writer. In England, the initial Tolstoy works to appear were mostly religious pamphlets, and the Christian-propaganda novel *Resurrection* was the biggest seller of all his books. Poet laureate Alfred Tennyson, who named his dog "Karenina,"[46] was absorbed with Tolstoy's Christianity, as was Robert Louis Stevenson, who felt it meshed with his own ethics-based religiosity.[47] For the men of this generation, Tolstoy was a moral shepherd leading a wayward Europe back to religion.

Increasingly, though, what appealed about Tolstoy was his rejection of the established church. All over Europe (and America), neo-Protestants read Tolstoy as a modern Luther, provoking conservatives to disparage him as an anarchist rebel against Christianity. This was just what mesmerized the French Symbolist writers, who were uninterested in Tolstoy's literary technique but fused his evangelical and altruistic anarchism with Nietzschean egoism.[48] Typical of this entire generation of European intellectuals, the Dutch painter Vincent van Gogh, nursing utopian expectations of universal justice, gained a sense of spiritual liberation from reading Tolstoy.[49]

The task of proselytizing for the Tolstoyan gospel of spiritual liberation was taken up by Romain Rolland (1866–1944), French Nobel laureate, novelist, playwright, socialist, pacifist, and enthusiast of Asian religions. "To many of us the novels of Tolstoy were . . . the wonderful mirror of our passions, our strength, our weaknesses, of our hopes, our terrors, our discouragement."[50] Tolstoy's influence was fundamental to Rolland's idealistically humanitarian and righteously indignant worldview. Disillusioned with Western civilization, Rolland at various times became a worshiper of Stalin and one of Gandhi's main European apostles. But the first of the many idols to offer him salvation from the capitalist, spiritually empty West was Tolstoy: "In the gloomy twilight of the later nineteenth century [he] shone as a star of consolation, whose radiance attracted and appeased our awakening spirits."[51]

Rolland did not have to point out that that star was in the East, for the general perception among the European intelligentsia was that Russia was part of the mysterious Orient, which held the secrets of higher spiritual truth. The seeming kinship of Tolstoy's philosophy with Asian religions helps to account for his popularity in these circles. De Vogüé was only one of the Frenchmen who saw him as being endowed with the highly prized "spirit of Buddhism" and the "contemplative mistiness of the ancient Oriental asceticism."[52] Havelock Ellis's *The New Spirit* (1890), the Magna Carta of the English New Age movement, attributed Russian onion domes to vestigial Hinduism and identified Tolstoy as the exemplar of a culture that was the "natural mediator between Europe and Asia."[53] An English biographer said straight away that Tolstoy was a combination of Moses, Jesus, and the Buddha.[54]

Tolstoy was associated with the Orient because of the significant role he played in introducing Asian religious thought to the West. He wrote extensively on ancient Chinese civilization, for he felt it would help him to expose the falsehood of the Western faith in progress. His publishing house, Posrednik, produced editions of Confucius, Laozi (founder of Taoism), and other Chinese philosophers. Tolstoy himself edited some of them, and all this wisdom from the East was distributed throughout Europe.[55]

Tolstoy's religio-philosophical ecumenism contributed to dramatic new trends in twentieth-century theology. In 1915, Hermann Hesse, himself partly responsible for the West's dalliance with Asian thought, attributed to Tolstoy the belief that all religions were at bottom similar expressions of a universal humanity.[56] And owing a great deal to Tolstoy was the Theosophical movement, one of the many spiritualist, occult, Asian-oriented religious alternatives to Christianity that emerged at the turn of the century. The Theosophy sect was cofounded by Helen Petrovna Blavatsky (1831–1891). Born to a rich German-Russian aristocratic family, she rebelled against her family, divorced her husband, traveled in the Middle East, Africa, and India, and moved from Russia to Paris, New York, and finally London. Her obesity, ragged clothing, chain smoking, penchant for hashish, claims of communicating with spirits, phony Hindu scholarship, and filthy language did not hinder her influence. The religion she founded at a séance in Vermont grew to have a following in the tens of thousands and a major cultural impact. Blavatsky and her followers created their own unique cult of Tolstoy. They chopped up bits of his pantheist metaphysics, death worship, and Christian ethics—above all passive resistance to evil—with pieces of Asian religious thought to make an esoteric stew emitting aromas of Russia, India, and the murky pagan netherworld.[57]

Theosophy, Tolstoyan Christianity, and the occult, often all packaged together, had a vigorous following in the first four decades of the twentieth century in Germany. The fascination Tolstoy held there was like a deep philosophical well from which its anti-positivist thinkers drew water.[58] Tolstoy's major German publisher was the Eugen Diederichs Verlag, the leading far-right press in the country after its founding in 1896. Diederichs (1867–1930) came to hate capitalism after his father's business was ruined in a recession. His messianic urge to save Germany from the spiritual and cultural crisis it had been plunged into by association with the West led to a vision of the mystical Russian soul, and eventually even Bolshevism, as sources of Germanic salvation. His publication of adulatory works on Dostoevsky and the fifty-volume complete edition of Tolstoy (1900–1912) fit in with his line of books, including Nietzsche, Hesse, the *I Ching*, Nordic mythology, neo-Romantic philosophy, and Germanic youth-movement literature—all offering a utopian message of escape from the modern world. Diederichs and other Tolstoy devotees helped to generate the occult-tinged worldview that prepared the soil needed for the irrationalist, anti-Semitic, and anti-Christian spirit of National Socialism to take hold.[59]

Closely related to the rise of antiestablishment irrationalist and religious movements was a concurrent revolution taking place in European attitudes toward sex. The sex-obsessed Tolstoy was considered both hero and villain of this revolution. His novella *The Devil* was one of the earliest "documents of sexual realism"[60] in European literature, although it was as censorious of lustfulness as his *Kreutzer Sonata*. Tolstoy's purpose was to condemn the sex drive, but his bold treatment of the subject is often what drew the attention: British lending libraries initially banned some of his fiction as sexually explicit, and American religious conservatives attacked his works as "salacious" literature, as bad as dancing and décolletage dress fashions.[61]

The sexual liberation literati were even more intensely engaged with Tolstoy, either applauding his willingness to write about carnal appetites in his fiction or arguing against his denunciation of them. German sexologist and homosexual advocate Dr. Magnus Hirschfeld wrote articles on Tolstoy's fiction and included him in a discussion of masturbation in a textbook on sexual disease he wrote for physicians.[62] Classicist John Addington Symonds, one of the first Britons to openly defend homosexuality, wrote that Tolstoy would help the dominant English middle class to overcome its "ostrich fear" existence stifled in the "gas of dogmas."[63] His associate Havelock Ellis (1859–1939) went a step further with Tolstoy. Ellis was a physician who took up cultural criticism and psychology. The author of the first English scientific study of sexuality, he was one of Britain's best-known proponents of sex education, birth control, women's suffrage, and the decriminalization of homosexuality. His book *The New Spirit* (1890) was a dithyrambic essay on behalf of the spiritual-sexual dimensions of modern literature. "Some form of physical enlargement," he wrote, whether "singing, dancing, drinking, sexual excitement," is always encountered in religious worship. Tolstoy is a good example: he "brings us face to face with religion" and "sexual excitement," for in Russia the ancient, primitive ways have not yet been suppressed by bourgeois civilization. "Tolstoi expresses in . . . extreme form the deepest instincts of his Sclavonic [sic] race" and offers us the keys to the liberation of sex and soul.[64]

It was left to novelist D. H. Lawrence to spread sexual views like Ellis's beyond elite intellectual circles to mass awareness. But he did so by taking issue with Tolstoy. In fact, he "came to self-realisation . . . in some part through wrestling with Tolstoy."[65] Lawrence despised Tolstoy's cramped religiosity. Carnal fulfillment for Lawrence was a positive, curative force: through it human instincts were released that would allow men to overcome the atomization and alienation brought on by the repression and competitiveness of the capitalist era. Lawrence's twentieth-century Romanticism and antirationalism, informed by current trends in psychology, settled on sex as the precondition for the revival of human community. He could not forgive Tolstoy for suppressing the "phallic splendour" in his work and turning a libidinous character like

Nekhlyudov in *Resurrection* into a self-denying "lump of half-alive elderly meat."[66]

Lawrence's own epics of socioerotic emancipation were in part written to negate the sexual-ascetic aspect of Tolstoy. His most infamous work, *Lady Chatterley's Lover* (1928), a sexually explicit novel that was banned nearly everywhere upon publication, is in its entirety a critical dialogue with *Anna Karenina*. Lawrence repudiates Tolstoy for condemning Anna Karenina to death after she breaks the flawed, man-made social code of marital fidelity by following her instinctive nature to an affair with Vronsky. He shows Tolstoy how *Anna Karenina* should have ended, by giving Connie Chatterley a new life when she escapes her death-through-marriage and commits adultery with Mellors. His heroes fornicate in the rain and adorn their naked bodies with wildflowers—expressions of spontaneity, union with nature, and departure from modern civilization. It is not a complete rejection of Tolstoy, for Lawrence endows Mellors with peasantlike traits, and the entire work is an antimodern, antibourgeois invective. But unlike *Anna Karenina*, where Anna and Vronsky are linked with Western modernity, in *Lady Chatterley's Lover* the adulterers are associated with the hallowed instinctual, unrepressed, preindustrial world.

Still, for all Lawrence's frustration with Tolstoy's sexual repressiveness, Tolstoy was one of the first to treat the theme of sex in an age that was just beginning to validate the irrational drives of humankind. German playwright Bertolt Brecht assessed Tolstoy more fairly by placing him next to Frank Wedekind and August Strindberg as one of the "great educators of the new Europe"—by which he meant that the Russian writer taught the Modernists to spurn Victorian mores and take a candid approach to sexuality.[67]

More directly in synch with Tolstoy's intentions was the growth of a vegetarian and animal rights movement. Vegetarianism grew like a mushroom after the steady rain of back-to-the-land "alternative" ideas fell on England in the 1890s. It was one feature of the urban, middle- or upper-class intellectuals' idealization of the vanishing rural world they were cut off from, and Tolstoy's name gave it a credibility it had not had before.

The dedicated leader of the vegetarian movement in England was the socialist Henry S. Salt (1851–1939), master at Eton College and prolific advocate of authentic living, protection of wildflowers, and animal rights. Salt used Tolstoy's writings on nonviolence and vegetarianism to justify his opposition to "savages"—his name for meat eaters. He entered into correspondence with Tolstoy, who wrote an introduction to Salt's work *The Ethics of Diet*. He was further inspired by Kropotkin's *Mutual Aid* to press for interspecies "sociability." In 1891 Salt founded the Humanitarian League, whose goals were to fight cruelty and injustice to all living creatures. This was the first institution dedicated to the promotion of humane treatment of animals and antivivisectionism—as well as opposition to blood sports, the wearing of feathers and furs, floggings in schools, and (because of the pain) vaccinations.[68] Out of the Humanitarian League also grew the English Penal Reform League, founded in 1907 by Arthur St. John, an officer who read Tolstoy in Burma and resigned his commission to push for prison reforms such as the introduction of discretionary sentencing and bail.[69] Tolstoy's philosophy of love helped to motivate all these vegetarians, defenders of animals, and Humanitarian League members to action.

Salt's Humanitarian League fought for nonviolence across the board and was part of a larger international pacifist movement whose ranks swelled partially because of familiarity with Tolstoy's writings. Coming out of socialist, sectarian, and nonconformist traditions, pacifism had a long history separate from Tolstoy. And few European pacifists agreed with the absolute rejection of war that he or Anglo-American Quakers advocated: almost all rallied around their flags in the summer of 1914. But Tolstoy's strident antiwar discourses helped "to make pacifists of many whose ideas on war had hitherto been inchoate and undecided," before and especially after World War I.[70]

The most prominent pacifist organization of the twentieth century was the Fellowship of Reconciliation. FOR, which still exists today, was founded during World War I by Henry Hodgkin (1877–1933), a former missionary in China who, like many other English Quakers attracted to radical politics, pacifism, and social reform, became a follower of Tolstoy. Another of its founders and longtime leaders was Muriel Lester (1884–1968), a lifelong Tolstoyan who eventually forged a link between Gandhi and Western pacifists. FOR headquarters ended up in the Netherlands, which was home to the biggest pacifist movement in Europe and the strongest contingent of Tolstoyan war resisters outside of Russia.[71]

Hammer together spiritualism, sexual liberation, and vegetarianism with pacifism, anarchism, and maybe Esperanto and you build the intellectual structure of the many "simple life" utopian communes that went up in the late nineteenth and early twentieth centuries. Tolstoyism provided the common blueprint for these communes that appeared in every country of Europe. The first and most numerous were in Russia; the longest lasting were in Bulgaria, where they disappeared only during the Second World War. But Germany, Switzerland, and England were the locations of the most noteworthy developments.

Tolstoy was the prophet of the English New Life movement, so named after the Fellowship of the New Life whose Tolstoyan anarchist/Christian socialist creed committed its members to living close to nature, engaging in Tolstoyan bread labor, and creating an alternative to the capitalist hell. The self-appointed high priest of Tolstoy in England was John C. Kenworthy (1863–1946), a former businessman turned anarchist who called himself a pastor and tried to put Tolstoy's social and religious ideas into practice. He founded the Brotherhood Church in 1894 in Croydon, the vegetarian and countercultural center where the Fellowship of the New Life had its headquarters. Brotherhood churches and their communitarian experiments multiplied across England, providing meeting places for radical socialists and spiritualists. Kenworthy started a journal, *The New Order*, to report on communes around the world, and when that folded in 1899, he joined forces with Tolstoy's deputy Vladimir Chertkov and founded the Brotherhood Publishing Company to issue Tolstoy's works; after Kenworthy was committed to the insane asylum where he would die, Chertkov renamed it the Free Age Press, which published all manner of countercultural writings. From his Croydon church base, Kenworthy founded a vegetarian food co-op in north London in 1894 and a utopian commune with twenty-three acres and sixty-five members governed by bread labor and other Tolstoyan precepts at Purleigh in 1897. Kenworthy was a member of the Land Colonization Society, which helped people to settle on rural communes; here he associated with Ebenezer Howard, Raymond Unwin, and other Kropotkinite proponents of garden cities. Separate from Kenworthy's, other Tolstoyan communes appeared in England, notably at Whiteway in the Cotswolds and in Essex.[72]

The English Tolstoyan communes are evidence of the discontent with modernity that existed among the educated elite even in this birthplace of industrialization, the most urbanized nation on earth. In Germany, where the disruptions of modernization had come later, extremist attempts to apply Tolstoyism were to be expected. The antimodern, bohemian fringes of both the socialist and proto-Nazi movements looked to Tolstoy as an idol. Through Gustav Landauer, the leading German interpreter of Kropotkin, Tolstoyan thought influenced the early German ecology movement and prompted the establishment of anarcho-religious and anarcho-socialist communes in the 1920s. Members of neo-Romantic, anti-Marxist, antibourgeois, anti-Semitic German youth movements also quoted Tolstoyan calls for a return to nature and in the same breath cried for German expansionism. This ideological syncretism was common among the movements that rejected modern Western civilization; Tolstoy's rural Populism was one of the ideologies below the surface of many.[73]

It was in Switzerland that the members of the international counterculture came together between 1900 and 1920, at a free-love, mystical, anarchist, sun-worshiping, vegetarian community named Monte Verità—Mountain of Truth—in Ascona, a resort town near Locarno. Its mélange of Tolstoyism, eroticism, and neo-paganism had something in common with the German youth movement, but its membership was far more intellectual/avant-garde, and it became one of the breeding grounds for modern sexual liberationism, experimental dance, and conversion to Asian religiosity. Nudism was an option, but vegetables were a must: with the advice of the Slovak Tolstoyan Albert Skarvan (1869–1926), the community opened a meat-free restaurant and hostel and published a vegetarian journal. Among the many regular residents or visitors were Kropotkin, who spent his winters there, Max Weber, D. H. Lawrence, Isadora Duncan, Carl Jung, and Hermann Hesse. Less well known Theosophists, God seekers, and protohippies flocked there too. Although not all were full-fledged followers of Tolstoy, most of them revered him as a spiritual guide, an anarchist, a pacifist, and a dietary deity. They simply discarded his asceticism![74]

The main thrusts of Tolstoy the prophet's influence in Europe are in the realms of religion, vegetarianism, sexual consciousness, pacifism, and countercultural communalism. His influence worked in complex ways, as all intellectual forces do. His ideas were part of a welter of often contradictory utopian and anti-Western beliefs floating around Europe at the time, and some of his followers consciously and unconsciously trampled on integral pieces of his creed. But all of them were consistent in seeking from him alternatives to the modern industrial and political system.

The Prophet in Asia

At the very same time that Europe's passion for Tolstoy was on the rise, Asian intellectuals were starting to exalt him too. His writings encapsulated in highly readable form the Russian philosophical stress on the illusory nature of Western progress, and the virtues of either backwardness or delaying the onset of Western modernization, ideas that reverberated throughout the non-Western world. He wrote in praise of Asian values and denounced the exploitation, oppression, and militarism of imperialism and autocracy. He urged non-Westerners and non-Christians to transform their societies by taking up pacifism and nonviolent resistance. For all these reasons Tolstoy gained followers in Asia.

Japanese interest in Tolstoy was even stronger than in Dostoevsky.[75] Tolstoy corresponded with many Japanese, and his opposition to the Russo-Japanese War boosted his popularity among intellectuals. Blaming his works for an alarming rise in radicalism among the young, between 1905 and 1915 the government launched a campaign against Tolstoy and other authors whose works undermined the ideal of "wholesome reading beneficial to public morals."[76] But his social influence continued to swell between 1912 and 1926: theatrical productions of his works drew sizable crowds, and he was regular fare in the popular press and scholarly journals. *Torusutoishugi* was the name given the Tolstoyan lifestyle in Japan, adoption of which was far more common than might be expected: as a Japanese intellectual reminisced, "In my youth there was hardly a young man who had not to some extent read Tolstoy and had not been influenced by his thought."[77]

The Japanese idealized Tolstoy differently from the Europeans. For the former, he was not mystical and exotic but familiar and easily digestible: there was a perception that he was close to Zen Buddhism or traditional Japanese philosophy. And many Japanese were experimenting with Christianity at the time; Tolstoy, a Christian who seemed one of their own, made the attempt easier.

The religious attractiveness of Tolstoy converged with his appeal as a socialist. Opposition to Meiji industrialization, militarism, and Westernization was led by socialists, pacifists, and anarchists encouraged to various degrees by Tolstoy's works. Abe Iso (1865–1949), the father of Japanese parliamentary socialism; the poet Kitamura Tokoku (1868–1894), the first Christian pacifist in Japan; and Kotoku Shusui (1871–1911), the anarchist-socialist-pacifist leader (also a Kropotkinite) each advocated his own version of Tolstoyism to help critique the course of government-led modernization. They were not all Christian-oriented—Kotoku, for instance, understood modern war less as an ethical/religious issue than as a by-product of capitalism. And for many socialists, Tolstoy's rejection of violence rendered him useless. But by now it should be clear that one did not have to accept or even understand Tolstoy in full to call oneself a follower.

Understandably, Tolstoyism (mixed with Kropotkinism in many cases) was a potent force in Japanese agrarianism, which was as much a part of the local ideological scene as back-to-the-land movements were in the West. Enthusiasm for Tolstoy was a major reason for the rediscovery of the Japanese countryside, just as his popularity in the first place owed a lot to his belief in the peasantry as a panacea for the ills of civilization. In Japan, as everywhere else

Tolstoy was popular, agricultural communes patterned after his ideas sprang up in the first two decades of the century; one such establishment, the Farmers' Institute of Love, mixed Buddhism, Christianity, and Tolstoyan theology. Reformist Buddhist followers of Tolstoy also founded communitarian religious settlements.

Agrarianism and the simple life were prominent themes in Japanese literature of the day, with obvious links to Tolstoy. But he had a wide popularity for other reasons as well, especially among the young. As one of them put it, "Seldom in modern literary history had there been anything written on love and death that was so terse yet so deeply moved the heart" as Tolstoy.[78] Japanese writers and critics took sustenance from Tolstoy both philosophically and stylistically. Two of the many authors heavily influenced by Tolstoy bear mention, for they were among the leading literary lights of their generation: Mushakoji Saneatsu (1885–1976) and Tokutomi Roka (1868–1927). Tokutomi was an antimodern writer who made the pilgrimage to Yasnaya Polyana in 1906 and for a while lived off the land in Tolstoyan fashion; the self-observation of his novels and the antiauthoritarianism of his thought are both features influenced by Tolstoy. Mushakoji was the most representative member of the neo-Idealist, antinaturalist White Birch (Shirakaba) school of writers, so named as a symbol of Russia and mark of dedication to Russian literature. A repentant nobleman who merged Christian and Zen elements in his novels and plays, Mushakoji identified with Tolstoy. In 1918 he founded a Tolstoyan commune called the New Village, which, dedicated to brotherly love, pacifism, and peasant life, initiated a rural uplift movement.

However much Tolstoyism was a negative reaction to the Westernization of Japan, by 1912 a contemporary newspaper could look at it as a sign of the strength and success of the government's modernizing policies: Tolstoy and Ibsen were "no longer foreigners"; in partaking of global culture, Japan had left its isolation and become a "province of the world."[79] With similar effect, Chinese and Korean students brought knowledge of Tolstoy from Japan back to their homelands.

In the Islamic nations too, Tolstoy gained a good-size readership, and his ideas mingled with other intellectual influences to produce a heady cultural fermentation in a region just beginning to move toward modernization. In Turkey, his works were being translated as early as the 1890s, and they grew even more popular as Turkish intellectuals set on mounting their own uprising sought to comprehend the meaning of the 1905 Russian revolution. Stage productions of Tolstoy were increasingly common, and by the 1940s many Turkish novelists spoke of him as their literary authority. Beginning at the turn of the century in Lebanon, Palestine, Egypt, and Tunisia, Arabs could read translations of Tolstoy produced by Orthodox seminary students. If a Russian traveler can be believed, inhabitants of the tiniest Egyptian villages knew his name and considered him as some sort of wise man. Many Arabic newspapers covered his death as front-page news and indicated that all manner of people mourned his passing. By the 1920s his works were well known, through extensive translations and theatrical performances. His influence on all modern Arabic fiction was significant and paralleled Dostoevsky's: as Egyptian novelist Mahmud Taimur explained, "The heroes of Tolstoy's novels are so close to us people of the East in spirit that only our names differentiate us."[80] Taimur succinctly expresses the reason why the non-Western embrace of Tolstoy, Russian literature, and antimodern, anti-Western Russian ideas was possible.

Nowhere in the non-Western world was Tolstoy so important as in India. His works were available there beginning in the 1870s. Like the Japanese and Chinese, Indians cast Tolstoy in their own image. They saw Hindu elements in his worldview that made him seem close to them and distant from the West. From the late nineteenth century to the postindependence era, his writings helped to stiffen Indian disillusionment with Europe and promoted among the educated an intellectual idealization of the lower classes and the village community.[81] Of the many novelists he influenced in that period, Premchand (1880–1936), an initiator of modern Hindi and Urdu prose fiction, was closest to him: his works blasted British tyranny, exposed the exploitation suffered by the rural poor and untouchables, and proposed socialism combined with inner spiritual reform as the solution to the problems of India.[82] But, of course, it was Mohandas Gandhi (1869–1948) who was the major carrier of Tolstoyism to India and, by example, to the wider world.[83]

The full revelation of Tolstoy to Gandhi took place in stages over the course of more than ten years in England and South Africa. Gandhi went to London to study law in 1888, left with his degree in 1891, and returned periodically thereafter. He had promised his mother he would not eat meat in England; his dietary restriction brought him into contact with British vegetarians, and he drew close to back-to-the-land, countercultural figures like Henry Salt, Kenworthy, and Chertkov. He encountered Theosophists, who introduced him for the first time to the *Bhagavad-Gita* and the exotic India fad. He became familiar with antimodern literature influenced by Russian Populism. And he began to read Tolstoy, first on vegetarianism, then on religion and politics.

Gandhi's reading of Tolstoy was a crucial step in his transformation from insignificant lawyer to Mahatma—"Great Soul"—and liberator of the Indian people. Gandhi moved to South Africa in 1893, where he suffered the humiliating treatment whites meted out to resident Indians. By the time he left in 1914, he had become a vocal advocate of equal rights for the Indian community and a thorn in the side of the authorities. At the same time that he was experiencing South African racism firsthand, he read Tolstoy's works, which, he wrote, "overwhelmed me." Compared to them, all other books "paled into insignificance."[84] Although Gandhi also drew on Thoreau, Ruskin, the Sermon on the Mount, the British suffragettes, and Indian theology, Tolstoy with his echoes of Hinduism was the writer who was most integral to the formation of his strategy of political action. The fusion of Tolstoyan thought with Gandhi's instinctive reaction to injustice in South Africa and India eventually rocked the British Empire.

Gandhi's disillusionment with Western civilization, membership in the British counterculture, and conversion to Tolstoyism led him to experiment with "alternative" lifestyles. Besides adopting strict vegetarianism, he renounced wealth, sexual intercourse, and false teeth. And he shunned Western clothing for the loincloth and shawl of the Indian peasant. Inspired by Tolstoy, Gandhi tailored a powerful political symbol out of his appearance and personal behavior in order to identify himself with the masses and mobilize the Congress Party, which he led. Eventually, nationalists throughout the

world would see the strength of that symbolism and take to wearing their own native dress in conscious or unconscious imitation
of Gandhi and Tolstoy.

Gandhi translated his ideas and inclinations into reality first by
founding a series of Tolstoyan communes that were to be models
for the future organization of Indian society. In South Africa he
established the Phoenix community near Durban and Tolstoy
Farm near Johannesburg; they were the precursors of his Indian
ashrams at Sevagram and Sabarmati. Gandhi's aim was to "im-
plant the spirit of Tolstoy, and then of country life, and of the way
to make the best use of it."[85] He applied the principle of bread
labor, which "came home to me upon reading one of Tolstoy's
essays. . . . Tolstoy made such a deep impression on my mind, and
. . . I began to observe the rule [of laboring for one's own suste-
nance] to the best of my ability. And ever since the Ashram was
founded, bread labor has been perhaps its most characteristic feature."[86] Beyond this, vegetarianism was required of residents, and
killing animals, even snakes, was forbidden. The communes produced their own *khadi*, or homespun Indian cloth, using a traditional spinning wheel.

Gandhi's personal habits, ashrams, and anarchist communitarianism give an indication of his view of the ideal India that would
take shape after the achievement of *swaraj*—self-rule. But first British rule would have to be eliminated, and to accomplish that, Gandhi developed a strategy based on Tolstoy's philosophy of peaceful
nonresistance and the example of Tolstoy's civil disobedience. He
coined a name for this strategy out of classical Sanskrit words, *satyagraha*, which he defined as the power "born of Truth and Love
or non-violence."[87] Gandhi wrote that in South Africa he became
a "humble follower" of Tolstoy, who taught him to realize the "infinite possibilities of love."[88] His strategy required passive resistance against the British authorities, an approach that he believed
would come naturally once people mastered themselves through
chastity, poverty, and truth, and rejected all the corrupting ways of
Western civilization. This mastery of self—*swaraj*—would steel the
individual for the punishment that noncooperation with the British

authorities would bring. The inward freedom gained would result in outward political freedom: "If man will only realize that it is unmanly to obey laws that are unjust, no man's tyranny will enslave him."[89] Echoing Tolstoy's critique of both the tsarist autocracy and its Bakuninist enemies, Gandhi argued that human fallibility justified a nonviolent strategy: *satyagraha* "excludes the use of violence because man is not capable of knowing the absolute truth and, therefore, not competent to punish."[90] To a great extent these assumptions were derived from Tolstoy, who in 1909 called Gandhi's efforts in South Africa "the most important work now being done in the world."[91]

With the experience in practical politics he gained in South Africa, Gandhi returned to India in 1915 and created a mass movement for Indian independence. By 1921 he was the undisputed opposition leader there, and his calls for boycotting British manufactures, and for noncooperation with all governmental political, judicial, and educational institutions, were increasingly heeded. His own fearlessness and repeated imprisonment encouraged thousands to break the law and accept prison terms during his major *satyagraha* campaigns of 1920–1922, 1930–1934, and 1940–1942.

Gandhi's program was the first instance in history of peaceful nonresistance put to practical use. But as his movement grew, differences between Gandhi and Tolstoy emerged. Unlike Tolstoy, Gandhi was a shrewd political operator who compromised with reality. When Tolstoy was still alive, he critiqued Gandhi's nationalism for contradicting his commitment to a nonviolent, stateless society. As an anarchist utopian, Gandhi did feel the state would eventually disappear as noncoercive, noncompetitive, decentralized village communes preempted it. But he did not consider it possible to abolish the state immediately: when he was participating in the negotiation of terms for the British withdrawal from India, this was never in the cards.[92]

But Gandhi's pragmatism had its limits. His utopianism prevented him from coming up with viable solutions to India's intractable problems of poverty and religious tensions. And ironically, just as his village-centered economic policies were sidelined by politicians attracted to Stalinist central planning, so his life was tragically snuffed out by a Hindu extremist linked to Russian-inspired terrorists.

Tolstoy in America

It is sometimes assumed that Tolstoyism as a political strategy died with Gandhi.[93] But in America, Tolstoyism made a distinct contribution to Progressive Era reformism and the later Civil Rights movement that grew out of it.

Like Europe, America had its share of occultists, Theosophists, anarchists, and simple-lifers who took after Tolstoy by forming utopian, usually vegetarian, communes. The largest Tolstoyan community in the country was in Muscogee County, Georgia, where some five hundred people joined the Christian Commonwealth, led by the Reverend Ralph Albertson (1866–1951), a former Congregational minister turned Tolstoyan anarchist, a friend of Jane Addams, and eventual volunteer in a White Army unit fighting the Bolsheviks in northern Russia.[94] The thousand-acre socialist commune was run on the principle of bread labor and lasted from 1896 to 1900 before it fell apart, a victim of bitter infighting and a typhoid epidemic. Tolstoy corresponded with its members and thought of sending the Dukhobors there. Through the entire twentieth century, Tolstoy inspired similar back-to-the-land, anticapitalist communal experiments in the United States.[95]

But Tolstoy's importance in America went well beyond utopian settlements: an entire generation of cultural critics and social reformers were swayed by his views in the late nineteenth and early twentieth centuries. As the Midwestern novelist Hamlin Garland wrote, his contemporaries received from Tolstoy "utterances of such apostolic austerity that they read like encyclicals from the head of a great church—the church of humanity. . . . We quoted Ibsen to reform the drama and Tolstoy to reform society. We made use of every available argument his letters offered."[96]

Garland was a friend of the leading American realist novelist of the 1880s, William Dean Howells, who was the main promoter of

Tolstoy in the United States. Born in Ohio, Howells made a name for himself as a literary authority in the intellectual circles of New York and Boston, and became rich off popular works such as *The Rise of Silas Lapham*. He considered Shakespeare to be inferior to Tolstoy, "incomparably the greatest writer of fiction who has ever lived."[97] Howells gave his idol mass publicity in the 1880s and 1890s through a column he wrote for *Harper's Magazine* and as editor of the *Atlantic Monthly*. Along with Mark Twain, Charles Eliot Norton, William James, and others, Howells was an increasingly radical critic of industrial America, the city, and the materialism of Gilded Age America. In their discontent, some of these men turned to Jefferson, some to Emerson; Howells did too, but his long-lasting quest for a utopia suitable to America ended with his discovery of Tolstoy.

Howells did not share Tolstoy's hostility toward democracy or toward all of Western civilization. But he agreed with his critique of urban industrial society for its having abandoned the ethical teachings of Jesus. The Tolstoyan aspects of Howells's thought appear most clearly in one of the major American utopian novels, *A Traveler from Altruria* (1892–1893), in which he advocates physical labor, social equality, brotherly love, and simplicity.[98]

Partly thanks to Howells, nonrevolutionary but reformist intellectuals and political activists of all sorts received stimulation from Tolstoy—those historian Peter Frederick terms the "knights of the golden rule."[99] Samuel "Golden Rule" Jones, mayor of Toledo, Ohio, from 1897 to 1904, worked under a portrait of Tolstoy (next to Walt Whitman's); he donated a power plant to Albertson's Christian Commonwealth, refused to prosecute prostitutes, and replaced policemen's guns and heavy clubs with light canes. Henry Demarest Lloyd, the journalist and social critic known for his attacks on Standard Oil and American big business; B. O. Flower, founder-editor of the leading muckraking magazine *The Arena*; Vida Scudder, scholar, feminist, and founder of the college settlement-house movement for women; and other quasi-socialist, sometime Christian reformers were all motivated to do what they did by a common moralistic religious creed at least in part stemming from and agreeing with Tolstoy.[100]

What unified the Tolstoyism of all these figures was a desire to create cooperative, humanitarian alternatives to the modern city, or at least to alleviate its suffocating poverty. No wonder Tolstoy appealed to the reformers of the Progressive movement—he himself was a muckraker: his book on the Moscow poor, *What Then Must We Do?* (1886), opened the eyes of Americans as much as of Russians to the suffering of the indigent and the horrors of the slums. Tolstoy's call for social action in this arena was heeded by Jane Addams (1860–1935), feminist, peace activist, and social reformer. Linked to Christian Socialist circles in England, inspired by Kropotkin, and responding to Tolstoy, Addams forsook polite society, went "to the people" like a Russian Populist, and founded Hull House in an immigrant slum neighborhood of Chicago. Hull House did more than dispense charity and banking services to poor immigrants. Addams lived there and offered classes, clubs, and arts-and-crafts activities—all in line with interconnected English and Russian "alternative" philosophies. She went to see Tolstoy in 1896 and hosted Kropotkin in Chicago. Upon her return from Russia, she introduced bread labor to Hull House, and until her schedule prevented it, she worked in the bakery every day.

Although Addams became a staunch defender of Tolstoyan non-resistance and pacifism, she was not convinced of the practicality of all facets of Tolstoyism. At Yasnaya Polyana Tolstoy criticized her for not wearing the clothing of the people—to which she responded that she served a multiplicity of ethnic groups, each with a different costume. Moreover, she needed to attract, not scare off, wealthy supporters. She believed not in rejecting and overthrowing the existing system, but in working within it as the best way of achieving practical improvements to society. She had misgivings about Christianity and anarchism, but did yearn for a secularized kingdom of heaven on earth. Tolstoy's philosophy of action on behalf of human solidarity helped her to understand what it would look like, and her invention of social work in America was part of the vision.[101]

Besides Addams, many of the followers of Tolstoy among Progressive reformers were pacifists and anti-imperialists—the most famous being William Jennings Bryan and, for a time, Clarence Darrow. Interestingly, neither of them seems to have been aware of the contribution made to Tolstoy's own outlook by the writings of the nineteenth-century New Englanders William Lloyd Garrison and Adin Ballou—who provided a native source of American pacifism alongside Tolstoy. For post-1880s American antiwar activists, Tolstoy's pacifism was of a piece with his Russian Populist, Christian socialism: not only a necessary antidote to the crass materialism of the day, but a reaction against "big stick" American militarism and, later, against World War I.

So visible was Tolstoy as a critic of U.S. government policy and an inspiration to other critics of it that President Theodore Roosevelt felt the need to denounce him when hailing American expansionism. Roosevelt had a keen literary sense and was well read in European literature. He once remarked that it would be "a bad thing . . . not to profit by the lofty side of [Tolstoy's] teachings."[102] But the other side was dangerous: Tolstoy, he charged, "makes a pretence of shoe-making in order to attract attention to himself; [and] dresses like a clown for the same purpose." Many of his novels were "dirty and obscene," and there is in him "a dark streak which tells of the moral pervert." Fully unacceptable as a guide to men of affairs, luckily his hysterical, insane works have "swayed or dominated only the feeble folk and the fantastic folk" in the United States.[103]

But America's rough-riding foreign policy and Roosevelt's cult of manhood stimulated a rather large pacifist response and assertion of Tolstoyan principles. Clarence Darrow (1857–1938) was an American member of the Humanitarian League and at one time a Tolstoyan pacifist. The renowned defense attorney and Progressive social activist read and lectured on Tolstoy. He published a book dedicated to Tolstoyan nonresistance in 1902 and cited Tolstoy in the courtroom in defense of labor agitators and strikers fighting government persecution. Although he gave up on Tolstoyan pacifism after the 1914 German invasion of Belgium, he continued to refer to him on those occasions when he condemned violence in the treatment of criminals and pressed for reform of the American legal system.[104]

Darrow's most famous role as defense attorney—at the trial of John Scopes for teaching evolution in Tennessee—brought him head-to-head against a member of the prosecution team, William Jennings Bryan (1860–1925), an opponent of Darwin, advocate of Christian teaching in schools, and ardent Tolstoyan.[105] The politician from Nebraska and unsuccessful Democratic candidate for the presidency was a fundamentalist and antiplutocratic populist who saw both Jefferson and Tolstoy as saints. Already an admirer of Tolstoy as the "apostle of love," he became a pacifist after the Spanish-American War, and in 1903—aged forty-two—he went to see Tolstoy at Yasnaya Polyana. There he charged his Christian activist batteries and in the next year's presidential campaign took a Tolstoyan position in attacking the "big stick" policy of his Republican opponent Roosevelt. Yet Bryan was not consistent in his pacifism. He believed that in some cases war was necessary for humanitarian purposes, and as secretary of state (1913–1915) in the Wilson administration, he sanctioned the use of American military force in the Caribbean. But he did push for treaties of reconciliation and negotiation as measures that might reduce conflict, and he resigned his office to protest the American drift toward war against the Germans.

World War I produced a new, more strident phase of American pacifism, also closely related to Tolstoy. One major center of the movement in the United States to emerge at this time was the previously mentioned Fellowship of Reconciliation. FOR opened a branch in the country to agitate against American entry into World War I. Under the leadership of A. J. Muste (1885–1967), an ex-minister in the Dutch Reformed Church who turned to pacifism after reading Tolstoy (then temporarily abandoned it in favor of revolution after reading Trotsky), FOR in the 1940s became a locus of radical Protestantism in this country and the largest organized body of war resisters in the world.[106]

The moralistic and reform-minded Progressive followers of Tolstoy were the first to introduce the defining features of the American Civil Rights movement—its presuppositions regarding race relations and its strategies. And in this regard, the encounter with Tolstoy changed the face of modern America. But Tolstoyism also came to America indirectly, through Gandhi's impact on the black intellectuals who were attracted to him from the 1920s on. "If humanity is to progress," declared Martin Luther King, Jr., "Gandhi is inescapable. . . . We may ignore him at our own risk." King heard a lecture on Gandhi at Howard University, read books by him, and was greatly impressed with the *satyagraha* campaigns. King's views of peaceful resistance, as they evolved, eventually came to mirror those of Gandhi, who he said "furnished the method" for the Montgomery bus boycott and the nonviolent African American rights struggle. Like Tolstoy facing the Russian terrorists, like Gandhi facing Indian insurgents, King also faced black radicals who called for struggle "by any means necessary," in the words of Malcolm X.[107] King contrasted nonviolence with the black power movement as Tolstoy and Gandhi had attacked militant organizations in Russia and India. He saw in Gandhi the aspirations of Jesus for universal freedom, renewal, and human reconciliation—all echoes of Tolstoy as well. But it was only an echo, for King did not write a word on Tolstoy or credit him with any influence; it is not altogether clear that he even read him.[108] Yet although a Tolstoy-King tie exists via Gandhi, a direct link exists through Tolstoy's inspiration of the earliest civil rights advocates, King's teachers, and most of the major organizations involved in the struggle.

People concerned with race matters at one time looked to Tolstoy as a guide. Henry Codman Potter, an Episcopal bishop and president of the American Colonization Society from 1892 to 1899, advocated the return of black Americans to Africa, a move he regarded as beneficial to them. It was from reading Tolstoy that Potter came to believe in the possibility of redeeming blacks and relying on them as missionaries in their ancestral homeland. Edward Alfred Steiner was Potter's contemporary: born a Hungarian Jew, he became an ordained Congregational minister after emigrating to America. His pastoral work centered on the black slums of Springfield and Sandusky, Ohio. He visited Yasnaya Polyana and eventually preached the Tolstoyan brotherhood of man and opposition to prejudice from his pulpit as professor of religion at Grinnell College. On these matters Steiner was close in spirit to the patrician New York judge Ernest Howard Crosby, whose conversion to Tolstoyism and challenge to Western imperialism brought him to denounce Anglo-Saxon superiority, the idea of racial inequality, and the shabby treatment of African Americans—which few other whites questioned at the time.[109]

Thus by the turn of the nineteenth century Tolstoy was recognized as a voice against American racism. Black journalists wrote articles about him, and Booker T. Washington sent him material on the Tuskegee Institute.[110] Black scholar-activist W.E.B. Du Bois acknowledged it: Tolstoy was a rare person of courage and conviction "who had before him a vision of simplicity, poverty, unselfishness and peace, such as would transform the world and make it anew. . . . Very few men have dared this straight and narrow path. Very few men will dare. But it remains before the eyes of all seers and prophets, a Path."[111] Du Bois shared that vision with black and white intellectuals who followed Tolstoy to nonviolent struggle on behalf of racial justice for African Americans in the early twentieth century; out of that environment Martin Luther King, Jr., emerged.

Philosophically, King owed much to the greatest theologian of the American social gospel, Walter Rauschenbusch (1861–1918), a Baptist minister and professor at Rochester Theological Seminary. His influential assertions that economics and politics should be rooted in notions of Christian justice would be embedded in the New Deal long after his death. Under the influence of Tolstoy and Crosby, Rauschenbusch decried American racial divisiveness as warping the country's sense of justice and love. He denounced lynchings as counter to the spirit of God and urged a passive resistance crusade for social justice. An anthology of his work was edited in the late 1940s by Morehouse College president Benjamin E. Mays, who introduced him to King, then his student. At Crozer Theological Seminary in Chester, Pennsylvania, King read still more of Rauschenbusch. It was to the Tolstoyan aspects of Rauschenbusch's thought that King was indebted; in this way Tolstoy assisted secondhand in directing King along his path toward nonviolent resistance.[112]

King also built on the experience of his predecessors and contemporaries in civil rights activism. His Southern Christian Leadership Conference, founded in 1957, coupled the principles of nonviolence with direct-action tactics. But this did not come out of the blue—it was the product of a long tradition within the NAACP (National Association for the Advancement of Colored People), the Urban League, and CORE (Congress of Racial Equality). These organizations were founded by Tolstoyans and had antecedents in the Tolstoyan-related pacifist movement. Two leading figures in founding the NAACP and Urban League were John Hayne Holmes (1879–1964) and William English Walling (1877–1936). Holmes was a Unitarian minister and Christian-socialist follower of Tolstoy who was the founder of the American branch of the Fellowship of Reconciliation as well as the American Civil Liberties Union and, eventually, an early Vietnam War protester. Walling, who according to Langston Hughes was more responsible for the NAACP than anyone else, was the scion of a wealthy, formerly slave-owning family in Kentucky. Involved in Addams's settlement-house movement, he was a social reformer and journalist, and he married a Russian Jewish woman who had been a revolutionary in her youth. On a two-year trip to Russia following the 1905 revolution, Walling came to settle on Tolstoy's anticapitalist, religious-utopian beliefs as divine truth and the hope for mankind. Soon after returning to America, he witnessed an Illinois race riot, which led him to compare the plight of blacks in the United States to that of Jews in Russia. Meshing the two circumstances, he looked to Tolstoy for part of the answer to the problem of American blacks; the NAACP and the Urban League were among the results.[113]

CORE had a similar Christian-socialist, Tolstoyan-pacifist heritage. It was founded in 1942 by James Farmer, then race relations secretary for the Fellowship of Reconciliation and a leader of the NAACP. He was a black minister, a labor organizer, a promoter of crafts industries among blacks, and an admirer of both Tolstoy and Gandhi. He formed CORE with the support of other FOR members and University of Chicago students interested in the application of Gandhism in America; it was from one Chicago branch of FOR that CORE emerged. With help from the Fellowship of Reconciliation, CORE organized chapters nationwide and took part over the course of the 1940s, 1950s, and 1960s in various nonviolent sit-ins, rides of reconciliation, and southern freedom rides all designed to challenge segregation and Jim Crow laws. It was after witnessing the effects of these Tolstoyan-Gandhian tactics and after discussions with FOR members in the midst of the Montgomery bus boycott in 1955 that King committed himself to nonviolent resistance.[114]

The success and public attention generated by the Civil Rights movement's application of nonviolent civil disobedience led to its adoption by other protesting segments of American society. Gloria Steinem recognized the Tolstoyan heritage of the Gandhian tactics she advocated for the feminist movement.[115] The student protests of the 1960s and Cesar Chavez's crusade on behalf of farm workers imitated the Civil Rights movement in their application of direct action and Gandhism as well, although probably without consciousness of the Tolstoy connection. But as with literature, vegetarianism, sexual attitudes, theology, communalism, and other Modernist and antimodern manifestations, the ubiquity of passive resistance techniques is testimony to the transformative impact the Russian "genius and crank" Tolstoy had on the entire twentieth-century world.

For some, Tolstoyism was a promise of heaven on earth; for others, it served a limited purpose as either an innovative literary technique or a pragmatic, nonviolent tool to effect change in unjust societies. And in between these extremes was a wide variety of interpretations and combinations of functions; for Tolstoy's followers made of him what they liked, just as the international audience did of Bakunin, Kropotkin, and Dostoevsky. But however Tolstoy was construed—or misconstrued, as the case may be—what was common to all who came under his influence was an attraction to components of his Russian Populism and spiritualism. Hostility toward science and technology, which had not produced the happiness its champions had promised; idolization of the simple, spontaneous lives of the lower classes, who were unspoiled by the artificiality of civilization and uncomplicated by thinking; belief in the virtues of economic backwardness as a vestige of a precapitalist golden age; a sense of the Russian peasant in his village as the embodiment of soulfulness: these were the strands of his thought that were generated in Russian circumstances and summed up or anticipated the reaction of the whole world to the stresses of modernization. At one and the same time they offered a highly individualistic, anti-statist vision and a cooperationist/communitarian/collectivist vision, which taken whole or separately promised release from the established world order and worldview.

Destroying the Agents of Modernity:

Russian Anti-Semitism

WHEREVER THE process of industrialization occurred in the nineteenth century, among portions of the population it elicited feelings of anxiety, fear, and revulsion as it ineluctably altered the familiar topography. Baffling new rules of economic life had to be learned, the urban landscape was transformed, aesthetic sensibilities were offended, and old social elites lost ground to new forces. One group in particular seemed associated with these pernicious changes: the Jews, who appeared as the quintessentially evil representatives of modernity, whether as financiers, traders, or revolutionaries. Although the intellectual seeds of modern anti-Semitism were sown by nineteenth-century French and German intellectuals, they found fertile soil in tsarist Russia. Its Russian practitioners then went on to shape twentieth-century anti-Semitism throughout the world.

Judeophobia has ancient origins in pagan and Christian religious disputes with the Jews. But the late nineteenth century marked the rise of a new kind of anti-Semitism in Europe, which was connected to the dramatically changing circumstances of both Jews and Gentiles. As Jews were closely identified with the capitalism and culture of the modern city, they often bore the brunt of popular displeasure when the increasingly investment-oriented economy took a cyclical downturn. Partly a function of antimodernism, anti-Semitism was especially strong in the Russian Empire, which, by the nineteenth century, had become the home of the world's largest Jewish population. The industrializing spurt induced by the tsars unsettled the social order and produced a large contingent of extremist, anticapitalist rejectionists, some of whom aimed their malevolence at Russia's Jews.

For many centuries there were few Jews who lived in the Russian Empire, but with the annexation of eastern Poland in the late eighteenth century, Russia found itself master of approximately half a million of them. In 1791 Empress Catherine the Great restricted Jewish access to the Russian interior. Her decree allowed them to live only in those regions where Jewish communities had at one time existed in the distant past, or on lands recently taken from the Turks where they were needed as settlers. Thus the Jews were confined to residence in the Pale of Settlement ("pale" here meaning fence or boundary)—the northwestern and southwestern frontier provinces of the empire, stretching from the Baltic Sea to the Black Sea through Lithuania, eastern Poland, Belorussia, Ukraine, Bessarabia, and South Russia. The Pale plus central Poland, annexed in the early nineteenth century, was to become the vast Jewish ghetto of the empire.[1] The Pale conveniently enabled Catherine's successors, who were far less tolerant than she, to impose a Jewish apartheid.[2]

An anti-Semitic worldview took shape as the stability of the traditional economic and political arrangements in Russia was giving way to an untried and uncertain future. Between the 1870s and 1890s, a fantastical fear of the Jews grew apace.[3] Throughout this period following the emancipation of serfdom, segments of the bureaucracy and the educated public fretted that the Jews would upset the social stability of the countryside by enslaving the peasants through drink and loans. Competition from Jews spelled doom in the minds of tradition-bound Russian merchants. All the while, through the agency of the periodical press, tsarist society was receiving a transfusion of fresh anti-Semitic ideas from Germany and France. Konstantin Pobedonostsev, the tsarist-appointed head of the Russian Orthodox Church and reactionary ideologist of the regime, expressed a common view: "The Yids . . . have engrossed everything, they have undermined everything, but the spirit of the century supports them. They are at the root of the revolutionary socialist movement and of regicide, they own the periodical press, they have in their hands the financial markets, the people as a whole fall into financial slavery to them; they even control the principles of modern science and strive to place it outside of Christianity."[4]

The government dealt with its phobia by instituting ever more repressive measures against the Jews. Armenians, Poles, Tatars, and other ethnic groups were also subject to discriminatory policies to keep them in line, but specific to the Jews were more than a thousand pages of restrictive legislation. According to these laws, the government imposed quotas on secondary school and university admissions that limited Jews to 10 percent of the student body in the Pale, and 3 to 5 percent elsewhere. A low ceiling was placed on Jewish ownership of rural real estate and participation in stock exchanges, mining, and the oil industry. In the army, Jews were prohibited from serving as combat officers, band conductors, or pharmacists. The freest Jewish professionals were prostitutes, who could live anywhere in the empire as long as they could prove they were plying their trade. To add injury to the insult of the repressive regulations, the police frequently rounded up and expelled Jews from cities where they were not allowed to live but had previously been tolerated: thirty thousand suffered this fate in Moscow in 1892, and Jews were deported from a score of other towns as well.[5]

Government discrimination against the Jews seemed justified by the fact that they were overrepresented in trade, commerce, and towns. As elsewhere in Europe, tradition and regulations had kept most Jews from landowning and farming. By the 1890s, of the 5.2 million Jews in the Russian Empire, more than 80 percent lived in urban centers, either large cities or the small- to medium-size market towns called shtetls. By contrast, most non-Jews lived in the countryside. Jews made up 40 percent of the commercial population of the entire empire, even though they constituted a mere 4 percent of the total population! The Jewish presence in this sector of the economy was felt even more strongly in southern Russia, the fast-growing and fast-industrializing region where big, heavily Jewish cities like Ekaterinoslav and Odessa were located.[6]

While some Jews were indeed very wealthy, for every successful Jewish entrepreneur there were thousands upon thousands who were suffering, pushed to the margins by the modernizing economy.[7] In Odessa, which had the most prosperous Jewish community in the empire, more than half the Jewish population were destitute. In the rest of the Pale, the unemployment rate among Jews was 40 percent or more—these were the multitudes of luckless Jews who in Yiddish were called *luftmentshn*—people who live off nothing but air. As for the employed tradesmen, they were mostly engaged in peddling used clothing or other junk items, and their turnover and profit margins were low. Thirty percent of the Jewish workforce of the Pale were involved in small-scale and backward cottage craft production as tailors, coopers, cobblers, and the like. In the shtetls there were far "more tailors and shoemakers than there ever could be buyers," one former resident recollected.[8] Far from being some capitalist vanguard, such Jewish "manufacturers" were ruined by factory production, in which only a very small number of wealthy Jews were involved. But the anti-Semites feared all Jews as potential lords of commerce.

Just as menacing as Jewish capitalists was the presence of Jews in the revolutionary movement. Like many other other ethnic minorities in the empire, young Jews became revolutionaries largely to protest their plight under the rigidly autocratic, Russifying regime. Until the 1870s, relatively few Jews were involved. That changed, however, with the onslaught of anti-Semitic "Jim Crow" legislation and the initiation of violent pogroms. Russian Jewish membership in radical Populist circles in the 1870s and 1880s stood anywhere from 8 to 40 percent of the membership, depending on the group. The formation in 1897 of the General Union of Jewish Workers in Lithuania, Poland, and Russia—known as the Bund—further expanded the field of Jewish radical activity. Both a revolutionary political party within the Russian Marxist movement and an illegal Yiddish trade union organization, the Bund could bring thousands of Jewish workers into the streets. By 1904, there were approximately 100,000 Jews in left-wing organizations across the empire, a small percentage of the Jewish population of 5 million, but a larger percentage of participation than for any other ethnic group.[9]

Sergei Witte, the finance minister and great industrializer whose wife was a converted Jew, may have understood what drove Jews to become revolutionaries: as he explained to the Austrian Zionist leader Theodor Herzl, "I think that it is the fault of our government. The Jews are too oppressed."[10] But the last two tsars, Alexander III and Nicholas II, and many officials, were deaf to this argument. Vyacheslav von Plehve, the interior minister, spoke for them in 1902 when he pinned responsibility for insurgency throughout the empire on the entire Jewish population: "There is no revolutionary movement in Russia, there are only Jews who are the true enemies of the government."[11]

Thus the Jews appeared to be pathogens in the Russian body politic. Many within the Russian ruling class associated them with aspects of modernity that were eating away at traditional social hierarchies and modes of existence. Already despised for their religion, they were now seen as the agents of change in a poor, rural, autocratic empire whose aristocratic elite could not well comprehend what was happening to its world. Although the tsarist government was the primary sponsor of modernization, some within it tried to slow or stop the process; for them dislike of the Jews was inseparable from their dread that Westernization would debilitate Russian society. The anti-Semitic worldview was to a large extent a reactionary delusion that the repression or even elimination of the Jews could immunize Russia against modernity.[12]

The paranoid demonization of the Jews by members of the Russian government and elite saturated the mass press, which in this highly unstable society legitimated the eruption of pogroms, violent anti-Jewish riots.[13] Isolated pogroms had occurred previously—for instance, in Odessa in 1821, 1849, 1859, and 1871—but in new circumstances they erupted wherever Jews lived in the empire. These "southern tempests," as they were called by Jewish writers, occurred in three main phases, 1881–1884, 1903–1906, and 1915–1921.[14] In city after city, town after town, the pogroms burst forth: 259 in 1881, 45 in 1904, 650 in 1905–1906, and more than 1,000 in the chaos of World War I and the civil war that followed the Bolshevik takeover.

Each phase was more violent than the last. The marauders gruesomely mutilated many of their prey, ripping open the bellies of pregnant women, driving spikes through a victim's limbs, eyes, and brain into a makeshift cross, or torturing children to death in front of their parents. In the pogroms of the 1880s, 20,000 Jews lost their homes and 100,000 suffered property loss of some form. In April 1903, perpetrators of the Kishinev pogrom murdered 50 Jews, injured 500, and destroyed hundreds of shops and homes. Altogether in the waves of terror that swept Jewish neighborhoods of the empire in 1905, more than 3,000 died and 5,000 suffered serious injury. Horrific though that seemed at the time, it was mild compared to the affliction brought on by war and the collapse of the old regime. Jews who lived in the main theaters of the wars were victims of looting, rape, revenge, and blood sport by gangs of deserters and troops in the rear. The number of Jewish casualties exceeded 100,000; so unimaginably great was the devastation that the London *Jewish Chronicle* termed it a "holocaust of Jews in Russia."[15]

Contrary to what many people once believed, the tsarist government did not orchestrate the pre-1917 pogroms. It was more startled than pleased by them. Even the wholeheartedly anti-Semitic Tsar Alexander III, who once said he could not concern himself with relieving the poverty of the Christ-killing Jews, did not want to see the pogroms repeated. The autocratic regime feared that these manifestations of spontaneous activity on the part of the populace could both boil over into a mass antigovernmental rebellion and threaten vital foreign investment. Thus more often than not, local police tried to put down the pogroms by arresting or shooting the perpetrators. Many attempted to protect the threatened Jewish populations. Unfortunately, though, the poorly trained and understaffed provincial police forces were usually no match for the murderous mobs.

The popular image of Russian peasants and government-commanded Cossack troops rampaging through Jewish villages is a false one (at least before World War I and the revolution). The overwhelming majority of late tsarist-era pogroms took place in cities, where local merchants, shopkeepers, and artisans feared intense Jewish competition and believed that by attacking Jews or encouraging attacks on them, they were resisting alien forms of capitalism. But it was migratory unskilled day laborers who had the most blood on their hands. This was a horde of rough young men who had left their dreary peasant communes for unskilled railroad, dock, or factory work in the booming and squalid southern cities. Hungry, hard-drinking, crowded into filthy flophouses, they found psychological compensation for their difficult existence in hatred of the Jews, some of whom competed with them for marginal jobs, while others were their pawnbrokers and vodka vendors. Brutalized and impoverished, sullen and angry, they were prey to feeling victimized by the exploitation or competition of Jews, their supposed social inferiors. For similar reasons anti-Semitic students and underclass criminals joined in the assaults on Jews when the opportunity arose.

Such were the elements that came together to produce anti-Jewish riots. Religion played only a small role, serving primarily to rationalize violent actions taken for other reasons. First and foremost the pogroms were a result of urban uprootedness, disorientation, and disarray at a time of unprecedentedly rapid economic and political change with which the Jews were identified, and for the hardships of which they were blamed.

As for the Jews themselves, the pogroms were stunning and dashed their hopes for acceptance. Together with the oppressive tsarist legislation, the pogroms provoked downtrodden Russian Jewry to break with centuries of tradition and escape the dire circumstances of Jewish life.

Thousands of Jews refused to endure their fate in the Pale, joining revolutionary parties or entering the Zionist movement, which initiated the Jewish settling of Palestine. An even more common response was to emigrate to western Europe and America. Three million did so between 1882 and 1914, creating vibrant Yiddish communities where none had been before, but also prompting rising xenophobic anti-Semitism in these places. Among the bugbears of the anti-Semites were several female Russian-Jewish revolutionaries who gained international fame: Anna Kuliscioff—born Rozenstein—a former Bakuninist who became the leader of the Italian Socialist Party; Rosa Luxemburg, the Marxist theoretician murdered after the left-wing Spartacist uprising in Berlin in 1919; and Emma Goldman, the incarnation of anarchism and sexual liberationism, eventually expelled from both the United States and the USSR.[16] Jewish revolutionaries such as these, along with the Zionists and Russian-Jewish émigrés, seemed to confirm Russian anti-Semitic accusations about the existence of an international Jewish conspiracy, a charge soon carried to the ends of the earth by the Russian Black Hundreds.

The pogroms were largely spontaneous explosions of anti-Semitic violence set off when specific local incidents threw sparks into the highly combustible, anxiety-laden atmosphere of modernizing Russia. Largely, but not entirely, spontaneous, that is: the stepped-up violence of the second wave of pogroms owed a great deal as well to the organizing activities of protofascist political parties that appeared after the turn of the century. It would be their eventual function in modern history to spread the techniques and ideas of Russian anti-Semitism around the world.

A militantly anticapitalist and rabidly anti-Semitic Russian far-right movement took shape with the formation of the Union of the Russian People (URP) and various rival offshoots.[17] These were only the most prominent of the many patriotic organizations appearing as mass politics came to Russia in the early twentieth century, and especially during the 1905 revolution. Collectively they came to be known as the Black Hundreds. Among the major personalities associated with them were the combative and profane anti-Semites Dr. A. I. Dubrovin, the founder of the URP, and the far-right parliamentary deputies in the newly created Russian State Duma, Nikolai Markov and Vladimir Purishkevich.

As Witte put it, the views expressed by the Russian far right amounted to "sewage from all the cesspools" of Russian ultranationalism.[18] They denounced capitalism, socialism, the West, and the very parliament that gave them a platform from which to voice their malevolent beliefs to the nation. Their instinct was to champion Russification, Orthodoxy, and autocracy. But they came close to the Russian Populist-anarchists, Dostoevsky, and Tolstoy in seeing Russia as an agrarian utopia whose rural communes and handicrafts economy were disappearing under the assault of modernity.

Despite having a fully reactionary political ideology, the Black Hundreds were not typical conservatives, for they loathed the status quo and sought to destroy it. In the words of one adherent, "To be a conservative at this time means to be at least a radical or, rather, a revolutionary."[19] But although one can find points of contact between the far right and far left, or the far right and traditional conservatives, it was the radical right's mono-obsession with the Jews that was its most distinctive feature. They discerned an "international dark force" that was responsible for the chaos—in other words, the Jews, who were to them "the greatest evil."[20] Black Hundred anti-Semitism can be contrasted with the Judeophobia of Dostoevsky, who argued that the Jewish adoption of Christianity was sufficient (and necessary) to solve any of the problems connected to them. European racist assumptions about the Jews as a biological rather than religious category were now in ascendance, and the far right believed that baptism would not keep the vile Jews from serving the Antichrist. Converted or not, the Jews would conspire through their "international Israelite union" to control the press, the land, Russia, even the world.[21] They were convinced that "a legion of devils has entered the gigantic body of Russia and shakes it into convulsions, torments it, and mutilates it. . . . The name of this legion is *Jew*."[22]

What measures would succeed in stopping the demons? Removing whatever liberties the Jews still enjoyed in the Russian Empire was a bare minimum, but that would leave the situation largely unchanged. In the Russian parliament, URP deputies suggested a final solution. Praising the ancient Egyptians for enslaving the Jews, one called for a Russian equivalent: confining the Jews in coercive labor camps.[23] Purishkevich wanted to deport the entire Jewish population to Kolyma, the most remote, inhospitable Arctic region of the empire. Markov and others, though, would not be satisfied until "all the Yids down to the very last will be killed."[24]

The pogroms and the URP's anti-Semitic cult all mark the Black Hundred phenomenon as a transitional phase in the history of the European right between old-fashioned reactionary movements and dynamic modern fascism. At least a decade before its counterparts in other countries, the Russian extreme right came close to formulating a strain of national socialism. Its alliance of old elites and resentful masses; its radical rejectionism; its reliance on violence as its chief political tool; and its demagogic anti-Semitism all anticipated the future fascist movements of France, Germany, and Romania.

Individually, none of these elements was unique to Russia, but appearing as they did in combination and before the catastrophe of World War I, they were indeed extraordinary, and their presence was a sign of an overwhelming Russian crisis of civilization. The Black Hundreds were held back from achieving full-fledged fascism only because of the continued existence of the tsarist regime, loyalty to which restrained their extremist subversiveness. The collapse of political and social stability after the war cut away such restraints elsewhere in Europe. Conditions were then ripe for true national socialism to emerge, and the Black Hundreds played a significant, in some cases formative, role in the process—far more than has often been recognized.

Many prominent Black Hundreds fled westward after the Russian Revolution, carrying their hate-filled baggage into Germany, France, the United States, Manchuria, and other ports of refuge. With them they brought a forgery known as the *Protocols of the Elders of Zion*, which was to become a powerful and adaptable vehicle for the transmission of Russian anti-Semitic ideas to the wider world.[25] After World War I, millions of copies were in circulation; they sharpened popular hostility toward the Jews and made a momentous contribution to the worldview of Adolf Hitler, among many other enemies of Jewry.

The *Protocols* were purportedly the secret resolutions of international Jewish leaders, a game plan for the domination of the world and enslavement of the *goyim*—Yiddish for Gentiles. Some of the *Protocols*' publishers claimed that they were transcripts from meetings of the Alliance Israélite Universelle, but most pointed the finger at the First Zionist Congress and attributed the wording to the two most important Zionist leaders, Theodor Herzl and Ahad Ha'am. This uncertain origin might be expected to raise suspicions of fraud, but for millions of people incapable of making sense of the adverse currents of the modern world, the *Protocols* raised suspicions of the Jews. How could they doubt Jewish ruthlessness? What the Jews whispered behind closed doors was now captured here in print: "The *goyim* are a flock of sheep, and we are their wolves."[26]

According to the *Protocols*, Jews would achieve their ultimate goal of world domination by throwing European society, politics, and economics into disarray. To this end the Jews were systematically undermining Christian morals through promotion of the evils of progressive education, crass materialism, prostitution, and alcohol consumption. They were fostering the powerful and disruptive ideologies of Marxism, Darwinism, and anarchism. They were rendering existing rulers impotent through control of the press and advocacy of both parliaments and revolution. They were sponsoring all the terrorist activity that had suddenly become such a plague on the continent. And they were working to upset Europe's global power through the alliance of America, China, and Japan—all Jewish strongholds. Time and time again we are told that the Jews were mobilizing Freemasonry as a screen for their conspiracy.

It was financial cunning that supposedly enabled the Jews to destabilize European society in these ways. The *Protocols* had the elders of Zion acknowledge that they had eviscerated the traditional economy with the depredations of Jewish financial institutions, unrestrained capitalism, and the gold standard. As if that were not enough, they were sucking the fiscal blood of the state through foreign loans and fomenting unrest by purposely precipitating economic crises throughout Europe. Their control of world capital was allowing the Jews to monopolize industry and trade, and that was the key to their political strategy: "What we want is that industry should drain off from the land both labor and capital and by means of speculation transfer into our hands all the money of the world, and thereby throw all the *goyim* into the ranks of the proletariat. Then the *goyim* will bow down before us, if for no other reason but to get the right to exist."[27] At that point, the "Super-Government" of the Jews was to emerge, and it "will be of such colossal dimensions that it cannot fail to subdue all the nations of the world."[28]

The careful reader of the *Protocols* will also find in it a subtle defense of the hierarchical tsarist Russian social and political order, which the rising tide of modernity was eroding. The Jewish elders state that until recently, the "one and only serious foe we had in the world" was the Russian autocracy, with its "majestic inflexibility of might."[29] But now it, too, was under threat by liberal democrats, revolutionaries, and economic modernizers like Sergei Witte, the Russian finance minister whom reactionary aristocrats and Populist intellectuals alike despised for fostering the expansion of heavy industry. Although the text does not mention him, the underlying message—which would have been apparent to anyone familiar with the politics of the day—was that Witte, who introduced the gold standard and raised foreign investment, was a tool of the cunning Jewish bankers, themselves allied with the Jewish revolutionaries, and that his policies would bring the Jews to power. The *Protocols*' author clearly expected to play on the anti-Semitism of Nicholas II and the ruling elite, alert them to the dangers of modernization, and encourage a shift toward reassertion of the traditional attributes of autocratic, Orthodox Russia.

It has long been known that the *Protocols* were a forgery, a reworking of earlier French, German, and Russian antecedents. The Jewish plan to take over the world was an old story in Germany and especially in France. The French right had long disparaged Freemasonry, with its secret societies, as anti-Catholic. French anti-Semites saw Masonic lodges as covert Jewish houses of devil worship—"synagogues of Satan"—and it is from them that the author of the *Protocols* would borrow the accusations against "Yid-Masonry."[30] Books making these and other conspiratorial claims appeared from the 1860s on, and these imported anti-Semitic calumnies were popular in Russia and plagiarized in the *Protocols*.

But there was also a vast native literature with a conspiratorial, anti-Masonic, anticapitalist edge.[31] Literally thousands of publications associated Judaism with all things evil and reflected the paranoid perception of Jews as all-powerful. Among the authors writing in Russia in the second half of the nineteenth century who produced antecedents of the *Protocols* were the following: Osman Bey, an anti-Semitic publicist of Anglo-French origin raised in Constantinople, who made a career in Russia writing of world conquest by the Jews and calling for their extermination; Yakov Brafman, a

Jewish convert to Christianity and an unsuccessful missionary among the Jews of Lithuania, who introduced the idea that Jewish communal institutions formed an underground state within the state which was scheming against Russia and Christendom; and the Pole Ippolit Liutostansky, a syphilitic former Catholic priest who had been defrocked after being tried for rape, became an Orthodox monk, and produced numerous Jew-baiting works with accusations of conspiracy. The publications of these scribblers had gained a large audience among educated Russians by the late nineteenth century. They fed the government's illusion that the revolutionary movement was part of a systematic international Jewish conspiracy, and they were rehashed and refined by the author of the *Protocols*.

Remarkably, however well known the antecedents to the *Protocols* are, the paternity of the most influential anti-Semitic text of modern times is still uncertain. Any one of the initial publishers of the *Protocols* might have had a hand in their production. There is no proof of their appearance before 1902, when they were discussed in *Novoe vremia*, a conservative St. Petersburg newspaper. The first full publication of the *Protocols* came when the infamous pogromist of Kishinev, Pavolachi Krushevan (1860–1909), serialized them in his St. Petersburg paper, *Znamia* (The banner), in August and September 1903. According to a leading expert on the *Protocols*, the Italian scholar Cesare G. De Michelis, this neatly coincided with the arrival of the Zionist leader Herzl in St. Petersburg for official discussions with Witte, and it may have been the immediate reason for their publication; he notes that allusions to Herzl's Zionist manifesto, *The Jewish State* (1896), appear throughout the *Protocols*. A text similar to *Znamia*'s was printed anonymously by two different presses in late 1905. Not long after, Krushevan's associate, Georgii Vasil'evich Butmi de Katsman (1856–?), a Bessarabian anti-Semite who was one of the major anti-Witte, anti-industrialization publicists in Russia and a leading member of the Black Hundreds, published the first of several variants of the *Protocols* in book form. Called *The Enemy of the Human Race* and printed by the Typography of the School for the Deaf and Dumb, it was dedicated to the URP. De Michelis's linguistic analysis of the earliest extant texts finds heavy Ukrainian elements in the wording of the *Protocols*. Given Bessarabia's proximity to Ukraine, the implication is that Butmi and/or Krushevan may have been responsible for their creation.

But the version of the *Protocols* to gain international prominence first appeared in late 1905 and was produced by the Russian minor aristocrat Sergei Aleksandrovich Nilus (1862–1929).[32] As a young man, Nilus spent years in France. He was at first attracted to Nietzscheanism and anarchism, but his predispositions against modernity and urban civilization soon led him back to Russia and toward the mystical strains of Eastern Orthodoxy that were popular in turn-of-the-century educated society. He became a priest, conducted research on saints, miracles, and devils, and expected the imminent end of the world with the coming of the Antichrist. The agents of Apocalypse were, of course, the Jews. Nilus shared the opinions of Butmi and Black Hundred theologians: Witte's support of industry, stock markets, and liberalism signified that he was a "creature of the Jews"; Orthodox monasteries and the peasant village were the last uncorrupted bulwarks of defense against the Jewish conspiracy whose existence the *Protocols* proved.[33]

It is unclear how and when Nilus received the *Protocols*. Many pieces of the puzzle are still missing, and we know for sure only that Nilus revised and published them. He initially included them in the second edition of his work of esoteric Orthodox patristics, *The Great in the Small*, published at Tsarskoe Selo in December 1905, to which he then added a new subtitle: *The Antichrist as a Near Political Possibility*. It is this edition of the *Protocols* that anti-Semites of the world still peddle.

Thus not only is the author unknown, but the publishing history of the *Protocols* remains murky to this day. Nonetheless, whoever conceived and wrote them, it is clear that this was a work of malignant genius generated by the paranoid anti-Semitism of early-twentieth-century Russia. To some extent, the person responsible only supercharged European ideas, then exported them westward in more potent form. But like Bakunin, Kropotkin, Dostoevsky, and Tolstoy in their respective intellectual realms, the producer of the *Protocols* was also reinterpreting Russian experience in a way that had universal appeal. In so doing, he made another signal Russian contribution to the antimodern, antirationalist strains of twentieth-century culture. For like other works of Russian thought that gave off an aura of mystical, higher Truth to foreign audiences, the *Protocols* had the effect of divine revelation for those who harbored anti-Semitic inclinations.

The Black Hundreds and *Protocols* Abroad

The *Protocols* did not stand out in Russia, where thousands of other anti-Semitic publications circulated between 1906 and 1914. But they received increasing notice during the Russian Revolution, which allegedly bore out the *Protocols'* predictions. The Jews Trotsky, Kamenev, Zinoviev, Sverdlov, and Radek were prominent leaders of the new government. The regime's opponents believed that the revolution was the fulfillment

6. Sergei Nilus. Courtesy of the Wiener Library, London.

of the Jewish conspiracy, that the Red Army was carrying out the orders of world Jewry. The facts showed a different picture: in 1922 the overall Jewish membership of the Bolshevik Party was a low 5.2 percent; and only 19,500 Jews—0.72 percent of the total Jewish population—belonged to the ruling party.[34] But in those apocalyptic times, truth and balance did not matter. Anti-Bolshevik officers of the White armies fighting in the civil war distributed the *Protocols*, which helped to encourage the mass murder of Jews in the civil war's pogroms.

As the Bolsheviks vanquished their adversaries, one and a half million Russians fled the country. Hundreds of thousands settled in China, Turkey, Czechoslovakia, Yugoslavia, England, or America. But the largest contingent made their way to Germany and then, because of political and economic instability there, shifted to France, where 400,000 Russians had settled by 1928. Most émigrés struggled to achieve routine lives. But not all were ready to give up the fight. Among the refugees were politically active ex-Black Hundreds and other supporters of the White armies, who formed what was in effect an international *anti-Semitic* conspiracy. With the zeal of missionaries, the far-right apostles of Russian anti-Semitism publicized the *Protocols* and its "proof" of Jewish intrigue to rally the world against Russia's communist rulers. Although important for the anti-Semitic cause in many places, their most consequential ventures were in France, Germany, and the United States.

The enthusiastic reception of the *Protocols* in France can be best understood in the context of the interaction that took place between French and Russian anti-Semitism beginning in the 1880s—not coincidentally, the same time the "invasion" of Russian literature was underway. A fin-de-siècle commentator in France attributed his nation's surly, modern form of anti-Semitism to Russia and Germany, a "foreign import . . . taking as its slogan: 'France for the French.' "[35] Of course, that was an exaggeration: the country had a rich anti-Semitic tradition of its own out of which French fascism eventually emerged. But questions involving Russia and Russian Jewry did agitate French anti-Semites at the time.[36]

At its most basic level, the stepped-up anti-Semitism of late-nine-teenth-century France was a reaction to the steady stream of Jewish immigrants from Austrian Galicia and the Russian Pale. In the nov-els of Zola we read about the uncertainties, fears of proletarianiza-tion, and resentments the French felt in their rapidly changing soci-ety; the appearance of Yiddish-speaking newcomers compounded these emotions to provoke a hysterical and irrational anti-Semitic backlash in the country that had been the first in modern history to extend civil equality to its Jews.

Negative French attitudes toward Jews were also intricately bound up with foreign affairs. After defeat in the Franco-Prussian War of 1870–1871, French archchauvinists agitated on behalf of a Franco-Russian alliance as the mechanism for bringing injury to Germany. To that they linked the problem of Jews and Freemasons. Not only were there preexisting suspicions of Jewish-Masonic con-spiracies: now French Freemasons came out against the Franco-Rus-sian alliance because of St. Petersburg's hostility to the expansion of the Masonic order in Russia. And French Jews, sympathizing with their oppressed coreligionists in the Russian Pale, were none too pleased with the alliance. The Rothschilds, among other Jewish financiers, made loans to the Russian government contingent on improved treatment for the country's Jews. The conditions were thus in place for many people to perceive Jews and Freemasons working together to undermine France's best opportunity to gain revenge against Germany and resuscitate French glory.[37]

Among the figures lobbying for the creation of the Franco-Rus-sian alliance and viewing matters in just this way was Juliette Adam (1836–1936), proprietress of *La Nouvelle Revue*, an eminent jour-nal of literature and opinion. Her review published Turgenev and other Russian writers, contributing to the Russian fever of the day. Here and in her salon, she worked ceaselessly to convince French society of the virtues of joining hands with the Russian autocracy. Adam had been a republican, but like many in French society at this time, she was haunted by France's military disgrace and became an extremist. By the time of the Dreyfus affair she was not only fanatically anti-German but also anti-Semitic. She editorialized about an international conspiracy of occultists, Freemasons, Marxists, and Germans, all manipulated by a Jewish syndicate, one of whose representatives was Dreyfus.[38]

The development of Adam's stance on Russia owed much to Élie de Cyon (1843–1912), a distinguished but roguish professor of physiology first in Russia, then in France, who had given up science to become a Parisian journalist. Born a Jew, Cyon was a reactionary Russian monarchist who had converted to Orthodoxy and eventually Catholicism. In the 1880s, he edited various nationalist journals, including Adam's, and in this capacity helped to warm French opinion to Russia. As a Russian agent, he worked to facilitate the Franco-Russian financial courtship that soon blossomed into alliance. But his close ties with the German-Jewish banker Gerson von Bleichröder, Bismarck's financier, raised official French and Russian suspicions of double dealing. When the Russian government dissolved its relationship with Cyon, he began to launch vicious press attacks against Witte, whose negotiations with Germany he warned were prelude to the Russian abandonment of France. Although Cyon does not seem to have believed in anti-Semitic conspiracy theories, nonetheless he cynically aided and abetted them by denouncing Witte's modernization policies and revealing the latter's close ties to Jewish bankers and industrialists. French anti-Semites fed off this news dished out by Cyon and warned that Witte was a puppet of the international Jewish syndicate. Some now even started to oppose the Franco-Russian alliance as a Jewish plot; Adam herself was rethinking her position until Witte's bribes changed her mind.[39]

As a direct result of contact with Cyon, Édouard Drumont also dramatically shifted his position on the Franco-Russian alliance. A vigorous anticapitalist, leading anti-Dreyfusard, and the most extreme of contemporary Jew-haters, Drumont (1844–1917) published a popular and scurrilous newspaper, *La Libre Parole* (Free speech), which lamented the demise of the shopkeepers of old Paris and their displacement by Jews. In the mid-1890s, the paper lashed out at the Franco-Russian alliance as an instrument that the Rothschilds and international Jewry had contrived to achieve the domination of Europe. He attacked Tsar Nicholas II as their "shabbas goy" and Witte as their "valet" for expanding capitalism and introducing the gold standard in Russia, thereby spreading anarchy and strengthening Jewish control of the world economy.[40] Cyon helped to focus Drumont's antimodern, anti-Semitic tirades on Russian matters; in turn, Drumont helped to set the tone for the *Protocols*, which partially drew on his writings.

By the end of the century, the amalgamation of French and Russian Judeophobia was well underway. Russian press coverage of Drumont and Dreyfus whipped up tsarist anti-Semitism, which at the same time also conditioned the French right's stance on the Jewish "problem." French anti-Semites viewed the 1905 revolution in Russia as part of a broader Jewish-socialist-Masonic conspiracy to undermine European governments. The anti-Semitic paper *La Croix* (The cross) called for a "Russian" solution to be applied to French Jewry: revocation of civil rights, legal controls, surveillance, and pressure to emigrate. Others, though, felt that the Russian experience was a lesson in frustration. Better to expel the Jews from France than be faced with a Gallic Pale of Settlement.[41]

The increasing radicalism of French anti-Semitism went hand in hand with the rise of extreme-right nationalist and fascist movements. While native factors were primary in the process, Russian anti-Semitism in various forms greased the way. Georges Valois (1878–1945), the founder of one of the first French fascist parties, Le Faisceau, became an anti-Semite in Russia. Like Mussolini, Hitler, and the Russian Black Hundreds, he epitomized the early-twentieth-century fusion of revolutionary and reactionary strivings, and well before the First World War he had hoped to unite the radical left and right. An antimodernist through and through, he pursued a lifelong quest to reverse the disintegration of the community of Frenchmen. To this end he had been a left-wing revolutionary anarchist and syndicalist in his youth, but turned to far-right anti-Semitism and monarchism while spending a year (1902–1903) in Russia as a tutor to an aristocratic family whose estate was in the Jewish Pale. Previously a Dreyfusard, now he learned that Jews were capitalist conspirators against the masses, and anti-Semitism the natural defense of the aggrieved lower classes. Back in France, he joined the right-wing Action Française in 1906, but his royalist nationalism turned into French fascism as he continued to mix revolutionary syndicalism, devotion to the workers, and hatred of the Jews. In 1925 he broke with the monarchists and formed Le Faisceau, which although modeled after the Italian Fascist Party, was closer to Nazism in its attitude toward Jews, a reflection of Valois's Russian-derived obsession with the Jewish conspiracy. Ironically, after the Nazi takeover, Valois became a libertarian communist and denounced anti-Semitism. For his leftist activism and criticism of the Vichy regime's treatment of Jews, he was arrested and interned in a Nazi concentration camp, where he died.[42]

Valois's movement was one of several fascist or semifascist leagues that emerged simultaneously in France. Embroiled in intellectual and personality disputes, they lacked the unity that had brought their German and Italian counterparts to power. But in common they had all agitated for years against the Jews. In this they were substantially aided by the *Protocols of the Elders of Zion*, not only insofar as it was directly anti-Semitic but also because it seemed to link Jews with communism, the alternative preoccupation of many French fascists.[43]

The first French edition of the *Protocols* was a translation from the Russian published in 1920 by the influential Catholic priest and conspiracy theorist Monsignor Ernest Jouin (1844–1932). Born into a family of artisans, as curé of Saint-Augustin parish in Paris in the late 1880s and early 1890s he was a principal figure in the nationalist cult of Joan of Arc. Only in 1909, at the age of sixty-five, did he join the crusade against Jews and Masons, under the influence of the massive number of Catholic publications and organizations devoted to these issues. By 1912 he had created La Ligue Franc-Catholique (Free-Catholic League, a play on Freemasonry). The league's journal, *La Revue international des sociétés secrètes*, was one of the two main anti-Semitic tribunes between the wars, the other being *L'Action française*. Although its subscribers numbered only two thousand when Jouin died, it was the reading of choice among Nazi sympathizers.

Since before the First World War, Jouin had been spreading the gospel of Russian anti-Semitism. His paper gave heavy publicity to right-wing Russian accusations that the Jews engaged in ritual murder. After 1917, he followed the Black Hundred party line in publicizing Bolshevism as a sinister plot of "Judeo-Masonry," wrote glowingly of the Russian far right, and was connected to extremist émigré circles in both Germany and France. Interestingly, Butmi himself had sent Jouin his edition of the *Protocols* before the war, and it is this version that Jouin published in French translation in both his journal and a separate compendium, *Le Péril judéo-maçonnique* (1920). Quoting the *Protocols* as often as he did the Bible to support his belief in the evil of the Jews, Jouin sowed contempt from his ecclesiastical seat. Despite this, Pope Pius XI soon appointed him to high papal office as a protonotary apostolic, and in 1957 Jouin's supporters proposed his beatification.[44]

The *Protocols* were continuously in print in the decades to come, alongside numerous faux *Protocols* and other Russian radical-right anti-Semitic publications. L'Action Française and other right-wing royalist or fascist leagues like the Croix de Feu took up the cause and elaborated on the *Protocols* in their voluminous literature. The fiction of the anti-Semitic novelist and eventual Nazi collaborator Louis-Ferdinand Céline also helped familiarize the nation with the *Protocols* and the corresponding view of America and the USSR as the bastions of Jewish power. The writer Léon Daudet, a violently anti-Semitic Action Française militant, summed up the opinion of the French right wing: "Don't imagine that these *Protocols* are a fiction, an ingenious invention, a polemical trick. They are a document, nothing more or less."[45] But though the French fascists brandished the *Protocols* vigorously, their thrusts were repelled until the arrival of Hitler, whose own anti-Semitic armory was originally equipped by Russian Black Hundreds.

Nowhere were the *Protocols* and the Black Hundred emigration more fatally successful than in Germany, where they helped to shape Nazi ideology and practice.[46]

Although the transmission of the *Protocols* to Germany is still partly veiled in fog, it is known that the first to publish them there, in a Russian journal, were two right-wing, anti-Bolshevik fanatics who arrived in Berlin in 1919: the assassin Pyotr N. Shabelsky-Bork and Fyodor V. Vinberg, a Russified German who had been an officer in the tsar's Imperial Guards and a URP member. Believing the revolution to be the work of the Devil and his Jewish minions, Vinberg now spread his view that the eradication of the Jews was desirable.[47]

The first German-language publisher of the *Protocols* was in close contact with this circle, as well as with Nilus's son. Ludwig Müller, alias Ludwig Müller von Hausen, issued a translation of the Shabelsky-Bork/Vinberg text in January 1920 under the pseudonym Gottfried zur Beek. Müller, a military officer and adviser to General Erich Ludendorff, had from 1912 on edited a Berlin anti-Semitic monthly associated with the Pan-German League. After the war he joined the Germanenorden, a secret anti-Semitic terrorist organization that was involved in the 1922 assassination of Walther Rathenau, the Jewish foreign minister of Germany whom the radical right targeted as one of the "elders of Zion."[48]

Sales of the *Protocols* were brisk, feeding off and fostering rising anti-Semitism in Germany. Müller's edition was reprinted six times in 1920 alone, and several times a year thereafter. A version issued by the Russian-born Nazi ideologist Alfred Rosenberg appeared in 1923. The next year, the old German anti-Semite Theodor Fritsch, having written articles on the *Protocols* as early as 1919, published his own edition. Henry Ford's *International Jew* was also translated. All in all, between 1920 and 1933, the year Hitler came to power, there were thirty-three editions of the *Protocols*, each one selling hundreds of thousands of copies throughout Germany and Austria. And countless imitations followed every edition.

One would think that German anti-Semitism had no need to take sustenance from such foreign sources.[49] During the nineteenth century, antiurban and anticapitalist sentiments deriving from Lutheranism, Romanticism, and the Prussian Junker ethos spread throughout society and commingled with lower-middle-class resentments to make Germans across the board suspicious of Jews. On top of that a steady stream of bearded and caftan-clad eastern European Jews—*Ostjuden*—came through Germany as they emigrated from Russian Poland, the Pale of Settlement, and Austrian Galicia. By 1910, around seventy thousand had stayed, and many Germans saw them as bizarre, backward, unsanitary hucksters or revolutionaries, a racially inferior but cunning and dangerous subspecies of humanity. Their numbers were not high (13 percent of all Jews in Germany, where 1 percent of the total population was Jewish) and they assimilated quickly, but it felt like an invasion of Russian Jews. As one observer commented in 1895, "Like the Chinese to California came the Jews to [Germany]: diligent, frugal, numerous, and thoroughly hated."[50] Moreover, among them were Rosa Luxemburg and other Jews of the Russian Empire who had entered the ranks of German socialism and loudly advertised their radicalism. Thus even without the *Protocols*, in German eyes the Jew was an outsider, the antithesis of Germanness, and a disruption to the harmonious community of Aryans.

Before the war, if Germans showed little sympathy for the Jews, their negative feelings were largely latent. But a Teutonic-consciousness movement was growing, which blamed the problems of imperial Germany on Jews and espoused anti-Semitic stereotypes along with Pan-German nationalism. Theodor Fritsch and other leaders of anti-Semitic völkisch political parties brewed Jewish conspiracy theories at the turn of the century and ranted about the deadly threat Jews posed to Germany. Nonetheless, although cultural and student circles were coming to be saturated with Judeophobia, popular electoral support for these parties was on the decline in the relatively stable first decade of the new century.

The cataclysmic World War brought what had been subliminal to the surface. Between 1914 and 1924, Germany (and Austria) experienced major trauma: military defeat and a humiliating peace imposed by the victors, the downfall of the monarchy, economic collapse and hyperinflation, and revolutionary uprisings in Berlin and Munich. In this setting, anti-Semitism gained the respectability and mass support it had not had before. Anti-Semitic publications and political rallies intensified their invective: it was the Jews and their alleged agents who had stabbed Germany in the back; it was the Jews who profited when the rest of the nation suffered; it was German and Russian Jews who led the Munich Soviet Republic (in fact, although the most visible personalities were Jewish, they were still a minority within the leadership). The *Protocols* substantiated the evil designs of the Jews; Alfred Rosenberg insisted that "millions suddenly found in [them] the answer to so many otherwise unintelligible phenomena of the present."[51] They also gained legitimacy through the endorsement of military officers like Ludendorff, whose attachment to the *Protocols* symbolized the refusal of German elites to accept responsibility for the nation's defeat.

The *Protocols* made sense to the Germans because they combined all of the anti-Semitic fears of past generations. But the Russian Black Hundred (or Baltic German) émigrés who brought them to Germany also added new and potent content to the mythology: portraying Bolshevism as the most ominous accomplishment of the Jewish conspiracy, they warned that the Jews would now try to escort the Grim Reaper from the slaughterhouse of revolutionary Russia to Germany. So effective was this widely publicized interpretation of the *Protocols* in stepping up the level of fear and hatred that, in interaction with the events of the day, it helped many Germans to focus on the Jews as their most implacable enemy. Among those who as a result became die-hard anti-Semites was a vagabond war veteran named Adolf Hitler.

The standard view of Hitler holds that his anti-Semitism first erupted in Vienna, where he lived as a tramp from 1908 to 1913. This city was home to 175,000 Jews—including many newly arrived *Ostjuden*—who dominated the capital's artistic life, medical and legal professions, and press. In reaction, Austrian anti-Semitism was even more vigorous and scurrilous than the German variety. Anti-Semitic newspapers and demagogic politicians spoke openly of freeing Austria from the Jewish yoke, if necessary by resorting to Russian-style pogroms. Hitler, nursing resentments over his poverty and artistic failure, is supposed to have breathed this hatred in with the air. He himself wrote in *Mein Kampf* that he was first sickened at the sight of a Jew in Vienna.

When he wrote this in 1924, he was perhaps trying to burnish his image by backdating his struggle against Jewry. Recent research shows that although he shared run-of-the-mill prejudices against Jews, he also had Jewish friends and kept up a warm correspondence with his family's Jewish doctor in Linz. At that time, Hitler's developing xenophobia was directed more against the Slavs who were also present in large numbers in Vienna and a focus of abuse by the right-wing press.[52] Even during the world war, when he clearly expressed his dislike of non-Germans, he had no negative reactions to the many Jewish officers he interacted with at the front.[53]

Hitler became an anti-Semite only in 1919, after the suppression of the Bavarian Soviet, which the radical right worked overtime to denounce as a foreign, Russian-Jewish, Bolshevik takeover. It was in Munich that the ideas about Jews he had first heard in Vienna came out of dormancy and developed into an all-encompassing, fanatical worldview. And it was to a large extent because of Russian right-extremists and *The Protocols of the Elders of Zion* that they did.

Among the refugees from Bolshevik Russia were a sizable number of Baltic Germans, hailing from territories absorbed into the Russian Empire in the eighteenth century. They took readily to German völkisch ideas and distributed mementos of Russian anti-Semitism throughout the new homeland. One of them was Alfred Rosenberg (1893–1946), who transformed German anti-Semitism in 1919 and was directly and indirectly responsible for radicalizing Hitler's perceptions of the Jews.

Rosenberg was born in Reval (now Tallin), Estonia, to a middle-class family of mixed Baltic, German, and uncertain ethnic origin. He studied architecture in Riga until the war forced him to evacuate to Moscow. There he read the *Protocols* in early 1917 and entertained anti-Semitic fantasies as he sought to make sense of the turbulence of the Russian Revolution and his own fate. He came to Munich in January 1919, where he led a derelict existence, immersing himself in studies of Hinduism and Judaism. Rosenberg was convinced that international Jewry operated from the new Jerusalem of Moscow, and that now these vermin were taking over Germany.[54]

In Munich, Rosenberg established a close—and historically pivotal—relationship with Dietrich Eckart (1868–1923), a bohemian playwright who became Hitler's first political mentor and author of the song that gave the party its slogan, "Germany, awake!"[55] Eckart, a longtime alcoholic and morphine addict, blamed Jewish critics for the failure of his plays and, in line with his antimodern tendencies, became an anti-Semite. During the war and German revolutions, his hatred grew to pathological dimensions. In December 1918 Eckart founded *Auf gut Deutsch* (In good German), a Munich paper whose purpose was to encourage the fight against Jewry as the precondition to the revival of the German spirit. Shortly thereafter, Rosenberg became his close collaborator.

Much of the editorial line of *Auf gut Deutsch* came from Rosenberg's regurgitation of the anti-Semitic content of the Russian Black Hundred émigré press, above all the *Protocols*, which heightened the fears of Jewish domination felt by Eckart and the Munich völkisch circles. Rosenberg's first article for *Auf gut Deutsch*, "The Russian-Jewish Revolution," appeared on February 21, 1919; Eckart called it a revelation in explaining that not just capitalism but also communism and Zionism were parts of the same Jewish plot to plunge the world into chaos and achieve global domination. Following Rosenberg's lead, Eckart announced that Russia was the "Christian-kosher-butchering dictatorship of the Jewish world savior Lenin," and he endorsed the *Protocols* as essential for anyone who "wants to get to know Judaism from the ground up."[56]

From February 1919 on, Jewish Bolshevik conspiracies would be the main theme of Eckart's paper, which gained a larger and larger circulation as the Bavarian Soviet revolution wore on. During the spring and summer of that year, well before they were published in German, Munich anti-Semitic groups were absorbed in discussions of the *Protocols*. Thanks to Rosenberg, who continued to publicize and interpret the *Protocols* in his torrent of writings, the entire German far right saw Marxism, Social Democracy, the Russian Revolution, and Jewish world conspiracy as one and the same. The Russian far-right anti-Semitic ideas he had imported were paramount in shaping the views of many Germans toward both Jews and the events in Munich that in turn encouraged so many to accept anti-Semitism. The fact that these were new additions to the rhetoric of German Judeophobia can be seen in their *absence* on a list of anti-Semitic accusations rebutted in mid-1919 by a leading Berlin Jewish newspaper.[57]

The Rosenberg-Eckart dogma had a metamorphic effect on the founders of the Nazi Party. The party had its direct origins in the Thule Society, an organization formed to promote Aryan purity

7. Alfred Rosenberg, 1920. Courtesy of the Bildarchiv Preussischer Kulturbesitz, Berlin.

and to fight the Jewish, communist, and liberal enemies of Germany. Neither Eckart nor Rosenberg was a member, but they were closely associated with it and gave invited lectures on Bolshevism and Jewry at its meetings. The society sponsored the creation of a political party to spread its racial supremacy ideas to the masses. The initiators of the German Workers' Party (DAP) were the sports journalist Karl Harrer and the railroad locksmith Anton Drexler. From March 1919 on, the DAP endorsed the *Protocols*, and Drexler integrated their perspective in his writings and speeches, which linked German socialism with Jews and the Jews with Bolshevism: its conspiratorial message is the overriding point of his testament, *My Political Awakening* (1919). The specific focus of this book reflects the rapid assimilation of the Russian Black Hundred outlook by German proletarian anti-Semites; it aroused Hitler's interest in the DAP, which during 1920 he would come to lead as the NSDAP or Nazi Party.[58]

Between 1919 and 1921, Hitler rose from obscurity to become master of the Munich anti-Semitic underworld and from there vaulted to national prominence. More than any others it was Eckart and Rosenberg who discovered Hitler and transformed him in this early phase of his career from an angry but directionless young man into a virulent and politically successful racist rabble-rouser. Before these two trained his mind on the menace of Jewry, Hitler was, as he put it, "intellectually a child on the bottle."[59] Eckart would have been important to Hitler regardless of the Rosenberg connection: as their friendship developed in the fall of 1919, he polished Hitler's manners and reduced the seediness of his appearance by having him trim his moustache and wear a trench coat. Furthermore, Eckart's strong belief that his protégé was the German messiah imparted to Hitler powerful psychological affirmation that fostered his self-stylization as "der Führer."

But Eckart's ideological mentoring of Hitler cannot be separated from that of Rosenberg, who first met Hitler in September 1919 at Eckart's home and joined the DAP later that year. Rosenberg's career as a venomous anti-Semitic journalist flourished under the wings of Eckart, who in 1921 became the first editor of *Völkischer Beobachter* (German racial observer), the main Nazi newspaper;

throughout this period, Rosenberg was the decisive contributor to the paper. Under the influence of Rosenberg and partly in reaction to the *Protocols*, in 1920 Eckart articulated the earliest Nazi proposals for the extermination of the Jews.[60] He later wrote, in a *Protocols*-inspired fictitious Socratic dialogue with Hitler, *Bolshevism from Moses to Lenin* (1924), that to prevent the success of the eternal Jewish-Bolshevik striving for world domination, "the whole race [of Jews] absolutely must be killed!"[61]

Eckart and especially Rosenberg provided Hitler with anti-Semitic literature and sharpened Hitler's growing animosity toward Jews in late 1919 and 1920. Above all it was Rosenberg's explication of the *Protocols* that gave the unemployed German corporal the weltanschauung that determined his political life. By the fall of 1919 Hitler was reading Eckart's *Auf gut Deutsch*, where he would have seen extracts from the *Protocols*. He read the full text itself almost as soon as it was available in German in early 1920.[62] His speeches, political platform, and policy from that point until the end of his life reflected their influence: although much of the Nazi Party's growth in this period can be attributed to Hitler's spellbinding oratorical skills, it was also his full absorption of Russian Black Hundred rhetoric that made him stand out amid the crowd of German anti-Semites and völkisch nationalists.

The teachings of Eckart and Rosenberg gave Hitler what he thought was a keener insight into politics and current affairs. In 1920 it dawned on him that he could expand the Nazi Party into a mass movement by making the Jews the main demons rather than incidental ones, as the DAP had tended to view them previously. Echoing Rosenberg, he decried the Jewish Bolshevik butchery whose victims numbered in the tens of millions and foreshadowed what was to come: the Russian Revolution had given world Jewry a dictatorial political base, a counterpart to its control of the modern European economy. From Russia, Hitler claimed, it would launch its struggle with Germany, which Jewish leftists and capitalists had already infiltrated.[63] He had by this time begun to call for the "removal" of the Jews; although he did not spell out precisely what that meant, he made it clear that it would be radical, bloody, and far more systematic than the Russian-inspired pogroms which many others on the German far right invited.[64]

And the *Protocols* were never far from Hitler's mind. It is too much to claim, as some have, that he learned concrete conspiratorial political techniques from them.[65] What he did get, however, was a sense of both the deviousness of his supposed enemy and the links interconnecting Jews, Russian Bolshevism, and the global conspiracy. As he underlined in *Mein Kampf*, "*in Russian Bolshevism we must see the attempt undertaken by the Jews in the twentieth century to achieve world domination.*"[66]

Rosenberg and the *Protocols* thus "provided the keystone to the edifice of Hitler's ideology" as well as many of his domestic and foreign policies to the very end. They presented him with the "image of an indomitable foe" that only relentless struggle under his leadership could challenge.[67] If in the impending conflict he failed to defeat Bolshevism on Russian soil and exterminate the Jews, evil would triumph and Germany would perish. It was the *Protocols*, especially as interpreted for him by Rosenberg, that roused him to take up this apocalyptic mission which was arguably the ultimate cause of World War II and the Holocaust.

As a mark of his respect for the foremost publicizer of the *Protocols*, in 1923 Hitler shoved Eckart aside and gave Rosenberg the editorship of *Völkischer Beobachter*, in effect making him the chief ideologist of the Nazi Party. As time went on, Hitler's ardor for Rosenberg cooled, but throughout the 1920s Rosenberg was the main conduit through which the effluent of Russian anti-Semitism flowed into Germany. Not only did he provide commentary of his own in *Völkischer Beobachter*, he (and earlier Eckart) also made the paper available to other right-wing ethnic-German refugees from Russia, including his friend from Riga, Max Erwin von Scheubner-Richter (1884–1923), soon Hitler's main political aid and fundraiser, who used it for his like-minded propaganda. This prompted Hitler's joking reference to the paper as the "Baltic edition."[68]

From this source as well as myriads of independent publications, the *Protocols* polluted the minds of many others besides Hitler. Much of the officeholding Nazi leadership was obsessed by the idea of a Jewish conspiracy.[69] The *Protocols* motivated Ernst Röhm, the founder of the paramilitary Storm Troopers (SA), to launch assaults on Jews. Heinrich Himmler, chief genocidal mass murderer of the regime, as early as 1919 wrote that a book he had just read which drew from the *Protocols* "explains everything and tells us whom we must fight against next time."[70] The cynical Joseph Goebbels, who called Rosenberg's serious philosophical efforts an "ideological belch,"[71] scoffed at the notion that Jewish bankers of the West were in league with Russian Bolsheviks. But he did not hesitate to instruct his propaganda ministry to exploit the *Protocols*, which by 1935 were required reading in all German schools.

For the Nazis could justify their persecution of the Jews with reference to the Jewish world conspiracy. Julius Streicher's *Der Stürmer* (The stormtrooper), whose banner slogan was "Bolshevism is radical Jewish domination," often excerpted the *Protocols*, explaining that they offered proof of the Jewish plan to enslave the Germans. To foil this plot, it called for the extermination of the Jews, which to Streicher and other Nazi leaders was an obligation. Once it was accomplished, they believed, a golden age would ensue for Germany under the Third Reich. At the basis of all Nazi anti-Semitic belief and rhetoric, the *Protocols* helped to extinguish lingering goodwill toward the Jews, and—primarily among the leadership—to rationalize their annihilation.

As if the *Protocols* and the labors of Rosenberg were not enough, other far-right Russian émigrés in Germany made contributions to the notion of the Final Solution. Another link between the Russian radical right and the Nazi movement was Grigory Schwarz-Bostunich (1883–?), a lawyer, scurrilous playwright, Theosophist, and Black Hundred member from Kiev whose occultism and clinical paranoia centered on fear of tobacco and Jews. A friend of Rosenberg, Scheubner-Richter, and Vinberg, he entered the NSDAP in 1931 and became a confidant of Himmler, through whose patronage he became a high-ranking officer in the SS and its leading expert on Jewry and ritual murder. In best-selling German books, he wrote of "Mongoloids and other subhumans" assisting bloodthirsty "Jewish Soviet gorillas" in world conquest. Although his claims were so ludicrous that even the SS eventually stopped taking him seriously, his early ties with Himmler helped to affirm the latter's intention to exterminate the Jews.[72]

Schwarz-Bostunich gained an international audience for his writings through the Weltdienst (World Service), the Nazi international news and information agency that propagated anti-Semitism abroad. Secretly financed by Rosenberg's NSDAP foreign political office, the Weltdienst was seen as an answer to the "Hebrew International," or Comintern, the Soviet bureau for the export of revolution. Much of its propaganda was based on the *Protocols*, which the agency also distributed in local languages throughout Europe, America, the Middle East, and North Africa. The "specialist" on Jews for the Weltdienst was none other than the former Russian URP leader Nikolai Markov (1866–1945), who worked in Germany after the revolution to combat the "dark forces" of the world through eradication of the Jews.[73]

To be sure, the Holocaust had ample German sources independent of Russian Black Hundred influence. The peculiarities of German culture, the crises of the day, the popular mood, the psychopathology of the individual Nazi leaders, the governmental mechanism of the Third Reich all coalesced to make it possible. And it cannot be forgotten that specifically German proposals for Jewish extermination had been aired for decades, although only on the very fringe of the Pan-German movement.[74] But far more than is usually recognized, Rosenberg and the other radical right-wing émigrés from Russia altered the nature and rhetoric of German anti-Semitism, making the ultimate, murderous end more likely.

Of the many spin-offs of the *Protocols* circulating in Germany, one was an American work that had been translated into sixteen languages and had millions of readers around the world. The book was *The International Jew* (1920), ostensibly by Henry Ford, who with this global blockbuster became as important in the mass production and marketing of anti-Semitism as he was in that of automobiles. Hitler, who used it in *Mein Kampf*, asserted, "I regard Heinrich Ford as my inspiration."[75] But in truth *The International Jew* was ghostwritten, and the brains behind it was a Russian Black Hundred émigré who had sold Ford on the *Protocols* in Detroit.

Anti-Semitism in the United States, as in Britain, was weaker than on the European continent. The political leadership was more tolerant, the population more prosperous, and antimodern, antiliberal sentiments less prevalent. But anti-Semitism was on the rise by the early twentieth century as the boatloads of Russian-Jewish immigrants came ashore. During the post–World War I Red Scare, American Jews were tainted when rightists described Bolshevism as a Jewish crusade against Christianity. It was at this time that the *Protocols* appeared, uncritically endorsed by anticommunist Americans eager to drum up support for military intervention in Russia against the Lenin government.

The main American edition of the *Protocols*, translated in New York, was commissioned by Boris Brasol and published in 1920 as *The Protocols and World Revolution* for use in a Russian far-right propaganda campaign. Brasol (1885–1963) was the leader of the Black Hundreds in the United States. In the 1920s and 1930s he was a member of the German-American Bund and a Nazi agent who traveled frequently to party headquarters in Berlin.

Born in the Ukrainian town of Poltava, Brasol joined the Bolshevik Party in 1905. But, like so many other contemporary antimodern extremists, he switched from one side to the other and entered government service as a prosecutor with pronouncedly anti-Semitic and reactionary views. Working in Kiev, he was a member of the local Black Hundred affiliate. When the revolution broke out, Brasol was on a war mission to London, where he came into contact with American officers who arranged for his entry into the United States. By 1919 he was an adviser to the chief of the U.S. War Department's Military Intelligence Division, whom he convinced of the truth of the *Protocols*.

Brasol was now gaining respectability as a knowledgeable anticommunist. Sensitive to his audience, in certain settings he toned down his anti-Semitism. But in others he circulated the *Protocols*, denounced the Bolsheviks as agents of a German-Jewish conspiracy, and blamed the Jews for the murder of the tsar. Brasol's edition of the *Protocols* was a commercial failure, but success came once he joined forces with Henry Ford. Then Brasol could boast that his publication of the *Protocols* and *The International Jew* had "done the Jews more injury than would have been done to them by ten pogroms."[76]

Ford's hostility toward Jews might seem paradoxical given his personification of the very modernity that anti-Semites usually rebelled against. But Ford, in fact, was imbued with a specifically American form of antimodernism. As a Midwestern nativist, he defended the chaste virtues of agrarianism, small towns, and manual labor against the loathsome big city and stock exchange, both associated with Jews. According to some of his associates, who explained his "Jew-mania," Ford was subject to bouts of paranoia and had the political sophistication of a child. As immigration from Russia swelled the ranks of Detroit's Jewish community, Ford sympathized with a local Aryan movement that campaigned against race pollution. He made it no secret that he feared the takeover of Ford Motor Company by Jewish financiers and penetration by Jewish communist labor organizers. The American press's spiraling attacks on Ford for his anti-Semitic calumnies only increased his belief in the existence of a hydra-headed Jewish conspiracy.[77]

Knowing of Ford's views, Brasol made contact with him. The *Protocols* impressed Ford so much that he tried to communicate with Nilus in 1925 or 1926.[78] It was under Brasol's influence that Ford came to see Bolshevism as a front for Jewish machinations. He published the writings of other Russian right extremists and put Brasol on the staff of his newspaper, the *Dearborn Independent*, where the former member of the Black Hundreds assisted its anti-Semitic editor, William Cameron, in the production of *The International Jew*.

This was a version of the *Protocols* designed specifically for the American public. Interspersed with excerpts from the original text were passages illustrating the activities of a purported Jewish conspiracy in the United States. As the Jews had introduced prostitution, gambling, and liquor to the United States, they sabotaged efforts to pass Christian laws that would curtail these vices. With their "demonic shrewdness," they had acquired control over baseball, Hollywood, Coney Island, and the popular music industry.

From these seats of power they were corrupting American youth with "theatrical degeneracy," lascivious movies, and black jazz, that "satanic" Yiddish "moron music." Sport clothes, socialism, sex education, and the concept of ethnic tolerance were all further manifestations of Bolshevism, whose five-pointed red star was a Star of David in disguise.[79]

Ford promoted the idea that the Jews were a threat to America as energetically as he did his cars. *The International Jew* ran as a serial between 1920 and 1922 in the *Dearborn Independent*, subscriptions to which he badgered his auto dealers across the country to sell as another trustworthy "Ford product."[80] He had the book version printed in an initial press run of half a million copies. After the U.S. government denounced it and a Jewish boycott of Ford Motor Company products went into effect in 1927, Ford allowed his associates to sign a recantation on his behalf. But this was purely in the interest of his company: he never abandoned his belief in the Jewish conspiracy.

The experience of World War II discredited these attitudes in the American mainstream. But if they withered there, they remained alive on the radical fringe, which has shown long-term brand loyalty to Ford. And outside of America, *The International Jew* continued to expand its market share after 1945, a remarkable achievement for an ideological tract first manufactured in the time of the Model T. This work served as a link between tsarist Russian anti-Semitism and its post-1945 counterparts.

The *Protocols* and *The International Jew* have continued to appear since World War II in every nation of Europe, North and South America, Australia and New Zealand, South Africa and North Africa, the Middle East, and various other parts of Asia. They can still be purchased today in countries with a large Jewish population, like Argentina, or in Japan, where the Jewish presence is almost nonexistent. Throughout the Islamic world, the *Protocols* have served as "the most important single vehicle" for the transmission of widespread anti-Semitic conspiracy theories.[81] A search of the World Wide Web will reveal hundreds of sites devoted to defending the validity of the *Protocols*. ·

———

Russian anti-Semites shared the mood of those nineteenth-century Russian thinkers who were hostile toward the urban, bourgeois economy, averse to parliamentarism, and bedazzled by the Russian cooperativist peasant village. Their fighting spirit was reminiscent of the revolutionary intelligentsia's, and they similarly blurred the distinctions between right-wing and left-wing, socialism and nationalism. The main difference was that the anti-Semites looked to the past and were tormented by apocalyptic fears of the present, while the radical left intellectuals were forward-looking, with secularized messianic expectations of the future. The radical right's delusional Jewish conspiracy theories kept its followers from understanding how to stay afloat in changing times. But along with the other figures we have examined, Russian anti-Semites carried that curious yet alluring mixture of modern and antimodern ideas originating in their homeland to the wider world. Their appeal coincided and often overlapped with that of the anarchists, Dostoevsky, Tolstoy, and also the Russian avant-garde, which at the same time was a leading force in the twentieth-century artistic revolution.

Conveying Higher Truth Onstage:
Ballet and Theater

AROUND 1900, Russian avant-garde artists entered into a period of frenzied experimentation that did much to foster Modernist culture. For about two centuries Russia had imitated European arts from the periphery; now it surged into the forefront with Diaghilev's ballet, the theater of Stanislavsky and Meyerhold, the abstract painting of Kandinsky and Malevich, and the revolutionary designs of the Constructivists. These artists devised radically new aesthetic forms to correspond with their philosophical beliefs. As they did, they initiated many of the twentieth century's new trends in the fine arts across the globe. But it is a great irony that an equally lasting legacy of these artists was to be found in realms of mass culture such as Hollywood movies, fascist propaganda, and Western commercial advertising, which borrowed the images of modern art but voided the original antimodern, revolutionary, or metaphysical content.

Diaghilev

The first true Russian Modernist movement appeared in 1898 with the publication of the *World of Art* journal (*Mir iskusstva*) under the leadership of Sergei Diaghilev (1872–1929).[1] One of the great impresarios of modern times, Diaghilev was the major figure of the Silver Age, the resplendent initiatory phase in the history of Russian avant-garde art.

Diaghilev was born into a music-loving, minor-aristocratic family in the northern Russian town of Perm. He moved to St. Petersburg to continue his education and there became part of a circle of friends that included the soon-to-be-renowned artists Leon Bakst (1866–1924) and Alexander Benois (1870–1960). The group, which became the core of the *World of Art* movement, had fostered among themselves a discriminating love of music, dance, and painting alongside scorn for what they saw as the stagnant Russian art of the day. They yearned for the revival of Russian art as a bulwark against the dominance of western European, bourgeois culture. Diaghilev's genius was for spotting and deploying artistic talent. From the mid-1890s on he organized pioneering art exhibits that brought modern European art to Russia and vice versa. In 1898 he created the lavish *World of Art* magazine. With Diaghilev as host, the sumptuous banquet of Russian Silver Age art commenced.

According to Benois, this first phase of avant-garde Modernism, associated with the *World of Art*, arose during a "spiritually tormented, hysterical time."[2] For decades religion and metaphysics had been discredited by the radical intelligentsia, but now they were back in fashion as many grew tired of atheism and also reacted against the stepped-up pace of industrialization. Among the educated, Orthodoxy competed with esoteric forms of mysticism, from Theosophy to sex-as-salvation theories. And Neoplatonic Idealism was in the air, a philosophical stance imported from Germany that, in opposition to spirit-denying Western empiricism and materialism, downgraded a turbulent earthly reality in favor of what was imagined to be a perfect heavenly realm.

The artistic and literary branch of Idealism was known as Symbolism, a neo-Romantic movement prominent in late-nineteenth-century France that the Russians, characteristically, borrowed and took to utopian extremes not dreamed of in Paris. Like Dostoevsky, Henri Bergson, and other contemporary antirationalist intellectuals, the Symbolists rebelled against the scientific worldview and the corresponding naturalist or realist schools of writing and painting, choosing instead to explore the irrational or metaphysical forces that seemed to be at work beyond physical reality. Building on their assumption that the terrestrial world was imperfect in comparison with the spiritual realm of the Ideal, they forswore direct depictions of objects or human behaviors and favored suggestive, dreamy representations in order to give a glimpse of that Ideal higher reality. If art continued to copy nature, its full potential would never be realized. The poet Konstantin Balmont declared that "the [realist] is still in bondage to matter; the [Symbolist] has departed for the realm of the Ideal," where he penetrates the "mysterium of the world."[3] Especially in Russia, artistic synthesism was the Holy Grail of the Symbolists. If all the various arts were refractions of one divine truth, combining them in a *Gesamtkunstwerk* (total work of art) would open the eyes of man to God and the secrets of the universe. This vision, partly taken over from German composer Richard Wagner, was the "aesthetic counterpart of [their metaphysical and earthly cravings for] wholeness."[4]

The *World of Art* was the first major forum for these views in Russia. Diaghilev and his associates differed widely in many of their aesthetic likes and dislikes, but as a whole they stood for beauty, mastery of technique, and artistic freedom against what they saw as the stale and pedantic painting of the realist school and the utilitarianism of intelligentsia art critics. The *World of Art*'s enemies were wrong, however, to accuse it of "art for art's sake." The members of the *World of Art* were a part of the Russian intelligentsia; although very much interested in pleasing the eye with their pictures, they also sought the transformation of the world through art.

In their view, art involved spiritual revelation. Diaghilev wrote that artists were visionaries whose "genius" gave them the capability of transcending the world and grasping the "mysteries of . . . divine nature." We the artists acknowledge "only in ourselves the divine authority" to resolve those "terrifying" truths.[5] It was incumbent upon the artist, therefore, to reveal his wisdom through art so as to regenerate humanity. Bourgeois civilization especially stood in need of a spiritual boost through doses of artistic beauty.

These ideas paralleled and were influenced by European aesthetic developments, which the *World of Art* tried to interpret for Russian readers. But Silver Age Modernism also owed much to native intellectual sources, in particular Dostoevsky and Tolstoy, whom Diaghilev named as "gods of *World of Art*'s Olympus" alongside Wagner, French Symbolist painter Pierre Puvis de Chavannes, and writers Charles Baudelaire, Gustave Flaubert, and Henrik Ibsen.[6] The two literary-philosophical giants were the forefathers of the entire Russian avant-garde movement, and it will become apparent throughout this chapter and the one that follows that their artistic views were all-pervasive. Diaghilev and the *World of Art* admired Tolstoy's desire for authenticity in art, his accentuation of art's ability to communicate emotions and reveal divine mystery, and his adoration of Russian folk traditions. Dostoevsky's antirealism and his conviction that "beauty will save the world" were equally a felt presence.[7] From Dostoevsky, Tolstoy, and other philosophers of the spirit, the *World of Art* inherited its peculiar understanding of artistic freedom. This was not the individualism of the West, which Diaghilev and Benois disparaged as a variant of capitalism and liberalism.[8] Rather, it was a spiritual freedom that they had in mind: one that would subordinate personality to a higher, collectivizing force.

Diaghilev's ambivalence toward the West was accompanied by messianic expectations of Russian culture. His magazine did a lot to make Russians aware of modern European art, but he was at bottom a Russian nationalist whose purpose was not to Europeanize domestic art but to remedy its defects through exposure to contemporary trends. Not unlike the Russian Populists, Dostoevsky, or Tolstoy, he was "fanatically" certain that Russia's backwardness was a virtue, and that "Russian talent," whose "gigantic might" derived from its "youthfulness and spontaneity," would surpass all others. Its calling was nothing less than to transfigure all European culture, which was in "desperate need of Russian art."[9]

What Diaghilev intended to introduce to Europe was the *World of Art*'s Modernist smorgasbord of antimodern, antirealist fantasies, counteractants to "Americanism, railroads, telegraphs, telephones, all this modern brutality and vulgarity" that Benois denounced as "serving the Devil."[10] The subject matter *World of Art* painters and illustrators preferred was nostalgic, opulent, and dreamy: Russian folk art and pre-Petrine Russia in the work of Ivan Bilibin; Rococo St. Petersburg for Benois and Konstantin Somov;

Louis XIV's Versailles for Benois; classical antiquity and the biblical Middle East for Bakst. In line with Silver Age antirationalism, Bakst and Somov especially delighted in erotic themes. And each of them sometimes broke away from these "cloudlessly idyllic" utopias[11] to depict more irrational and disturbingly violent scenes.

Through his *World of Art* activities, Diaghilev played a major role in launching the early phase of the Russian avant-garde. But had he restricted himself to that, he would not have become one of the foremost figures in the initiation of modern global cultural life. This distinction he achieved through the creation of the Ballets Russes. If dance anywhere in the world is today artistically vital and innovative, it owes something to him. His ballet company, moreover, fulfilled his expectation of "initiat[ing] a new era of the theatre . . . for all of Western Europe" and beyond.[12]

Prior to Diaghilev, many European ballet troupes had sunk into artistic torpor. Their art was often formulaic, with dancers doing the same pointed-toe spins regardless of the music and wearing the same tutus and tiaras whether the ballet was about Baroque France, the Russian countryside, or ancient Greece. Sets were insipid backdrops. Sneering at productions as "ponderous and tasteless" "animated kaleidoscope[s]" full of "tricks, window-dressing, posing, false paints, and glitter,"[13] Diaghilev rebelled against the established ballet and initiated a revolution in dance, music, stage settings, and costume design.

But why the ballet? It had to do with the *World of Art* group's hoped-for agency of all-encompassing unity, the *Gesamtkunstwerk*, "the idea for which our circle was ready to give its soul." Ballet seemed "the most consistent and complete" expression of this idea, requiring as it did the application of almost all branches of art.[14] Dance, furthermore, held a special place for Symbolists because it was a nondescriptive and suggestive means of expressing pure emotion. Without any connection to reality, dance was the earliest kind of artistic abstractionism. Benois, a ballet addict since childhood, felt that the concreteness of words in librettos and scripts brought operas and plays "down from heaven to earth." Ballet, on the other hand, had a "liturgical quality," "something truly divine and mystic."[15] Diaghilev's conception of the Ballets Russes was in accord with these sentiments: "The essence and the secret of our ballet lies in the fact that we have renounced ideas in favor of an elemental spontaneity. We wished to find an art through which all the complexity of life, all feelings and passions, could be expressed apart from words and ideas—not rationally but elementally."[16]

8. Sergei Diaghilev. From *Vanity Fair*, May 1916.

The formation of the Ballets Russes in 1911 was preceded by Diaghilev's "export campaign" of Russian neonationalist music and opera to western Europe.[17] As he lost interest in the *World of Art*, he preoccupied himself with making a splash in Paris. The Franco-Russian Alliance was in full march, and France and much of the rest of Europe would soon tire of Wagnerian fare, that "Viking world of bearded warriors drinking blood out of skulls," as Diaghilev put it.[18] He sensed that the moment was right for seduction by the Russian spirit.

Diaghilev gave Europe a Slavic alternative to German musical domination. In 1907 he arranged for a season of "Russian Music through the Ages" at the Paris Opéra, featuring music by Tchaikovsky, Rimsky-Korsakov, Rachmaninoff, Scriabin, and others (in the same year he also introduced Stravinsky to Russian audiences). Following the success of that series, in 1908 he staged an elaborate production of Mussorgsky's opera *Boris Godunov*. In these and subsequent programs Diaghilev established the popularity of Russian composers, who have occupied a place in Western repertoire ever since.

But all this paled before the "Ballets Russes de Serge Diaghilev." It was the French-Jewish impresario Gabriel Astruc who put the idea of organizing a ballet series in Paris into Diaghilev's head. In 1909 and then again in 1910 Diaghilev brought together the stars of the Russian Imperial Ballet, among them some of the greatest dancers of all time: Adolph Bolm, Michel Fokine, Tamara Karsavina, Vaslav Nijinsky, and Anna Pavlova. Astruc's promotional efforts lured the rich and famous to the Théâtre du Châtelet for the first season.

Following these two years of what Countess Anna de Noailles called "dazzling, intoxicating, enchanting, seductive performance,"[19] Diaghilev formed his own company in 1911. From that point until his death in Venice in 1929, the Ballets Russes was a dominating presence among world stage productions. It was no easy task managing such an enormous undertaking and maintaining its status. Of necessity, the troupe led a stressful, peripatetic existence as it brought its performances to Paris, London, Monte Carlo, and every other major European city, as well as America and Argentina; ironically, it never performed in Russia owing to official ostracism of Diaghilev before 1917 and Diaghilev's hatred of communism afterward.

Beleaguered by financial problems, Diaghilev was often consumed by the desire for commercial success. At the same time, he wanted to remain unchallenged as the cutting-edge leader of Modernism in Europe. He was determined "not to be less modern than [Italian Futurist Filippo] Marinetti," he told Nijinsky in 1917: "Futurism [and] Cubism . . . are the last word [and] I do not wish to lose my place as an artistic guide."[20] For these reasons he strove to make his ballets both as luxurious and as controversial as possible. The aura of scandal surrounding his open homosexual love affairs with Nijinsky and other male dancers only brought more welcome publicity to his productions.

But Diaghilev's purely artistic commitment and astuteness cannot be denied. That was clear in his choice of choreographers: Fokine (1880–1942) and Nijinsky (1890–1950) before the war; Léonide Massine (1895–1979) from 1915 on; and in the 1920s Bronislava Nijinska (Vaslav's sister, 1891–1972) and George Balanchine (1904–1983). Despite their rigorous classical training at the Imperial Russian Ballet School, they all rejected academic dancing as "idiotic" and disdained its "open umbrella" costumes.[21] Contrary to earlier dance conventions, which Fokine identified as "acrobatic tricks designed to attract applause, and formal entrances and pauses made solely for effect," they attempted to convey the quintessence of the music and the theme of the ballet through the physical movements of the body. They created dance steps to signify the forces of nature and impassioned emotions. No longer were ballerinas to mime the story line with their hands. Now they would use their entire bodies to express psychological or metaphysical meaning. Fokine outlined his choreographical principles: "There shall be but one thing—the aspiration for beauty. Through the rhythms of the body the ballet can find expression for ideas, sentiments, emotions. The dance bears the same relation to gesture that poetry bears to prose. Dancing is the poetry of motion."[22] To see their ballets, to quote Stravinsky, was "to see the music with one's eyes."[23]

It was Nijinsky who consummated Diaghilev's and Fokine's hopes for the Ballets Russes, as a dancer perhaps more than as a choreographer. Before going insane in 1917, Nijinsky had become a supercelebrity. Technically he was magnificent, renowned for his leaps that seemed to defy gravity. Fully absorbed in his roles, he showed the necessity of acting talent in dance, but he also made the art more abstract and less mimetic, as he sought to capture the essential core of reality. As Lady Ottoline Morrell, an English patroness of the Ballets Russes (somewhat pompously) told him, "When you dance, you are not a man—you are an idea. . . . You have read Plato no doubt?"[24]

The themes of the early ballets came right out of the Silver Age. They were lush, emotionally frenzied, otherworldly, antimodern, hedonistic but also anti-individualist productions—in which the corps of dancers often played as significant a role as the principals in order to express collectivist intent. According to its decorator, Nikolai Roerikh, the paganistic *Rite of Spring*, which premiered in 1913, signified metaphysical unity, the connection of "our earthly existence with a Supreme."[25] In the Oriental, Middle Eastern, and classical Dionysian ballets (e.g., *Cleopatra*, *Scheherezade*, *The Blue God*, and *Afternoon of a Faun*), sado-eroticism, necrophilia, masturbation, and androgyny—Nijinsky's other stage specialties—loomed large as the company's desire to shock the public intertwined with its belief in eros as a primeval, creative, spiritual force, the expression of subconscious truths and oxygen for a stifling civilization. With the same intent, the ballets with Russian settings—including *The Firebird*, *Petrushka*, and *The Golden Cockerel*—emitted a sense of primitive vitality as they integrated urban carnival and rural folk motifs in music and dance.

Once the troupe's preeminence in European ballet was established, Diaghilev was able to pick his collaborators among the international avant-garde. Georges Braque, Giorgio de Chirico, André Derain, Juan Gris, Henri Matisse, Pablo Picasso, and Georges Rouault all designed Ballets Russes sets, as did Mikhail Larionov and Natalia Goncharova, Russian artistic exiles with a Slavic-primitivist style. Experimental musicians Jean Cocteau and

9. Vaslav Nijinsky, in *Scheherazade*. From *Vanity Fair*, May 1916.

Erik Satie composed jazz ballets for Diaghilev. With these artists at his side, Diaghilev was able to position himself as one of the initiators of innovation in European culture.

But his main thrust after the war was in the direction of neoclassicism and Tchaikovsky revivals. Repelled by the Russian Revolution, Diaghilev began to favor reactionary "imperial" style ballets that glorified the golden age of the eighteenth- and nineteenth-century Russian aristocracy. For his part, Stravinsky, the main composer for the Ballets Russes and an anti-Semite, passed through a period of intense Slavophilism and then turned to fascism, calling himself the Mussolini of the musical world and eventually currying favor with the Nazi regime. In the 1920s, the anti-Westernism and anti-individualism of the Ballets Russes' earlier Symbolist period remained alive in these new forms, and the troupe came to lead the "conservative wing of the avant-garde."[26]

Learning about this transition may surprise those who know something of the uproar at early performances of *The Rite of Spring* or are aware of Stravinsky's reputation as one of the great experimental composers of the twentieth century. But Stravinsky detested the atonality of his rival Arnold Schoenberg, which he denounced as musically anarchic, and not long after the war he embraced a Modernist strain of neoclassicism. This suited Diaghilev, who feared that discordant music would turn audiences off.

It was far easier for Diaghilev to keep his artistic trendsetter status through costume and set decors. The public could tolerate more experimentation here, and this caused as great a sensation in Europe as the music. Although many Russian and European artists worked for the Ballets Russes, Bakst was the central figure and, before his untimely death, as much of a star as Nijinsky or Stravinsky. Bakst furthered the antirealist revolution that would make Russian stage design foremost in Europe. What he did was to break up the standard two-dimensional backdrop—in effect a big painting—by using a host of visual perspectival tricks such as design on a diagonal axis and asymmetry to achieve a more convincing three-dimensional effect. He then applied vivid, riotous combinations of colors to heighten the themes of the ballet—in accord with both

Russian art traditions and the Symbolist belief in a consonance between specific colors and emotions. Unlike the next theatrical generation, Bakst did not strive to eliminate the boundaries between audience and stage, but his innovations made that next step possible. And he viewed the body as a dynamic, kinetic force whose movement and features he amplified with semirevealing costumes. In this way Bakst helped to liberate the body onstage and, as we will see, in daily life as well.[27] All in all his sets transported the viewer into "the irreal, romanticized world of theater totally at variance with the commonplace of everyday life."[28]

"So barbaric, so luxurious"

Nothing like it had been seen before. The European dance and theatrical avant-garde had engaged in projects with some similarity to Diaghilev's, but none of them had gained the widespread popular appeal of the Ballets Russes. Its audience consisted of artists, intellectuals, sophisticated cosmopolitan aristocrats, and wealthy local Jews, who, on top of loving the ballet, sought acceptance through cultural patronage and viewed the Ballets Russes as a counterweight to Wagner's Bayreuth. Members of the middle class also flocked to the performances, where they gained exposure to Modernist culture for the first time. What the *New Statesman* wrote about London in 1925 applies everywhere: Diaghilev

has done more than anyone to make the arts popular. . . . He is the Apostle to the Philistines. Thanks to him not only are the airs of Scarlatti, Schumann, Chopin, and Rimsky-Korsakov whistled in the bathrooms of thousands who never go to serious concerts, but the idiom of contemporary composers such as Stravinsky receives the appreciation that only familiarity can breed. Thanks to him, too, the crowd has positively enjoyed decorations by the best and most ridiculed living painters. He has given us Modern Music without tears and Modern Painting without laughter.[29]

Reactions to the Ballets Russes were different in each country. France gave it the warmest reception.[30] Before the war, Diaghilev's company helped to cement Franco-Russian solidarity; afterward it retained its popularity in Paris and also on the Riviera: next to gambling it was Monte Carlo's "greatest magnet" in the mid-1920s.[31] In all of its phases the Ballets Russes captivated the French artistic and intellectual elite. A few French nationalist critics attacked it as un-French or Jewish and, during the war years, charged that it was tainted with enemy Turkish and even German attributes.[32] Beginning with the startled reaction to *The Rite of Spring*, many others just denounced the ballets as base or bewildering. But

10. Leon Bakst, costume design for the ballet *The Tragedy of Salomé*. From M. N. Pozharskaia, *Russkoe teatral'no-dekoratsionnoe iskusstvo kontsa XIX-nachala XX veka* (Moscow, 1970).

their shouts were barely perceptible above the din of approbation and acclaim. The same critics who touted Dostoevsky and Tolstoy raved about the ballet, and the enthusiasm of Debussy and Ravel ensured its standing. The work of both of these composers was wholly infected by the exoticism of Russian music. As a conservatory student, Debussy had made trips to Moscow and combined the "Oriental" flavor of its music with other Asian and Iberian elements in his work. In collaboration with Diaghilev he produced the vehicle for Nijinsky's fame, *Afternoon of a Faun*. The Ballets Russes also inspired Ravel to begin writing ballets and operas.[33]

During and immediately after the war, the mood of French music changed, but the Ballets Russes' reputation evolved in tandem.

11. Leon Bakst, costume design for Nijinsky's role in *Afternoon of a Faun*. Cover of *Comoedia Illustré*, May 15, 1912.

Hardened by the carnage, many musicians could no longer abide the atmospherics and "sauce" of Debussy and neo-Romanticism. The critic Jacques Rivière was a political conservative whose writings urged artists to adopt an avant-garde aesthetic. *Petrushka*, he argued, was the ideal model for all art: pure and simple, but with an underlying power and anti-individualistic, anticivilizational thrust. Protofascist art journals of the early 1920s praised Stravinsky along similar lines; one, *Montjoie!*, hailed him as the messiah of French music.[34]

In the visual arts the reception and impact were even stronger. The Impressionist painter Pierre Auguste Renoir was "enchanted."[35] Aristide Maillol and Auguste Rodin did sculptures of Nijinsky. Kees van Dongen, Amedeo Modigliani, and countless other painters turned to the ballet for subject matter.[36] Matisse may have jealously appraised Bakst's work as an insufficiently structured "explosion of color," but Picasso and others felt that the sets and choreography of the Ballets Russes confirmed their own experiments with primitivist forms and partial abstractionism.[37]

Without the Ballets Russes, it would have taken longer for the public to be conditioned to modern art. Although Bakst's coloration was clearly influenced by Matisse and French Fauvism (as well as Russian folk art), he is the one who first made these bold tones known to a broad audience. Because of the Ballets Russes, Russian Modernist painting was more highly regarded in some circles than that of Picasso, Matisse, and Braque: in 1914 Guillaume Apollinaire, the Polish-French poet and critic (who later coined the term "Surrealism" in a review of Diaghilev's ballet *Parade*), complained that museums were already purchasing the works of Russian avant-garde artists while "the new French painters . . . continue to reap nothing but ridicule."[38]

In England, the Ballets Russes was slower to take effect, but when it did, the reaction was similar to that in France: "To an English public weary of English things and already longing for whatever was savage and untamed, the wildness of [the Ballets Russes was] like firewater to an innocent native."[39] In 1911, the wealthy pharmaceuticals manufacturer Sir Joseph Beecham, together with his conductor-son Thomas and Lady Ripon organized the Russian ballet's English premiere at both Covent Garden and the Coronation Gala of George V. Subsequently, Beecham the younger arranged for the ballet to return in 1914, as it did regularly thereafter.

Whereas Richard Strauss had failed to arouse much enthusiasm among the English, Diaghilev succeeded, at least after a while.[40] Critic Arnold Bennett was wildly enthused right away, as was the Bloomsbury intellectual Leonard Woolf, who later equated the Ballets Russes' impact on European civilization with that of Einstein, Eliot, Freud, Joyce, Picasso, and Proust. Only after the war did the rest of his circle warm to the Russian ballet, at the same time that the Dostoevsky fad took hold. Virginia Woolf spoke ecstatically about the performances, Lytton Strachey had homosexual fantasies about Nijinsky, and economist John Maynard Keynes married one of the ballerinas, Lydia Lopokova. Havelock Ellis, speaking for the English socialist counterculture, saw it as a sign of a coming renaissance from Russia: "It is . . . significant that Einstein was immediately preceded by the Russian ballet," he wrote in 1923.[41] Earlier, he had made a wartime analysis of "the psychology of Russia" for the *New Statesman* based on Ballets Russes performances. The "mighty subconscious energy" and "inborn" democracy of Russia, he concluded, gave rise to orgiastic forms of dance and music that would never appear in such a regimented, unspontaneous culture as England's.[42]

The dandies of English society also rallied behind the Ballets Russes.[43] The iconoclastic aristocratic poets and critics Edith, Osbert, and Sacheverell Sitwell were already enthralled in the teens. In the twenties, they were joined by Harold Acton and other rich, precious youths in rebelling against uptight, old-fashioned Victorian and Edwardian mores. They idolized Diaghilev and Nijinsky, who seemed to sanction their sexual exploits and love of American cocktails, jazz, modern painting, and experimental poetry. They listened to the ballet music on gramophones and went to the performances; other concert-goers complained of incessant homosexual flirtation at the Ballets Russes.

The influence of the Ballets Russes was also felt among the American expatriates who led a branch of the radical English avant-garde. Not all of them were enamored of the ballet: unaware of Diaghilev's anticapitalist credentials, harsh, puritanical, antiestablishment figures such as poet Ezra Pound and novelist-artist Wyndham Lewis reviled the Ballets Russes for its opulence and the adoration it received from high society. But *The Rite of Spring* "more than anything else" confirmed Imagist poet John Gould Fletcher in his intention to "risk everything in order to become a modern artist": a "determination to make and accept every kind of experiment, and not flinch from any novelty."[44]

Even more profoundly affected was T. S. Eliot, who became enraged at members of the audience for snickering at *The Rite of Spring*. A Neoplatonist, he believed in the doctrine of impersonality or dehumanization in art, according to which the artist strives for universal truth in his creations by extinguishing the involvement of his personality. Thus he was already sympathetic to the underlying assumptions of Diaghilev's choreography, which he said helped him understand how to represent men, women, and events as poetic symbols of unchanging reality. Like ballet, he wrote, his verse was the "art of simplification of current life into something rich and strange." He saw himself as poetry's Stravinsky and in *The Waste Land* sought to re-create the mood of *The Rite of Spring*, which he understood as having transformed the primitive "rhythm of the steppes into the scream of the motor-horn, the rattle of machinery, the grind of wheels, the beating of wheels, the beating of iron and steel, the roar of the underground railway, and other barbaric noises of modern life."[45] For Eliot, the brutishness of mankind was a constant through all periods of human existence. Although not an accurate measure of Stravinsky's messianic Slavophilism, Eliot's interpretation was in keeping with the antimodern tone of European intellectuals, and with their frequent misunderstandings of Russian thought.

Such a mood was largely alien to the United States, and the reception of the Ballets Russes here had a distinctively American tang. Convinced that American culture needed to be elevated to the European level, Otto Kahn, the German-Jewish financier, arts patron, and chairman of the board of the Metropolitan Opera, arranged the 1910–1911 tour of Anna Pavlova through the United States,

Canada, Mexico, and Cuba. She and her partner Mikhail Mordkin had stopped performing for Diaghilev and formed their own company because they could not stand working with their rivals Karsavina and Nijinsky. During one of his dances in New York, Mordkin accidentally threw a sword into the audience, piercing a man's skull. But the show went on, the incident gave them free advertising, and ticket sales soared.[46]

Under Kahn's auspices, Diaghilev also came to America for two seasons in 1916, when his troupe made appearances in the major cities of the Northeast, Midwest, and West Coast. These shows were dogged by racists, Christian moralizers, and philistines. *Scheherezade* ended with black men embracing white women in the harem; "Even to Northern minds," the *New York Tribune* editorialized, "the spectacle was repulsive."[47] Complaints from Catholics in New York instigated a police vice-squad investigation that forced Diaghilev to moderate the orgiastic parts of *Afternoon of a Faun*. In the heartland, the *Kansas City Star* interviewed a policeman who told "Dogleaf, or whatever his name is," that "this is a strictly moral town and won't stand for any of that highbrow immorality." He warned him to keep the show "toned down to the decency of a high class city": if it was "too rank," he would "close it down."[48] Elsewhere in the Midwest, an engineer from Dayton, Ohio, who saw Nijinsky perform told a reporter, "How I'd like to take a sock at that guy! Why doesn't he *work* for a living?"[49] Still, the Ballets Russes was a smashing popular success. Newspapers gave its arrival front-page headlines, and it played before sellout crowds. Americans were ignorant of the philosophical message and found the Russian names strange, but like British and French audiences, they came in droves.

The odd man out was Germany. Before the war, the Ballets Russes was popular, received extensive news coverage, and garnered rave reviews by leading critics. Expressionist painters of Die Brücke (The Bridge) group dashed off canvases of Berlin nightlife featuring Russian dancers. Modern art patron Count Harry Kessler and Austrian author Hugo von Hoffmannsthal joined with Diaghilev to produce a Richard Strauss ballet, *The Legend of Joseph* (1914), the first German work to appear at the Paris Opéra since

1870.[50] But in postwar Germany things were different, and the Ballets Russes was remote from the mood of the day. The avant-garde and intellectuals were too somber, angry, and radical to enjoy it. For the far right, only the Teutonic apocalypticism of Wagner could satisfy. On the left, German artists took heart from Russia's revolutionary avant-garde. Those Germans who did like the Ballets Russes followed the logic of critic Carl Einstein. Relating the company to Dostoevsky, Tolstoy, and Lenin, he argued that it signified, as they did, a new kind of politics and morality that came from the East: in Russia, he wrote, the Orient is a reality, not a "dream" or an "exotic construction."[51]

Of course, this view of Russia *was* very much an exotic construction, a figment of the Western imagination that reflected either discontent with the vulgar bourgeois status quo or a sense of superiority over the non-European races. In any case, it was that perception of Russia as representing the exotic Orient which lay behind much of the fascination with the Ballets Russes in Europe. A French critic spoke for his contemporaries when, writing before the war, he came to this conclusion about its meaning: "Having remained barbarians in a Europe whose every fiber is civilized, the Russians now have the most richly creative, beautifully developed inner selves. As fresh, avid, and sincere as children, they give themselves over entirely to feverish soul-searching." He and others repeated these platitudes over and over: in contrast to Russia, Europe seemed "old and worn out";[52] the Russians with their Oriental, Slavic souls had deep wisdom, instinct, and primal wholeness, and all of this was apparent in their precivilized, frenzied dancing that must have come straight off the vast, mysterious steppe. Following this logic, in 1911 the London *Times* wrote that the Ballets Russes was an "aesthetic revolution" which has "revealed new faculties and means of salvation in ourselves."[53] Diaghilev believed that Russia offered a higher, more holistic truth than did Europe, and, at least before his neoclassical phase, he catered to the desire for Russian barbarism. His programs played it up, stating that the Slavs were the bearers of Eastern culture in the West.

But it was more than an Asian aura that Diaghilev presented. Hand in hand with it, the Ballets Russes offered elegance, sumptuousness, eroticism, and aristocratic snobbishness. And this image coexisted comfortably with the soulful Oriental one; as Arnold Bennett wrote in 1910, he "never saw anything so beautiful, i.e. so barbaric, so luxurious at the same time."[54] In the mind of the bedazzled audience, it was all part of an exotic Russian treat that—for the price of a theater ticket—provided a momentary chance to flee the humdrum world.

By accelerating a fad for luxurious, Oriental styles, the Ballets Russes transformed French and English fashion and interior design from 1910 to the mid-1920s.[55] At the time, the Ballets Russes was said to be a tempest from the steppe blowing away tired old tastes, and it is impossible to imagine the post-Edwardian, post–Belle Époque look without reference to Bakst. Suddenly Oriental boudoirs became stylish. Rich and often jarring colors and bold patterns appeared in household and restaurant decor. The muted tones of Morris-influenced wallpapers and fabrics went out of fashion. Somerset Maugham's 1919 novel *The Moon and Sixpence* captured the spirit: " 'What wonderful cushions you have,' said Mr. Van Busche Taylor. 'Do you like them?,' [Mrs. Strickland] said, smiling. 'Bakst, you know.' "[56] Bichara and other perfume makers marketed new, heavily scented products with exotic names, promising in their ads that they would convey "the voluptuous feelings of the Ballets Russes and . . . conjure in our memories the choreographic and decorative seductions of *Scheherezade*."[57] These ballets also gave women license to wear costume jewelry that previously would have been considered garish. Diaghilev's companion, fashion designer Coco Chanel, was the first to break this barrier, and soon Cartier, too, was putting sapphires and emeralds and rubies together in combinations after Bakst's costumes.

In clothing of the period, Bakst and the Ballets Russes helped to do away with older fashions by popularizing exotic motifs and eroticizing the female body onstage—thereby doing its bit to assist in the overthrow of Victorian sexual restrictiveness.[58] The styles were merchandised in Paris by Chanel, Paul Poiret, and the houses of Callot and Patou, and in London and New York by the Diaghilev admirer Lady Duff Gordon, proprietress of the house of Lucile. These were the *hauts couturiers* who first liberated women's bodies from the confines of the corset by designing clothing in conscious imitation of Bakst's costumes. At first it was his amalgamation of Near Eastern and Asian features that they reproduced. *Vanity Fair* reported on Parisian fashions in 1913: "The Oriental waist has invaded the domain of the tailor-made to a remarkable degree. Everywhere one sees loose-fitting waists, like Oriental chemises or Russian blouses, drawn into a sash of velvet or satin."[59] Geometrical, butterfly, or dragonfly patterns on velvet gowns and lingerie, silk and bead embroidery, feather adornments, wing sleeves, belted blouses, "harem" style pantaloon gowns, culottes closed at the ankle, and Cossack boots were further features of the Ballets Russes-, Bakstian-, or faux Russian-peasant-style of these design-

12. Post–World War I French fashions under Ballets Russes influence. From C. Spencer, *The World of Serge Diaghilev* (New York, 1979).

ers. So were the turbans that replaced brimmed hats and were the forerunner of the close-fitting, Art Deco–inspired toque, the signature headgear of the flappers of the later 1920s.

Coco Chanel, a dominant force in the Parisian fashion and perfume industries, was an intimate of Diaghilev and lover of Stravinsky.[60] In her fashion designs, she moved in the direction of comfort and sexual freedom by designing ready-made casual outfits, eliminating any sign of the waist, and raising the dress above the ankle. Under the influence of Bakst, whose simple, utilitarian costumes for tennis players in the ballet *Jeux* (1913) captured the dynamism and kineticism of sport (akin to dance and so also of interest to him), she began to design tennis and skating clothes that corresponded to, encouraged, and profited from the middle class's vigorous pursuit of leisure. Chanel herself was responsible for the costumes in another Diaghilev ballet about tennis, *Le Train Bleu* (1924).

The revolutions in clothing that the Ballets Russes precipitated were widely advertised in fashion magazines. In fact, the Ballets Russes was the single most important influence on the graphic arts of *Vogue* and similar publications. Georges Lepape, Paul Iribe (eventual husband of Chanel), and Georges Barbier are the best known of the many French Art Deco artists who came under the spell of the Ballets Russes, and they introduced colorful, lithe Oriental and other exotic motifs into their work as a result. Bakst, too, designed dresses for *Vogue* and illustrated one of its covers, and the magazine gave constant publicity to his ballets in its French, English, and American editions.[61]

In fashion, the Ballets Russes' sway was strong and at times preeminent, but it coexisted with many other influences. In dance, though, it stood almost alone, and its impact was wide and varied. In Europe, North and South America, and Japan, Diaghilev revived interest in classical ballet, assisted by the enormous outpouring of writing on his productions. An entire generation of dancers learned from the Ballets Russes, having seen the shows or at least the ubiquitous photographs in women's magazines. Lady Diana Cooper reminisced that she "bought ballet shoes, puckered up my sylphide skirts, . . . and went to [Russian ballerina] Lydia Kyasht to be taught to glide like a Russian peasant, flickering a provocative red handkerchief."[62]

13. Leon Bakst, women's clothing designs for Lord and Taylor department store, New York, 1924 (drawings of models by Harriet Meserole). From William Packer, *Fashion Drawing in Vogue* (London, 1989).

The Ballets Russes also spawned new ballet companies. Marie Rambert, the Polish-born grande dame of British ballet, danced for Diaghilev, then set up a dance school in London and the Rambert Ballet. Former Diaghilev dancer Ninette de Valois (born Edris Stannus of Ireland) established her own school and the Vic-Wells, later Royal, Ballet in England. Alicia Markova (born Lilian Marks), prima ballerina of the latter company and student of Rambert's, cofounded the Markova-Dolin Ballet with Anton Dolin (born Sydney Francis Patrick Chippendall Healy-Kay). If ballet flourished in Britain, it was because of these dancers and their association with Diaghilev—who for marketing purposes required non-Russians in his company to adopt pseudonyms.

Similar developments took place elsewhere in Europe as well as farther afield in Argentina, Turkey, and Japan—all beneficiaries of the visits of the Ballets Russes or of exiled Russian dancers founding ballet companies and dance schools.[63] In the case of Japan, the 1922 tour of Anna Pavlova and her troupe—rivals to the Ballets Russes—stimulated both an awakening of interest in European classical ballet and the freeing up of dance styles in traditional Kabuki theater. Some nationalist critics denounced ballet as a form of Western corruption, but despite that, Kabuki actors learned new ways of moving onstage by observing Pavlova and the other Russian dancers coming through Japan in this period.[64]

In America, too, the dance renaissance of the twentieth century originated with Diaghilev and offshoots of his ballet. Russian-Jewish impresario Sol Hurok brought the "Monte Carlo Ballets Russes," a remnant of the original, to New York in 1933–1934; many of its dancers stayed, forming dance companies and schools.[65] In 1933 as well, the wealthy modern art and dance patron Lincoln Kirstein—who saw himself as the American Diaghilev—invited the Ballets Russes's Russian-Georgian choreographer George Balanchine to the United States, where he worked on productions for Broadway, Hollywood, and the Metropolitan Opera, and in 1949 formed the New York City Ballet. Balanchine's protégé Jerome Robbins, famed for his choreography of musical hits such as *West Side Story* and *Fiddler on the Roof*, acknowledged the importance of the Russian dance training he and many others had received from Balanchine, who at the same time encouraged the full integration of American rhythms.[66] Diaghilev dancer Adolph Bolm played only a slightly lesser role in Chicago and Los Angeles.[67]

Diaghilev would have been appalled to know that Balanchine adapted so well to musical theater and the movies, for he tried to keep his ballet from having any association with the philistine (non-Russian) masses. Yet his impact on popular culture in Europe and the Americas was fundamental. First of all in popular dance: through the subject matter of its productions, the Ballets Russes opened the door to the embrace of an array of exotic lower-class and foreign music and dance impulses. The adaptation of urban street-fair culture in *Petrushka*, for instance, inspired French composer and dramatist Jean Cocteau to look elsewhere for similar kinds of cultural inspirations. He found it in "Russian-Jewish American" and American Negro jazz music. The Diaghilev-Cocteau ballet *Parade* (1917), with music by Erik Satie, was the first concert performance of jazz in France and initiated a new direction for the French musical avant-garde, which after the war rebelled against the Romanticism of Debussy and the hated Germans. They did so by focusing their art on everyday life and using either neo-classical or jazz sounds.[68]

Once the Ballets Russes had paved the way, the jazz craze hit Paris. Thanks largely to Diaghilev, the Europeans and Americans had learned of dancing as a form of self-expression with innuendos of sensuality. Partly because of Bakst, their freedom of movement on the dance floor was made possible by the new, less restrictive clothing fashions. And the Russian ballet had stoked their craving for "all things rare and exotic." This is when the African American Josephine Baker achieved fame as a dancer; she had learned from exiled imperial Russian ballerinas by watching them perform at the Folies-Bergère in Paris. This is when the Argentine tango and popular American ragtime dances like the turkey trot entered the scene; even in the United States, they were made more acceptable to the middle class after Russian ballerinas awakened a general interest in dancing. Pavlova herself at first praised the turkey trot as a kind of folk dance until she suspected it of undermining the purity of ballet. For a time, Russian peasant dancing also caught on, but with its knee drops and kicks the *kazachok* was too physically demanding for most people.[69]

In addition to its impact on popular dance, the Ballets Russes helped to shift the direction of American popular theater and film. Russian productions inspired a short-lived rage for exotic Oriental styles in the music halls, on Broadway, and in Hollywood. But the more permanent impact of the Russian ballet on these arenas was in elevating the importance and quality of dance. Eventually, a virtual dance invasion would occur, as Russians fleeing communism emigrated here. Besides teaching students in the proliferating dance schools, they performed in vaudeville or the premovie shows called "prologs" where in the 1920s and 1930s millions of Americans would see them.[70]

But Russian dancers had already established a beachhead in America before World War I. Not long after the Pavlova-Mordkin tour of 1910–1911, a rip-off of the Ballets Russes appeared in vaudeville; its eventual impact on American film would be enormous. In 1909, the Russian-Jewish immigrant Morris Gest had gone to Paris with vaudeville star Gertrude Hoffman to attend performances of the Ballets Russes. They knew a winner when they saw one and offered big money—far more than Diaghilev could pay—to dancers and choreographers to perform in a "Saison Russe" in America. Pavlova and others refused to lower themselves by working in vaudeville, and Lopokova quit midstream after Hoffmann added a tacky showgirl revue and comedian routine to her performance. But Theodore Kosloff (1882–1956), Karsavina's preferred Ballets Russes dance partner, had no such qualms. He served as dancer and choreographer, directing the first of many pirated versions of Diaghilev's productions with the help of local artists and dancers using fake Russian names. Bakst's lawsuit against him failed in the American courts, there being no copyright on sets or costumes in those days. Kosloff then formed his own troupe, the Imperial Russian Dancers, which lasted through 1917 on the Keith-Orpheum vaudeville circuit. In the summer of 1916 he broke Palace Theater box office records and performed Stravinsky for the first time in the United States, where plebeian audiences heard his music before the highbrows did! Kosloff knew how to sell his wares in America: he explained Stravinsky's music as making "Russians happy in our art, because in that we have a sense of freedom which we do not enjoy in life."[71] In relating Russian avant-garde art to political freedom, Kosloff was foreshadowing the way in which Russian and other varieties of abstract painting would be defended much later.

Even more significant for American culture, Kosloff also worked for the movies, bringing Ballets Russes dances, costumes, poses, and decorative style with him to Hollywood.[72] He played no small role in the movie industry's embrace of dance in the 1920s and helped to create the very concept of the sound musical of the 1930s and 1940s. He did so both as a teacher and in collaboration with the great filmmaker Cecil B. DeMille (1881–1959), one of the showmen responsible for establishing the feature film and securing the global reputation of Hollywood. DeMille was the first producer to showcase dance in his movies, which were lavish, luxurious productions whose sets, costumes, and choreography were often directly imitative of the Ballets Russes. Impressed with Kosloff's dancing and Michelangelo-like bearing, he used him as actor, dance arranger, art director, and general adviser in almost every one of his films of the 1920s.

Having lost his investment wealth in Russia owing to the revolution, Kosloff settled permanently in Hollywood and opened several dance schools, where he taught aspiring actresses how to express themselves through ballet movements—an essential skill in silent film. His close relations with teenage pupils periodically led to charges of statutory rape, but his reputation did not suffer. Among Kosloff's students were actresses who would dominate American movies or Broadway musicals for a generation: Joan Crawford, Agnes de Mille, Marilyn Miller, Pola Negri, and Gloria Swanson, all of whom relied on training and choreography by Kosloff to impart to their viewers a grace of movement and heightened sensuality. One of his students, "imperial Russian" ballerinas, and underage lovers was Natacha Rambova (born Winifred Shaughnessy of Utah), who eventually married Rudolph Valentino. By means of clothing that was designed in imitation of Bakst to reveal the power of her husband's body, and through dancelike movement inspired

14. Natacha Rambova and Theodore Kosloff. From Michael Morris, *Madame Valentino* (New York, 1991). Courtesy of Michael Morris.

by Nijinsky and Kosloff, she made Valentino into a Hollywood star and heartthrob of America in the early 1920s.

Douglas Fairbanks, Sr., was another movie idol and filmmaker of the 1920s who borrowed freely from the Ballets Russes. Known as "Mr. Pep," he was the symbol of American masculinity, and his dynamism on the screen stemmed partly from his observation of the ballet. "Watching him move," his wife Mary Pickford said, "was like watching the greatest of Russian dancers." His 1924 film *The Thief of Baghdad* epitomized Hollywood's attempt to secure for itself a middle-class audience and his concern to raise film to the level of "Art." The movie was a reworking of *Scheherezade*, whose lavish costumes, Oriental sets, and monumental scale were through and through derived from the Ballets Russes. But in America, male dancers were still often seen as oddities, and it would have been unimaginable to suggest anything like Nijinsky's androgyny. Fairbanks, in the role of Ahmed, shows his sexual certainty by engaging in he-man stomping, as opposed to the corrupt royal suitors whose ballet movements display their effeminacy. The orgiastic components of the Diaghilev original are also replaced, in true American style, with sentimental romance, and the general theme—in contrast to the apocalyptic eroticism of *Scheherezade*—is very American: "happiness must be earned" through hard work and strength of character.[73]

The Thief of Baghdad highlights the way in which Russian ideas were often distorted by those who adopted them. But despite that, it should be clear from all of the preceding that through the Ballets Russes Diaghilev succeeded far beyond his expectations in enriching both the high and the low culture of the twentieth century.

The bold new innovations in Russian theater did so as well, and to no less an extent.

Stanislavsky and Meyerhold

The genius of both Stanislavsky and Meyerhold on the stage grew in soil prepared by Russian society and culture.[74] Russia's rulers had relied on parades, spectacles, and theater to teach dynastic loyalty and civilized manners to their rough-hewn aristocrats. Emulating their sovereigns, provincial nobles took up acting and established their own estate theaters, in which frivolous distraction mingled with the pursuit of status and instruction of the peasants. In these circumstances, Russian theater flourished. Add to that the nineteenth-century intelligentsia's desire to reach out to the downtrodden lower classes and transform society in accord with "higher truth," and the impulses behind the theatrical approaches of Stanislavsky and his onetime protégé Meyerhold come into focus.

Much like Dostoevsky and Tolstoy, the two directors are often pegged as poles apart, but in reality they shared many of the same assumptions. Regardless of their differences, they were utopian Modernists of the theater who, like Slavophiles, Populists, and the neo-Orthodox, imagined a new, undivided community of elite and masses in place of the current lamentable reality. Even after the Russian Revolution, both remained true, deep down, to the basic position of Russian Symbolists such as Vyacheslav Ivanov. Combining elements of the Silver Age with Wagner and Nietzsche, Ivanov saw art as a form of religion, and the theater as a temple in which poet and crowd, dramatist and spectators, would be united in mystical ecstasy, as he assumed had occurred long ago in classical Greek drama or medieval passion plays. But the goal was not limited to reforming the theater. Rather, it was to promote the creation of a new, more spiritually and emotionally conscious humanity that could break free of the rationalism and commercialism imposed upon it by modern civilization. What Ivanov and other Silver Age thinkers fantasized, Stanislavsky and Meyerhold, each in his own way, attempted to realize.

Stanislavsky (1863–1938) was born Konstantin Alekseev, the son of a French actress married to a wealthy Russian textile manufacturer. He grew up attending the theater on his father's estate and acting in amateur productions. The pseudonym Stanislavsky he took from a retired Polish actor in order to avoid using his family name in experimental and farcical productions. In 1885 and 1890 he attended the realistic performances of the Meiningen Company, a German theater troupe on tour in Russia, which impressed him and opened his eyes to the deficiencies of contemporary dramatics. He also took part in productions at Abramtsevo, the arts colony of his cousin, the patron Savva Mamontov. Here he was exposed to Russian operas and plays, aesthetic theater design, a contempt for banal performances, the synthesist desire to fuse music, sets, and action, and the notion of transcending literal realism for artistic truth—all to remain integral components of his outlook until the end.

Stanislavsky's mission to upgrade the theater gradually dawned on him as he spent the next decade producing scores of plays in Moscow. He achieved success in partnership with Vladimir Nemirovich-Danchenko (1858–1943), a Moscow landowner, playwright, critic, and drama teacher whose reformist proposals had been rejected by the Imperial Theater. Having seen Stanislavsky's productions, Nemirovich-Danchenko invited him to a midafternoon meeting at the Slaviansky Bazaar restaurant on June 21, 1898; their tête-à-tête lasted until 8:00 the next morning and culminated in the creation of the Moscow Art Theater (MAT). This rendezvous initiated the modern era in the history of world stagecraft.

"Our program was revolutionary," Stanislavsky remarked: "we rebelled against the old way of acting, ... the whole spirit of performance and the insignificance of repertory."[75] He and Nemirovich-Danchenko did not want theater to be taken lightly. It was to be a collective undertaking, a *Gesamtkunstwerk*, in which everything would be subordinated to the whole and consciously keyed to the play's themes—and the director would take charge of all activity connected to the process. The sets, costumes, and makeup—some designed by Benois, Bakst, or other *World of Art* figures—were to look natural and authentic. Music was to establish the mood. Performances would no longer be a venue for stars to hog the stage and interrupt the play while bowing to the applause of spectators. "There are no small parts, there are only small actors,"[76] Stanislavsky announced: no matter how insignificant-seeming, all served the purposes of the playwright and director in achieving "truth onstage." In performance, he banished all triteness, artificiality, false emotions, and routine. Actors would be committed and highly disciplined artists seeking to convey the inner emotions of their characters. They would read and discuss the play in advance in order to grasp its central thematic purpose, what Stanislavsky called the "trunkline of action." Actors would then listen to lectures on related subjects, visit relevant historic sites, and for days on end wear their costumes and live their parts.

With his high-minded expectations of the theater, Stanislavsky required the spectators, too, to take performances seriously. He and Nemirovich-Danchenko were the first to insist on darkening the seating area to encourage concentration on the show, to lock out latecomers, and to require absolute silence of audiences that had been accustomed to chattering among themselves and shouting to the actors. The verisimilitude of the acting and sets generated a positive reaction from audience members, who quickly warmed to the new style of theatergoing.

Later, Meyerhold and some of the Silver Age mystics and avant-gardists condemned the Moscow Art Theater for its outdated realism. Its naturalistic productions, they said, were proof of its superficiality and lack of concern for deeper truths, higher realities, and artistic experimentation. The criticism is wholly undeserved. Stanislavsky was well aware of the negative result of early MAT productions in which props and costumes were authentic but so cluttered the stage that they drew attention away from the content of the play. It was difficult for him and his company to break free from the surface realism of decor and acting that had brought them popular success. But he agreed with Anton Chekhov when the latter remarked that "a real nose stuck through a portrait instead of a painted one is natural enough, but does not constitute art."[77]

Chekhov (1860–1904) was in effect the third partner of the Moscow Art Theater, and that fact, too, establishes the MAT in the ranks of the Modernist rather than the realist movement. Nemirovich-Danchenko had to persuade a reluctant Stanislavsky to produce Chekhov, but once he did, in 1898, the company gained national and international fame. The MAT also staged plays by Shakespeare, ancient Greek dramatists, Ibsen, Hauptmann, Gorky, and Tolstoy, but primarily it was known for its Chekhov plays, *The Seagull*, *Three Sisters*, and *The Cherry Orchard*, all critical successes. The seagull became the emblem of the MAT, and the world gained an enduring contribution to its theatrical repertoire.

On the surface, the Chekhov plays may seem to be done in the realist mode, but in fact they are intense, tightly written psychological dramas, with symbolic, tonal, and absurdist features that prompted leading representatives of the later avant-garde to claim them as antecedents of their own experiments in writing.[78] Like his stories, Chekhov's plays are "small epic poem[s] in prose,"[79] devoid of all superfluities, in which words are often less important than silences, and subtle body gestures reveal inner thoughts. People are bundles of contradictions, dramatic events are replaced by inaction, and the stories often lack clear-cut resolution, as in life itself. With their irony, shifting moods, and intimations, they required a new style of minimalist and understated acting, which Stanislavsky introduced, altering the course of theater everywhere.

As with Chekhov, Stanislavsky's central concern was human psychology: "Those who thought that we strove for naturalism on the stage are mistaken. . . . Always we sought for inner truth, for the truth of feeling and experience."[80] Nemirovich-Danchenko called the mind-sets of the characters in a play the "second level," but it was the first order of priority for MAT actors, who were trained to apprehend the "inner truths" of their roles. Capturing what they perceived to be the genuine emotional state of their characters required actors to project themselves into their imaginary lives, to feel their parts as much as memorize the lines. They did so by digging up memories from their own personal psychological experiences, "living through" their characters' lives, and creating for them a subconscious thought process, an "inner monologue," to correspond to their spoken parts. Hinduism, too, was pressed into the service of the stage: Stanislavsky required yoga exercises to reduce physical and mental tensions that prevented actors from becoming one with their characters. These were the main facets of what Stanislavsky called his "System," the means by which the MAT was to become a "theater of authentic emotion."[81]

Stanislavsky formulated his System on the basis of an understanding of psychology that was very much pre-Freudian and in tune with the Silver Age—a detail that escaped his later American proponents. He drew partly from French psychologist Théodule Ribot's study of emotions and memory, then circulating in Russia. But Tolstoy was the overriding influence.[82] The connections between the MAT and Tolstoy were many: the company produced his works, the directors were in frequent contact with him, and the eventual head of their acting workshop, Leopold Sulerzhitsky, was a Tolstoyan disciple who, having taken vows of poverty and love, lived homeless in Moscow parks before attaching himself to the theater as his commune. Stanislavsky often repeated Tolstoy's observation that "the theatre is the most powerful pulpit of our

15. Konstantin Stanislavsky. From Vladimir Nemirovitch-Dantchenko, *My Life in the Russian Theatre* (New York, 1968).

times."[83] In accord with Tolstoyan didacticism, he averred that the MAT as a Russian enterprise had a moral mission to build a better life and transform the world: it "cannot and does not have the right to serve pure art alone; it must . . . be the teacher of society."[84] Following Tolstoy's aesthetic philosophy, MAT's founders expected the emotional sincerity of the acting to "infect" the audience with both empathy for the character and a quasi-religious catharsis. Their approach to acting took inspiration from Tolstoy's fiction, especially his "creative affection for . . . his own characters."[85] Stanislavsky's System was rooted in the principle of Tolstoyan metaphysics that the divine is present in all things. Actors were to feel their parts, obliterate their individuality, and search within themselves for experiences that were universal to all mankind. Stanislavsky called this a "spiritual technique": creativity in acting, he felt, hinged on entering the "spiritual atmosphere," even "renounc[ing] materialism and attain[ing] incorporeality"; only then might an actor express "the sorrow of the world, the feeling of the secret of existence, [and] the eternal."[86] Here once again we see the ubiquitous hope among the Russian intelligentsia for human and metaphysical unity, based on presuppositions about human psychology that were very different from the individualistic assumptions prevalent in the West.

Contrary to the image fabricated by its detractors, not only was the MAT innovative in its day; it continued for a long time to evolve as Stanislavsky, wary of falling into the artistic trap of rote and routine performance, increasingly moved away from concern with externals to exploration of invisible and irrational forces. He and Nemirovich-Danchenko produced antirealist, metaphysical, or Symbolist plays such as Maeterlinck's *Blue Bird* and Dostoevsky's *Brothers Karamazov* with stylized or minimalist sets to encourage concentration on the spiritual atmosphere and the characters' inner emotional tensions. In 1905 they created a workshop for experimental performance called the Theater Studio. As Stanislavsky explained,

Realism and [depicting] the way of life have outlived their age. The time has come to stage the unreal. Not life itself, as it occurs in reality, must be depicted, but life as is vaguely perceived in fantasies and visions at moments of lofty emotion. . . . The power of the new [drama and set design] . . . lies in its combination of colors, lines, musical notes, and the rhyming of words. They create general moods that carry over to the public unconsciously. They create hints that make the most unobservant person create with his own imagination.[87]

That statement could well stand as the credo of the entire artistic avant-garde from Diaghilev to Kandinsky; certainly it encapsulates the views of Meyerhold, who served a brief tenure as the Studio's first director.

His time there was short because Stanislavsky fired him. Despite the broad overlap in their Russian Silver Age expectations of Modernist drama, the two parted company over the ways and means of rendering reality in the theater. The most radically inventive director in Russian theatrical history, Meyerhold was driven by an unslakable thirst, almost a mania, for creative and iconoclastic means of revealing higher truths through stage performance.[88] Why was it important to him? Even more than his mentors at the MAT, Meyerhold was an antimodern, antibourgeois utopian who spoke of the theater as healing and purifying a sick, evil society. Its "great mission," he told Chekhov in 1901, was the "reconstruction of everything which exists around us."[89] In his eyes, attaining truth in the theater was essential because the revolutionary transformation of mankind would come not through politics but through art.

Vsevolod Meyerhold (1874–1940) was born Karl Meyergold, son of a well-to-do German Lutheran vodka distiller in the steppe town of Penza. A childhood memory of theater and street fairs, his mother's love of art and music, and aversion for his strict businessman father all pushed him toward the choice of acting as a career. Identifying with Russian culture, he converted to Eastern Orthodoxy and Slavicized his name. He became a student of Nemirovich-Danchenko and played leading roles at the Moscow Art Theater. Between 1902 and 1905 he produced plays in the MAT style in the provincial towns of Tiflis and Kherson, then entered the Stanislavsky Studio.

After his termination there, he committed himself to fighting all vestiges of realism in the theater. This orientation was accentuated by knowledge of the antirealist productions of Georg Fuchs at the Munich Art Theater and Wagnerian theories of synthesism and transmittal of emotional effects to the audience. But it also came from Russian Symbolism and from Tolstoy, who had taught that in order for art to infect the spectators with truth, "one should reveal little, leaving the spectator to discover the rest for himself."[90] Meyerhold finally landed in 1908 at the Imperial Theater in St. Petersburg, where he spent the next ten years as a director. Simultaneously, he conducted his most audacious experiments under the pseudonym Doctor Dapertutto in cabarets, theater workshops, and private homes—including that of his guru, Vyacheslav Ivanov. At this time he was already dreaming of a collective theater with both spiritual and socialist overtones.

But it was the revolution of 1917 that gave the Master—as his actors called him—license to smash all conventions and refashion the Russian theater; this is when Meyerhold became a militant Communist and began to diverge most clearly from the style of the MAT. He cochaired the theatrical section of Proletkult, an early Soviet agency aiming to proletarianize culture and bring theater to the masses, and formed a pro-Communist lobby called Theatrical October, which published articles attacking bourgeois traditionalists in the theater and urging the politicization of all drama. He developed a pedagogical curriculum in his drama workshops and was given his own theater. Here he presented an array of European satire, German Expressionist works, Russian classics that he updated and Sovietized, and new Soviet drama by avant-garde writers such as Alexander Blok, Sergei Tretyakov, and Vladimir Mayakovsky, whose experimental, apocalyptic, and utopian antibourgeois works stood in relation to the Meyerhold Theater as Chekhov's did to the MAT.

Meyerhold sought new ways of practicing his art in tune with revolutionary times and in the 1920s became the leading force behind Soviet experimental theater, as director and teacher. But the Stalinist regime soon soured on the old leftist avant-garde as too independent and cerebral, and in the 1930s it began to badger him. His theories and productions were never sufficiently ideologically correct or propagandistic in the ways the authorities deemed acceptable—and by having Stalin's rival Trotsky himself take the stage in a 1923 production, he made matters worse. Early in the century, Meyerhold had stated that the director's function was to reveal the "world of the soul."[91] After the revolution, he substituted for that the world of the revolutionary proletariat, but in effect it was the same utopian hunger for what many Russian radicals perceived as lacking in Russia and the bourgeois West: an Ideal realm of order, unity, and harmony. Despite his endorsement of Communism and renunciation of mysticism, at heart he remained a Silver Age Symbolist, a devotee more of Ivanov than of Marx.

Until it was already too late, Meyerhold refused to adhere to Socialist Realism, the official artistic formula established by the dictatorship in the early 1930s, and his radical productions were alien to the tastes of Stalin and the other narrow-minded nonintellectuals within the party leadership. They preferred the MAT, whose performances the aging Stanislavsky and Nemirovich-Danchenko, under pressure from above, made more naturalistic than ever before. Tacking the name Gorky onto the MAT in honor of the chief collaborator in Soviet literature, the government made it the official Socialist Realist theater. Stanislavsky resented the state's interference more than his partner did, and he bravely defended Meyerhold in public. But to no avail. The curtain descended during the Great Terror. In 1938 the government shut Meyerhold's theater down. The following year the secret police arrested the unreliable maverick. Beaten and tortured for weeks, he was executed in 1940. His wife, the actress Zinaida Raikh, was brutally murdered in their apartment.

The government had smeared Meyerhold as a "formalist," which was the slur it used against those avant-garde artists and composers who aroused suspicions of disloyalty by not going over to Socialist Realism. In his case, although the political charges were a sham, the term "formalism" as applied to his art was valid. His was the theatrical equivalent of Russian avant-garde tendencies in the visual arts, which strove to depict not the despised visible world but a higher reality that only the artist could recognize and convey. Rooted in Neoplatonic Idealism and Symbolism, the theory of formalism held that an artist could communicate meaning best not by representing nature as we see it, but by achieving an abstract or unconventional treatment of a subject through manipulation of the forms or media or devices of art. In painting, this produced an emphasis on color or texture instead of illustration; in poetry sounds and tone instead of narrative content; and in theater overt artifice or "theatricalization" instead of naturalist illusion.

Why try to represent the world as we see it if it was impossible to do so adequately? The best way to leave the audience with an understanding of the path to truth was through "stylization" and the "schematization of the real" in a retheatricalized theater.[92] Let the spectators see that what was taking place onstage was not the ephem-

16. Vsevolod Meyerhold. From Nikolai Volkov, *Meierkhol'd*, vol. 1 (Moscow-Leningrad, 1929).

eral life they knew, but a play that distilled the essence of reality to unveil permanent, eternal truth as the artist-director saw it.

In Russian avant-garde parlance, all of that required "making strange," a term we encountered in the Tolstoy chapter, referring to the great writer's way of making a reader see something from a fresh, unfamiliar perspective. This became the forte of all the innovative radical Russian artists of the day. In order to communicate what the artist saw as the true essence of his subject matter, the "thing in itself," he deformed it until it no longer appeared as it did in nature. The point was to gain a better understanding of reality that, once achieved, would inevitably lead to the destruction, then reconfiguration, of wicked modern bourgeois society. Meyerhold introduced this defamiliarization technique in the theater, whose effect he explained thus: "Your imagination is activated, your fantasy stimulated, and a whole chorus of associations is set off. A multitude of accumulated associations gives birth to new worlds."[93]

Everything he did in the theater was a form of "making strange." He diverged sharply from the MAT's psychological approach and eliminated realist acting and set design by adopting the grotesque, fantastic, artificial, carnivalesque devices of prenaturalist theater, street fairs, Kabuki theater, and commedia dell'arte—Italian improvisational comedy. Performing pantomime, wearing masks with frozen expressions, or contorting their own faces, his actors played archetypal theatrical roles and communicated "extracts"[94] of emotions rather than an infinite number of subtle feelings as in naturalistic theater. To enhance the effect of artificiality and prompt the audience to see things in a new way, he "bared the device": that is, he refused to hide stage mechanisms like light fixtures, ropes, scaffolding. And he eliminated almost all props—for instance, stacking two chairs to represent mountains, as in traditional Chinese theater. Imparting a political and philosophical moral, Meyerhold's productions employed telegraphic speech, monologues, and a jarring style that would later become common to virtually all modern avant-garde theater. All of this might have been acceptable to Stanislavsky, but he refused to accept Meyerhold's attempt to bend all components of a performance to his will as director. Whereas MAT actors were given free rein to develop the emotional dimensions of their roles, Meyerhold gave his none, as he wanted to eradicate psychological analysis and anything else that smacked of life as people lived it.

Hence the importance he placed on rhythm and physical movement in acting and actor training, "the most powerful means of expression in the creation of a theatrical production."[95] He was interested not in telling a story but in getting concepts across to his audience, and dance motions he felt were the most effective method of doing so. He saw them as a concise expression of inner emotions and the state of the characters' souls; but he was uninterested in the individual and understood the coordinated rhythmic movement of the corps of actors as a demonstration of "prerational" and/or East Asian mentalities and the much-coveted collective society that he hoped would replace the disharmonious Western individualist model.[96]

Meyerhold's understanding of rhythm and dance as abstract forms capable of expressing supreme emotional and universal truths was close to that of the Ballets Russes, which, of course, had much the same intellectual ancestry. Meyerhold danced alongside Nijinsky and Karsavina in the 1910 Diaghilev ballet *Carnival*, and he learned the basics of choreography from Fokine. After 1917, he justified rhythm with reference to Communism. His system of actor training, which concentrated on dance, gymnastics, reflexes, and other forms of motion, he called "biomechanics." He related it to Constructivism in the arts, Pavlovian psychology, Trotskyite labor theories, and Taylorist scientific management of industry, all then in vogue among Bolshevik utopian intellectuals. Like all other realms of life, acting was to be made a highly organized, efficient, and collective activity. The actor must control his body as the factory worker does his tools. "The artist," he proclaimed, must "become an engineer."[97]

But despite all his attempts to square what he was doing with the radical formulas of the Russian Revolution, Meyerhold never really discarded his original Diaghilevian point of view: biomechanics were essential, he said, primarily for expressive purposes:

"The art of the actor is the art of sculptural forms in space."[98] This principle that he took over from modern ballet has more to do with fin-de-siècle Symbolism than it does with Communism. Following the trail blazed by the Ballets Russes, his productions transmitted ideas, concepts, and moods through the abstract medium of dance.

Meyerhold's revolutionary innovations in set design were of the same order; his French biographer calls him the inventor of twentieth-century staging insofar as he destroyed and redefined traditional theater space.[99] One might assume from such productions of his as Mayakovsky's propaganda play *Mystery Bouffe* (1918 and 1921) that Meyerhold was primarily dedicated to promoting communism. He *was* committed to this, but politics were never of the utmost importance to him, and much of what he was trying to do went back to an earlier phase in his formation as director. Before and after 1917 he believed that the first step toward the unification of humanity and transformation of society was to follow Vyacheslav Ivanov's prescription for a "spiritual theater" in which the audience did not just watch a spectacle from the sidelines but participated in sacred performance as in classical antiquity, when the world seemed whole, and art, religion, intellectuals, and the masses seemed one. If Stanislavsky erected a "fourth wall" in the theater through which the audience peered silently into the lives being acted out onstage, Meyerhold tore it back down to fuse the spectators (i.e., the people) and the performers (i.e., the artistic intelligentsia). The audience he therefore considered the theater's "fourth dimension," a concept he took from other mystically inclined Russian intellectuals with roots in the Silver Age.

Before the revolution, Meyerhold had borrowed from the Ballets Russes for the visual effect of the sets, at one time commissioning designs from *World of Art* veterans, Bakst included. But he also went much further in eliminating all vestiges of illusionism. He did away with the traditional proscenium stage by means of uneven floor spaces, a ramp that jutted into the audience, and acting in seating areas—anything to suppress the barriers between stage and audience. For the same reason, again predating all other avantgarde directors, he introduced directional lighting to spotlight certain objects for effect and allow set changes under cover of darkness in one area while the action continued in another. He was also the first to project slogans and captions onstage as in silent film. After the revolution, he renounced mysticism and replaced Ivanov's idea of stage as temple with the utopian Bolshevik notion of the stage as a machine for acting, relying on the factorylike designs of the Constructivist artists Lyubov Popova (for *The Magnanimous Cuckold* and *Earth Rampant*), Alexander Rodchenko (*The Bedbug*), and Varvara Stepanova (*The Death of Tarelkin*). But wasn't that a new kind of temple, a new kind of mystical communion for the dawning age of the revolutionary industrial proletariat? "I am happy about the revolution," he had declared. "It has turned the theater upside down. And only now is it possible to begin the work of building a new altar."[100]

"True Resurrection and transformation"

Because Stalin violently halted the creative surge in Russian theater that had begun in the Silver Age, the lasting impact of Stanislavsky and Meyerhold occurred abroad, where almost no theater went untouched by their accomplishments. Sooner or later, actors in such diverse lands as Brazil, China, France, Italy, Holland, Turkey, and Wales became fully conversant with Russian theatrical theory, and stagecraft and repertoire changed dramatically as a result. But England, America, Japan, and Germany best illustrate the global trends.

Before the founding of the MAT, several European theaters had made the first moves toward directorial control and stage realism: The Meiningen Company in Germany (1874), André Antoine's Théâtre Libre in Paris (1887), Otto Brahm's Freie Bühne in Berlin (1889), and J. T. Grein's Independent Theatre in London (1891). Over the next two decades, the writings and productions of Adolph Appia (Switzerland and Germany), Jacques Copeau (France), E. Gordon Craig (England), and Georg Fuchs (Germany) instituted antinaturalist acting and set design with parallels to the Meyerhold Theater. But their labors made little impression on the public until the Russians took the stage and grabbed the attention of the world; with that came the sea change in theater.

The widespread influence of Russian theater in England[101] was the result of developments after World War I: the pessimistic mood; the counterculture's Russian fever; and the decision of director Theodore (originally Fyodor) Komisarjevsky to exile himself to London after the Bolshevik revolution. Although Stanislavsky and, to a lesser extent, Meyerhold had begun to affect dramatic productions in Germany and the United States in the decade preceding World War I, English theater, steeped in stodgy traditions or basking in the West End's commercialism, had remained ignorant of them.

It took the war to open British eyes to the Russians' theatrical revolution, although the spirit of the Ballets Russes had already stimulated some new directions, as witnessed, for instance, in Granville Barker's Shakespeare productions. The postwar mood of disillusionment changed the initial negative perception of Chekhov as bland, melancholic, and incomprehensible; eventually he would occupy the position just below Shakespeare in English-language repertory. George Bernard Shaw was the first to come around, reading Chekhov as a commentary on both the decline of the English aristocracy and bourgeois futility; he patterned his 1919 play *Heartbreak House* after him. He was followed by the antiestablishment intellectuals connected to A. R. Orage's journal *New Age*: short-story author Katherine Mansfield, who introduced the Chekhovian style into English writing, and her husband John Middleton Murry, the Russophile gadfly. Orage sent his theater critic, Huntly Carter, to Moscow in the early twenties. This Theosophist and socialist utopian sent back some of the earliest descriptions of Russian avant-garde dramatic productions. Widely read in theater circles throughout the West, he explained his subject as the agency of the "true Resurrection and transformation of Russia" that had taken place under communism. He wished the same might take place in the West.[102]

It was the Russian émigré Komisarjevsky (1882–1954), however, who made Chekhov accessible to London audiences and was the main interpreter of Russian theatrical developments there. Considered a lesser light at home, he won fame in England by pretending to be the heir to Stanislavsky, who in fact had rejected his application to perform with the MAT. He believed the purpose of theater was not to entertain but to impart "spiritual comfort and warmth of togetherness."[103] But to sell English audiences on Chekhov, he turned the plays into maudlin anglicized melodramas. Besides that, he was the first director to have actors perform Shakespeare in modern dress, a widely copied innovation.[104]

By 1940, Komisarjevsky had established himself in the United States, whose acting community had undergone a conversion to Russian-style dramatics after the American apostles of Stanislavsky crusaded against the twin idols of commercialism and entertainment onstage. But Hollywood and Broadway, far from being vanquished, only gained strength as they appropriated the theatrical theology and weaponry of their foes.[105]

In the United States, proponents of "serious," socially aware drama sparked a revolt against commercial theater and wooden acting, beginning around the turn of the century. Those involved were estranged from Gilded Age America and, being theater people, saw theater as the source of salvation. They turned to the Russian example to find out how an omniscient intellectual elite might shepherd society out of the wilderness of capitalism and bourgeois taste. Overlapping with the Progressive Era and the early formation of an American avant-garde, the "little theater" movement originated in Chicago with the founding of Jane Addams's Hull House Players (1901), followed a decade later by theaters in several other states. Among the enthusiasts were playwrights George Cram Cook and his wife Susan Glaspell. They formed the Provincetown Players (1915), located on Cape Cod before moving to New York's Greenwich Village. The troupe gained fame for staging the early plays of Eugene O'Neill, an admirer of Chekhov and a gloomy Modernist who dwelt on the repressiveness of puritanical America and the psychological harm endured by the individual in modern, materialistic society.[106] A decade later, in the midst of the Roaring Twenties, social reformer Elizabeth Reynolds Hapgood and her husband Norman, the muckraking editor of *Collier's*, *Harper's*, and *Hearst International* magazines, set out to found the University Players at a party hosting Nemirovich-Danchenko. Opening in 1928, this was to be a "Moscow Art"–type summer stock company based at Falmouth, Massachusetts, and run by college theater students—among them the youthful Stanislavsky devotees Henry Fonda, James Stewart, and Joshua Logan, eventual producer/director of *South Pacific* and numerous other postwar stage and film hits.[107]

The trend represented by the two Cape Cod playhouses—widely imitated in communities all across America—owed something to western European examples. But Russia was the primary stimulus. The earliest glimpse of Stanislavskian psychological acting in the United States came in 1905 when Paul Orlenov and his wife Alla Nazimova arrived to perform for Russian-Jewish audiences in New York. Orlenov was an aristocratic stage manager fleeing Russia as a subversive, and Nazimova was a Yiddish actress from Odessa who had performed bit parts with the MAT. Their press agent was the famous anarchist Emma Goldman who, using the pseudonym Emma Smith, milked Andrew Carnegie and J. P. Morgan for the funds needed to sponsor the events.[108] Orlenov, gleefully advertising himself as a suffering Russian artist and victim of a phony Black Hundred assassination attempt, was the first to stage Chekhov and Gorky in America. So successful were the shows that they propelled Nazimova (1879–1945) into Hollywood stardom as a silent film actress and bathing beauty. She owed her financial success to her ability to veil her rank commercialism with an aura of taste and style she brought with her from Russia, anticipating the way Hollywood in general would co-opt the Stanislavsky legacy.[109]

American audiences did not get to see the real thing until much later. Oliver Sayler, a drama critic for papers in Indianapolis and Boston, had been to Russia after the revolution and churned out articles reporting that Soviet theater had achieved the spiritual revolution promised but not fulfilled by classical Athens, Renaissance Italy, and Wagner's Germany.[110] He urged Morris Gest, the impresario responsible for Kosloff's counterfeit Ballets Russes, to arrange the MAT's American tour, which commenced at Al Jolson's Fifty-ninth Street Theater in January 1923. Despite the fact that not a single performance was in English, box-office receipts broke all existing Broadway records. Over the next sixteen months, the company put on 380 Russian-language productions of thirteen plays in twelve cities.[111] That was followed in 1925 by the arrival of Nemirovich-Danchenko's Musical Studio; both had an immediate impact on acting and repertory in the United States.[112]

It was not only because so many people saw them perform. Elizabeth Hapgood began to translate Stanislavsky. His manual *An Actor Prepares* (1936), which she had published, sold in the hundreds of thousands and in the next thirty years went through more than twenty printings. This and other works were the bibles of acting technique, "read and re-read by all serious American drama students."[113] Even earlier, two of the actors performing with the MAT had remained in the States and begun to teach the Stanislavsky System. They were Richard Boleslawski (1889–1937) and Maria Ouspenskaya (1876–1949), who both joined the American Laboratory Theater (ALT) in New York from 1923 until they moved to Hollywood later in the decade. There, he became a director for MGM and Fox studios, and she a successful actress. Boleslawski's lectures were the earliest authentic source of information about Russian acting techniques available in the United States; indeed, the ALT was formed specifically to propagate them. One of his students reminisced that those attending his lessons on Stanislavsky felt that they were witnessing the "coming of a new religion which could liberate and awaken American culture."[114]

Among those students were Elia Kazan and Lee Strasberg, both of whom played a major role in the creation of a "distinctive American style of acting."[115] In his memoirs, Kazan writes that he, Strasberg, and their associates were "all Russophiles then."[116] Strasberg, who had made the decision to become an actor upon seeing the MAT performances of 1923 in New York, became the most stringent disciple of Stanislavsky in the United States. Together with like-minded idealists, including director Harold Clurman, another Boleslawski student, Strasberg and Kazan formed the Group Theater in 1931 as a stage collective dedicated to acting as an exploration of inner emotional impulses, and to plays of social significance.

During the Great Depression it went in for politicized productions in the Meyerhold vein.

Here and at the subsequent Actor's Studio, founded after the Second World War, Strasberg emerged as the high priest of what he called the "Method," his own version of Stanislavsky's System, which introduced Freudian elements nonexistent in the original and gave preference to "the mumble, scratch, and slouch" as the means of revealing character in performance.[117] Among his students were Marlon Brando, James Dean, Paul Newman, and Marilyn Monroe; she, one might be surprised to know, spoke often of Stanislavsky, whose ideas Strasberg had drilled into her.[118] The Method approach was also apparent in Kazan's blockbuster stage productions of Tennessee Williams and Arthur Miller, both playwrights who considered Chekhov to be their dramatic forebear.[119]

The "Method" was widely criticized for shifting focus toward individual emotions and away from the play as a whole, as well as for Strasberg's rigid, Freudian interpretation of the MAT, which diverged from the latter's metaphysical emphasis. Still, the "Method" became the most widely taught drama technique in American acting schools. For some observers it is ironic that although Stanislavsky had intended artistic commitment to replace the quest for wealth and stardom among actors, even the most dedicated and politicized adherents of the MAT approach in America easily succumbed to the lure of Hollywood and Broadway.[120] That may be true, but there is another side to the story: wholesale adoption of Russian theatrics significantly raised the quality of American film and popular theater and conditioned mass audiences to embrace cerebral drama such as offered by O'Neill, Williams, and Miller.

In Japan, too, Stanislavsky and the MAT played a leading role in modernizing theater in the Meiji and Taisho eras, that period of rapid change when the country's intelligentsia also warmed to Russian anarchism, literature, and painting.[121]

After the turn of the century, Japanese theatrical personalities with knowledge of European drama and a desire to capture the traumas of contemporary life onstage attacked Kabuki, the traditional Japanese theater, for its clumsy, stylized acting and outmoded sets. The main figure in the development of Shingeki, or the modern theater movement, was Osanai Kaoru (1881–1928), founder of the Free Theater (1909–1919) and the Tsukiji Little Theater (1924–1929). In 1912–1913, he left Tokyo to spend nine months in Europe. It was Moscow that impressed him most. Although he did not comprehend a word of Russian, he was able to see Stanislavsky's company perform and meet the director; he had wanted to do so since 1910, when he staged a version of Gorky's *The Lower Depths*, guided by postcards of the MAT production. Upon returning to Japan, he wrote authoritatively on the MAT's stage effects and acting style, and used his memory of what he had observed to direct the plays of Chekhov, as well as more Gorky and Japanese works in the Russian manner. One of his star actresses— Higashiyama Chieko—was a Japanese diplomat's wife who, living in Moscow, had became entranced by its theater.

Osanai and his reform-minded compatriots were taken with Chekhov in a way that reflected Japanese Modernist sensibilities. For them, his plays offered subtle critiques of an authoritarian, class-based, industrializing system, while escaping the notice of censors. Like the rest of Russian literature, Chekhov's works could be interpreted as non-Western insofar as they seemed to subordinate the individual to the group. When toward the end of his career Osanai reconciled with the traditionalists and called for a synthesis of Kabuki and Shingeki, he saw the suggestiveness and gesturing of Chekhovian drama as providing a bridge between the two schools.

By the time of Osanai's death, Japanese drama schools and theaters were rearing an entire young generation of actors on Chekhov, Stanislavsky, and also Meyerhold, whose borrowings from Kabuki made him particularly accessible to the Japanese. After the war, as in so many other nations, the Stanislavsky System came into its own in theater and cinema. Filmmaker Kurosawa Akira serves as the best example. As a youth he regularly attended Osanai's productions, which left a lasting impression on him. Later, he directed several films based on Russian classics reset in Japan and adopted the whole array of Stanislavsky's techniques to extract from his actors an inner awareness of their roles.

If in Japan, America, and England Stanislavsky's importance grew steadily, in Germany his prestige was initially strong, but conditions there were such that interest in the MAT waned over time. The Moscow Art Theater received accolades from the press, the public, and Kaiser Wilhelm on its sold-out 1906 German tour through Berlin, Dresden, Düsseldorf, Leipzig, Prague, and Vienna. Playwright Gerhard Hauptmann wept during the performances and proclaimed the actors the "gods of art."[122] But the MAT's indirect influence had already begun several years earlier, thanks to Max Reinhardt (1873–1943), the Viennese-Jewish actor who had become Germany's most renowned theatrical director. Brilliantly eclectic, he kept his ear to the ground for the latest innovations, especially those coming out of Russia, whose theater he held in the highest regard. He had his first big triumph in Berlin with three hundred performances of Gorky's *The Lower Depths*, which he selected after learning of its success at the MAT; Chekhov and Tolstoy soon also entered his wide international repertory. Reinhardt corresponded with Stanislavsky and followed his example to help raise the quality of German acting. A few years later, his shows would begin to mirror Diaghilev's antinaturalist ballets and extravagant sets.[123]

The next time the MAT visited Germany, however, in late 1921, it met with almost complete indifference. This contrasts with the enthusiasm of its followers in the United States and England; but, then, in the aftermath of the war, German culture had been radicalized to an extent not seen elsewhere in the West. It was Meyerhold who stole the show in the avant-garde theater community of the Weimar Republic.[124]

To be sure, twentieth-century avant-garde theater all over the world was indebted to Meyerhold, who led the way in abandoning all "external realism . . . in favor of a 'true' super-realism, which depicts the essence rather than outward appearance."[125] This was especially true of nonrepresentational political theater in the United States and elsewhere, which borrowed techniques from Meyerhold much earlier than is often recognized.[126] But nowhere was his voice so resonant as in Germany, where his two greatest emulators were Erwin Piscator (1893–1966) and Bertolt Brecht (1898–1956).

Both of these men who were among the fathers of experimental Modernist theater borrowed to a significant degree from Meyerhold's stage.[127] Piscator and Brecht drew on rich German theatrical theories and innovations going back to Wagner, but many of the features of Weimar's avant-garde dramatics associated with their names also came from Meyerhold: machinelike Constructivist sets, exposed stage mechanisms, flashing lights, projection of newsreels or captions, a greater emphasis on stylized and depersonalized acting—in other words, many of the devices of retheatricalized theater. These were for them the means of production onstage, capable of raising the political consciousness of spectators and expressing the politically militant, anticapitalist, anti-individualist, pro-communist themes of the plays they presented.

One scholar has denied that Piscator knew much of Meyerhold's work.[128] Brecht himself never acknowledged his debt to it, perhaps because of his ego, perhaps because of the dangers involved for an East German communist to link his name to Meyerhold, executed as an "enemy of the people." But Meyerhold's accomplishments had been highly publicized and praised for years in Germany. Piscator's literary collaborator, Dadaist writer Franz Jung, had traveled to Russia immediately after the revolution. He and others brought back news of Meyerhold, upon whom the German avant-garde's utopian expectations were projected. Numerous reports circulated in drama journals, socialist newspapers, and lectures hosted by German-Soviet friendship organizations. Many were completely fantastic: this great Eastern theatrical genius, some of the accounts claimed, had brought theater into the streets, achieved true unity between actors and spectators, and offered salvation from the woes of modern existence.

The same press celebrated Meyerhold in 1930 when he brought his company to Berlin (performing, among other works, Tretyakov's *Roar China!*), and no one involved in theater could have missed the posters, accompanying speeches, and extensive reviews. After that, the avant-garde cultural elite of Germany and the world streamed to the Meyerhold Theater. Lee Strasberg, Gordon Craig,

Diego Rivera, André Malraux, Chinese director Mei Lanfang were among those making the pilgrimage to Moscow in the next few years. So were Piscator and Brecht.

By that time Brecht was already quite familiar with Meyerhold. At the Munich Kammerspiele he had become close to Asja Lacis, a Soviet actress who had worked with Meyerhold and went back and forth between Germany and the USSR. In the early 1920s, Brecht learned the particulars of Russian avant-garde theater from her and her husband, the actor Bernhard Reich. In 1928 Brecht and Soviet cultural commissar Anatoly Lunacharsky met in Berlin and discussed Meyerhold. Brecht saw the 1930 performances of the Meyerhold ensemble and garnered even more information about it during visits to Moscow in 1932, 1935, and 1936. In 1935 he stayed in Moscow with Meyerhold's associate, the playwright Tretyakov, and together they visited Victor Shklovsky, the literary critic who coined the term "making strange" (in Russian *ostranenie*). Tretyakov (and possibly Shklovsky) explained the significance of the expression to Brecht, and from that point on, Brecht began using a German translation of the term, *Verfremdungseffekt*, which became the mantra of his theater and its many international offshoots. Translated into English as "alienation effect," the term lost its connection to the original Russian concept. Thereby was the Russian paternity of the defamiliarization technique obscured.

Peter Brook, the leading postwar British director, once stated that "Brecht is the key figure of our time, and all theatre work today at some point starts or returns to his statements and achievements."[129] In light of the preceding, it seems time to revise that assessment to take Meyerhold and Stanislavsky into account.

Russian theater and ballet left a distinctive imprint on the cultural life of the twentieth century. In painting and design, too, the Russian artistic revolution extended to the entire world.

CHAPTER 7

Abstract Art and the

Regeneration of Mankind

FROM 1910 on, Russian visual artists cease-
lessly pushed the limits of the artistic firmament, creating abstract,
formalist works in order to zero in on what they assumed to be, in
the words of Kandinsky, the universal "truth which only art can
divine [and] . . . express."[1]

It would be impossible in the space available to unravel every
strand linking Russian and world avant-garde artists.[2] Here we will
focus attention on those Russians who had the greatest effect on
the development of modern art: Vasily Kandinsky, the practitioner
and theorist of abstractionism; Kazimir Malevich, the founder of
Suprematism; Alexander Rodchenko, the most eminent Constructivist; and El Lissitzky, who amalgamated Suprematism and Constructivism and was the disseminator-in-chief of Soviet avant-garde
art to the wider world.

All four believed that art could depict philosophical verities,
"lofty emotions beyond the reach of words."[3] And artists more
than any other subspecies of man possessed the ability to grasp
those truths. "Priest[s] of beauty," they expected their art to point
humanity in the direction of the light that only they as artists perceived.[4] To do so, these heirs of the Russian Silver Age and witnesses of European Post-Impressionism opted for the formalist aesthetic of abstractionism.

Their Neoplatonic Idealism, collectivism, and attachment to either anarchism or Marxism marked them as members of the Russian intelligentsia longing to see the fractures of society overcome.

However, their artistic radicalism also had a complex relationship to their social origins as outsiders in a nation dominated until 1917 by the St. Petersburg elite. Like many members of the avant-garde, they were of non-Russian or mixed ethnic heritage and spent most of their lives outside of the prerevolutionary capital.[5] Kandinsky (1866–1944) was born into a wealthy tea-merchant family in Moscow and grew up in the volatile boomtown of Odessa. His ancestry was a mixture of Russian, Baltic German, and Mongolian. Malevich (1878–1935), born and raised in Ukraine, was of Polish origin; his father was a factory foreman in the sugar-processing industry. Rodchenko (1891–1956) was born in St. Petersburg but moved with his family to Kazan, a Muslim Tatar center on the Volga River. A descendant of serfs from the Smolensk region, his father was a stagehand, his mother a laundress. El Lissitzky (1890–1941) was a Jew who grew up in a middle-class family in the Belorussian city of Vitebsk and attended gymnasium in Smolensk, just outside the Jewish Pale. The artists' provincial and (excepting Kandinsky) non-privileged backgrounds reinforced the lack of sympathy they felt for existing cultural norms, and attuned them to the seismic changes taking place in this society.

Each one of them developed within the broad framework of European Post-Impressionism and owed a large artistic debt to French Cubism, Fauvism, or German Expressionism.[6] But they should not be seen, as they so often are, as merely advancing toward abstraction on a course predetermined by the evolution of Western art. For what distinguished them from their European counterparts and indeed placed them in the driver's seat of artistic Modernism the world over was their origin in imperial Russia, whose social and intellectual climate conditioned their art.

Russian abstractionism did away completely with the three-dimensional naturalism that had prevailed in the arts since the Renaissance. Maurice Tuchman has argued that it was *spiritualism* that caused the emergence of abstract painting, even the geometric variety which bore a similarity to Cubism.[7] The majority of French avant-garde painters were like Picasso and Braque: they rearranged earthly subject matter but never thought of renouncing it altogether. Whereas French artists by and large were uninterested in the occult, the supernatural was the core of most avant-garde art in late imperial Russia. By 1910 the theories and experiments passed down from Dostoevsky, Tolstoy, Russian folk art, Theosophy, the *World of Art*, the Ballets Russes, the MAT, and Meyerhold had congealed into an antirealist aesthetic involving formalism, primitivism, "making strange," distortion, simplification of design, vibrant coloration, and avoidance of surface appearances, all with the purpose of grasping and relaying the essence of universal truth. "Our providential time," prophesied Kandinsky, "is the time of the *great liberation*, liberation . . . from the superficial."[8] The Russian avant-garde fully believed that abstract art forms established a bond with a higher, collective consciousness which represented the underlying unity of mankind and, in making people aware of that, prepared them for spiritual and/or revolutionary transformation.

The first Russian to leave earth behind in his art was Kandinsky, whose abstractionism materialized between 1909 and 1911 in Schwabing, the bohemian arts district of Munich.[9] On this "spiritual island" in the sea of the bourgeoisie, he first obliterated recognizable subject matter in his paintings, works that, in his words, surge with overrunning masses of "primordial color" and the "archipelagic scatter" of paint. He described the effect he was trying to achieve: "Burning zig-zag rays split the air. The skies burst. The ground cleaves." "Space trembles from thousands of voices. The world screams." And these "moments of sudden illumination," he explained, "reveal[ed] with blinding clarity new perspectives, new truths."[10]

Kandinsky mistakenly maintained that he "was the first to break with the tradition of painting existing objects."[11] In truth, others had done so earlier: nineteenth-century Theosophists (during séances) and various artists of a metaphysical bent, including Mikalojus-Konstantinas Ciurlionis of Lithuania, French painter Robert Delaunay, the American Arthur Dove, and Frantisek Kupka, a Czech. But their accomplishments were little known outside their own small circles, whereas Kandinsky's international fame warrants his reputation as the true initiator of abstract art.

Kandinsky did much to establish that reputation himself, as an avant-garde impresario, theorist, and pedagogue. As founder of the Munich Neue Künstlervereinigung (New Artists' Association) in 1909 and two years later the Blaue Reiter (Blue Rider) group, he had become the organizer of Munich Expressionism—his role model, interestingly, being Diaghilev.[12] His own works were shown alongside his confederates' at their various exhibitions, receiving publicity when the press attacked them as the dribblings of the "incurably insane."[13] From 1912 until 1918, Kandinsky's works were marketed by Herwarth Walden, whose leading-edge Berlin Expressionist gallery and journal, *Der Sturm*, guaranteed Kandinsky sales and attention throughout the war years in Germany (despite his return to Russia). In this period his works also traveled to France, Holland, Russia, Switzerland, and the United States.

The *Blue Rider Almanac* and Kandinsky's manifesto of abstractionism, *On the Spiritual in Art*, were both published by the countercultural Piper Press of Munich in early 1912 and sold well.[14] Within two years, the latter went through four German editions. Prior to the appearance of the complete English translation in 1914, Alfred Stieglitz's *Camera Work*, the journal that introduced modern art to America, excerpted Kandinsky's manifesto. So did the British equivalent, Wyndham Lewis's *Blast*, which complimented Kandinsky on his "Blavatskyish soul," referring to the founder of the Theosophical movement.[15] The appearance of a Japanese edition in 1924 is testimony to the rapid globalization of Kandinsky's reputation.

Through Kandinsky's paintings and writings, Russian abstractionist aesthetics floated into the world's consciousness for the first time. Yet it is often assumed that he was more a product of Munich than of Moscow. He did begin his formal study of painting in the former city, under the Slovene painter Anton Azbé, and was not immune either to the occult atmosphere of Schwabing or the artistic styles of German Expressionism and French Fauvism. If there was any place that was prepared for Kandinsky's art and ideas it was Munich.[16] But his Germanness should not be overemphasized: most of Azbé's students and many members of the two art associations led by Kandinsky were Russians, including David and Vladimir Burliuk, Alexei Jawlensky, and Marianne Werefkin. More important, Kandinsky arrived in Germany at age twenty-nine, fully formed as a Russian radical intellectual.

Moscow was his aesthetic homeland, as he stated, "the origin of my artistic ambitions."[17] Originally trained as a lawyer, Kandinsky was drawn by the Populist anarchism of his youth to undertake ethnographic and legal studies of the Russian peasantry. He loved the pagan-Christian syncretism and rich colors of folk art, which he rated higher than academic painting and took to be a sign of the Russian village's spiritual superiority to the rationalist civilization of the West.[18] Not only did this experience encourage him to paint religious and fairy-tale themes; it also pushed him toward abstractionism. Russian peasant artworks, he said, emphasized color to such an extent that "the image in them becomes dissolved."[19] He also compared the effect of his abstract paintings to the misty air in Russian steam baths and to pagan-Slavic shamanistic trances.[20] Of course, all this reflected his Russian Silver Age dissatisfaction with modernity, which he frequently denounced in his writings on art. In his view, "the soul was sick" in the materialistic bourgeois epoch; only abstract art, which was unfettered by earthly objects and revealed the artist's intuition of transcendent truths, could heal it.[21]

Kandinsky's abstractionism was also related to his affinity for synesthesia, an aspect of Symbolism central to his own artistic vision. This was the assumption that correspondences existed among the various branches of the arts, in particular that painting could replicate the psychological effect of music or poetry and vice versa. The concept was derived from the mystical Platonism of Symbolist aesthetics, which assumed that all of the arts were but different emanations of a single divine truth. Kandinsky felt "that painting could develop just such powers as music possesses," and gave his earliest abstractions symphonic titles such as *Composition* or *Improvisation*.[22] The purpose was to achieve "psychic effect" and, through the "spiritual vibration" and "spiritual values" produced by combinations of colors and shapes, to bring the viewer into closer contact with the cosmos as intuited by the superior mind of the artist.[23]

These notions of synesthesia came partly from German Romantic aesthetic theory, as interpreted by Rudolf Steiner, who, with his Russified Baltic-German wife, founded the Anthroposophy cult, a heretical branch of Theosophy. Popular among a segment of the Russian avant-garde, he preached that the "cosmic mission" of a human elite—among them Russian artists—would penetrate the mysteries of the universe and reintegrate humanity with it to achieve universal love as divined by Tolstoy.[24] Kandinsky's Russian roots in the Silver Age made him receptive to these ideas. But they eventually placed him at odds with artist-revolutionaries in Communist Russia.

He returned to his motherland at the start of World War I, and, though he later denied an interest in such a lowly thing as politics, he was initially full of utopian zeal for the Russian Revolution. He participated in various Soviet governmental arts institutions but, unlike many artists, could not reconcile his neo-Romanticism with the materialist ideology and proletarian-oriented aesthetics of the new regime. In 1921 the Bolshevik government sent him to Berlin, as it did other cultural figures, on a mission to establish sympathy for the USSR among German artists. Feeling more at ease there, he stayed, having been invited to join the faculty of the Weimar Bauhaus, the radical design institute.

Back in Germany, his style shifted away from unshaped liquidity to a preference for distinct lines and geometric forms, especially circles: "I love circles today in the same way that previously I loved . . . horses—perhaps even more, since I find in circles more inner possibilities."[25] This new style corresponded to the theory he taught at the Bauhaus associating specific shapes with specific colors, sounds, and moral values.[26]

He never abandoned his mystical utopianism. In line with many postwar European trends, he remained a philosophical Idealist seeking to eliminate the subjective from his art to reach permanent, elemental reality—as he put it, the "illusion of cosmic infinity" on canvas.[27] His goal at the Bauhaus was to create "new men," artists

17. Vasily Kandinsky, *Yellow-Red-Blue* (1925). Courtesy of Artists' Rights Society, New York.

who would usher in the forthcoming "epoch of the spirit."[28] And he never lost his belief that salvation would come from the East— that is, from Russia.[29]

When the Nazis came to power, Kandinsky, an anti-Semite like so many other Russians of his background, tried to stay in Germany by urging that control of the Bauhaus be given to Alfred Rosenberg, but as a "degenerate" artist and suspected Russian communist he was forced to leave.[30] After he settled in France in 1934, the influence (which he denied) of his friends Jean Arp, Joan Miró, and other Abstract Surrealists led him to increasingly soften his geometricity with the inclusion of amoebalike biomorphic shapes. He died in 1944; soon thereafter, his works began fetching prices approximating those of Picasso.

The geometrical attributes of Kandinsky's Bauhaus years had begun to appear during the Russian Revolution, when he fell under the influence of the Suprematist painter Malevich, also one of the earliest abstractionists.[31] Malevich was more like the younger generation of Russian avant-garde artists than was Kandinsky. Although apparently warm and lighthearted in person, in his writings he comes off as a rough-edged, angry figure who would attack his artist-enemies in the crudest of terms. He heaped contempt on Benois (in a personal letter) as an "old elephant" and exhorted his peers to "spit on the old dress [of *World of Art* painting] and put new clothes on art."[32]

Malevich had little formal education of any kind but apprenticed as a painter in Moscow studios. He passed quickly through a variety of Post-Impressionist phases. His preferred subject matter was rural Russia, but around 1913 he turned to urban scenes that are among the most effective evocations of movement in modern painting. Simultaneously, he produced absurdist paintings with collage effects that indicate his growing interest in transcending the limitations of rational thought.

These stylistic shifts were way stations en route to the extreme form of abstractionism he arrived at in 1915 and exhibited for the first time in Petrograd at *0,10. The Last Futurist Exhibition*. His *Black Square* so excited him, he said, that he could not eat or sleep for an entire week after it was conceived. This was followed by hundreds of drawings and paintings of one-color geometrical shapes, including a barely discernable, off-center white quadrangle delineated on top of the canvas's painted all-white background. Other works followed, with squares and circles menaced by triangles, pierced by lines, and overlapped by rectangular planes, all seeming to float in space.

The square, Malevich declared, was the "icon of reductivism."[33] He treated it as a work of sacred art, appropriating the position that Orthodox icons held by hanging his paintings of plain squares high in the corners of rooms according to Russian peasant custom. He took inspiration from the bold colors and flat forms of traditional Russian religious painting. His geometrical abstractions were neo-Idealist icons, beacons along the "crossroads of . . . celestial paths."[34] The square stood for the pure, Ideal universe of which the Silver Age dreamed—hence his choice of the term Suprematism to describe his art, from the Latin *supremus*, meaning ultimate or absolute. *White Square on White* (1918) depicted absolute nothingness, the ultimate reality farthest removed from the earth: "I have conquered the lining of the heavenly. . . . Sail forth! The white, free chasm, infinity is before us!"[35]

Besides Orthodox iconography and the Modernist viewpoint we are already familiar with, Malevich's paintings manifest his fidelity to the Theosophical theories of Pyotr Ouspensky (1878–1947), a Russian mystical philosopher, and Charles Howard Hinton, an Anglo-American mathematician and inventor of a baseball-pitching machine. They argued that the third dimension was a misperception of reality on the part of modern man's shallow rationalism. True reality existed in a higher fourth dimension, and art was a means of making it visible to the masses who could not easily comprehend it. Following their lead, Malevich reasoned that if the third dimension was an illusion, it would be better to avoid it in

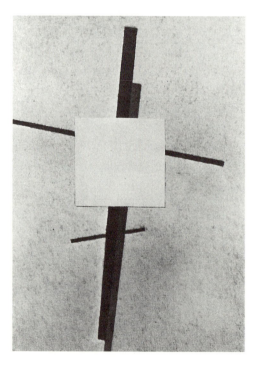

18. Kazimir Malevich, Suprematist painting (1919). From El Lissitzky and Hans Arp, *Die Kunstismen* (Erlenbach-Zürich, 1925).

one's artwork and instead visualize objective reality in two-dimensional painting, which he understood as an "expression of passage into the fourth dimension"![36] He felt that he was a messiah chosen to lead the way there through painted squares: "Tens of thousands of years have prepared my birth," he proclaimed.[37]

Malevich, whose hostility to modernity was a product of the Russian Silver Age, expected that contemplating the higher, immaterial realm would help "overcome our endless progress." In other words, it would bring to an end the chaos and conflict associated with modern technology and capitalism, which have "held up at every step the path of [man's intuition]," the "kernel" of the boundless universe planted inside him.[38] Like many other members of the Russian intelligentsia, he harbored a delusional understanding of freedom and the individual. Deprive man of private property and he will be liberated from earthly concerns, he thought, able to gain the "maximum freedom" that comes from submitting himself to the "infinity of space" glimpsed in those paintings of squares.[39]

Perhaps not surprisingly, Malevich was slow to grasp the threat posed by the Communist dictatorship to his art. For a few years after 1917, he spread his Suprematist message with missionary zeal at the Vitebsk School of Art directed by Marc Chagall—whom Malevich elbowed out in an academic/ideological power play. He and his students, wearing armbands with black squares, decorated the streets with Suprematist shapes, to the befuddlement of the masses whose collective consciousness they were supposed to raise. His designs, when applied to porcelain, architectural models, and propaganda posters, did, however, appeal to the avant-garde artists, who also attended his lectures and read his proclamations. But under the Stalinist dictatorship, this mystagogue and political anarchist found himself increasingly sidelined, yet also forbidden to emigrate. In 1935, he died of cancer, borne to infinity in a coffin of his own design, adorned with the Suprematist black circle and square.

Malevich may have become persona non grata, but the geometrical designs of Suprematism were taken over by Constructivism, the ascendant avant-garde current within early revolutionary Russia.[40] This movement took shape between 1913 and 1921, originating in the three-dimensional "constructions" of Malevich's rival and admirer Vladimir Tatlin (1885–1953), once a Ukrainian sailor, and two Russian-Jewish brothers originally from Bryansk, Naum Gabo (1890–1977) and Antoine Pevsner (1886–1962). Alexander Rodchenko and El Lissitzky soon became the most visible practitioners of Constructivism, but by the early 1920s it had attracted so many artists and architects that this chapter can only hint at its diversity and complexity.

Constructivists renounced easel painting as a relic of the bourgeois age that they were expecting to shove into oblivion. Tatlin started out as an antinaturalist neoprimitivist painter, but on a trip to Paris in 1914, he met Picasso, whose collages inspired him to move beyond paints; this indicates the strong influence French Cubism exerted on the Constructivists. Tatlin began to create reliefs and three-dimensional objects out of metals, cardboard, virtually any available materials. The others followed his lead. Their early formalist experiments—abstract, volumetric, dimension-defying metal or wooden sculptures and mobiles called spatial or hanging constructions—strove to capture a sense of the dynamism of modern life as in Russian and Italian Futurist painting; to convey perfect universal realms outside of nature; and to combine the various media and genres of art as expressions of synthesism.

After the Russian Revolution the movement as a whole hitched itself to Bolshevik ideology and touted a utilitarian, antiaesthetic notion of art dedicated to the proletarian masses. The artists believed their work should entail a "new conception of the beautiful" reflecting and glorifying the machine, heavy industry, and Bolshevism.[41] They imparted to their creations a modernistic geometric look—leaning heavily on Suprematist shapes—and preferred to make them out of politically correct industrial materials (although often enough only wood was available). To quote Lissitzky, "*Iron* is strong like the will of the proletariat, *glass* is clear, like its conscience."[42] Some declared, "Death to art!" because it was "indissolubly linked with theology, metaphysics, and mysticism."[43] Disavowing the artist-mystics of the capitalist dark ages, they thought of themselves as "Constructivist technicians" ushering in the new dawn of Communist industrialism.[44]

What most distinguished them from their avant-garde predecessors was the Constructivists' effort to design and build a new world. But despite this and their adamant Marxist disdain for the ethereal in art, the Constructivists' outlook was not that far removed from the Russian Silver Age. They approached their art with a spiritual intensity that almost seems to have negated their professions of atheism and materialism. Industrialism, Tatlin mused, was a "modern Messiah."[45] What else was all their talk of merging art and life, studio and factory, and devotion to the proletariat but the old Populist and Silver Age rhetoric of universal unity clothed in Constructivist fabric?

To a great extent the same was true of their aesthetics. Central to their art was a concern with *faktura*, or that the surface texture and materials used in their "constructions" reveal intrinsic properties of "Communistic expression" and "elements of industrial-culture."[46] But what they were doing was no different from the endeavor of their formalist precursors: attempting to capture the inner essence of an object in order to glimpse absolute Truth, and "making strange" through the artistic manipulation of texture in order to convey a new perspective on reality, to render visible the invisible "building blocks of the world."[47]

The sociopolitical didacticism of the Constructivists was also similar to the Russian avant-garde going back to the *World of Art*. Their reverence for industrial technology coexisted with a fierce hatred of bourgeois capitalism and suggested a utopian conviction that Russia, unlike the West, could construct a perfect, collectivist society. Their shift away from the anti-industrialism and anarchism of the earlier avant-garde was a result of the formation of a Marxist regime with a pro-industrial ideology and little tolerance for anyone who disagreed with it. The most fantastic "revolutionary dreams" swept the land, and the artists, in an ecstasy of Bolshevism, clamored for social engineering.[48] Witnessing the destruction of the old regime at the hands of the Bolsheviks, the Constructivists acted with the conviction that they as artists now had the chance to refashion the world in accordance with their visions. Lissitzky announced that the purpose of the artist was "not to embellish life,

19. El Lissitzky, *Proun 1 E: The City* (1921). From Sophie Lissitzky-Küppers, *El Lissitzky* (Dresden, 1976). Courtesy of Artists' Rights Society.

but rather to organize it."[49] Constructivists believed that geometrically composed works of art created out of modern materials would "urbanize the psychology of the masses" and foster an environment conducive to the establishment of Communist collectivism.[50]

Lissitzky's "Prouns" exemplify both the persistence of the Silver Age mentality and the new transitions taking place within the early Soviet avant-garde. Having once converted from the Orthodox Judaism of his youth to Suprematism, after 1917 Lissitzky forsook that faith, too, for Constructivism. All of the components of the movement—*faktura*, "making strange," revolutionary didacticism, Suprematist geometricity, synthesism—were at play in the Prouns. A sui generis art form whose name stood for "Proekt utverzhdeniia novogo" (Project for the Affirmation of the New), these

were large-scale Malevichian architectural models, futuristic geometrical drawings, and three-dimensional reliefs displayed in a series of rooms either on stands or attached to the walls. Lissitzky
conceived of them as "true model[s] of perfection" that would
stimulate viewers' extrasensory perceptions of both the fourth dimension and the Marxian dialectic, the lights within that bespoke
the promise of a revolutionary heaven on earth.[51]

Rodchenko, too, labored in his studio to prepare the consciousness of the masses for the new era. He devised multifunctional,
collapsible, modular furniture, each piece of which was to serve a
variety of uses, whether as seat or shelf. These and all his other
designs for the working class were pared down to the basic skeletal
apparatus: the stool in his worker's club, consisting of three thin
planks spaced around the semicircular seat and armrest, looks like
the wooden undergirdings of a chair. To some extent, the point was
to economize on the use of materials, the better to provide for the

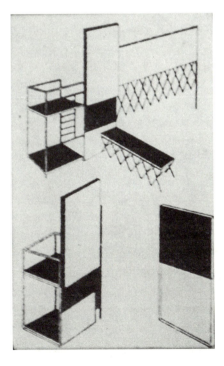

20. Alexander Rodchenko, designs
for folding furniture. From *Sovremen-
naia arkhitektura*, no. 1 (1926).

masses in a poor society. But the true purpose was to surround the proletariat with modern, geometrical objects that were, to the extent possible, nonindividualistic in function so that the working class might more easily acclimatize to a collective existence in the socialist age. The same motive lay behind Constructivist textiles and ceramics—often decorated with distinctly Suprematist forms.

The hugely influential innovations of Rodchenko and Lissitzky in typography and photography amplify the didactic and politicized aesthetic of Constructivism as well as its continued debt to Suprematism. Typography and photography appealed to Constructivists as machine-based branches of art. Lissitzky, a former Hebrew calligrapher and book illustrator, applied the geometrical forms of his teacher Malevich to the printed page. Rodchenko, too, acknowledged that Suprematism influenced his own contribution to this bold new visual language that revolutionized graphic design throughout the world. Block letters; separation of text and images in a sharp-edged, geometrical, often asymmetrical layout; flat colors;

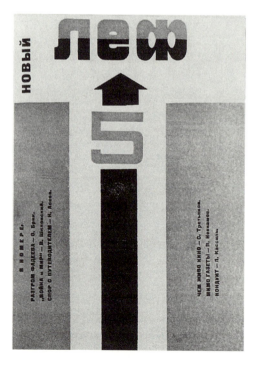

21. Alexander Rodchenko, the new typography. Cover of the journal *Novyi lef* (May 1928).

and superimposition of bold triangles, squares, circles, arrows, or exclamation points to emphasize headings or blocks of text: all of these were the features providing a strong, declamatory, and modern-looking alternative to the traditional overcluttered printed page with its ornate lettering. Rodchenko and Lissitzky wanted the ubiquitous presence of these new graphic principles in the mass media to have a steady subliminal effect on the consciousness of the people.

In photography the goal was also to act upon the outlook of the masses. Conveying a new perspective on reality was common to all aspects of Constructivism and is implicit in the concept of *faktura*. Rodchenko was a master of this as well as the defamiliarizing technique in photography. He had been inspired by Berlin Dadaism to try his hand at photomontage. But finding that he lacked photographs, he began to shoot them himself; his technique was to take pictures of recognizable objects from completely unexpected angles, eliminating normal notions of perspective. Published in popular magazines and avant-garde journals such as Mayakovsky's *Lef*, his photographs, he maintained, would ready people for the new revolutionary society by encouraging them to look at the world in a new light. Utilizing the new photography, Rodchenko, El Lissitzky, and fellow artist Gustav Klutsis (another former Malevich student) produced compelling Modernist propaganda posters, often allied with photomontage and Constructivist typographical styles.

By the late 1920s and early 1930s Constructivism had run its course. Together, Soviet disinvestment in consumer goods production; the petit bourgeois cultural tastes of the apparatchik elite; the dictator's preference for bombastic "Stalinist Gothic" architecture; and the one-party state's mistrust of artists who did not toe the Socialist Realist line all did the movement in. Disabused of their utopian ideals and under pressure from the regime, but also motivated by a negative impression of Western capitalism during the Great Depression, Lissitzky and Rodchenko deployed Constructivist photographic and graphic arts techniques in the service of the state, idealizing the forced industrialization of the Five-Year Plans in their propaganda art.

The Russian avant-garde was dead, but its artistic style survived after being taken over by the Soviet regime, intent on "rebranding" itself as supermodern. As will become apparent, it served remarkably similar functions abroad, in both fascist and Western capitalist settings.

"The objects of our environment have become repulsive to us"

Kandinsky's original impact on European Modernism predated World War I and was concurrent with that of the Ballets Russes. After the great conflagration of 1914–1918 it merged with the Russian Revolution's promise of redemption and the art of Suprematism and Constructivism to permeate in some fashion or other nearly every form of abstract or formalist art.

22. Alexander Rodchenko, photograph of glassware, in *Novyi lef* (March 1928).

Aside from the impression his own writings and paintings made, Kandinsky's influence seeped into the avant-garde through the filter of Swiss Dadaism, which gave rise to, or at least set the rebellious tone of, many trends in modern art down to the late twentieth century.[52] It originated in the Cabaret Voltaire, founded in Zurich in 1915 by a number of draft-dodging poets and artists, chief among them a German, Hugo Ball (1886–1927). The Dadaists insisted that war and capitalism had debased European civilization and corrupted its languages and art forms: "God is dead," declared Ball, "a thousand-year-old culture disintegrates. There are no columns and supports, no foundations any more—they have all been blown up."[53] Like philosopher Ludwig Wittgenstein at the same time, he concluded that renewal required rejection of established culture and creation of a completely new language. With much of the rest of the counterculture, he extolled primitivism as an escape from an insane modern world. And he conducted radical linguistic experiments with poems of pure sounds which, without any preconceived meaning—that is, the taint of civilization—were supposed to contain traces of primal sacred truth.

Ball was a German pacifist whose politics had led him to read Bakunin, Kropotkin, Tolstoy, and from there the works of Russian Symbolists and occultists. By 1912 he had befriended Kandinsky in Munich. Ball said Kandinsky brought him "liberation, solace, redemption, and peace."[54] Impressed by Kandinsky's prognostications of salvation through abstract art, Ball applied the Russian painter's antirepresentationalist, transrational concepts to poetry. Referring to Kandinsky's art, he wrote that "the image of the human form is gradually disappearing from the painting of these times. . . . This is one more proof of how ugly and worn the human countenance has become, and of how all of the objects of our environment have become repulsive to us. The next step is for poetry to do away with language for similar reasons."[55] He went beyond Italian Futurist Marinetti, another influence on him, who had freed up syntax; Ball and the Swiss Dadaists separated words from all accepted meaning in order to convey, in Kandinsky's terms, those spiritual "inner sounds."

The Cabaret Voltaire's eclectic and bizarre readings, performances, art exhibits, and publications often featured Kandinsky's works. His influence spread directly through the many cultural figures who saw them, and indirectly via the output of the Dadaists themselves—to Surrealism, for instance, whose name came from Apollinaire's description of a Ballets Russes production as "beyond real." In connection with Kandinsky's participation in a Paris exhibition featuring the Surrealists, the *Sixième Salon des Surindépendants* (1933), Jean Arp identified him as a "leader of the Surrealist procession."[56] While this statement was true in the sense that Kandinsky's antirealist artistry had helped to set that movement in motion, it was clear at the time that much also separated him from it. The philosophy of the Surrealists, leaning heavily on Freud, left most of them ill at ease with Kandinsky's underlying Idealism and formalism. Their emphasis on the randomness of the individual human psyche was completely alien to Kandinsky, who thought of his art as a manifestation of an unchanging spiritual realm; if their understanding of "inner necessity" was psychoanalytic, his was metaphysical.

Dissociating himself from Surrealism, Kandinsky, then in his geometric phase, labeled his art "concrete" to signify that it represented permanent higher reality. So did his fellow European abstractionists of the interwar years, most of them neo-Idealists who endeavored to portray the constants of an orderly universe rather than the chaos of a world gone to pieces or the dreams of the fickle mind. In the painters' war that ensued between Surrealists as chroniclers of ever-mutating subconscious processes and abstractionists as scrutinizers of the eternal Absolute, Salvador Dali derisively dismissed Kandinsky as a second-rate painter who "might have made marvelous cloisonné enamel cane heads."[57] According to Joan Miró, others called his paintings "woman's handiwork."[58]

The hostilities went far beyond Kandinsky versus the Surrealists. It was an internecine conflict that divided Modernist artists into the opposing camps of inward-looking emotionalists and upward-looking Idealists. The Russian avant-garde fought alongside western European formalist allies. These artists spearheaded a broad abstract-art front eventually termed the "International Style" (coined by American architect Philip Johnson), but which can also be called "Constructivist" to more accurately reflect its origins. With the Soviet avant-garde, the German Bauhaus, French Purism, and the Dutch *De Stijl* movement were the proponents of this machine-precise, geometrical aesthetic that more than any other typified twentieth-century design.

Although the leading figures of the French variant, Le Corbusier and Amédée Ozenfant, were intimately familiar with developments in Russian art and publicized them in their influential journal *L'Esprit nouveau*, they reached a similar Modernist outlook and design scheme independently, with only minimal reference to the Russians (although both spent significant amounts of time in Russia).[59] Not all aspects of avant-garde activity were dependent on Russian antecedents. But it is a different story with the Dutch and Germans: certain sectors of their avant-garde art were closely tied to Kandinsky, Malevich, and Russian Constructivism.

By coincidence, the two most unlike countries of Europe, Russia and Holland, were also the two nations whose avant-gardes most fully embraced abstractionism.[60] The background of Piet Mondrian (1872–1944) suggests that the reason for this lies in an analogous spiritualism. Mondrian's grid-pattern abstractions—as important as Malevich's painting in inspiring all later minimalist geometric art and design—were the culmination of a quest for the essence of absolute truth corresponding to his religious journey from a rigorous Dutch Calvinism to Theosophy and Anthroposophy. His artistic evolution followed, moving from Symbolism and Cubism to complete antinaturalism. Many of Mondrian's artist-contemporaries took a similar path, so that his metaphysical painting was paralleled by abstractionist and formalist developments in Dutch furniture and architectural design that also initially had little to do with Russia—except that as countercultural socialists, most of these artists were attracted to Russian-anarchist communitarianism and, later, communism.

But Russian avant-garde art soon flooded the country. Mondrian had been the major theoretician of the journal *De Stijl* in its first

few years after 1917, but once he departed for Paris, its founder,
Theo van Doesburg (1883–1931), came out from under Mondrian's shadow to become one of the evangelists of abstractionism
in Europe. Van Doesburg's artistic career was bound up with the
Russians. The influence of Kandinsky in Holland had grown apace
between 1912 and 1914 with publication of his book and center-
stage showings at modern art exhibitions in Amsterdam. After
reading *On the Spiritual in Art*, van Doesburg abandoned his con-
ventional approach to painting, became a Mondrian acolyte, and
visited Kandinsky in Munich. By 1920 he and *De Stijl* architect
Cornelis van Eesteren had discovered El Lissitzky, whom van Doesburg found to be working "in our spirit."[61] Through both Lissitzky's own followers in the Netherlands and the publicity van Doesburg gave him, Russian Constructivist influence on the Dutch
avant-garde of the 1920s was pervasive. Van Eesteren designed his
famous antiperspectival, primary-colored, block-like houses as re-
alizations of Lissitzky's Prouns; van Doesburg amalgamated the
principles of Malevich and Mondrian in his "Elementarist" paintings—geometrical abstractions with a diagonal emphasis derived
from Suprematism to insinuate spiritual uplift. All of the radical
artists of *De Stijl* believed that the transformation of soul and society was contingent on man's direct interaction with abstract art;
this idea, too, they took over from the Russian formalist artists.

In the immediate aftermath of the Russian Revolution, the art
of the *De Stijl* group was stimulated by positive impressions of
early Bolshevism—as well as by familiarity with Kandinsky, Malevich, and other individual Russian painters. This was the case
throughout the avant-garde movements of the world, made up as
they were of antiestablishment rebels. But it was the Germans who
exhibited the most frenzied enthusiasm for the Russian Revolution
and its art.[62]

Many of the Weimar German avant-garde artists had once had
allegiances to anarchism or Theosophy, but after 1917, they turned
to the Red Star in the eastern sky for guidance and revelation. The
socialist utopia was making the great experiment, promising to fulfill their political and aesthetic ideals by obliterating the line sepa-

rating art and life, thereby creating a new man, a new society, a new world. And these German artists fully sympathized with the Russians' relentless hatred of the Western bourgeoisie. Defeat and deprivation had both radicalized and rejuvenated them. Never before in Germany had it been possible to believe that intellectuals and artists would have a hand in creating a completely new society, a feeling left-wing French artists could only envy, as victory in the war had sustained their bourgeois society.[63]

The Russification of art went much further in Germany than anywhere else. Even before the end of the war, exaggerated news of the Russian avant-garde's art for the masses poured into the country. Exuberant German artists fired off letters of greetings to their comrades in Russia and in 1918, inspired by developments there, formed a Workers' Soviet (council) for Art, the Arbeitsrat für Kunst. The chairmen of this organization besotted with utopian collectivism were two architects, Bruno Taut and Walter Gropius, who, confusing dictatorial Bolshevism with libertarian anarchism, assumed that Lenin's goal was to dissolve the state in defense of the freedom of the individual and the principle of nonviolence.

At first, it was the rebellious and liberating mood rather than the specifics of Soviet Russian political and aesthetic philosophies that German artists latched onto. Berlin Dadaists, for example, defined their rejectionist movement as "German Bolshevism" and proclaimed, "Art is dead! Long live the new machine art of Tatlin!"[64] Echoing German interpretations of Dostoevsky, they spoke of the "the embryo of God" existing in "the new European man . . . born in Russia" who they were convinced would soon destroy the "soulless force of the materialistic and militaristic machine."[65] Later, when they actually came to know something about Russian avant-garde art, some of them, like George Grosz—whose main concern was to caricature German brutishness—lost interest; others, like Kurt Schwitters, became Constructivist followers of Lissitzky; and still others took to Socialist Realism.

The Germans became more familiar with Soviet art after 1920. Fairly reliable information appeared in books and art journals, and exhibits and galleries showed the works themselves. Many German artists traveled to Russia—including Grosz, who came back disillusioned. And from the other direction, refugee artists streamed into Berlin—Chagall, Gabo, Kandinsky, and others—disheartened with the turn of events in the Communist dictatorship. There were so many that by 1922 Berlin had virtually supplanted Moscow as the center of the Russian avant-garde.

But not every Soviet artist was an exile—for instance, El Lissitzky, who preached the artistic word of revolutionary Moscow. Having studied in Germany before the war, he had preexisting ties there. With several other Russian-Jewish artists and a Soviet secret-police operative, he assisted in arranging the *First Russian Art Exhibit*, which displayed a thousand pieces of Soviet avant-garde art at the Van Diemen Gallery on Berlin's Unter den Linden in 1922. This was the first Soviet cultural event in Germany since the signing of the Rapallo Pact between the two outcast nations of Europe, and over the next decade it was followed by regular Russian-German joint artistic ventures: steady release of collaborative publications with European artists, guest lectures, Proun exhibits, Soviet propaganda displays, and rallies of international Constructivists which brought together avant-garde artists of that tendency from as far away as Japan. And although centered there, the activity was not limited to Germany: Dutch Communists arranged to bring the Van Diemen exhibit to Amsterdam's Stedelijk Museum in 1923, and the Russian pavilion at the Paris Art Deco exhibition of 1925 made a big splash with the unusual designs of Russian Constructivists Rodchenko and Konstantin Melnikov.[66]

The Kremlin was the invisible hand facilitating these initiatives that linked the Russian and German avant-gardes and helped to lay the groundwork for geometrical abstractionism in modern art. It did so through Communist front organizations, the arts section of the International Workers' Relief (IAH in Germany), and various Societies of the Friends of the New Russia, all under the control of German Comintern member Willi Münzenberg. It was not that Lenin cared about the Soviet avant-garde. But Münzenberg had convinced him to use its international prominence to win sympathy for the USSR among the German and other European intelligentsias so as to balance the influence of anti-Bolshevik émigrés:

"We exist for one purpose—to wage the broadest propaganda campaign for Soviet Russia."[67]

The political results of these efforts are not of concern to us here. But the Van Diemen exhibit and others like it showed the German avant-garde that modern art had made a "breakthrough" in revolutionary Russia, according to filmmaker Hans Richter: "We . . . suddenly saw in the East a whole generation of new artists and ideas for us." Paul Westheim, the leading Berlin critic of the day, hailed these expressions of "eastern barbarism," and German left-wing artists agreed with Lissitzky that the "art of the future" was a "constructive, anti-individualist art" that promised a new epoch both in the arts and for humanity.[68] Precisely these assumptions also activated the German Bauhaus, which, in achieving the "ambitions of the Russian Constructivists," became the main "breeding place" of the International Style.[69]

Through its adaptation by the Bauhaus, Russian avant-garde art can be considered one of the progenitors of twentieth-century applied arts and architecture. During the 1920s this acclaimed German industrial-design school and workshop developed many of the patterns that still prevail in Modernist building types, housewares, furniture, and graphic arts. The Bauhaus is responsible for helping to build the close relationship that exists between artistic design and mass production; both this and its impersonal, severely minimalist, geometrical architectural and design style were to a large extent derived from the aesthetics of Constructivism and related Russian avant-garde currents.[70]

The Bauhaus was established in 1919 in line with German antecedents and the outlook of German intellectuals, but Russian elements were also strong in all phases of its existence. Located in Weimar (later in Dessau, then Berlin), it was to be the successor to the Saxe-Weimar Grand Ducal Applied Arts School headed by Belgian artist Henry van de Velde, who recommended Gropius (1883–1969) to carry on his legacy as its principal. Gropius had pre–World War I professional affiliations with both the German General Electric Company (AEG) and the German Werkbund, a nationalist association of architects, designers, and industrialists dedicated to raising the artistic quality of buildings and manufac-

tured goods. Within the Werkbund, he belonged to the radical socialist faction, which sought to provide cheap but aesthetic mass
housing and factory goods for the working masses.

Influenced by the Blaue Reiter's aspirations toward artistic synthesis and the spiritual unity of mankind, Gropius understood art
as an ethical category that, when applied to industry, would counterbalance the immorality, exploitation, and alienation of capitalism. He and his comrades hoped to transcend the class conflicts
that seemed to plague imperial Germany and all other bourgeois
societies. Some German socialist artists wanted to turn the clock
back and replace the factory system with medieval craft guilds. But
others—Gropius among them—developed a cult of American technological efficiency (shorn of its capitalist underpinnings), which
coexisted with a reverence for Russian Constructivism as a revolutionary art that promised integration between industry and the
masses and an egalitarian, cooperationist future for mankind.

At the time of the school's founding, Gropius was a Bolshevik
sympathizer prominent in both the Arbeitsrat für Kunst and the
Society of Friends of the New Russia. He grew less enamored of
the Soviet system over the course of his nine-year tenure at the Bauhaus and muzzled his school's socialism to ensure the inflow of
commissions from industry, but he remained committed to his original principles. His successor, the Swiss architect Hannes Meyer
(1889–1954), was an Arts and Crafts anarchist until converted to
the International Constructivist Style by his reading of both Le Corbusier's *L'Esprit nouveau* and *ABC*, a building-design magazine
founded in Basel by the ubiquitous Lissitzky and Dutch architect
Mart Stam. Meyer's eventual commitment to communism was such
that after leaving the Bauhaus, he emigrated to the USSR.

If the Bauhaus was initially conceived, according to its founding
manifesto, as a "cathedral to socialism" with only partial reference
to the Russian Revolution, the avant-garde aesthetics of Russian
Constructivism and Suprematism soon came to dominate. Gropius
had been fully informed about developments in Moscow by contacts within the leftist art organizations to which he belonged. He
redirected the Bauhaus's focus away from its initial anarchist-lean-
ing, handicrafts-oriented Expressionism and toward the industrial,

geometric formalism of Constructivism, which he expected would be better able to foster a new collectivist humanity and an industrial system that, tamed by art, benefited man rather than exploited him. The Constructivist style, furthermore, encouraged the full development of the design forms with which he and a few other like-minded German architects and industrial artists had already begun to experiment before World War I.

Gropius also hired Kandinsky to offer basic courses on color theory, abstract form, and analytical drawing; through his teaching, Kandinsky transmitted the Constructivist agenda he had absorbed in Moscow before reemigrating to Germany. The presence of this anti-industrial spiritualist artist at the bastion of what became the severely impersonal International Style is often explained away as stemming from Gropius's wish to hire a "big name" for the struggling school, an avant-garde star whom writers on Russian art had proclaimed throughout Germany as the "Russian Messiah," a "most daring Conquistador . . . of the metaphysical zone," even the "stormtrooper" of the avant-garde.[71] But this explanation overlooks Kandinsky's antipsychological neo-Idealism and shift away from his fluid prewar abstract style. By this time he was closer to the practitioners of the Constructivist/Bauhaus/International Style than to any other avant-garde faction (although he did feel that his intuitive approach separated him from the Constructivists, who denied the soul). Even if he maintained Silver Age doubts about factories, all of his courses at the Bauhaus conveyed trends he had adopted from Constructivism and Suprematism, above all that geometric forms were the most concise and direct means of artistic expression.[72] Partly through his instructional activities, the Bauhaus came to adopt the formal language of the Russian avant-garde and channeled it to much of modern industrial design.

The versatile Hungarian-Jewish artist Laszlo Moholy-Nagy (1895–1946) was another intermediary between Russian Constructivism and the Bauhaus after he was hired in 1923.[73] Hungarian "alternative artists" (mostly anarchists) had come into regular contact with their Russian counterparts during the short-lived post–World War I Hungarian Soviet Republic. Budapest art publications beat the rest of Europe to the press with coverage of Russian developments, and, when the Hungarian Communist regime fell, various artists fled to Berlin with news of the Moscow avant-garde—well before any Russian representatives got there. Moholy was close to these artistic circles, knew the work of Malevich and Lissitzky by 1919, befriended the latter in Berlin in 1921, and corresponded with Rodchenko beginning in 1922. A year later he co-authored a book surveying Russian avant-garde trends with which he sympathized: a neo-Idealist, he felt that individual artistic expression should be eliminated so that art could depict universal constants. By moving the masses to a higher level of consciousness, art would liberate humanity from its narrow perspective, enabling it to comprehend the unity of life and regain wholeness. Following this doctrine, he began taking photographs under Russian formalist, "making strange" influence that challenged visual conventions, and he and Rodchenko shaped each other's photography at different stages. Moholy's work and theoretical writings sparked the Weimar German New Photography movement, which soon led the entire genre worldwide into a new era. Similarly, his kinetic sculptures were indebted to the designs of the Russian Constructivists-in-exile Gabo and Pevsner. Moholy's merit as an artist is indisputable; but a large part of his oeuvre, which by itself served as a pillar of the International Style, consisted of forms he had adapted from the Russian avant-garde and the Constructivist wing of Dadaism.

Just as Moholy's talents cannot be denied, the native genius of Gropius must be given its due, as must the independent German industrial-architectural design traditions tapped by the Bauhaus. However, it is undeniable that the trademark style of the Bauhaus was stamped by the impact of Soviet avant-garde art—reinforced by van Doesburg and the Dutch *De Stijl* group once they, too, aligned themselves with Constructivism. As Marina Dmitrieva-Einhorn points out, the Suprematist square (she might have added the triangle) was the basic Bauhaus form. It "was imprinted on all the design projects of the institute, from Marcel Breuer's metal chairs to the cups, textiles, and lamps." "What luck," critic Paul Westheim sardonically remarked, "that [Malevich] . . . did not patent [his square]."[74] The famous Bauhaus building and Gropius's home, both in Dessau, with their quadratic block design and flat roofs—two

23. Walter Gropius, Gropius house, Dessau, Germany (1925–1926). Courtesy of the Bauhaus-Archiv Berlin.

of the prototypes of International Style architecture—were built in accordance not only with German Werkbund antecedents but also with the geometricity of Russian Suprematism and Constructivism that Lissitzky was purveying throughout Germany. The same was true of the work of architect Ludwig Mies van der Rohe, Meyer's successor as Bauhaus director and the progenitor of the (much maligned and now ubiquitous) International Style high-rise with glass walls seemingly wrapped around its four corners. Mies first began designing pronouncedly geometrical structures without relationship to their surroundings after being struck by the shapes and abstract, "self-referential" nature of Lissitzky's Prouns.[75]

Some readers familiar with the Bauhaus may raise the objection that its art was functionalist rather than formalist. Like many of the Russian Constructivists, most Bauhaus artists and architects did strive for a design that emanated from and revealed the functions of the building or object created rather than one that showed off the whims of the artist or hid the structure under the ornamentalism typical of preceding epochs. But what function did strictly geometrical forms serve? Even some of the progenitors of this type of architecture admitted that it was an ideological nod toward Russian avant-garde prototypes, a "propaganda gesture" implying rejection of anything associated with the practices of the reviled current-day reality and asserting the utopian future society that modernistic design would cultivate.[76] According to Berthold Lubetkin, the Russian Constructivist architect who was among the first to initiate the International Style in Britain, the point was really not to fulfill any functional purpose but, rather, to make a *socialist statement* through buildings that shared as few features of the "bourgeois aesthetic" as possible, in order to "create a powerful impression on the ideology of the masses by every plastic means which the imagination can demand."[77] The International Style was a lot like church architecture: the structure itself was formed into the emblem of the creed. As van Doesburg explained, the quadrangle "is the token of a new humanity. The square is to us what the cross was to the early Christians."[78] The Russian Constructivist designs that the Bauhaus had adopted were geometrical, industrial-like icons, symbolizing transcendence of the dilemmas of capitalism and modern bourgeois existence.

But although the International Style originated with artists intent on escaping from modernity, it quickly evolved into the best visual means of identifying with, even celebrating, it.[79] This contradictory dual function is what made the designs of the Bauhaus and its close relative Russian Constructivism especially attractive as propaganda art and architecture in Nazi Germany and Fascist Italy, where an antirationalist, antimodernist, nationalist socialism coexisted with a utopian cult of modern technology.[80] It served much the same mixture of symbolic purposes for the far right as for the far left: the techno-Spartanism of International Style buildings could pronounce the departure of a revolutionary society from capitalism and at the same time display that it was "decisive and virile," in contrast to the dithering bourgeois democracy just overthrown.[81] It even fit in as the modern—and less expensive—version of the imposing neoclassical architecture of parade-ground buildings, and in fact the two styles could be easily combined. And like International Style architecture, Constructivist/Bauhaus graphic arts were unsurpassed at creating illusions for the masses. Both the Nazi and Fascist propaganda apparatuses hijacked many of the strikingly effective techniques and imagery of the Russian avant-garde.

But didn't Hitler, with his narrow tastes and broad hatreds, destroy the resident avant-garde for spreading the contagion of degenerate cultural Bolshevism? Wasn't the Bauhaus smeared in the Nazi press as an "alien" and "Jewish" "Spartacist-Bolshevik institute" whose "artistry [was that] of the mentally ill"?[82] Indeed so, but there were those in the Nazi movement who identified with the avant-garde as radically antimodern. An early article in the Nazi paper *Völkischer Beobachter* praised the Bauhaus for its disdain of individualism and its encouragement of inexpensive factory-produced housing estates for the masses.[83] And although the rule for Nazi residential developments was that they look Teutonic and rustic, the Bauhaus/Constructivist style was often adopted for industrial, military, and low-ranking party buildings as emblematic of the technical prowess of the Third Reich. A solid contingent of prominent official Nazi architects had even been on the Bauhaus staff, including Herbert Rimpl, a former assistant to Gropius.

Some Nazi propaganda artists borrowed even more directly from the USSR. Lissitzky had fused all the stylistic novelties of the Russian avant-garde for Weimar German audiences at the *Pressa International Exhibition of Newspaper and Book Publishing* (Cologne, 1928), the German Werkbund's *Film und Foto* exhibition (Stuttgart, 1929), and the Soviet pavilion at the *International Hygiene Exhibition* (Dresden, 1930). He designed and arranged gallery rooms, wall decorations, display cases, posters, photographs, and lettering by applying all the tricks of Constructivism, including his own Prouns and typography, to publicize Soviet art and society. The event lodged itself permanently in the artistic memory of professional circles, as attested by Third Reich propaganda posters and advertisements done in the Lissitzky-Rodchenko-Klutsis style and by the 1933 admission by the Nazified German Werkbund that its propaganda exhibition designs came from Lissitzky's.[84]

Despite these inroads, traditional imagery and design predominated in Nazi Germany; as in Russia, that was what the masses were more comfortable with and the leadership preferred as expressions of national culture, as opposed to the universality of the International Style. The balance was somewhat more in favor of the avant-grade in Italy, where from the beginning of the century the Russian counterculture had had a subversive effect on art.[85] The Italian radical intelligentsia had relished Russian Symbolist poetry—some of it published by Marinetti—and Italian Futurism was nourished on the rebellious spirit of Russian thought. Futurist typographical style (as opposed to other aspects of its aesthetic) came straight from Moscow. In the 1920s as well, the Proletkult movement to Bolshevize art for the masses received inordinate amounts of attention in the radical and mainstream Italian press.

Once Mussolini recognized the Soviet regime in 1924, Soviet artists were regularly represented at the *Venice Biennale* art exhibitions, where they crowded out other foreign contributors with the encouragement of Il Duce, who (at least before World War II) used patronage of the avant-garde to show wary social and intellectual elites that he was a man of culture and not the thug they believed him to be. Fascist art critics routinely praised and analyzed the large selection of Constructivist and Suprematist works on display in Venice, as they did after the Milan Decorative Arts exhibition of 1927. The *Mostra della Rivoluzione Fascista*, the exhibition celebrating the tenth anniversary of the March on Rome, which ran from 1932 to 1934 with countless thousands attending, gave a barometric reading of the rising level of Russian avant-garde artistic influence. Modernist architect and painter Giuseppe Terragni (1904–1943) was the man responsible for its design. Thoroughly familiar with the work of El Lissitzky and other Soviet Constructivists, this court artist to Fascist officialdom applied their visual effects—sometimes plainly, sometimes in combination with homegrown Futurist configurations—in his poster graphics, photomontage images, exhibition spaces, and other decorative features of the propaganda extravaganza.[86]

If the inextricably intertwined Russian avant-garde and Bauhaus aesthetic idiom was co-opted rather than extirpated in the fascist

24. El Lissitzky, entrance to Soviet pavilion at the *International Hygiene Exhibition*, Dresden, 1930. From Sophie Lissitzky-Küppers, *El Lissitzky* (Dresden, 1976). Courtesy of Artists' Rights Society.

25. Giuseppe Terragni, 1919 room at the *Exhibition of the Fascist Revolution*, Rome (1932). From *Ausstellung der faschistichen Revolution* (Rome, 1933).

nations, it flourished in the open environment of the Western democracies, where in the 1930s and 1940s exiled German and Russian artists sought refuge en masse and were able to give free rein to their individual artistic instincts. Yet below the surface one finds a curious convergence. In the United States from the Great Depression to the Cold War, there was also co-optation of international Constructivist aesthetics, by government propagandists as well as by image-makers seeking to mobilize public opinion and market products on behalf of "modern" corporations.[87]

The process began during the Great Depression when both the reputation of big business suffered and sales lagged. Industry wanted to show the public it was economically beneficial and efficient, both to induce consumer spending and to reduce popular support for the New Deal. In 1935, the mouthpiece of Republicanism and big business, magazine publisher Henry Luce, stated the argument for adopting International Style architecture: "Unless chaos is to intervene, a new order must be consciously created."[88]

With their fingers on the pulse of American consumer psychology, and in keen competition for declining numbers of shoppers, department stores were among the first to associate themselves with that new order. They had long kept abreast of trends in art for display ideas and now eagerly adopted Modernist designs. Russian-Jewish immigrant artist Louis Lozowick (1892–1973) had visited the USSR in the 1920s, returning as a publicist with firsthand knowledge of Soviet Suprematism and Constructivism in art and theater; as one of the few Americans to witness the Russian revolutionary artists at work, he was a sought-after authority in the 1920s and 1930s. His abstract constructions for the New York Lord and Taylor department store windows in 1926 conformed to his theory that the Russian avant-garde machine aesthetic captured the spirit of the modern era and should be applied wherever possible, even in the setting up of mannequins. Some avant-garde art advocates in the museums acknowledged that department stores were giving the public first-time exposure to the new art forms, breaking the ice for their acceptance in American society.[89]

This was only part of a far broader range of activity underway among American advertisers and graphic artists—originally known as practitioners of commercial art. Of course, stylistic diversity was the rule here, and nostalgia for older American forms was common. But by 1929 Modernist art copy, typography, and photography were "rampant" in advertising, according to a trade journal.[90] The depression was a challenge met by vastly expanding marketing budgets and the birth of the packaging industry. Both of these related venues provided employment for large numbers of artists, many of whom liked the paycheck but also believed that this mass art merging industry and aesthetics was superior to the egoism of fine arts, and that through it they would modify bourgeois consciousness and reform society: they agreed with German museum director G. F. Hartlaub, who understood commercial art as a "truly social, collective, real mass art: the only one we now have. It shapes the visual habits of that anonymous collectivity the public. Little by little an artistic attitude is hammered into the mass soul."[91] On the business side, it was not just a matter of suckering shoppers but also a reflection of the capitalist utopianism that insisted only profit-seeking corporations could establish a permanently stable, harmonious society.

The two utopias overlapped in their eager adoption of the Bauhaus or *De Stijl* aesthetic, which derived from Russian avant-garde prototypes. Block lettering, geometrical layout, unconventional photography, and abstract designs rarely appeared in advertising or packaging before the 1920s but now became common under the influence of German, Dutch, and Russian graphic art that trade magazines and exhibitions publicized in the United States: "Mod-

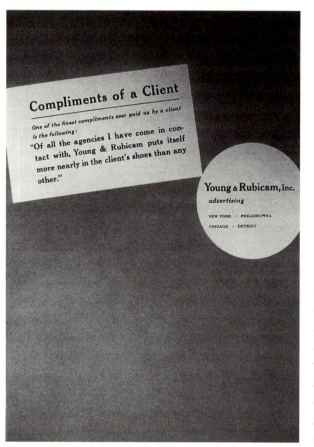

26. Suprematism in American corporate graphic design. Young and Rubicam, Inc., advertisement from *Fortune*, January 1933. Courtesy of Young and Rubicam, Inc., New York.

ernism turns merchandise," declared the West Virginia Pulp and Paper Company's *Westvaco Inspirations for Printers.*[92] Rodchenko and other Constructivists had successfully applied their art to commercial graphics on behalf of Soviet state-run enterprises, and in Germany El Lissitzky himself did famous advertising designs for Günther Wagner's Pelikan Ink firm. Lissitzky's disciples among Dadaists, European Constructivists, and Bauhaus artists followed his example. One of them, the German Jan Tschichold (1902–1974), published a text that became the world standard on typography, and stated therein that virtually all the innovations came from Kandinsky, Malevich, Lissitzky, and Soviet Constructivism. To him the clarity and precision of their exact geometric forms when applied to lettering and layout would purify life and give a sense of universal unity amid technologically driven earthly chaos; to the marketers who applied them in the service of sales, the style conveyed a product's features and implied its modernity with a minimum of text, effectively catching the attention of lower-middle-class consumers flipping through a magazine or newspaper. This was a Western capitalist adaptation of the avant-garde technique of expressing the concept or essence.[93]

In packaging, the revolution began in the mercantile city of Chicago, the capital of American industrial design. Here was the headquarters of the Container Corporation of America, owned by Walter Paepcke, a visionary who believed in the vanguard role of business (as opposed to government) in art patronage and humanist reformism, but who also knew how to sell his boxes: "I want to give people the idea that our company is a new and progressive, modern operation. And I don't need a lot of text to do that if [I] can do it with art."[94] His CCA advertisements featured the signed work of modern artists from around the world, and the clients who used his packaging—which incorporated, as he put it, the Modernist "visual vocabulary"—included almost every major consumer-goods enterprise in the country. He also sponsored Bauhaus artist Moholy-Nagy and others, whose art figured prominently in his plans. With some trepidation the anticapitalist Moholy left Europe and moved to Chicago to head the New Bauhaus (later renamed the Institute of Design), which Paepcke had funded.

Through his educational activities on behalf of industrial arts, from 1937 until his death in 1946, Moholy contributed to familiarizing America with the Bauhaus aesthetic—and through it that of the Russian Constructivists as well as other closely related Modernist art movements.[95]

Making a similar contribution were Mies van der Rohe, who emigrated to Chicago in 1938 to serve for twenty years as director of the architecture and design college at the Illinois Institute of Technology, which merged with the Institute of Design after Moholy's death; Gropius, chairman of the architectural department at Harvard University's Graduate School of Design from 1937 to 1951; Russian-born International Style architect Serge Chermayeff (1900–1996), Moholy's successor in Chicago, Gropius's in Cambridge, and finally professor at Yale University; Bauhaus painter, Kandinsky protégé, and Malevich admirer Josef Albers (1888–1976), art teacher at Black Mountain College, the experimental arts school near Asheville, North Carolina, then chairman of the design department at Yale; and many other German and Russian avant-garde artists. Most of these men, not long after coming to America, accepted the embrace of corporate capitalism, softened their radicalism, and settled for raising the ethical consciousness of Western society and/or improving the aesthetic quality of industrial goods through antitraditionalist International Style formalist art and architecture. Parallel developments took place in postwar western Europe with the return of various artists from exile and the continentwide revival of pedagogical institutions inspired by the Bauhaus, whose prestige rose higher than ever as mythic cultural opponent of the Nazis.

The modernistic International Style became more and more common after the Second World War. In architecture, it symbolized in Europe a socialist break with the past and in America the technological prowess and financial muscle of big corporations. Housewares and furniture, too, were increasingly stamped by Bauhaus/Russian Constructivist aesthetics, replacing the faux-functionalist, faux-aerodynamic "streamlined" Art Deco objects that represented the ultimate in modernity to 1930s America. This updated "technostyle" came from a variety of sources that are difficult to isolate.[96] Suffice it to say that in the United States, the starkly geometrical, metallic furniture of Knoll Associates International and even the more supple furnishings coming out of the Cranbrook Crafts Academy retained more than a vestige of Russian Constructivist design, just as the squares, rectangles, lines, and triangles that seemed to float in nothingness in the paintings of Malevich and the pottery of the Suprematists came to adorn the fabrics and ceramics that so typify the aura of the 1950s.[97] Mass production of such goods rose with the economic boom of the 1960s, and still today one encounters Malevichian shapes adding a flourish to styrofoam soft-drink cups, carpets, newspaper ads, wallpaper, Crest toothpaste tubes, and many other items.

So what had once been oppositional and metaphysical had become either decoration for the middle class or an affirmation of capitalist might. If any of the old utopianism was left, it was now a reflection of a self-assured postwar American optimism. No wonder art historian Timothy Clark calls the alliance among avant-garde, advertisers, and corporations the "bad dream of Modernism."[98] But then again, largely because of this relationship, Modernist art succeeded in entering mass consciousness, transforming (for better or worse) the aesthetics of industrial design and the urban landscape, and leaving behind a style that reflected both the triumphs and the horrors of the twentieth century. Without the support of American corporate giants (and, across the Atlantic, the builders of western European social welfare states), it would likely have remained the arcane design fantasy of a fairly obscure sect of artists.

While corporations in the United States adopted the industrial design and architecture of the Constructivist/International Style, the federal government gave Abstract Expressionist painting quasi-official status as the fine-arts style of Cold War America in the propaganda battle waged against Soviet Communism. It was then that abstract painting entered the mainstream of popular taste, and the avant-garde rebels unintentionally emerged as guardians of the status quo and designers of colorful nonrepresentational decorations for the bourgeoisie.[99] Kandinskian aesthetics and Cold War anticommunism are the keys to the story.

The very term "Abstract Expressionism" was initially coined by Museum of Modern Art director Alfred Barr to describe the early painting of Kandinsky. But clearly, postwar artists such as Franz Kline, Lee Krasner, Barnett Newman, Robert Motherwell, Jackson Pollock, and Mark Rothko were not second-rate imitators of Kandinsky, for they generated a movement of great vitality and originality. In canvases fervidly, even sensuously, splashed with lush layers of paint, streaked with tormented lines, or blotched with amorphous expanses of color, they bared their subconscious impulses, their angst at the destruction of war, and their revulsion at the conformity of the middle-class masses. Socialism, anarchism, Blavatsky, Freud, Sartre, Jung, and Zen swirled together like differ-

27. Suprematism in 1950s American housewares design. Creamer, from the author's collection.

ent-colored paints; American Indian, Kandinskian, or Surrealist art forms they admired as the aesthetic equivalents of these philosophies of irrationalism and anticapitalism. Self-liberation and self-assertion through art was their Romantic, rebellious, intensely individualist, Existentialist vision, which—in the light of politics in the 1940s—accompanied both a pessimistic foreboding of human and cosmic strife and a desire to purify the world by expressing through their art the deep truth of unity not readily apparent—as Pollock put it, the "inner world . . . of [the] rhythm of the universe, of the big order."[100]

The Abstract Expressionists' outlook was a bit of an intellectual jumble. One can see how the psychoanalytic-tinged, self-absorbed elements differed from Kandinsky's Silver Age mysticism, and yet there is also something quite similar to him in their Idealist, universalist views of existence and the messianic seriousness with which they approached their art. Indeed, the nongeometrical spiritual painting of Kandinsky formed one of the many basic pigments of Abstract Expressionism.

Kandinsky's influence on the American avant-garde dated back to before World War I, beginning with the New York *Armory Show* of 1913, where his work was first shown, alongside paintings of the French and German avant-gardes—or, as Teddy Roosevelt called them upon seeing the exhibit, Europe's "lunatic fringe." The critics trashed Kandinsky's painting *Improvisation No. 27*, which one described as "fragments of refuse thrown out of a butcher's shop upon a bit of canvas."[101] But it appealed to the American counterculture, a group at that time dominated by women, Southerners, foreigners, and Jews, all "outsiders" hostile to the prevailing WASP-ish, masculine, rationalist, bourgeois voices.[102] In opposition to all this they turned to Emersonian Transcendentalism, Madame Blavatsky's Theosophy, and now Kandinsky, whose writings reinforced these spiritualist tendencies; in fact, his manifesto introduced many American artists to modern art.

Among his early American supporters was avant-garde promoter and photographer Alfred Stieglitz, who bought the just-mentioned painting of Kandinsky's and was the first to publish his writings here. Stieglitz gave his future wife, Georgia O'Keeffe, Kandinsky's

On the Spiritual in Art and the *Blaue Reiter Almanac*; she affirmed their fundamental importance for her painting: "[After reading Kandinsky], I found I could say things with colors and shapes that I couldn't say in any other way—things that I had no words for." Other early American abstractionists and experimental artists, like Marsden Hartley, felt much the same way.[103]

But it was really two women whose labors, in the face of artistic opposition and public ridicule, built a solid foundation in the 1920s, 1930s, and 1940s for the development of abstract art in America: Katherine Dreier (1877–1952) and Baroness Hilla Rebay (1890–1967). Dreier was a rich Connecticut patroness with Theosophist, feminist, and, until 1939, pro-Nazi leanings. After viewing the Van Diemen exhibit, she began buying works of the Russian avant-garde. Her modern art association, the Société Anonyme, held the first major Kandinsky exhibition in the United States, in 1923, and in 1945 the first after his death, along with many other shows devoted to Modernist painting and sculpture.[104]

Rebay, her rival, did even more. A wealthy Bavarian noblewoman, she was a teenage Anthroposophist and budding realist painter until Dadaist-Surrealist Jean Arp, during a brief love affair, introduced her to Kandinsky's painting, whereupon she converted to abstractionism. In 1927 she moved to New York, convinced that America would be more receptive to her (unimpressive) art. She quickly connected to bohemian society circles, eventually becoming chief art adviser to collector Solomon Guggenheim, and curator of the Museum of Non-Objective Art (later the Guggenheim Museum), which she persuaded him to establish in 1939. Although they purchased works by many artists, Kandinsky's were the heart of the collection. For Rebay, he was a messiah figure inspired directly by God, and as this was a temple (the name she originally proposed for the museum) of devotion to him, she had organ music piped into the viewing halls. In her words, "non-objectivity will be the religion of the future. Very soon the nations on earth will turn to it in thought and feeling and develop such intuitive powers which lead them to harmony." One of the avant-garde artists attracted to these views was Jackson Pollock (1912–1956), who had been raised by his parents to admire Russian socialism and discovered Theosophy on his own. In 1943 he worked as a guard and custodian at the Museum of Non-Objective Art; the exposure to Kandinsky and experiments Rebay initiated in drip painting were critical in the genesis of his own Action Painting technique.[105]

Pollock, Rebay, and Dreier were all connected to two other people important in the development of American abstractionism and the dissemination of Russian avant-garde aesthetics, John Graham and Arshile Gorky.[106] Graham (1881–1961) was the pseudonym of Ivan Dambrovsky, a Polish aristocrat from Kiev who had fought Bolshevism as an officer in the counterrevolutionary White army before fleeing to Paris. In New York by the early 1920s, he became a socialist, occultist, and collector of pre-Columbian art; for a time he was an administrator at the Rebay/Guggenheim museum. His influential 1937 book, *System and Dialectics of Art*, echoed Kandinsky's and Malevich's thought with added reverberations of Dostoevsky, Tolstoy, and the Jungian concept of the collective unconscious (another philosophy of neo-Idealism). The camera has made realistic painting obsolete, he explained; now art must be nonrepresentational in order to open "access to the unconscious mind" and "establish personal contact with static eternity." The abstract artist "leads humanity . . . to higher levels of knowledge and to heroic deeds," and certainly out of the impasse of industrialized, bourgeois-dominated Western civilization.[107] In addition to extolling Russian artists, whom he ranked among the greats of all time, he transmitted his excitement about the powers of Native American art—a Jungian-enhanced throwback to Russian Populist adoration of the primitive peasants—to the young artists he mentored, among them Krasner, Newman, Pollock, and also Gorky.

Arshile Gorky (1904–1948) was another entry point for Kandinsky's aesthetics in New York. An Armenian who had fled the Ottoman Empire during the massacres of 1915, he falsely claimed to be a relative of the famed Russian writer Maxim Gorky. A follower of Graham, Gorky viewed Kandinsky's works in the Guggenheim collection, and they confirmed his particular artistic proclivities. Through Gorky's painting style, the future Abstract Expressionists also absorbed the influence of French artist-refugees in New York during the war, a younger generation of less dogmatic Surrealists who were more open to abstract painting and incorporated in their work the protoplasmic features of Kandinsky's French years.

Kandinsky's style and philosophy were thus disseminated in America over several decades by a variety of abstractionist proponents. Uprooted from its native soil in tumultuous Russia, it did not grow on the far side of the Atlantic with the same characteristics that it had in, say, Germany. Although some of the Abstract Expressionists understood Kandinsky's earth-transcending spiritualism and Idealist formalism, mostly they interpreted his art as a solipsistic expression of his own subjective psychology. Heirs of the Surrealists, they saw his art as one of the forerunners of their own unpremeditated, "stream of consciousness" painting,[108] in opposition to the fully planned geometric abstractionism of Mondrian and Malevich, to whom in reality Kandinsky was closer than they realized.

But one feature Abstract Expressionists shared fully with their Russian ancestor: an antimodern sense that Western civilization, including America, had gone tragically awry. Humanity required radical aesthetic and political measures to rescue it, namely, their brand of abstract painting plus socialism or anarchism. Although also repelled by the Soviet Union, they stood on the far left of the political spectrum and seemed likely to suffer repression during the McCarthy era. Indeed, in 1949, the conservative Republican congressman from Michigan George Dondero informed the public that Kandinsky, in league with Trotsky, had unleashed the "black knights" of modern art visions to undermine the tsarist regime. Following that blueprint, he claimed, American abstract painters, allied with a "polyglot rabble" of "international art thugs" and the "effeminate elect"—that is, U.S. museum directors—had formed a "sinister conspiracy conceived in the black heart of Russia" to undermine American culture.[109] President Truman, who called the painters "lazy [and] nutty," agreed with Dondero that "modern art equals communism."[110] Yet despite the fear-mongering of the politicians and the Abstract Expressionists' subversive worldview, the U.S. government would soon champion them for propaganda purposes during the Cold War. Anti-Stalinist artists and art critics successfully re-created the image of these painters as individualist aesthetes who would have suffered under totalitarian systems but prospered in the land of the free.[111]

In the interwar years, most left-wing artists and critics in America, including the Abstract Expressionists in their youths, had opposed abstract art as mystical nonsense or disengaged art for art's sake. Instead they defended Socialist Realism as the socially committed aesthetic of the revered USSR. But Stalin's dictatorship caused a breach in the ranks of the artists, as it did among all left-wing intellectuals. As early as the 1930s in the United States, Russian-born abstractionists Ilya Bolotowsky and Mark Rothko were campaigning against Stalin and against Socialist Realism as the artistic manifestation of his tyranny. Many artists, still radicals, turned to Stalin's enemy, Trotsky, for guidance. It came in his 1938 essays (one co-signed by Surrealist André Breton and Mexican painter Diego Rivera) in the New York independent leftist journal *Partisan Review*. Eager to win radicals to his side and away from Stalin's, Trotsky denounced Socialist Realism as toadyism and called for the "complete freedom of art," whose very purpose, he said, was to challenge authority and bring on the true revolution.[112]

Regardless of Trotsky's various motives, his letters legitimized abstract art for New York intellectuals, who began to see it as an autonomous, critical, anti–status quo activity. That is how ex-leftist critics like Clement Greenberg, who "made" Pollock and the Abstract Expressionists, understood it and explained it to the American public. With similar effect, MOMA director Alfred Barr, by explaining abstract painting as just the sort of free expression that the Soviets could not tolerate, convinced magazine publisher Henry Luce to stop ridiculing the genre; soon coverage of the artists began appearing in *Time* and *Life*. Even Congressman Richard Nixon, who had once denounced abstractionism as communist, defended it as a symbol of the American way. Hoping to impress European intellectuals, the United States Information Agency and the CIA sponsored foreign exhibits of American abstract art and issued propaganda magazines on the subject, which had a noticeable impact on the direction of European painting.

In part, the U.S. government's propaganda battle with Russia sped up the acceptance of abstract art in America. But interior decorators, advertisers, and consumer-goods packaging had already done much of the work, by conditioning the eye of the public to the whole range of abstractionist modern art styles. This prepared the country to accept the critics' and journalists' Cold War–era depiction of the artists as energetic, inventive, autonomous, democratic, and modern, all the characteristics Americans associated with themselves after World War II. What about the mystical and politically revolutionary sides to the art? Well, who in 1950s America besides artists and a few intellectuals cared about that?

Australian historian Bernard Smith interprets the American espousal of formalist abstract art and International Constructivist Style design as an effort by a society with a colonial inferiority complex vis-à-vis European civilization to flex its homegrown cultural muscles but at the same time affiliate with Europe through adoption of "universal" art forms originating there.[113] In Japan and Latin America, too, Modernist art offered itself as a kind of aesthetic Esperanto whose advocates for a variety of reasons rejected the existing language of art. Both of these regions in the nineteenth and twentieth centuries contended with the problems of modernization, including rapid socioeconomic change and the related challenge posed by Europe and the West to national traditions and identities. And in both regions artists learned from the Russian avant-garde, which seemed to have worked out alternative artistic arrangements that promised to bring about a new society.

Japanese Modernist art began with the arrival of painter David Burliuk (1882–1967) in 1920. A former associate of Kandinsky's in Munich and contributor to the *Blaue Reiter Almanac*, Burliuk was a Russian Jew fleeing the revolution and headed for America. En route from Siberia, he stayed in Japan for two years, during which time he published on Russian abstract art and exhibited his own works and those of Malevich, Tatlin, and others. His primitivist, antirealist style had a revolutionary impact, as did the slap-in-the-face Russian avant-garde provocativeness that he urged on Japan's radical arts community. In the same year he left, St. Petersburg artist Varvara Bubnova (1886–1983) came to Tokyo. Arriving to visit a relative in 1922, she stayed until 1958, teaching and writing extensively on the principles of Soviet Constructivist art. Several Japanese artists also attended the International Constructivist-Dada Congresses in Germany, where they were introduced to the ideas of El Lissitzky and Kandinsky. One of them, Murayama Tomoyoshi (1901–1977), believed that art should create "the image of the age to come" and "reconstruct the world." On his return home, he formed the avant-garde group Mavo, many of whose members had been anarchists and were now gravitating toward Russian communism. Those who did believed that in all the world, only "Russia shines with the light of a white building!" However small in number, the Japanese avant-garde survived government persecution before the war and then flourished thereafter. Eventually it found a balance between native Zen motifs and Russian and other European influences, to create a powerful art that was recognizably Japanese but in its abstractionism also universal.[114]

In Latin America, too, mediation between native art and Russian and European aesthetic models was the norm for the avant-garde.[115] From Mexico to Chile, abstract art and the International Style in architecture took hold beginning in the 1940s and 1950s. This was largely a result of individuals unrelated to Russia except for their association with the European Constructivist movement. But it is noteworthy that two Russian immigrants, Lazar Segel and Gregori Warchavchik, were, respectively, the first Modernist painter and architect in Brazil, and that ex–Bauhaus director Hannes Meyer, after leaving Moscow, became director of the Instituto de Urbanismo y Planificación in Mexico City (1939–1949).

Even earlier in Mexico, gripped with revolutionary crises between 1910 and 1934, riven by ethnic and social divides, and ever wary of the United States, avant-garde painters had been grappling with questions of artistic as well as social change. Diego Rivera (1886–1957) is known for his ties to Cubism, but he was also a fixture among Russian painters (and women) in pre–World War I Paris and was fully charged with enthusiasm for Marxism and the art of the Russian Revolution. He and his conational, David Siqueiros (1896–1974), turned to mural painting, for which they are famous, partly out of adherence to the Russian Constructivist injunction against easel painting and to the movement's declaration of art for the masses. Rivera abandoned full abstractionism in favor of a narrative propagandistic art synthesizing Mexican traditional imagery and Socialist Realism while retaining an experimental and neoprimitive flavor taken over from both European and Russian Modernist painting.

Rivera's art is an example of the global adaptability of the Russian avant-garde idiom. The new artistic vocabulary was one result of the Russian intelligentsia's impassioned struggle to formulate alternatives to capitalist modernity. Russian avant-garde experimental forms in the visual arts as well as dance and theater expressed powerful visions of social renovation that the developing world, the industrialized democratic West, and midcentury totalitarian regimes alike readily borrowed. Like Russian anarchists, writers, visionaries, and anti-Semites, the Russian avant-garde appeared as wise men of the East offering access to higher truth. Rooted in the mysticism, messianism, and anti-Westernism of the Silver Age and Russian Revolution, Russian artists rejected urban-industrial-bourgeois existence and sought to remake society anew. This utopian ambition failed, and their art, in an ironic twist of fate, often ended up being appropriated to promote capitalism or dictatorship or a distinctly Western form of individualism. Yet by contributing to the transformation of culture in many parts of the globe, Russian art did help to shape the modern world, even if it could not overcome it. The Russian avant-garde gave twentieth-century humanity a new way of seeing and interpreting reality; along with Freud, Einstein, and the western European pioneers of modern art, it altered contemporary consciousness.

As in the realm of culture, twentieth-century politics cannot be understood without reference to Russia, whose communist dictatorship shaped recent history by prompting international animosity and adoration.

The Dream of Communism

FOR DECADES, Russian radicals dreamed of the revolutionary transformation of their country and the world. Many came to reject peasant-oriented Populism and anarchism and turned instead to Marxism with its urban, industrial, and working-class emphases. Among the diverse multitude of factions that proliferated within this wing of Russian socialism, the Bolshevik (later Communist) Party was one of the least expected to lead the revolution if and when it finally occurred. But over the course of 1917, this is the party that succeeded in riding the wave of mass discontent. In October of that year, under the leadership of Vladimir Ilyich Lenin, the Bolsheviks wrested power from the incapacitated Russian Provisional Government. After Lenin's death in 1924, Joseph Stalin vanquished his competitors for leadership of the party, which he turned into a submissive agency of his personal despotism.

A sizable contingent of the world's anti-Western intelligentsias saw Communist Russia as the embodiment of higher truth, the bearer of light from the exotic East, just as it had Russian anarchism, literature, and avant-garde art in the preceding decades. At the same time that this Russian cult peaked within the European countercultures, the myths surrounding Russia magnified the hostility of the West's political establishment, which perceived it as an alien force threatening modern civilization. Conservatives had at one time feared a global conspiracy involving Russian anarchist bomb throwers; in the wake of the Bolshevik uprising, anti-Russian hysteria shifted focus to the communists. The irony is that anticommunism became a far more powerful force than communism itself, which, at least in the West, turned out to be a paper tiger, to borrow a phrase from Mao.

The Bolshevik One-Party State

Unlike the previous figures and movements discussed in this book, the story of Russian communism is so well known that it is not necessary to recapitulate it here. It is, however, necessary to illustrate essential aspects of the Soviet political and economic system, for they provide the key to how Leninism and Stalinism transformed politics around the world.

Lenin's major innovation was the establishment of a one-party state in the guise of a fictitious democracy laying claim to mass legitimacy, something all twentieth-century political systems coveted. The new government theoretically derived its powers from the people, from the bottom up, through the soviets, which were local, regional, and national legislative organs. In reality, however, the elections were soon to be rigged, and the soviets became rubber-stamp institutions, part of a constitutional facade that concealed the true nature of the political structure. Real power flowed from the top downward, from the highly centralized Russian Communist Party, issuing orders from Moscow to every level of the government, whether bureaucratic ministries or soviets.[1]

Of course, the dictatorship did not function like a well-oiled machine. The Bolshevik leaders were revolutionaries without administrative experience. Long years of war and revolution had flung the enormous country into chaos, which would have presented any government with a daunting task. And the duplication of functions between party and government thwarted bureaucratic efficiency.

We must also keep in mind when considering the nature of this system that the Communists ruled not just through naked force but also by winning the active support of some of the populace, especially in the big cities. This was a repressive regime that mobilized the nation through fear and propaganda, but it was not just that. Many intellectual elements within society were hostile toward capitalism and predisposed toward Bolshevik authority. Among the masses, although some supported it fleetingly, others did so enthusiastically, in response to the vibrant popular culture it promoted, the educational and career opportunities it offered, and the social-welfare promises it made to a citizenry that had never been given center stage before.[2]

But we should not exaggerate the social welfare aspects of this system. In reality, the state-provided social benefits were inadequate across the board, all the more so when one considers that they were denied to many suspect categories of the population. In fact, the social benefits remained largely on paper before the 1960s, and those actually extended to the populace served not to improve material security but primarily to strengthen the regime's authoritarian rule. Attached to the guarantee of full employment in the exclusively state-owned economy, for instance, were the elimination of trade-union rights and the threat of losing one's livelihood for political noncompliance.[3] Furthermore, to the benefit of state interests, the government neglected the consumer sector of the economy in favor of heavy industry, and it disrupted, ruined, or liquidated thousands upon thousands of lives in its attempt to "build socialism," as the propaganda slogan went.

If we view the Soviet system primarily as a variant of the modern social welfare state, we risk downplaying the dictatorial and repressive elements of the communist regime.[4] Even if there was always some mass support, coercion eventually gave most people no choice but to cooperate, as the party systematically isolated and destroyed all potential political dissenters. Insecure in power, eager to ensure the survival of the revolutionary cause, and frustrated by the difficulties of administering the country, Lenin and, to an even greater degree, Stalin, initiated mass terror against their putative enemies.

To contend with the opponents of the regime—actual or potential, real or imagined—the one-party state institutionalized the terror, applying it selectively in some periods, indiscriminately in others. The secret police organs (the acronyms for which changed over time from Cheka to GPU, OGPU, NKVD, MGB, and finally KGB) were far more powerful than they had been in tsarist days. From the start the security agency was above the law, answering only to the Bolshevik leader. In the early years its branches often operated autonomously and all the more violently as they could not be punished. Under Stalin, it was the agency by which he ensured the loyalty of party members: even his closest associates knew what would befall them if they dared question his judgment. Stalin was "drunk with his own power"; as his henchman Vyacheslav Molotov put it, he had "succumbed to sickly suspiciousness."[5] Through the one-party secret-police state that he inherited from Lenin, Stalin blocked any potential checks to his absolute authority.

The system they established enabled Lenin and Stalin to make other radical new departures in social control and manipulation of the masses. Although scholars continue to disagree over the validity of the term "totalitarian,"[6] what is indisputable is that after seizing power, the Bolshevik Party *strove* for total domination over society. Even if it was not fully successful in this, it did achieve a degree of mastery over *politically relevant* behavior unprecedented in human history.[7] Out of a utopian urge to create a new socialist man and for the more cynical purposes of preserving the leadership in power, the Soviet autocrats attempted to throttle autonomous cultural life. They never completely succeeded, but the Bolshevik notion of turning people into "cogs" in the machinery of the socialist state gives an indication of their goal.[8] The government did establish a monopoly of information through strict censorship, suppression of religion, and its grip on education and mass communications. It further asserted its presence and authority through the establishment of party cells within all conceivable organizations of the nation, from recreational clubs to military units. To rally the population behind it, the regime whitewashed Soviet life and bombarded the multiethnic and largely rural citizenry with state-sponsored propaganda emphasizing national unity and technological accomplishments. It whipped up a crisis atmosphere by harping on the presence of threatening foreign and domestic nemeses. Official Marxist-Leninist ideology provided justification for state actions and helped the party leadership to identify potential political deviants. Mouthing of ideological slogans was a litmus test of loyalty to the regime. Under Stalin, suspected "doubters of the party line" had a very low survival rate.

Stalin added a theocratic and Russian chauvinist imprint to Soviet official culture.[9] The former seminarian from the remote Caucasus Mountains of Georgia endowed the nation with features borrowed from Orthodox Christianity. Party ideology served a catechistic function, propaganda posters took after religious icons, Lenin was glorified as a deity, and Stalin became the object of a personality cult accompanied by unrestrained official worship. More than a reflection of his personal psychology and despotism, these innovations indicate Stalin's deep sensitivity to the Russian popular mentality. The same was true of his exploitation of Russian nationalism, elements of which he melded with communism in a departure from Lenin—one that was analogous to the national-socialist fusions of Mussolini and Hitler.

All of these characteristics were combined in the cultural formula of Socialist Realism. Stalin required artists and writers to sing paeans to the successes of the Soviet system through adherence to the Socialist Realist canon, whose aesthetic was derived from neo-classicism, nineteenth-century naturalism, revolutionary utopianism, and official propaganda. The themes of Socialist Realism stressed party-mindedness, ideological commitment, and the heroic national spirit. According to a functionary of the regime, art and literature had to "speak to the broad masses in the name of the Party." The goal, as he put it, was "accessibility" to the largest contingent of the population, with "simplicity and clarity of form [being] . . . among the most important criteria of the new aesthetics."[10] Like avant-garde art, Socialist Realism sought to transform humanity, but abstractionism had no place in a cultural program designed to beguile the masses.

The economic system developed under Stalin also served the purpose of imposing the power of the party over society. The Communist Party was able to penetrate the daily existence of individuals as no government had previously been able to do thanks to the command economy initiated in 1929 with the introduction of the first Five-Year Plan. Stalin's government outlawed all private economic activity and with it any remaining vestiges of the capitalist free market. It then flung itself into a "bacchanalian orgy" of planning, a nationwide superindustrialization binge.[11] Entirely new urban agglomerations seemed to arise overnight from the dust as workers rushed to erect factory complexes and industrial towns— Soviet versions of Gary, Indiana, one of the fantasy dreamlands of the Kremlin's economic planners.

The inclination toward a centralized, planned economy had some roots in tsarist experiments with state-led economic-development projects such as the Trans-Siberian Railroad, as well as in Lenin's fascination with German economic coordination during World War I. But it was taken to unheard-of extremes because of the confluence of many different factors, including the utopianism of Bolsheviks desperate to escape the chaos and poverty of the capitalist free market through social engineering; Stalin's determination to strengthen Moscow's dominion over the distant reaches of its empire through the assertion of full governmental authority over the economic life of the nation; Stalin's alarm at the country's incapacity for modern war against potential capitalist adversaries; Stalin's psychological urge to prove that he was a great and powerful leader through the godlike transformation of his nation; and Stalin's attempt to legitimize the party dictatorship by showing that it was building a new society more advanced than that of the West.

In the short run, the Five-Year Plans achieved the political goals that were uppermost in the Soviet dictator's mind, and brought about the industrialization and urbanization of a largely rural society. But the costs to the long-term economic vitality of the USSR were high. The breakneck race to build and produce caused incalculable damage to the environment and public health. The individual's living standard was sacrificed to the good of the Stalinist state as the almost exclusive investment in heavy industry resulted in severe shortages of consumer goods and mass housing. The central planning agency set yearly production targets and rewarded managers for fulfilling them without concern for profit, loss, or competition. This sapped the country's entrepreneurial spirit: risk-taking innovation brought factory directors few benefits and, if it disrupted achievement of the numbers dictated from above, possible punishment. As a result, the country would be saddled with its inefficiently run 1930s-era smoke-belching, rust-belt factories for more than half a century. Impossible-to-achieve production targets and the propaganda needs of the state were expressed in falsified statistics that both symbolized the whole venture and belied the claim that the Soviet economic system was more rational than capitalism. It clearly was not: the shortcomings of the economy called forth the universal toleration of bribery, the routine theft of public goods for private distribution, and a ubiquitous black market run by organized criminal mobs with links to the government. Moreover, many of the most impressive construction projects could not have been completed without a steady supply of slave laborers from the concentration camps, hardly the sign of a successful modern economy. Lack of collective-bargaining rights, bad work conditions, and guaranteed employment to all workers ensured the low productivity of the labor force.

The entire industrialization campaign, furthermore, was contingent on the enserfment of the peasantry that formed the majority of the population. The Bolsheviks despised and mistrusted the peasants as capitalists. In an internal war initiated by Stalin that cost millions of lives, the government ruthlessly expropriated the peasants' property and forced them to join state collective farms, on pain of death or deportation to the Gulag. Stalin viewed it as the conquest of an enemy nation. He referred to the acquisition of peasant lands as "plunder" and imposed "tribute" on his foes by compelling them to deliver their agricultural production to the state.[12] This was intended to ensure that the supposedly anti-Bolshevik peasantry would supply the urban population with foodstuffs, easing Stalin's concerns about the cost and feasibility of the industrialization campaign he deemed vital to Communist power. Because forced collectivization crippled Russia's farming class, Soviet agriculture would be perpetually underproductive. But for Stalin it was the political gains that counted.

The country was thrust into turmoil and violence during the 1930s, yet Soviet propaganda proclaimed the destruction of traditional rural society as a desirable benefit of the Stalinist modernization strategy. Just as cynically, it depicted the planned economy as a triumph of Russian socialism and the political system as an egalitarian democracy that had forged among the peoples of the union a new Soviet identity transcending previous ethnic loyalties. The Russian Communist Party trumpeted the USSR under Stalin as the superior alternative to avaricious capitalism and the conflict-ridden Western parliamentary system. "Catch and overtake the West" was the official slogan of the day that defined Soviet Russia's international image. The aura of transformation that it fostered, as well as the political and economic forms that it devised, attracted supporters and imitators and terrified detractors the world over.

Adoration and Revulsion: Western Communism and Anticommunism

Discontented youth were drawn to the extremes. Throughout Western Europe and America, young intellectuals, estranged from bourgeois existence, proved receptive to the allure of Soviet Communism. "What an enormous longing for a new human order there was in the era between the world wars," Arthur Koestler once commented.[13] The left-wing Western intelligentsia's perceptions of the Bolshevik revolution were variegated, but they were in two respects consistent. One, they saw in it only what they wanted to see, and two, they carried forward prerevolutionary stereotypes of soulful Russia as repository of Eastern wisdom and collectivism. As before 1917, only the tiniest minority of observers saw Russia as akin to the West.[14] Had it been otherwise, the revolution would not have excited such messianic hopes and apocalyptic dread.

Before 1917 few people in the West had ever heard of Lenin or the Bolsheviks. It was the Populist-anarchists who had been romanticized by the media and thrilled progressives. Liberal "fellow travelers" cheered on the revolutionary movement's valiant struggle against the tsarist autocracy just as later celebrity intellectuals would express solidarity with Communist Russia. In England, the Russian terrorist and best-selling author Stepniak had formed the Society of Friends of Russian Freedom in the early 1890s, which counted among its members William Morris and Sidney Webb, the Fabian socialist and future Stalinist apologist. Those who belonged to the American branch included social activists and writers like Jane Addams, Samuel Gompers, W. D. Howells, Robert M. La Follete, and Mark Twain, who summed up the position of the group when he stated that Russian radicals should "make a bonfire of the Russian throne and fry the Czar in it."[15] Even Buffalo Bill showed his sympathy for the Russian left by dropping the "Cossack Extravaganza" from his Wild West Show to protest police repression during the 1905 revolution. At the same time and for the same reason, the Société des Amis du Peuple Russe was organized in France with the support of Anatole France, Georges Clemenceau, Pierre and Marie Curie, and Madame Zola.[16]

But the October seizure of power changed the allegiance of the intellectuals. The Russian Communist Party was the first radical group to succeed at making a revolution, and Bolshevism excited leftists everywhere—so much so that they redirected their affections toward it. In the United States, free-spirit bohemians of Greenwich Village like Max Eastman and John Reed, and for a time even the anarchist Russian-Jewish firebrand Emma Goldman, eagerly greeted the Bolshevik revolution. In France, former anarchists among the cultural vanguard who announced for communism after 1917 included André Breton, Fernand Léger, Pablo Picasso, Diego Rivera, Erik Satie, and Paul Signac; in Germany, it was the Dadaists and artists of the Arbeitsrat für Kunst. This shift within the progressive intelligentsia was spontaneous but in Europe soon facilitated by the Soviet agent and German communist Willi Münzenberg, who set up international organizations to rally prominent cultural figures behind the USSR: Hands off Russia lobbies, International Worker's Relief committees, and the Society of Friends of the New Russia.

The switch was not restricted to the radical-chic set: many of the leaders of the Western communist parties themselves had begun their political careers as anarchists. A number of the founders of the French and German communist parties had been anarcho-syndicalists who were bowled over by the Bolsheviks' success at making a revolution.[17] Sylvia Pankhurst, the militant suffragette and cofounder of the British Communist Party, was a former anarchist sympathizer. In America, William Z. Foster, leader of the Communist Party USA (CPUSA) and presidential candidate in 1924, 1928, and 1932, followed a not uncommon path in making the transition from American populism to IWW syndicalism to Leninism/Stalinism. He took to the latter because he understood it as a form of "anarchism made practical" that could impose a much-needed discipline on the ranks of revolutionaries.[18]

The movement from anarchism to Russian communism sometimes resulted from conscious revolutionary strategizing but often reflected ideological confusion. Few intellectuals understood that Lenin and Trotsky were autocratic. Most believed that the Bolshevik leaders were implementing the decentralizing anarchist agenda that had long been recognized as the hallmark of Russian radicalism. Socialist enthusiasts idealized the soviets as the political adaptation of the vaunted Russian peasant village, with its communal, participatory, localist features. Soviet Russia seemed to have achieved the primitive, direct democracy conjured up before 1917 in the writings of the Russian Populists, Tolstoy, and Kropotkin. In the words of John Reed, author of the ecstatically pro-Bolshevik eyewitness account of the revolution *Ten Days That Shook the World*, "No political body more sensitive and responsive to the popular will was ever invented."[19] The same misconceptions were held by the German insurrectionists of 1919 when they tried to galvanize society to revolutionary action through the formation of their own soviets (*Räte*). Likewise, Antonio Gramsci, cofounder of the Italian Communist Party, proposed establishing factory soviets (*consigli di fabbrica*) as a means of breaking down the mental wall that separated the revolutionary elite from the masses.[20] Most of these Western radicals were unaware that the Russian Communist Party authorities were stripping the soviets of power and using them as fronts for a highly centralized governmental structure.

Even more deeply entrenched than the sense that all Russian revolutionaries were anarchists was the image of the Russian soul. The Western intellectuals' understanding of Bolshevism and the October revolution was colored by a long-standing perception of Russia as a spiritual force, the key to earthly salvation. In the 1890s, the French chauvinist Juliette Adam had truly believed that the Franco-Russian alliance was a "mystical union transcending ordinary human associations."[21] Interpretations of Dostoevsky and Tolstoy indicate that these kinds of perceptions about Russia were widespread, and they were strongest among radicals who already anticipated a coming socialist millennium. According to Max Eastman, among Western communists and communist sympathizers, the Russian Revolution "had taken the place of Christ's second coming."[22] John Reed offered this testimony: "I suddenly realized that the devout Russian people no longer needed priests to pray them into heaven. On earth they were building a kingdom more bright than any heaven had to offer, and for which it was a glory to die."[23]

Reed may now seem naive, but such views were not at all uncommon. Arthur Holitscher, a wealthy but radical-socialist German travel writer, saw Russian Bolshevism as the emanation of a "magnetic, cosmic power."[24] Diego Rivera's wife, Frida Kahlo, the half German-Jewish, half Mexican painter, turned to communism for spiritual solace after the amputation of her leg, whereupon she painted Marx and Stalin as gods.[25] French novelist and (for a time) fellow traveler André Gide wrote, "I must admit it, what leads me to Communism is not Marx, it is the Gospel." "In the abominable distress of the present world," he stated in 1932 during the Great Depression, "new Russia's [Five-Year] plan now seems to me salvation. . . . And if my life were necessary to ensure the success of the U.S.S.R., I should give it at once."[26]

When it came to interpreting Soviet economic planning, supposedly rationalist intellectuals in the West were just as prone to messianic delusions as were Romantic radicals like John Reed. American thinker John Dewey, traveling to Russia during the Stalinist industrialization drive, felt "as if for the first time I might have some inkling of what may have been the moving spirit and force of primitive Christianity."[27] Overlooking the suffering of the Soviet citizenry, Sidney and Beatrice Webb claimed that Stalin was forging an entirely "new civilisation" with a truly democratic system of representation, mechanized large-scale farming, the abolition of profits, social equality, and centralized planning for both industrial production and community consumption.[28] Certainly for many intellectuals, the Great Depression justified their support of Communist Russia, which seemed to be advancing while the West was in decline. But the utopian outlook of Dewey and the Webbs indicates that communism functioned largely as a secular faith for the left-wing intelligentsia.

The USSR acquired a utopian halo partly in connection with the survival of the nineteenth-century Western attitude that Russia was primitive, exotic, and "Oriental," thus all the more intense spiritually, all the more likely to be considered the repository of true wisdom. "C'est l'Asie! c'est l'Inde! c'est la Chine!" Juliette Adam joyously proclaimed upon arrival in Moscow in 1882.[29] As one of her contemporaries wrote, "all Russians . . . have an Oriental mode of thinking, . . . [concerned with] universal existence."[30] Their "vigorous barbarism," argued another Frenchman, was humane and would contribute to the advance of civilization.[31] That was precisely the view of most left intellectuals after the revolution too. Far removed from the West, Russia was commonly seen as a "bridge to Asia."[32] Gide had been attracted to Dostoevskian Christianity because of its "contact between the Gospels and Buddhism";[33] at least until he observed the country firsthand, he thought the same about Russian communism. So did Nobel laureate Romain Rolland, the French novelist, Gandhian, and Stalinist, whose Russian wife was (unbeknownst to him) an agent of the Soviet secret police.[34] For Weimar-German Dadaist Franz Jung, the USSR represented an Asian-metaphysical-revolutionary force out of which would emerge "light," "equality and communal joy."[35]

It may seem as though the intellectuals had an astonishing capacity for fooling themselves. From 1917 on, against all the evidence, many of them denied that the Soviet government was a dictatorship terrorizing its populace. British playwright and Fabian socialist George Bernard Shaw insisted that Stalin was "simply secretary of the supreme controlling organ of the hierarchy, subject to dismissal at ten minutes' notice if he does not give satisfaction."[36] At the height of Stalin's purges, German author Lion Feuchtwanger wrote that people enjoyed "genuine" freedom in Russia, whereas in the West it was "bogus."[37] Every communist sympathizer in Europe and the United States would have agreed with Rolland's 1932 statement: "The murderous immorality of the [capitalist] . . . system must. . . . be destroyed. Now the USSR represents the only force, the only new social faith in Europe (or America) which is profoundly alive and fertile."[38] Of the many culture stars who made the pilgrimage to the Soviet utopia, their travels carefully stage-managed by the authorities, only a few—Gide, H. G. Wells, and Mary Poppins creator P. L. Travers among them—came away disillusioned.[39] Most praised the USSR to the heavens.

But the pro-Soviet Western intelligentsia were not as gullible as is often thought. By and large they hated their own capitalist society and wanted to stick it to the bourgeoisie. Even though most would not have wanted to live there, the Soviet Union offered revolutionary solutions to the problems of class conflict and poverty that had agitated the left intellectuals for so long. The Western defenders of Communist Russia were not liberals in the traditional sense: they valued egalitarianism, communitarianism, and abstract mankind more highly than they did the individual. That is why they had little trouble justifying the suppression of civil liberties, mass arrests, and political terror in Russia. And like Lenin, many were elitists disdainful of the masses on whose behalf they claimed to speak; if it was necessary to drag the backward petit-bourgeois peasants into modernity by forcing them into collective farms and liquidating rich rural families, so be it. Of course, some of the radical Western intellectuals were in denial about Bolshevik excesses, and none knew the true extent of the violence, but the fact remains that they wanted extreme solutions and were willing to tolerate brutal dictatorial methods as long as they struck a blow against the capitalist devils. Before 1917, progressives in the West had admired the violence of the Russian revolutionaries; now, too, they felt that the ends justified the violent means utilized by the revolutionary Russian government. Socialist tyranny was a small price to pay for the dawn of a new humanity.[40]

When leftist fellow travelers did start to have doubts about the Soviet Union because of the Stalinist show trials, their potential defection from pro-communist ranks was forestalled by the rise of Hitler, Franco, and Mussolini. The Western democracies seemed unable or unwilling to stand up to the threat of fascism, but Russia, they imagined, was a bulwark against this evil. Lest it work to the advantage of the right, Rolland and others like him refused to give the USSR any bad press even when they knew something of the persecutions taking place there. As exiled German novelist Heinrich Mann explained, referring to the Soviets, "the enemies of my enemy are my friends."[41] On the same grounds, after 1945 many leftists, like Sartre, continued to side with the Soviet Union or their Third World allies in dogged opposition to the dominant power of the capitalist United States.

Because the Soviet system attracted the allegiance of several generations of Western intellectuals and fellow travelers between 1917 and 1950, these years are often called the "Red" or "Pink" decades. But in many ways that is a mischaracterization, based on the overestimation of Russian communist influence made by both its supporters and its opponents. In reality, in no Western nation except Weimar Germany was communism as great a force outside the intelligentsia as is often thought.

Most socialists, anarchists, and even liberals initially hailed the Bolshevik revolution.[42] But far from sweeping the left-wing political movements in the United States and Europe, the Russian communist victory plunged them into debilitating internal conflict. Communist radicals quit the socialist parties, which, free of the extremists, then moved toward the political center. For moderate Western socialists, the ruthless dictatorship of the Russian communist state sullied the name of the left and frightened off voters. Although it urged diplomatic recognition of the USSR, the English Labour Party was hostile to the British Communists and dissociated itself from Bolshevism by arguing against revolution and for parliamentary democracy. The other democratic-socialist parties of Europe and also Australia did the same. Despite that, their liberal and conservative political opponents made every effort to paint them as "red."

One might have encountered Bolshevik slogans and red flags at post–World War I labor rallies, but the backing given Western communist parties by the proletariat was also surprisingly weak. Overall the working classes of the West showed little inclination to vote communist. There were some exceptions: traditionally volatile coal miners and dockworkers; several unions within the American CIO that Communist Party members controlled; and rising numbers of Germans between 1929 and 1933 (in the November 1932 parliamentary elections, the communists received 17 percent of the vote). But otherwise, workers had by and large bought into the capitalist system and were not going to support a party that sought to destroy it, even during the Great Depression. Typical was the American presidential election of 1932, when the Communist Party won 100,000 votes, its best performance ever, but nothing compared to the 22.8 million ballots cast for FDR. After World War II, the French and Italian communist parties, led by pro-Soviet functionaries and partly inspired by the enormous sacrifices made by the Soviet people during the war, grew as large as the other major parties but were never able to capture enough popular backing, even among the working class, to bring themselves to power.

Besides lack of popular interest, a major part of the problem was that rank-and-file Western communists were themselves often turned off by the party's behavior. The subjugation of all communist parties to Moscow, the Stalinization of the leadership, the dogmatism of party officials, and the witch-hunt atmosphere drove many supporters away. Revelations of the Great Terror caused the Soviet Union's following in the West to waver, and upon the consummation of the Nazi-Soviet alliance in 1939, communism appeared to many party members as "the God that failed."[43] After that they quit in a steady stream.

Not only was Russian-inspired communism a weaker force on the socialist left than is often assumed. Its impact on economics and social reform in the twentieth-century West has also been vastly inflated. The Soviet Union has been both blamed and lauded for inspiring the social welfare state, Keynesian economics, European economic planning, the New Deal, women's liberation, and the struggle for racial integration in the U.S. South. As a recent commentator writes after providing just such a list, "Communism made life difficult for Western establishments, and it is doubtful that reforms would have come when they did if the USSR had not existed. . . . Ironically, . . . the existence of the Soviet Union helped the capitalist West reform itself and avoid the bloody revolutions of the East."[44]

These arguments are inaccurate. The basic conceptions of Western economic planning or the welfare state owed little to the Soviet Union. These features of modern European and American history evolved from a social and political dynamic specific to each nation and were on the way to being developed before 1917; they then received further impetus in the aftermath of World War I demobilization, the Great Depression, and World War II. English Liberal leader David Lloyd George and the American politicians Woodrow Wilson, Herbert Hoover, and Franklin Roosevelt did all speak at one time or another of instituting radical reforms to stem the tide of revolutionary and working-class unrest affecting American or British society in the interwar era. But although the Russian Revolution heightened fears of class conflict throughout the Western world, neither the problem itself nor the proposed cures had much to do with Russian communism. Wilson and Hoover were already arguing *before* the Bolshevik revolution for government intervention in the economy, in part to prevent the kind of political chaos Russia had experienced because of the failings of the tsarist regime. Pro-labor legislation was to some extent intended to weaken the feared attraction to communism in the factories, but mostly it, too, resulted from a growing consensus in Western nations that it would boost social justice and economic productivity. In fact, far from frightening political leaders into social welfare and labor reform, Bolshevism had the opposite effect of delaying federal welfare measures in the United States, where opponents attacked them, unfairly, as Russian-communist inspired. And in every country of the Western world, governments and employers answered labor union demands with the accusation of Bolshevism, which then gave them the excuse to—often literally—beat back strikers.[45]

As for the impact of the USSR on Western economic policies, that, too, was minimal. In the 1920s and 1930s, segments of the intellectual and political elite increasingly felt that laissez-faire capitalism had failed, and that extensive government measures to regulate the economy and ensure social stability were necessary. The

Soviet Five-Year Plans received constant press coverage and fascinated everyone. But that was all they did. FDR's many critics may have smelled the "foul breath of communistic Russia" in the New Deal,[46] but its architects were pragmatists who considered Stalinist economics an unacceptable blueprint for American society, with its already advanced industrial sector. "God knows when I am going to get time to listen to a long recital on Russia," wrote New Dealer Harold Ickes, uninterested in hearing reports on the USSR.[47] Even the most radical among FDR's advisers, Rexford Tugwell, who was impressed with what he saw on a visit to the Soviet Union, felt that Scandinavia offered more relevant models to the United States. Indeed, if there were any foreign sources of reformist ideas adopted in this country, they came from capitalist Europe rather than Russia. They also traveled in the reverse direction, as France under the anticommunist socialist leader Léon Blum and other continental European nations of the 1930s began instituting "New Deals" in imitation of the United States.[48]

In England, too, modifications of the nineteenth-century liberal capitalist system took place without emulating the USSR. The father of the mixed economy and government economic management, John Maynard Keynes, was hoping to save capitalism, and in particular to achieve full employment, by correcting the flaws of the free market—but not by adopting the "illogical and . . . dull" ideas of Marxian socialism or Russian communism, which he felt had "no intellectual interest or scientific value."[49] Likewise, communism had negligible influence on the socialist policies of the Labour Party, which gave up thinking about economic planning precisely because it was not democratic. After 1945 the party came out for the nationalization of the heights of industry, but that was far different from the situation in the USSR, where all private commercial activity was outlawed. The precedent for nationalizing industry lay in the traditional British public ownership of the docks, and the inspiration came from preexisting utilitarian and technocratic strains of thought; the British Labour Party rejected the Soviet example as inapplicable. In Britain as in the United States, capitalism and state regulation of economic life were reconciled to achieve stability in a manner consistent with long-standing reformist projects that were on the way to fulfillment without stimuli from Russia.[50]

On the matter of women's liberation, the role of communism was no greater than in other realms. Soviet guarantees of gender equality and the abolition of restrictions on divorce and abortion did attract the attention of Western activists concerned with these issues. Norman Haire, president of the British section of the World League for Sexual Reform, announced that the sexual code of the USSR was a "fascinating experiment which we sexologists in other countries are watching with great interest."[51] But the agitation for women's rights was already underway before the rise of the Soviet Union and, like welfare reform, would likely have developed just as it did with or without the Russians.

Finally, in the American Southern Civil Rights movement, communists played only an ancillary role, despite the allegations of the FBI and white segregationists. It is true that many black radicals looked to Stalin as a "new Lincoln" for supposedly bestowing equal rights upon the minorities of his country.[52] And black and white communists were active (though so was the NAACP) in organizing among African American workers and sharecroppers in the Deep South during the 1930s and 1940s. But that was in spite of the Soviet Union, whose call for black territorial self-determination in the United States was so inflammatory that, in a rare display of autonomy from Moscow, the CPUSA refused to endorse it. Few African Americans were interested in communism at all, and even those prominent black intellectuals who made trips to Moscow and were considered pro-Soviet, like W.E.B. Du Bois and the Harlem Renaissance poet and novelist Claude McKay, expressed wariness of communist tactics. Both suspected the Communist Party (of Russia and America) of prejudice and warned against the indoctrination that prevented communists from attempting independent analyses of the state of race relations in the United States. There were exceptions, like Pan-Africanist Marcus Garvey in the post–World War I era, or singer-actor Paul Robson a generation later, but their enthusiasm for the Soviet Union had little impact at home.[53]

All in all, the proponents and antagonists of communism have significantly overstated its importance in the West. Yet what a reaction there was! Through much of the twentieth century, a fear of class war, creeping communism, and Russian conquest was recurrent and at times pervasive. Anticommunism affected almost all aspects of international relations, from Woodrow Wilson's Fourteen Points (in part a reaction to Lenin's call for a new world order), to the appeasement of Hitler (whom many saw as a lesser evil than Stalin), to the Cold War. Anticommunism shaped domestic affairs as well, and not just in the United States. What first comes to mind are the American Red Scare of 1919–1920 and the McCarthyite 1950s. But the (nonexistent) "Bolshevik danger" of 1919–1920 in Italy helped to pave Mussolini's path to power, and throughout the interwar years French police dragnets and deportations of suspected alien communists made American civil-liberties violations against radicals pale in comparison.[54] And none of this approaches the scale of the German dread of Russian-Jewish Bolshevism, which affected the fate of the Weimar Republic and the entire world.

But why all the fury and phobia of anticommunism if communism itself was so insignificant (outside of Germany)? Partly it was a reasonable response to Soviet terror at home and aggression abroad. Woodrow Wilson could have been speaking for any liberal Western leader when he expressed his repugnance at the Bolshevik regime: it meant "government by terror, . . . not government by vote. It is the negation of everything that is American."[55] Over the course of the subsequent decades, the understanding of communist Russia as "totalitarian" became fixed in the public consciousness as the antithesis of democracy and capitalism. The mistrust that this point of view implied was suspended during the World War II alliance with the Russians, but it was never far from the surface and revived with full force immediately thereafter.

During the Cold War, it seems that Stalin was more cautious in foreign affairs than was realized at the time, and the military capacity of the USSR was more limited than once thought. But the Soviet dictator, as a Marxist ideologue, was irremediably suspicious of his capitalist allies and wanted to establish as large a buffer zone around his country as he could get away with. "Whoever occupies a territory," noted Stalin in 1945, "also imposes his own social system. . . . It cannot be otherwise."[56] Manifesting the same paranoid obsession with security that led to the Great Terror at home, Stalin forcibly imposed Russian communist dominion over much of Eastern Europe. The closing of the Iron Curtain, inflammatory propaganda invoking East-West, communist-capitalist conflict, and the theft of nuclear secrets by Soviet espionage all raised the hackles of the West. It was not just that Russia set off balance-of-power alarm bells; with Hitler still painfully fresh in their minds, Western statesmen were determined not to fall into the same trap their predecessors had with the German dictator. As Truman's secretary of defense James V. Forrestal stated, "It seems doubtful that we should endeavor to buy [the Russians'] understanding and sympathy. We tried that once with Hitler. There are no returns on appeasement."[57]

These moral and strategic reactions to the problem of the Russian communist state were legitimate, even if sometimes flawed in execution because no one knew for sure how far abroad Stalin's ambitions lay. But they were preconditioned by a long history of concern about Russian tyranny and expansionism going back to the sixteenth century, increasing during the reigns of Peter the Great and Catherine the Great, and heightening even further in the nineteenth century because of Anglo-Russian and Franco-Russian imperial rivalries across Asia.[58] At the same time, Kaiser Wilhelm II and his General Staff saw Russia as standing in the way of German greatness, a giant whom they wanted to cut down to size. Because of the German menace, France and England reconciled with Russia between 1890 and 1914, ultimately fighting on the same side in World War I. American doubts about joining the side of the tsarist autocracy were obviated by its overthrow, but the tentative alliance did not survive the Bolshevik revolution.[59]

Early Soviet attempts through its Comintern wing to spread revolution to Europe and the colonies confirmed the deeply rooted suspicions held toward Russia, but a great deal of the communism phobia of Europe and America was bound up with internal anxieties. In the aftermath of World War I, patriotic passions and the fear of subversion were transferred from the kaiser's Germany to Lenin's Russia, and institutions geared up to suppress dissent easily shifted attention to the new enemy. In 1918 or 1919 came unprecedented levels of labor strife, short-lived but terrifying revolutions in central Europe, and, in the United States, a rash of anarchist bombings. Many people imagined that Bolshevik aliens were behind these events. The presence of large foreign populations alarmed anti-immigrant nativists, who saw Italian and eastern European Jewish communities as breeding grounds of radicalism. Similar attitudes were held toward the refugees from the Russian Revolution who flooded into western Europe after 1917. For the next two decades, France, as the center of this migration, witnessed murder, kidnapping, and cloak-and-dagger conspiracies involving Soviet spies, Trotskyites, and Russian royalists. French newspapers, films, and popular crime novels made them appear to be omnipresent extensions of the upheaval and atrocities taking place in the USSR.[60]

Woodrow Wilson again seemed to reflect the opinion of the entire Western establishment when he urged his nation to take all possible measures to stop Russian communism—the "poison of disorder, the poison of revolt, the poison of chaos"—from spreading abroad.[61] His attorney general, A. Mitchell Palmer, and the head of the General Intelligence Division (later FBI), J. Edgar Hoover, were both architects of the illegal roundups of alien radicals Wilson sanctioned in 1919–1920. They felt that a small group of revolutionaries could overthrow the American government just as easily as they had done in Russia. Already, they were convinced, immigrants, labor unions, and African Americans were "seeing red," as Palmer put it, and coming under Moscow's control.[62] Most European leaders believed there were similar trends in their own countries—or if they knew otherwise, cynically exploited popular fears thereof for political gain.

Negative stereotypes that were the mirror image of the radical intelligentsia's Russophilia also played a major role in accounting for the heightened fears of communism in this era. Bolshevism was thought to be another phase of the international anarchist conspiracy governments had been fighting for several decades. To the same degree that leftists had once adored anarchism, the establishment regarded it as villainous: Theodore Roosevelt called it a "a crime against the whole human race."[63] The English *Gentleman's Magazine* (1895) wrote that anarchists were the "very dregs of the population, the riff-raff of rascaldom, professional thieves [and] bullies."[64]

These same formulas were applied to Russian communism after 1917. "Sick," "born criminals," "anarchists" were the characterizations of Lenin and Trotsky appearing in the liberal French press.[65] American attorney general Palmer justified his crackdown on alien radicals by claiming that Bolshevism was the worst form of anarchism, the "creed of any criminal mind," for whom "robbery, not war, is the ideal." "Sinister" and "unclean," foreign anarchists "in the pay or under the criminal spell of Trotsky and Lenine [*sic*]" planned to foment revolution, destroy religion, and "replace marriage vows with libertine laws, burning up the foundations of society" in what would resemble a "prairie fire."[66] Films and editorial cartoons from 1900 to 1930 in the United States and Europe alike reflected and sustained these interpretations, depicting anarchists, communists, and Russians as one and the same, all disheveled, wildly gesticulating, bomb-throwing maniacs.[67]

Integral to this image was the perception of Bolshevism as a primitive, Asiatic phenomenon. This, too, reflected both the fascination and the repugnance with which Russia had long been viewed. Russians were seen as uncivilized Eastern barbarians from the moment they began interacting with western Europe. Elizabethans observed with distaste the "Russian grandees, dropping pearls and vermin" who made up the first Muscovite diplomatic mission to London in the sixteenth century.[68] A generation after Russian troops had defeated Napoleon and occupied Paris, the French marquis de Custine asserted that "there is between France and Russia a Chinese wall—the Slavonic language and character. . . . [Asia] commences" on the Russian border.[69] In late-nineteenth- and early-twentieth-century Germany, Baltic-German immigrant intellectuals like the popular writer and professor Paul Rohrbach, the conservative historian, columnist, and Wilhelmine courtier Theodor Schiemann, or the Nazi ideologue Alfred Rosenberg based their counsels of anti-Russian aggression on similar arguments, tinged with both contempt and fear.[70] These were not the only views of Russia at the time, but they were strong currents and nourished Germany's expansionist ambitions to its east. In Britain and the United States, opinions were not that different. In 1904 Sir Cecil Spring-Rice spoke of Russia rather than Japan as the real "Yellow Peril." His close friend and confidant, President Theodore Roosevelt, agreed.[71]

Once the Bolsheviks took charge in Russia, they bore the brunt of these barbarian-Asian stereotypes, which were the converse of the Russian soul mystique. Conspiracy theories suggesting that communism was an Oriental-Jewish plot were rife, and not just among proto-Nazi Germans. Wilson's secretary of state, Robert Lansing, for one, was convinced of their truth. Another common refrain among anticommunists everywhere was that "squads of Chinese executioners" were committing atrocities at the command of Lenin and Trotsky.[72] Typical were the imaginings of the best-selling French spy novel by Charles Robert-Dumas, *The Lead Idol* (1935): the Bolshevik secret agent Mâh Le Sinistre is a fanatical Mongolian who slits open his victims' bellies in seedy hotels and concocts perfumes with which he can seduce women and murder all the inhabitants of Paris. Serge de Chessin's *The Night Which Comes from the Orient* (1929) describes Russia (incoherently) as "a thick night, an integral darkness, a renewal of the Mongol invasion on a spiritual plane awaiting an apocalyptic raid from bolshevized Asia."[73] This was little different from the official assessments of American policy makers, whether in 1919, when J. Edgar Hoover called Russian communism the "most terrible menace . . . since the barbarian hordes overran West Europe and opened the Dark Ages," or 1945, when Averell Harriman, the U.S. ambassador to Moscow, accused the Soviets of launching the "twentieth-century barbarian invasion of Europe."[74]

Such views expressed the foreboding that decades of warfare, ideological conflict, and economic turbulence had aroused. And these views had a significant bearing on reactions to Fascism and Nazism. These right-extremist parties thrived on the Bolshevik bogeyman. In Italy and Germany, Mussolini and Hitler fanned the flames of middle-class and elite anxieties about Russian Bolshevism to win mass electoral support and gain the backing of political power brokers. Mussolini initially earned the respect of Western, anticommunist politicians such as Winston Churchill, who in 1927 proclaimed to Roman Fascists that "if I had been an Italian I am sure I should have been entirely with you from the beginning to the end of your victorious struggle against the bestial appetites and passions of Leninism."[75] After establishing his dictatorship, Hitler continued to harp on the threat of the "Red terror" to negate western European diplomatic opposition to his military buildup. British prime minister Neville Chamberlain, one of the authors of appeasement, saw Hitler as the lesser of two evils: should Hitler fall, he asked, "who will guarantee that Germany will not become Bolshevistic?" French premier Édouard Daladier, too, was convinced that if not for Nazi Germany, "the Cossacks [would] rule Europe."[76] Some French nationalists went so far as to believe that a French victory over Hitler would be worse than defeat, as it would mean the collapse of the Third Reich, the "main rampart against Communist revolution."[77] The irony is that the Italian and German dictatorships had cloned many features of the Soviet system that seemed so terrifying. In fact, this was the main legacy of Russian communism in Europe.

Communism and the New Forms
of Dictatorship

WHERE Russian communism was most directly influential was not in relatively stable democracies but within European and Third World authoritarian movements in nations where many were already receptive to Communist Russia's challenge to Western capitalism and imperialism. Here, would-be dictators customized the seductive techniques offered by the Soviet model. Created by Lenin and refined by Stalin, the one-party dictatorship and command economy would be Russia's most consequential bequest to twentieth-century history.

Fascism, Nazism, and the Soviet Model

Neither Fascist Italy nor Nazi Germany was a carbon copy of the Leninist/Stalinist state as the popular understanding of totalitarianism might suggest.[1] Their leaders were pragmatic revolutionaries, who, in their thirst for power, were willing to borrow from an eclectic variety of political sources. In ideology, the Russian nationalist elements increasingly present in the Soviet Union were counterbalanced by universalist and even humanitarian claims that were completely lacking in the purely chauvinistic belief systems of Mussolini and Hitler. Unlike the Bolshevik Party, an underground organization that seized governmental authority in the midst of revolution, the Fascist and Nazi Parties came to power partly through thuggish street violence, but by and large legally within existing parliamentary regimes—which they subsequently destroyed from within.

Nor as they evolved did the German and Italian dictatorships function precisely the way the Soviet Union under Lenin or Stalin did. National and international circumstances as well as the individual personality traits of the leaders shaped each society differently. Although Mussolini was the only one of the three dictators to openly proclaim that creating a totalitarian state was his ambition, Italy under his rule never endured the same degree of one-party control over life as in Germany and Russia. Il Duce had the upper hand but failed to fully neutralize the church, monarchy, or old social elites. Mussolini subordinated the Fascist Party to the Italian state apparatus, and, although some industrialists feared the imposition of a "black [i.e., fascist] bolshevism" in the economy, "corporatist" state interventionism did not undermine the existing capitalist structure.[2] Although Mussolini made a concerted effort at coercion and enticement to cow and mobilize the populace, the results he sought were elusive. Like a "chameleon," he often altered his policies to suit the demands of his various constituencies, who ended up shaping him as much as he did them.[3]

This contrasted with the do-or-die apocalypticism of Hitler, or the dogmatism of Lenin and Stalin, who sacrificed ideological consistency for political survival but nonetheless viewed the world through Marxist lenses. Although Mussolini violently suppressed enemies and dissenters, he did not resort to bloodshed on the scale of the Nazis or Soviets, whose leaders, on top of having the routine insecurities of dictators, had a Manichaean outlook and were hell-bent on liquidating those who appeared to represent the forces of evil.

On the surface, the mass terror unleashed in Germany and Russia makes these two dictatorships seem a totalitarian pair. But they, too, differed from each other in significant ways. Hitler's racial suprematism propelled his terror along a specific but limited path, against Jews, their purported Marxist allies, and other targeted minorities (Gypsies, homosexuals, Jehovah's Witnesses, etc.), as well as political opponents. Outside of these categories, the average German's chances of avoiding secret-police harassment were high. Russian state terror was another matter. No single ethnic group was targeted for extermination as the Jews were in the Third Reich. Arbitrariness was the rule as even the most loyal communists often fell under suspicion, and with them their families or close associates. Anyone might be arrested in Stalin's Russia, be they lowly peasant or high party official. Stalin, furthermore, enjoyed playing a sadistic cat-and-mouse game with some of his victims and closely directed the repressive operations of the secret police.

That personal detail highlights a major distinction between the overall political functioning of the two dictatorships. Stalin was an interventionist ruler who meticulously supervised the mechanisms of power, monopolized decision making, and inspired the bureaucracy through fear. He and his ministers constituted a well-defined, coordinating power center the like of which was lacking in Nazi Germany. Hitler, having retained his bohemian disposition, was completely uninterested in routine desk work and remained aloof from the day-to-day details of government activity. After 1933 he devoted the bulk of his work time to plotting wars of conquest. This allowed his devoted underlings wide latitude to operate on their own, establishing policies they interpreted to be consistent with their Führer's aims. Their efforts to win his attention and favor did not prevent them from pursuing departmental rivalries and corrupt personal agendas that quickly eroded the efficiency of both party and civil bureaucracies.

The distinctions pointed out here among Bolshevik, Fascist, and Nazi autocracies cast doubt on the validity of the hypothesis that these systems were three variations on a common totalitarian theme. Yet while the scholars on both sides of the dispute over this issue have engaged in elaborate comparative analyses of the three dictatorships, they have rarely attempted to ascertain the specific ways Fascist Italy or Nazi Germany learned from the Soviet Union.[4] And despite the very real divergence between them, there is sufficient evidence to show that the Leninist-Stalinist state provided Mussolini and Hitler, if not all of the materials needed, at least the basic blueprint for the erection of a regime seeking monolithic authority. Mussolini, Hitler, and their henchmen kept a close watch on developments in the Soviet Union and adapted its central methods of acquiring or holding onto power.

Italian fascism emerged from Mussolini's revolutionary socialism. Before founding the Fascist Party, Mussolini (1883–1945) had
been one of the leading Marxists of Europe. He called himself an
"authoritarian communist" and led a "truculent," maximalist
wing of the Italian socialist movement.[5] Like Lenin, he hated bourgeois political and economic institutions, saw violence as a desirable political tool, favored the creation of an antidemocratic party
led by professional revolutionaries, idolized the machine as a
model for social organization, and made a revolution in a relatively
underdeveloped European nation. So close in spirit was he that
Lenin lamented his loss to the right, and Trotsky considered him
his best pupil in the art of revolution.[6]

Mussolini's Marxism grew independently of Lenin and was
rooted in the political irrationalism and elitism of contemporary
theorists Gaetano Mosca, Vilfredo Pareto, and Henri Bergson, and
in the militancy of the anarcho-syndicalists. But there was overlap
between Mussolini and Lenin in the absorption of the insurrection-
ist ideas of the French socialist Louis Auguste Blanqui and in the
attraction to Russian radicalism. Mussolini, the son of a Bakuninist, had translated Kropotkin from the French and advocated political violence along the lines of Russian terrorists like Sophia Perovskaya, whom he heroized.[7] Moreover, living in Swiss exile
(1902–1904) at the same time the Bolshevik Party was formed, he
sought out the Russian socialists who had found refuge there, and
was familiar with their ideological disputes: "I can't remember
whether I met [Lenin] in Zurich with the others. . . . [but] we all
used to argue a great deal with one another."[8]

Although Mussolini eventually renounced the left, the radical
and conspiratorial orientation of his socialist days stayed with him
to the end. His intellectual, psychological, and political makeup
was such that he would be receptive to the techniques of Leninism
as he carried out the Fascist takeover of Italy. As his *Complete
Works* indicate, Mussolini's journalistic writings from 1917 on
comment frequently on Russian communism. Despite his expressions of disdain, he viewed it as being closely related to his own
movement. By the early 1920s, his writings depicted Soviet Russia
as an imperialistic autocracy favoring industrial interests and

mocked its leader as "His Majesty Lenin I."[9] But he also applauded the Bolshevik dictator for ruthlessly crushing his opponents.[10] Later, Mussolini praised the "crypto-fascist" Stalin for what he perceived to be his implementation of a national-socialist agenda.[11] And Mussolini applied lessons he had learned from the Russian Revolution at the same time that he whipped up anticommunist sentiment to justify the 1922 March on Rome which vaulted him into office. When once discussing the street fighting of his black-shirted *squadristi* and the Fascist occupation of government offices and telephone exchanges in the period leading up to his political triumph, Mussolini admitted that "our tactics were decidedly Russian."[12]

In his gradual consolidation of dictatorial power, Mussolini also had the "powerfully armed" Russian "superstate" in mind.[13] Referring to the communists, he stated in 1921 that "we, like you, consider necessary a centralized and unitary State which imposes an iron discipline on all individuals."[14] Asked a decade later whether "in Italy the Party and the government are simultaneously incorporated in your own person . . . [as] in Russia under Lenin," Mussolini replied, "I don't deny the similarities." "Here, as in Russia," he remarked, "we are advocates of the collective significance of life and we wish to develop this at the cost of individualism."[15]

Other Fascists admired Bolshevism too: their press was engaged in an extensive, complex debate on Soviet experience, and by no means were all the conclusions negative. Radical-right intellectuals like Ardengo Soffici felt the Fascists should follow the Bolsheviks in "trying the experiment of a plunge into refreshing barbarism."[16] Achille Starace, the Fascist Party secretary, envied the Stalinist regime and emulated it as he strove to expand his party's authority in the 1930s.[17] Fascist Party arts administrators openly sought emulation of the Soviet regime's impressive propaganda innovations in the arts and film. Mussolini himself summed up their sentiments when, intent on improving the quality of fascist propaganda films, he noted that "the Russians set us a good example there."[18]

Perhaps nothing gives a clearer indication of Mussolini's debt to the Soviet Union than the creation of the Fascist Party "Cheka." Named after the Bolshevik secret-police agency, this was the secret cell Il Duce organized in 1924 with his next-in-commands Filippo

Marinelli and Cesare Rossi. Its charge was to terrorize antifascist opponents, and, as in Russia, it was directly subordinate to the party leader and expected to act above the law. It was this organization that in June 1924 murdered Mussolini's most outspoken critic, the socialist parliamentarian Giacomo Matteotti. Although Mussolini continued to expand Fascist secret-police activity in the years to come, the fact that judicial pressure forced him to have the hit man arrested, effectively shutting down the "Cheka," indicates the gap between his powers and those of Lenin or Stalin.[19] But Bolshevism provided Mussolini and the Fascists with the measure of the kind of state they intended to create.

Mussolini's drive for monolithic power made a deep impression on Hitler (1889–1945). The Führer cult emerged in the mid-1920s out of the Nazis' hero worship of their leader and Hitler's own self-image as a Germanic version of Il Duce. In this regard, as in its overall negation of liberal politics, the Third Reich showed the influence of Italian fascism. But the Nazis came somewhat closer to realizing their totalitarian aspirations than did Mussolini's regime, and in part that was because they were more successful at integrating elements from the Soviet paradigm.

In an atmosphere of violent hostility toward the West, a pronounced segment of the far right in Weimar Germany had been receptive to the Bolsheviks. German anticommunism in this period followed the same patterns as in every other country, with the difference that the short-lived revolutions after World War I intensified the phobia. But many Pan-German intellectuals in the right-extremist camp, like the Dostoevsky disciple Moeller van den Bruck, mythologized the Russian soul and advocated a pro-Bolshevik foreign policy for Germany. Despite their opposition to the German left, they saw in Moscow the ideal partner for an anti-Western, anticapitalist alliance.[20]

A certain contingent of the freebooters within the paramilitary Freikorps, which gleefully participated in crushing the 1918–1919 left-wing uprisings in Munich and Berlin, also sympathized with Bolshevism. Many did join Freikorps units out of fear of revolution, but the "Red peril" gave a large number of these demobilized veterans an excuse to fight just for the sake of fighting. Among them were antimodern extremists whose hatred for the Weimar Republic and the West led them to espouse Soviet communism. They called Lenin a "great Führer" and themselves "Bolsheviks of the right." Friedrich Wilhelm Heinz, a Freikorps officer and, later, a Supreme Leader of the Nazi Stormtroopers (SA) in Western Germany, wrote in 1932 that "Russia . . . gave the example: . . . Attack! Attack with arms! Attack by terror and atrocities! Attack to the point of destruction!"[21]

Hitler knew his supporters well. Freikorps vigilantes entered the Nazi Party (NSDAP) out of attraction to its socialist agenda and violent radicalism, but they were tempted to join the German Communist Party (KPD) for the same reason. Aware that brown-shirted SA militants were drifting away from the NSDAP and into the communist camp, he was persuaded to go against his political instincts and instigate the Beer Hall Putsch of 1923 to appease hotheads who were thirsting for an immediate assault on the republic.[22] He also recognized that communist street fighters were hard-core opponents of Weimar democracy whom he could win over to the Nazi side.[23] In the aftermath of the 1933 Nazi takeover, while the KPD leadership was being pulverized in the concentration camps, rank-and-file ex-communists flooded into the Gestapo and SA, where they were known as "beefsteak" Nazis—brown on the outside, red on the inside.[24]

Hitler viscerally hated Bolshevism as a manifestation of the global Jewish conspiracy, and he was set on conquering Soviet Russian territory to provide Germany with the *Lebensraum* necessary to ensure its greatness. But he would also not refrain from imitating the communist enemy when he thought such a course would yield political advantages. "Power was Hitler's aphrodisiac,"[25] and to satisfy his urge, he applied what he understood to be Soviet methods of seizing power and exercising monolithic authority over society. Reading through his writings, speeches, and transcribed conversations, one finds Hitler harping on the theme that the Nazi Party must make itself in the image of the communists in order to match their strength and bring about "the revolutionary upheaval of an entire continent" as only political leaders like Lenin (and himself) were capable of doing.[26] The party newspaper, the *Völ-*

kischer Beobachter, explicitly compared Hitler to Lenin, the extremist Bolshevik "Führer" who "knew what he wanted to achieve and how to accomplish it."[27]

Munich, Hitler said, was the "Moscow of our movement."[28] From that base the Nazi Party would mimic both KPD and Russian-Bolshevik organizational patterns and mass-mobilizing techniques. The immediate goal was overthrowing the despised democratic government, and the means thereto was through a Leninist-style party: "History has always been made by an organized minority which seized power for the benefit of the majority," Hitler maintained.[29] The party's strategy, especially after the failed Beer Hall Putsch, would be not to make outright coup attempts but to capture power by winning the electoral support of the masses—as Jacobins had done in the French Revolutionary National Assembly and Bolsheviks in the soviets.[30] Gaining that support would be a matter of applying party demagoguery along the lines of Russian communism. As he wrote in *Mein Kampf*, Hitler believed that "the greatest revolutionary upheaval of the most recent period, the Bolshevist Revolution in Russia, was brought about . . . by the hate-fomenting oratorical activity of countless of the greatest and smallest apostles of agitation. The illiterate common people were . . . fired . . . solely by the glittering heaven which thousands of agitators . . . talked into the people."[31]

The Nazis revealed unique talents for these very tasks, but Hitler knew that however many people he won over to his movement, the opposition would also remain strong given the determination of the enemies of the Germanic race. From the beginning, therefore, it was clear to him that "the defense of [the party's] spiritual platform must if necessary be secured by strong-arm means." The French, Russian, and Italian Fascist revolutions were made by "fanatical faith[s]" that had assumed "the right to apply even the most brutal weapons" to ensure the "victory of a revolutionary new order on this earth."[32] The Nazi Party also assumed that right: "We cannot expect Germany's salvation from the present [parliamentary government], but only through a dictatorship brought through the sword."[33] Like the Bolsheviks and Fascists, the Nazis would form a "brutally decisive" government that would destroy its adversaries before they destroyed Germany.[34]

Once appointed German chancellor in January 1933, Hitler moved decisively to gut the Weimar Republic and annihilate opposition to the Nazis. The revolution began with the process of nazifying German institutions, designated *Gleichschaltung* (Coordination), a term whose banality belied its convulsive assault on political rivals and, indeed, all of autonomous society. Hitler soon succeeded in establishing a one-party dictatorship. Four main pillars of the system were to a certain extent modeled after the Russian communist system: the secret police, the party-controlled judiciary, mass propaganda, and the command economy.

Disposing of one's political opponents was not new to the twentieth century, and the Nazis needed no outside inspiration to figure out how to round up and torture theirs. Nonetheless, the kingpins of the Gestapo (secret state police) paid close attention to the repressive apparatus of the Soviet Union when establishing their reign of terror. Heinrich Himmler, the overlord of the Nazi police state, had once dreamed of emigrating to Soviet Ukraine to take up farming. He was fascinated with the tsarist Okhrana and Leninist Cheka, and studied the books about both security services that proliferated in the 1920s. Not long before the Nazi takeover, he boasted to a group of party leaders, Hitler among them, that what he intended for the opposition would surpass the ruthlessness of the Soviet state.[35] Once the National Socialist revolution was underway, Himmler and his assistant, the notorious Reinhard Heydrich, used information gathered on Soviet secret-police methods by the Weimar-era Bavarian police department's anticommunism section. The head of that department was Heinrich Müller, soon to be Gestapo chief.[36] The USSR was not the only inspiration for the system of repression that emerged under the wings of these men, whose personalities were also at play in its creation. Himmler was a true-believing Nazi fanatic; Heydrich was obsessively suspicious by nature and also envied the British secret service; Müller went to sadistic extremes to satisfy his masters. But all of them also applied what they had learned from the Russians.

With his totalitarian yearnings, Hitler continued to do so as well, balancing contempt for Slavs and Bolshevism with admiration of Stalin's brutal tenacity. "I have a book about Stalin," he told his military staff, "and one must say that that is one colossal figure, . . .

who asks: is the sacrifice of 13 million people too much for a great idea?"[37] Stalin "is a beast, but he's a beast on a grand scale," Hitler stated on another occasion. He "must command our unconditional respect. . . . He knows his models, Genghis Khan and the others, very well."[38] If only the Third Reich had access to a remote territory as Stalin did in Siberia, Hitler lamented: it would then be easier to conceal his treatment of imprisoned enemies of the regime![39]

These were not just idle musings. Although Stalin made bloody refinements to his own rule after observing Hitler's purge of the SA in 1934, the reverse was also true. After surviving the bomb plot of July 20, 1944, Hitler ordered a Stalinist-style purge to uproot the conspiracy (and catch other purported opponents in the same net). For propaganda reasons he decided against his initial impulse to hold Moscow-like show trials, but indicative of his line of thinking, he called Roland Freisler, the hanging judge presiding over the in camera proceedings, "our Vyshinsky," referring to the Kremlin's chief prosecutor during the Russian Great Terror.[40] It is relevant that before converting to Nazism, Freisler had gained fluency in Russian while interned as a World War I POW in Siberia, then served as a Bolshevik commissar until 1920. He is reputed to have applied his knowledge of Soviet methods as chief of the Third Reich's feared *Volksgericht* (People's Court).[41]

Soviet industrialization also conditioned the nature of the Nazi command economy.[42] Hitler's curiosity overflowed when he received reports about life in Russia.[43] According to an officer at Hitler's military staff headquarters, the Stalinist economy "enthused" both the Führer and his close advisers, who believed that "compared to it other economic systems could not compete."[44] Hitler marveled that "if Stalin had 10–15 years left to work, Soviet Russia would become the most powerful state on earth."[45] In preparation for war, Hitler in 1936 adopted a "Four-Year Plan," with Hermann Göring in charge. Both believed that this was essential lest Germany, in the words of Hitler, prove itself "incapable of surviving . . . in this modern age in which [the] Soviet State is [erecting] its gigantic plan."[46] The Nazis expected to achieve state planning and determine the nation's production priorities without resorting to the disruptive abolition of private enterprise that accompanied Russian forced industrialization. But like Stalin, Hitler intended to call the shots: "The basic principle of my party's economic programme . . . is the principle of authority. . . . Every owner should feel himself to be an agent of the State. . . . The Third Reich will always retain the right to control property owners."[47]

As in the Soviet Union, the state's coercive authority was accompanied by techniques of mass persuasion. The Nazi regime's attainments in this arena originated with the innate demagogic genius of both Hitler and his propaganda minister, Joseph Goebbels. But they also drew on World War I antecedents and the highly successful Soviet example. Goebbels, in fact, came out of the "National Bolshevik" faction of the early Nazi Party, which stood for an anti-Western alliance between Russian communism and German national socialism. A radical, antimodern intellectual, Goebbels had once immersed himself in both Dostoevsky and Marxist literature. He believed that "we have far more in common with Eastern Bolshevism than with Western capitalism," and he saw Hitler as a German Lenin.[48] Goebbels early on stifled his pro-Soviet sentiments when Hitler expressed his displeasure, but they surfaced in his ministerial activities. Film was the keystone of Goebbels's propaganda effort, and he explicitly urged imitation of Soviet cinematography. At his first address to representatives of the German film industry, in March 1933, he spoke about *Battleship Potemkin*, the stirring production of Russian director Sergei Eisenstein, as "a marvelously well made film, and one which reveals incomparable cinematic artistry. . . . This is a film which could turn anyone with no firm ideological convictions into a Bolshevik, which means that . . . even the most obnoxious [political] attitude can be communicated if it is expressed through the medium of an outstanding work of art."[49] Goebbels understood what the Soviets had accomplished in this regard and set out to encourage the same in Germany.

If the Soviet example inspired essential aspects of the Nazi Party's seizure of power and consolidation of dictatorial authority, in other realms there was no such inspiration. Evidence does not exist to support the contention that Soviet collectivization of agriculture, which resulted in the deaths of millions of peasants, served as a mass-murder precedent to the Nazi Holocaust.[50] Nor was Hitlerian racial genocide an extreme but preventive reaction to the threat of Soviet class warfare, as has been argued by German historian Ernst

Nolte.[51] The Nazi extermination of the Jews, with its focus on one ethnic group and the industrial efficiency of its gas chambers, establishes the Third Reich as a unique manifestation of evil in history. The Holocaust was encouraged to an extent by the paranoid allegations of émigré Russian anti-Semites that Bolshevism was the vanguard of the international Jewish conspiracy, a view that Alfred Rosenberg and company introduced to Germany. But Nolte goes too far in saying that without the example of the Gulag, the Nazi death camps would not have come into being. To simplistically link Russian communism and the Holocaust in this way is tantamount to relativizing, if not legitimizing, Hitler's crimes.

Despite this, however, and despite the different ways Nazi Germany and Stalinist Russia evolved, there were important similarities between the two regimes. And if we take into account the aspirations and policies of Mussolini, Fascist Italy deserves to be categorized with them. Although their distinct personalities, ideologies, national traditions, intellectual antecedents, and political circumstances gave different color to their movements, Mussolini, Hitler, and their Soviet communist mentors were cut from the same cloth. All were anti-Western, anticapitalist, antiliberal rejectionists. All sought (even if they did not equally achieve) full monopolies of power by means of police terror and the politicization of life. In many of the tactics they employed to gain and hold on to power, as well as their conceptions of the state, the Führer and Il Duce learned from the example of the Bolshevik leaders. But they did so *selectively*, with the result that they created their own mutations of the new form of absolutist tyranny whose prototype was the Soviet one-party dictatorship.

Communism and the Third World

German Nazism and Italian Fascism lay in ruins by 1945, but outside the Soviet Union and its satellites the Russian model of the one-party state survived in Africa, Asia, and, to a more limited extent, Latin America.

The Cold War was the context in which the Soviet archetype spread outward from its Russian and Eastern European base. One of the mechanisms by which the United States sought to "contain" the expansion of world communism after World War II was by forming armed alliances—NATO, CENTO (the Baghdad Pact), and SEATO—which encircled the Soviet bloc. Moscow then upped the ante in the late 1950s and 1960s by extending its power beyond Eurasia, building a navy with a global reach to breach the West's containment ring. This served only to confirm Western fears of Soviet global domination, and great-power competition escalated.

As part of the containment strategy, American statesmen sought to induce non-Western leaders to join forces against the Soviet threat. But the Russians were simply not a concern to Third World politicians, who were preoccupied with ongoing decolonization. On the contrary, just beneath the surface lay fears of American dominance through its military alliances, which the Third World suspected as a form of neocolonialism that would replace the departing British, French, and Dutch. The United States had immense postwar power, and as it intervened in Iran, Guatemala, and Vietnam, it appeared no longer as the traditional enemy of colonialism but rather as a supplanter of old European empires.

The United States initially so overplayed its hand in insisting that the entire world join the fight against communism that it helped to push some countries into the Russian camp.[52] It should be recognized that the United States did not simply "lose" the Third World: a predisposition toward Russia and socialism already existed on the part of the Third World leadership, and the desire to reduce dependence on the colonial powers was a major factor in orienting the newly independent nations toward the anti-Western communist bloc. Specific Western diplomatic démarches also explain why some moved closer to the Russians when they did. Egypt under Gamal Abdel Nasser, for instance, relied on an alliance with the USSR as a counterweight to the United States and Great Britain as these powers supported Nasser's enemy, Israel, in Middle Eastern conflicts during the 1950s and 1960s. India's first postcolonial leader, Jawaharlal Nehru, threw himself fully into the Third World nonaligned movement—in fact an anti-American association—after the United States gave preference to India's enemy, Pakistan, on the Asian subcontinent. Other Third World countries (e.g., the Yemen Arab Republic, Iran, Sukarno's Indonesia) flirted with the

Soviets as a way of gaining leverage against the United States, which they hoped would boost the amounts of economic and military aid it offered in return for their joining the anti-Soviet camp.

Whatever the specific situation, the Soviets under Stalin's successor Nikita Khrushchev (in power from 1953 to 1964) expected that aiding Third World nationalist movements would yield foreign policy and military advantages.[53] International relations were revolutionized as the world was partitioned into competing blocs, and the entire postwar era until the demise of the USSR was dominated by American-Russian rivalry.

But the appeal of the Soviet Union to Third World elites went well beyond temporary foreign-policy expedience. Its roots were established long before the Cold War, and in some regions before 1917. The Russo-Japanese War of 1904–1905, in which the two powers fought over control of Manchuria and Korea, was a disaster for Tsar Nicholas II. This was the first defeat in modern history of a European great power by a non-Western nation. In Europe's Asian colonies, this David-and-Goliath struggle gave subject peoples the first hope of one day being able to throw off their own oppressors. The Japanese victory over the powerful Russian autocracy made all colonial powers seem potentially vulnerable. In the words of Lord Curzon, British viceroy of India, "The reverberations of that victory have gone like a thunderclap through the whispering galleries of the East."[54]

At the same time, the Russian intelligentsia was beginning to exert cultural and ideological influence in Asia. Russian novelists and anarchists had followers across the continent, and the Russian radical movement seemed responsible for the 1905 revolution, which turned the country into a semiconstitutional monarchy. The events of these years had a worldwide impact, giving direction to constitutional movements and reforms in Turkey after 1905, China in 1911, and Iran, Afghanistan, and Korea in the same period. In all of these nations, some of the major catalysts to change were similar: regional newspapers, which closely followed developments in the tsarist empire; Russian radicals, who brought revolutionary ideas with them as they escaped persecution by fleeing to neighboring regions; and native students and "guest" workers, who returned home from Russia with a rebellious spirit after witnessing events there.[55] The Bolshevik revolution of October 1917 became an even more potent symbol of liberation. Russian anarchism had generated radical enthusiasm, but the Bolsheviks offered a proven model for making a revolution. Over time, as in the West, the anarchist movement hemorrhaged and Russian-inspired communist parties gained strength at its expense.

Through the 1920s and 1930s, the Soviet Comintern agitated for communism and national liberation in the European empires. As a tactic in the global anticapitalist struggle, Lenin and his subordinates explicitly encouraged the revolt of Asia against the West. Lenin's writings on imperialism established the theoretical rationale for undermining the capitalist powers by means of fomenting unrest in the colonies, which he considered to be the prop of the entire bourgeois political and economic system.[56] His works were translated and distributed abroad, but the gist of his thought was spread by Comintern propagandists, who in the early 1920s began calling for a "holy war" against British imperialism and the "liberation of the peoples of the East."[57] The Third World rapidly absorbed the Leninist perspective, which served to give theoretical expression to the emotions of native intellectuals.[58]

Although the Soviet Union did not involve itself extensively in the affairs of the colonial world until after the death of Stalin, through the image of the USSR as a communist Saint George fighting the dragon of the West, and through familiarity—however vague—with Lenin's anti-imperialist ideas, Russia had a formative impact on inchoate national liberation movements. It had this effect partially because many of those colonial subjects who had the opportunity to study in the European imperial capitals were converted to Marxism, which was current in left-wing intellectual and university circles (while, ironically, many of those who studied in Russia became hostile to socialism after experiencing it firsthand).[59] Aside from the experience of imperialism itself, other factors were also involved in encouraging Third World nationalism: European Romantic philosophy, Woodrow Wilson's emphasis on self-determination in the Fourteen Points, fascism, and FDR's anticolonialism. But Russia had at least as much relevance for the Third World as these other sources of inspiration; for the USSR stood in the vanguard of the struggle against the West, embodied a new ideal of justice, and seemed to be making a new, modern civilization out of a backward agrarian country.

Few if any Third World nationalists ever tried to adopt the Leninist model whole. Rather, they applied it creatively to their specific needs, as Lenin himself had done by pragmatically applying Marxism to a largely peasant country, making revolution before most Marxists would have predicted it was likely, and doing so heedless of the wishes of the bulk of the population. A Marxist from Chad, Maurice Adoum, speaking in 1962, seconded Lenin's viewpoint: "Marxism is not a dogma, it is a guide for action."[60] Leninist methods of seizing power and organizing the new society under the auspices of a one-party state could be applied anywhere, whether the intention was to make mass revolution or to effect a minoritarian insurrection, elements of both having been present in October 1917. After coming to power in Russia, the Bolsheviks had been forced by circumstances to abandon hopes for immediate world revolution and instead to focus on creating "socialism in one country." In this respect, too, Soviet experience had special appeal to development-minded Third World nationalists. All told, there was much to take from Bolshevism, which seemed to have succeeded in the struggle against a powerful political establishment by means of centralized party organization and by force of its leader's will. Moreover, as in the USSR, the Bolshevik ideology of Marxist internationalism did not hinder national interests from taking primacy.

The attraction of Russia transcended the political affiliations of Third World nationalist leaders. Whether they leaned to the right or the left, they could learn something from the Leninist experience. The Syrian foreign minister Khalid al-ʿAzm in 1960 summed up Third World perceptions: "Scratch a Bolshevik and you will find a nationalist."[61] Like Mussolini and Hitler, Third World rebels took from the Soviet example what they felt would best allow them to achieve their nationalist and power-political ends, which meant sometimes embellishing revolutionary ideologies with localisms and sometimes leaving ideology behind altogether. After all, Stalin himself had downplayed the concept of the class struggle in favor of Russian nationalism.

The earliest nationalist figures to embrace the single-party state model all had close connections with Russia. The first nation outside of Russia to take guidance from the USSR, in this case building a one-party dictatorship without communist ideology, was Turkey under Atatürk (Mustafa Kemal, 1881–1938). In the Ottoman Empire, Pan-Turkic and Young Turk ideas had arisen in response to the dangers represented by Russian Pan-Slavism as well as fears of emergent Pan-Arabism. Many Turkish intellectuals were also influenced by Russian Populist and Tolstoyan ideas about the common people.[62] Turkic Tatar émigrés, Turkish students, and World War I POWs returning from the tsarist empire spread knowledge of Russian intellectual currents. Many Turkish intellectuals interpreted the Russian Revolution as an anti-Western phenomenon, and this appealed to them at a time when their nation was under threat of dismemberment by the victors of World War I. They also assimilated the ideas of the Tatar Bolshevik leader Mirza Sultan-Galiev, whose political philosophy reconciled Islam, nationalism, and Leninist communism (for which creativity Stalin had him shot).

Although Atatürk himself persecuted communists and was wary of Russian designs on his nation, he suspected the Western imperialists even more and sought to circumvent the threat from this quarter by building a strong Turkish state with some limited borrowings from the Soviet Union: "If the Allies insist on partitioning Turkey," he stated in 1920, ". . . we will willingly accept . . . [Bolshevik help]."[63] With this in mind, he established a Russian-inspired one-party regime that eliminated rivals to his Republican People's Party. Although he also drew on World War I–era German economic practices, Atatürk was later impressed that the Soviet economy seemed to have avoided the Great Depression and therefore instituted a Five-Year Plan (1934–1938). Credits were provided by Moscow—the first time the Russians gave foreign aid to a developing nation, and the precedent for what later became a common Soviet Cold War diplomatic tool.

Atatürk used only select elements of the Soviet model, without appropriating the ideology. State economic investment was almost exclusively in consumer-goods production rather than heavy industry, and private enterprise was allowed to function outside the limited nationalized sector of the economy. Politically, state terror and show trials were applied on an extremely limited scale. This was an authoritarian but nontotalitarian regime that had no intention of restricting social autonomy beyond outlawing independent political activity. But Atatürk showed the rest of the non-Western world that a one-party state with a constitutional facade could serve nationalist and modernizing purposes—with or without Marxism.[64]

In East Asia, too, the same practical Leninism was an essential element in the nationalist struggle against imperialism and the establishment of revolutionary dictatorships. After 1917, more and more Chinese intellectuals turned to the Soviet Union for answers to their nation's problems. In the early 1920s, results of an opinion poll of Chinese students showed that by an overwhelming margin they considered Lenin the greatest man in the world outside their own country; they chose Sun Yat-sen as the greatest within China.[65] Like Atatürk, whom he admired, Sun (1866–1925) was an ideologically flexible nationalist with authoritarian tendencies who swiftly perceived the advantages to be had from emulation of Lenin. Sun was the founder of the Chinese Guomindang, a revolutionary organization that was fighting against the warlords who had hijacked the Chinese Republic. In order to prevail in the conflicts of the 1920s, Sun, even though educated in an American boys' school in Hawaii, turned to the Soviet Union to learn "Russian methods for the struggle" and to make the Guomindang "as well organized and as [disciplined] as the revolutionary party of Russia." Under the guidance of Russian Comintern agent Mikhail Borodin, the Guomindang reorganized itself along Leninist lines with a central command structure and party control of what Sun called its "revolutionary army." Sun's successor after his death in 1925 was Chiang Kai-shek (1887–1975), who mistrusted the Russians and broke with them two years later. An admirer of European fascism who was preoccupied with power-struggle techniques, he, too, had worked to introduce into the Guomindang such Soviet organizational principles as restrictive party membership and party preeminence over the governmental apparatus.[66]

Chiang's eventual chief rival was Mao Zedong (1893–1976), whose disciplined, Leninist party made an anti-Western, nationalist-communist revolution in a rural society. Mao deviated from mainstream Marxism even further than Lenin by rooting his movement almost wholly in the peasantry. Mao was influenced by Sun Yat-sen and early communist ideologist Li Dazhao, who perceived similarities between Russia and China as non-Western, underdeveloped nations, and wrote of the revolutionary effectiveness of Bolshevism. As Mao fought to establish himself in power and set up a functioning regime in the territory under his control, he duplicated and extended Soviet Communist Party organizational principles and mass mobilization techniques.[67]

Upon the defeat of his adversaries in 1949, Mao formed a dictatorship with many basic features derived from the Soviet Union, even if he never trusted and later turned against the Russians. Like his Soviet counterparts, Mao was a communist tyrant. He had absorbed the Leninist hatred of backwardness and faith in the redemptive powers of the Communist Party. He brooked no dissent within his own party or the rest of society. Mao's security chief, Kang Sheng, was a former Comintern agent who had received his training in Moscow in the 1930s from the OGPU and NKVD. Intimately familiar with the Soviet Gulag (while in the USSR he had routinely arranged the arrest of Chinese communist rivals), Kang Sheng is credited with establishing the Chinese Gulag, known as the Laogai. Having witnessed the Stalinist Great Terror, he initiated the murderous ideological purges of the Chinese Communist Party known as "campaigns of rectification" and institutionalized the use of torture to coerce confessions out of detainees. The Chinese security ministry (Gonganbu) was expressly patterned after the Russian secret-police agency; through the 1950s, portraits of Felix Dzerzhinsky, founder of the Cheka, adorned the walls of Gonganbu offices.[68]

Communist China also adopted from the USSR an emphasis on forced industrialization and centralized economic planning, with the purpose of modernizing society and harnessing the masses. The Great Leap Forward (1958–1961) and the agricultural collectivization campaign that preceded it were Mao's attempts to Stalinize the economy and deepen the revolution from above. These efforts to "build socialism in one country" differed in specifics from Soviet practices, but the original concepts were based on them. Even after the Sino-Soviet split of the early 1960s and the departure of Soviet economics advisers, the Chinese kept a modified variant of Soviet paradigms in enterprise management in place for at least two more decades.[69]

With totalitarian intentions of molding the populace, the People's Republic of China imported Soviet Socialist Realism as the mandatory cultural mode of the country, altered only superficially by Maoist and Chinese accretions. Official Soviet literature, art, and films were revered by Chinese communists as simultaneously European and anti-Western, proletarian and ultramodern. For the leadership, Socialist Realism provided a uniform ideological language with which to impose social discipline as it stressed the transformation of the nation by means of industrial technology and the wisdom of the Communist Party. More than an aesthetic technique and mechanism of social control, it reflected the party's utopian fantasy of leaving backward agrarian life behind and surpassing the developed world.[70]

Learning from Mao and Sun after sojourning in both revolutionary China and Russia was Ho Chi Minh (1890–1969), whose Leninist party eventually monopolized the nationalist movement in Vietnam.[71] A member of the French Communist Party by 1921, he left Paris to study in Moscow from 1923 to 1925, at which time he joined Borodin as a Comintern agent in China. Like Lenin and Mao, Ho was an "opportunist of genius."[72] For him and his early followers, many of whom were also educated in Russia, Leninism was an organizational doctrine that provided a means of winning the fight against French colonial power in his country as well as overthrowing capitalism; Marxism-Leninism was especially attractive insofar as it might further those goals. As Ho put it, "Only if the party is solid can the revolution succeed, just as only when the helmsman is firmly in control can the ship sail. If we want to have a solid party, it must have an ideology as its foundation, an ideology that everyone in the party must understand and follow. A party without an ideology is like . . . a ship without a compass."[73]

With this guiding principle, Ho cofounded the Indochinese Communist Party in 1930 and subsequently organized the Viet Minh national liberation movement. His arguments on behalf of a centralized party organization based on Leninist-Maoist principles and adapted for guerrilla warfare won over Vietnamese radicals, many of whom had once been anarchists. Their quest for individualism was supplanted by the feeling that order had to be imposed on society if the French were to be defeated. Under the leadership of Ho's Communist Party, the Viet Minh filled the vacuum left after World War II by the departing Japanese. Within ten years the French, too, had gone and Ho established his authority over North Vietnam, from which base the struggle continued against the American-backed regime in the south.

The nationalist revolutions of Turkey, China, and Vietnam owe a great deal to impulses derived from Lenin. Elsewhere in Asia, Africa, and Latin America, the Russian communist impact was not fully felt until the independence struggle commenced after World War II, but the ground was prepared in the interwar years. In Africa, the anticolonial, antiracist Pan-African movement was one of the channels by which Russian ideas were disseminated. Many of the major figures—George Padmore and Marcus Garvey, among others—either spent time in Soviet Russia or were to varying degrees under its influence at different periods of their lives. Padmore later became an adviser to Kwame Nkrumah of Ghana, the leader of the first black African state to achieve independence, who further promoted the Soviet model throughout his continent and the Third World.[74]

A similar process was occurring in Islamic North Africa and the Middle East. Nationalists in the Arabic-speaking colonies, secular-oriented and Islamic fundamentalist alike, overlooked for a time the fact that Marx and Lenin were both antireligious and even hostile to nationalism as a vestige of the bourgeois past. The Muslim Brotherhood (founded in Egypt) serves as an example. The anticolonialist and anticapitalist mood of Marxism-Leninism meshed with the organization's own sentiments, and Bolshevik theories of liberation and political organization offered a guide to action against both Western interests and Zionist Israel. To fight these enemies, a Syrian Islamic fundamentalist leader declared in the 1950s, "we will bind ourselves to Russia were she the very devil."[75] Of course, Nazism in its heyday attracted many of them for the same reasons, but after Germany's defeat the Soviet Union no longer had any competitors in the business of challenging the West.

In parts of colonial Asia and Africa the soil was thus prepared for the penetration of Soviet influence. After decolonization, since the Soviet Union represented the polar opposite of the Western system, affiliation with it signified psychologically that independence from Western overlordship had been achieved. And the Soviet government carefully burnished its image as a modernizing superpower defending the downtrodden and championing social justice against the twin evils of bourgeois democracy and capitalist imperialism. Variants of the Soviet model took hold in the Third World, though, not because it swayed legions of native idealists—although it often did that too—but because its techniques of governance met the demands of the professional politicians and revolutionaries who took over the bureaucratized, authoritarian states that the Europeans had (often rapidly) left behind. For this reason more than any other, the Soviet model provided no less than the vocabulary and grammar of Third World politics in the second half of the twentieth century.[76]

Most observers of Third World affairs portray the leaders of national liberation movements as opposed to the colonialists but not to the colonial state, which they were interested in taking over for themselves. A new native elite consisting of intellectuals, petty bureaucrats, and junior army officers had arisen under the tutelage of colonial powers desiring both to introduce reforms and reinforce their authority by creating a Western-oriented stratum among the population. These semi-Europeanized elements within native society came to be well aware of imperialist methods of control and corruption. They wanted their due at the same time that they were humiliated by their inferior social and political status and resented the alien whites who seemed to be plundering their nations.

What finally replaced the colonial state was a nativized bureaucracy whose powers were vastly expanded by a new modus operandi derived not only from the colonial state but also from imitation of Leninist political systems.[77] The leaders of many national liberation movements became heads of new governments, and the party machines they built up in the course of the independence drive became ruling parties, hostile to the traditional elites who were considered reactionaries and oppressors, and full of hate mixed with envy toward the imperialist West. Yet by virtue of their political status and modern education, they were themselves estranged from their own peoples. In addition to the state authority they inherited from colonial governments, they relied on the propaganda and coercive capacities of Leninism to maintain their power and foster political legitimacy in the eyes of the populace.

If the makeup of Third World states were as simple as a combination of two uniform categories—rulers and subjects—perhaps Leninist dictatorships would not have appeared. But the situation was far more complex. Just as the Soviet Union was an empire made up of more than a hundred different ethnic groups, so most African and Asian societies are segmented, artificial colonial constructs consisting of diverse ethnicities, languages, and religions. They are highly fragile political entities with strong centrifugal tendencies. In this circumstance a one-party government with a centralized economy provided organizational mechanisms that promised to preserve national unity. The Leninist-Stalinist, one-party, monolithic state appeared to have ended the divisive antagonisms in Russian society, and adaptations of it in the Third World achieved preeminence wherever natural conditions for nation building were the *least* auspicious. Leninism made it seem possible to bind nations through the illusion of popular sovereignty, mass mobilizing propaganda, nationalized economies, and police coercion.

Conflicts between ethnic groups, often in the guise of a struggle for broad-based social liberation, were one of several major reasons for the attraction to Leninist dictatorships in the post–World War II era. As in Russia (or Yugoslavia), specific ethnic groups in Africa and Asia in a number of cases utilized communist patriotism as a vehicle for (not always successful) attempts to establish dominance over often fractious multiethnic states. The Mbundu people in Angola did so via the MPLA (People's Movement for the Liberation of Angola), and the dominant Coptic Abyssinians in Haile Mariam Mengistu's post-1974 Ethiopia turned to socialism in part to win over the country's multiplicity of non-Christian peoples. In Burma and Vietnam, majority ethnic groups affiliated themselves with communism solely to fight imperialism and without regard to other issues, but minority relations within the two countries had some bearing on the situation after independence and the establishment of socialist dictatorships. In the Middle East, the Leninist inspiration was introduced partly by discontented minorities with close intellectual, political, and family ties to the USSR—in particular Jews, Armenians, and Kurds. And, although this is only one component of a complex phenomenon, the Leninist-style Ba'th Party was created in part because certain minorities—Syria's Christians and Shiite Alawites—saw a conspiratorial, centralized, revolutionary organization as the only way to bring down the despised old regimes and gain prominence for themselves.

Other vexatious domestic and foreign policy circumstances also made the adoption of Leninist politics and affiliation with the USSR more of a likelihood. In Africa the Soviet model was strongest where the problems were greatest and stability weakest, for example, in Angola, Mozambique, and Ethiopia, as opposed to Egypt, where its influence was significant but not nearly so absolute. In these three countries it was the government's instinct for survival in the presence of powerful internal opposition—ethnic or otherwise—that explains their strong identification with Leninism. In other cases, for instance, Benin, Congo-Brazzaville, and Tanzania, the threatening presence of militarily strong Nigeria, Zaire, and Kenya on their respective borders provided enough incentive. Status concerns were generally important too, especially in the Francophone colonies, where the French Communist Party had a prestigious aura composed of revolutionary intransigence, hostility to imperialism, and the glamour of Paris.

In some instances, Russian-sponsored "scientific socialism" was embraced to save non-Marxist revolutions from foundering. The best-known case is Cuba, whose leader Fidel Castro co-opted the local communist party even though, according to his brother Raúl, he had never been able to stomach reading more than a few pages of Marx in his entire life.[78] Add the hostility of a resented imperialist neighbor, itself locked in Cold War conflict with the USSR, and the choice was obvious. In most Latin American countries, Marxism-Leninism was not as influential as in Africa or Asia. Latin American states had received their independence a century earlier and had already developed a national consciousness and political-economic systems without reference to Russia. Some of the mid-twentieth-century South American dictatorships may have integrated a few Stalinist elements, but mainly they were imitating the Fascist dictatorships of Spain and Italy.[79] However, Cuba, and for a time Grenada and Nicaragua, consciously applied elements of the Soviet system and eagerly sought Moscow's patronage.

Generally, across the newly liberated Third World, as centrifugal forces grew stronger, and more and more elements of society became involved in the political process, governing became more difficult. Political bosses without any appreciation for or experience of parliamentary forms of government found that the easiest course was to take more power for themselves or their parties, which many leaders in any event had intended in the first place. Their tendency was to contend with difficulties by crushing their rivals and to introduce radical political and economic reforms for the cynical purposes of expanding state power and protecting the class interests of the new bureaucratic elite. In all this, they learned directly from the practices of Soviet rulers and the system they had established in response to often similar circumstances.

With a great deal of artistic license, a large percentage of Third World states followed the one-party model. They erected facades of democracies and established monopolies of power by nationalizing industries and applying secret-police "dirty tricks" to opponents—arrest, torture, and in some instances mass slaughter. None went as far as the Khmer Rouge in Cambodia, which liquidated almost the entire educated segment of the populace, but most were ruthless enough. They established monopolistic authority over the media and education. Pouring money into propaganda machines, they sponsored cultural production with partial derivations from Socialist Realism.

At the very least, they borrowed from Soviet discourse, in which complex realities were reduced to simplistic jargon: the people versus reactionary imperialists, mass spontaneity, the creation of a new man—all code phrases used to justify radical social engineering and crackdowns against enemies. It was often difficult to translate leftist buzzwords in native societies. Siad Barre's "scientific socialist" regime in Somalia plastered the country with hammers and sickles when attempting to please its Soviet benefactors[80] but had a hard time finding indigenous words that corresponded to our "revolution." At first it tried the Somali word *afgembis*, which means "tripping over oneself." This was then changed to *kacaan*, or "growing up," but it, too, proved unsatisfactory since in Mogadishu slang usage *kacaan* means "going to hell"![81] Notwithstanding such unwitting humor, everywhere these linguistic exercises were symptomatic of the onslaught of dictatorial repression.

One should bear in mind that none of these Third World one-party regimes was an exact replica of the Soviet exemplar, and few approximated an ideal of the totalitarian state. Indeed, few of the one-party states were ruled by a communist party, and some were outright hostile to the USSR. Even Soviet allies like Syria and Iraq ruthlessly suppressed local communists. In these countries, as in Algeria under the FLN (Front de Libération Nationale) and Egypt under Nasser, Soviet concepts and methods were often initially learned from local communist parties that were then dispensed with as dangerous rivals.[82] But whether they were formally communist or not, in all such cases Soviet inspiration has been operative at a basic level.

We can track the vicissitudes of the Soviet model by reviewing a sample of sub-Saharan African and Middle Eastern nations. In Ghana under the Pan-Africanist, nonaligned movement spokesman and semicommunist Nkrumah (1909–1972), ideology was a mishmash of angry and airy Third Worldism with Marxist phrasing thrown in. Two aspects of the Ghanaian political system introduced by Nkrumah were taken directly from the Soviets: the personality cult and security-service operations, neither of which prevented politics and economics from fast degenerating into the chaos that results from a brutal but incompetent dictatorship. Mobutu Sese Seko's rule over Zaire was similar in its despotic devastation of his country, although he skillfully managed to stay in power for more than thirty years. Mobutu (1930–1997) is a perfect indication that there were no ideological boundaries to the Soviet model—he was a client of the United States and by common understanding a "right-wing" dictator. Yet after seizing power in a 1965 coup, he established a regime in one of many Leninist styles, complete with governing Politbureau.[83] Senegal under Léopold Senghor (1906–2002) and Guinea under Sékou Touré (1922–1984) much more faithfully imitated Soviet forms in politics, economics, and ideology. Perhaps this is understandable: after the French departed, there were only fifty or so university graduates left behind.[84] How else could they have thought to manage but by adopting a one-party system that promised to extract order from chaos, modernization from backwardness, and abundant aid from a sympathetic superpower?

The most effective imitators of the Russians and the most dreaded of Third World one-party states were (and are) noncommunist Syria and Iraq, both nations jerry-built by the British and the French out of a mosaic of traditional ethnic and sectarian groups. From the 1940s on, the secular-oriented Pan-Arab Ba'th socialist parties absorbed some of the sentiments and all of the organizational techniques of Arab communism, put to good effect in the 1960s when they seized power in coups d'état. Thereafter they radically restructured society and retained power by murdering and torturing real and potential opponents on a vast scale. Hafez al-Asad (1930–2000) and Sadaam Hussein (1937–) can perhaps be portrayed as Oriental despots, but more accurately they should be seen as the closest heirs of Stalinism.

Both Asad and Hussein were, like Stalin, skilled political organizers with a lust for power, and some of the Leninist characteristics of the Ba'th Party were inherent in the ideas of its anti-Marxist founder Michel Aflaq (1910–1989), who saw the communists as his major competitors but admired their organizational talent and the Bolshevik transformation of Russia. Asad's brother, Rif'at, a major adviser in the formative years of his rule, was an open advocate of Stalinist-style terror and successfully urged its application in Syria against Islamic fundamentalists.[85] The KGB trained the Iraqi security services in torture techniques. The head of the Mukhabarat (the party intelligence agency), Fadhil al-Barak, was a Soviet Ph.D. and publisher of the *Protocols of the Elders of Zion*. Ba'th Party members from both countries shuttled for years to the USSR, where they became intimately familiar with all dimensions of communist rule. Under the guidance of Asad and Hussein they created in essence two neighboring Soviet-type states, with Ba'th Party cells in schools, universities, trade unions, and the military. For all practical purposes economic life, even when ostensibly governed by the private sector, followed the dictates of the party. Local variants of Socialist Realist propaganda displaced other artistic and literary forms. And in politics, autocratic centralism—enforced by the very real threat of jail, torture, or murder—secured the loyalty of the Ba'th Party to the leaders.[86]

In all the above cases, and many others around the world as well, Sékou Touré's statement expresses the Leninist attitude of Third World politicians in power: "The party constitutes the thought of the people . . . at its highest level and in its most complete form."[87] Leninism has proven a convenient and effective way for the few to dominate the many. Whether new elites were ethnic minorities or part of a new technological intelligentsia (the latter often represented by military officers), they were often virtual aliens in their own lands. Without dictatorship they could not stay in power, retain privilege and wealth for their families, or attempt to accomplish their other political goals. Almost everywhere in Asia and Africa the potential for democracy faded fast after independence (if it had existed in the first place, which is perhaps doubtful given the political legacy of colonialism). The majority of countries became one-party states with a disdain for governmental checks and balances, disregard for legal protection of the individual, and strivings toward ultra-rapid modernization, all impulses that inevitably produced tyrannies.

In economics as in politics hopes and reality parted company early on as the ready-made utopian edifices slapped together by the newly independent, developing nations turned out to have been anchored in the unstable subsoil of human nature. After independence came to the colonies of Africa and Asia between the late 1940s and early 1970s, the new nations saw in the Soviet Union what appeared to be an easy-to-follow recipe for administering multiethnic societies and quickly transforming traditional economies into advanced, self-sufficient ones. Although these states were already tethered by colonial practices to state-led modes of development, whatever the governmental or ideological system of the new regimes, they were almost universally impressed by the claims of Soviet centralized planning to have allocated resources fairly, efficiently, and productively.[88]

The leadership of the Third World was in a rush to bring their nations into the modern era, paradoxically desiring to reject the West but at the same time achieve its standard of living. In the words of a fictional African prime minister appearing in a Nigerian novel, "Ours is a country in a hurry. . . . We are committed to build more industries in these five years than the colonial government provided in half a century."[89] Partly, officials saw state economic management as a necessity: as former Malian planning minister explained, "You cannot be a capitalist when you have no capital."[90] But they were also blinded by their faith in socialism and the supposed successes of the Soviet Union. The new ruling strata of the Third World were by and large convinced that all they needed to do to achieve development was to overthrow the imperialists, accumulate investment capital—through expropriation, if necessary—and establish a central-planning agency. They failed to understand that the power and dynamism of the Western system had been attained only after centuries of cultural and technological preparation, and that it would be very hard indeed to remake their own societies overnight. But because they hated imperialism and capitalism, Soviet-inspired socialism seemed an attractive alternative to the market economies of the Europeans and Americans.

Naturally, the self-interest of the new elite as much as its idealism and understandable biases against the West lay behind the preference for Soviet-inspired economics. Local businessmen, for instance, in India and other countries where some development had taken place, often assumed that nationalization would eliminate foreign competition and, conveniently enough, also leave them with an economic monopoly over their nation's heavy industry. Throughout Asia and Africa, economies based on some derivation of Soviet principles would significantly bolster the wealth and power of the new ruling groups—even in a democracy like India. The postcolonial elites used the nationalized or planned economic sector to enrich themselves, to facilitate the control of the population dependent on their industries, and—via the huge bureaucracies that arose—to dispense the patronage that lubricated their one-party political machines. As in the USSR, inefficiency, waste, and corruption resulted from such an arrangement, but the survival of elite dominance was dependent on it.

To provide concrete evidence of their rapid success in modernizing the nation—evidence necessary to legitimize their dictatorial rule—the leaders of what were virtually all poor, financially strapped, agrarian countries took Russian aid and embarked on the construction of giant prestige projects—the dams, heavy industry, hotels, sports stadiums, and airlines the vision of which entranced so many Third World rulers. In most cases these white elephants imposed heavy fiscal burdens and yielded at best only meager returns for the nation at large. The Russians sometimes built projects unsuited to local conditions. Examples extend from beet sugar, sulfur, and phosphate plants in Indonesia, where there were no beets, sulfur, or phosphates, to a hydroelectric plant in Nepal on a river that is dry eight months of the year.[91] Even the Russian successes, like the Aswan Dam in Egypt and the Bhilai steel complex in India, were marred by unsafe building procedures that resulted in the loss of hundreds of lives. The former colonies' strategies for development were based on adoration of Western technology with a gigantomania learned first from colonial planners and then greatly enhanced by exposure to Soviet economics. This contributed to the undermining of economies already made fragile during the age of imperialism.

Most Third World countries did not fully eliminate private industry or agriculture, although generally the "commanding heights"—a 1920s Soviet term for key sectors of the economy such as banking, transportation, and utilities—were nationalized, and land and companies previously belonging to Europeans were often confiscated. Nehru, the first prime minister of independent India, had visited the USSR while the initial Five-Year Plan was underway. He opposed the violent side of Stalinist Russia but felt that the speed and planning of its industrialization campaign made it more relevant to India than was the European experience. "Soviet Russia," he wrote, "despite certain unpleasant aspects, attracted me greatly, and seemed to hold forth a message of hope to the world."[92]

Although Nehru did not outlaw entrepreneurial activity, and his planners tended to look more toward the West than the USSR for technical advice, he did subordinate private-property interests to the needs of the government in the Indian Five-Year Plan. In so doing, he may have successfully encouraged popular commitment to the new state at a time of political uncertainty, but he also entrenched a pattern of excessive state intervention in Indian economic development.[93] Similarly, Nasser's Egypt did not eliminate private enterprise, but a planning regime was introduced under Russian inspiration, and a large portion of the economy eventually came under state ownership.[94] According to a World Bank expert, in 1995 Egypt still had a largely "Soviet-style command economy . . . where 80 to 90 percent of GDP is . . . generated by the public sector."[95]

These cannot all be considered fully planned economies, to be sure, but more important is the fact that, like Nehru and Nasser, a majority of Third World leaders followed the Soviet Union in giving governments direct or indirect dominance over economic life, to the benefit of an elite group of bureaucrats and to the detriment of industrial efficiency and commercial vitality. Those nations that did set up carbon copies of the Soviet system—such as North Korea, Cuba, Vietnam, and Ethiopia—found that without massive Russian subsidies their economies would be a shambles. And developing nations like Algeria with mildly collectivist but partly private agriculture, or those which introduced total forced collectivization like Julius Nyerere's Tanzania, were all prone to agricultural crisis. Permanent underproduction and periodic famine became common features of much of socialist Asia and Africa after independence.

Africa and Asia are too complex and heterogeneous to warrant reduction of all of their problems to one cause. It is fair to argue, however, that the influence of Soviet-style economics was responsible for many grievous economic ills in the Third World in the second half of the twentieth century. The rapaciousness and benign neglect of the European colonizers had negative effects, as did the ineluctable entry into the world market system and runaway population growth. All of this helped upset the precarious equilibrium of traditional societies in the first place, including those not attracted to socialist ideology. But what also accounts for the steady and perilous decline of economic vitality outside the West in recent decades were the inimical Soviet-inspired policies favored by Third World rulers.

Over time the majority of Third World leaders themselves saw that Soviet development aid and economic programs were not going to yield the expected advantages. They turned instead to the West for more abundant financial assistance on easier terms, even though most of them maintained the political and economic status quo for the purpose of defending elite class interests, and even though a good many remained allies of the Soviet Union. To reduce their own costs, the Soviets actively encouraged this arrangement since it did not even usually entail the countries' renouncing socialist economics.

That did not mean, though, that these former colonies of Western Europe had reduced their new dependence on the USSR. On the contrary, over the course of the 1970s and 1980s, as the Soviet Union's economic disbursements declined, its military aid expanded, and so did the export of Soviet and East-bloc (especially GDR) secret-police technology since economic failure made many African and Asian governments even more likely to resort to Soviet-style coercive tactics against their own populations.[96] In all of the Third World in these decades the officer corps rose to political prominence. Many of Africa's officers were trained in Russia or its Warsaw Pact satellites, which partly explains the creation of Leninist clones in Benin, Congo-Brazzaville, Madagascar, Somalia, and Guinea-Bissau. These and other Third World regimes recognized after a time that they simply could not withstand popular discontent and survive without binding themselves closely to the protective

Slavic superpower offering a steady flow of arms and security assistance in return for diplomatic support against America and its allies.

This state of affairs finally crippled many developing nations, which with their sputtering socialist economies could ill afford to make preponderant investments in economically nonproductive police and military technology. Western military assistance to Third World countries was itself not always beneficial, but it is clear that Soviet aid by the 1970s kept its patrons in the Third World armed to the teeth and encouraged devastating warfare. Soviet military aid over the course of the postwar years made compromise and conciliation less attractive and less necessary. With the exception of conflicts between India and Pakistan in 1965 and 1971, every major war between Third World protagonists before the 1990s was started by a state armed by the Soviet Union. Certain that Russia would keep them afloat, many nations entered wars rather than reconciling with their neighbors. This helps to explain, for instance, why Egypt went to war so often against Israel. Russian arms gave Egypt the illusion of military superiority. But it gained little benefit and much pain.

In internal affairs the impact was to shatter all possibilities of democratic rule, prosperity, and social stability. Soviet support for the Third World apparatuses of repression enabled local tyrants to crack down on their opponents and build personal power bases rather than cohesive nations. The Soviet Union's zeal in buying friends through unlimited arms sales encouraged the proliferation of coups and civil wars, and, above all, wasted precious resources and steered investment away from productive tasks. Ethiopia epitomizes the worst excesses: Mengistu's army was six times the size of Emperor Haile Selassie's; between 1977 and 1985, years of dire famine and mass starvation, his regime purchased four billion dollars' worth of weapons from the Soviet Union. Thus did the combination of Soviet strategy and Leninist political concepts help perpetuate endemic poverty in many regions of the Third World.

The Soviet system was imported in the Third World to serve the practical and personal power ends of new leaders, who strengthened the colonial bureaucracies they inherited at independence in order to counteract the centrifugal tendencies of their societies and nourish their new class interests. The expansion of the state's political and economic role in Africa and Asia via adaptations of the Leninist model seemed necessary to compensate for political fragility. But in the end the system failed to deliver. It exacerbated the problems it had promised to cure, heightening poverty, spreading warfare and dictatorship, and deepening a state of dependence within the world economy.

It took the collapse of the USSR to make clear to its emulators around the world that their versions of the Soviet prototype were torpid, if not moribund. Among many Third World allies of the USSR and scientific socialist regimes, as well as in nations with only loosely derived components of the Russian model, there was a push for change after the 1980s. Many parts of Africa, Asia, and Latin America have seen multiparty elections, attempts to dismantle state industrial sectors, reduction of government intervention in agricultural pricing, anticorruption campaigns, and, as in Tanzania, admissions that socialism was a total failure. It is still too early to predict outcomes, and it may be that what results brings neither peace nor prosperity. But Third World political and economic life has entered a new period of ferment, facilitated in many ways by the end of the Cold War and the fall of Russian communism.

EPILOGUE

BEGINNING in the nineteenth century and continuing well into the twentieth, modernization transformed the world in a manner unparalleled since the prehistoric revolutions of the Neolithic and Bronze Ages. Traditional societies dissolved as they were integrated in an international communications network and market economy, as industrialization expanded, and as big cities drew populations off the land and out of small towns. Highly bureaucratized central governments asserted vastly expanded powers over their citizenry. Liberal ideologies challenged the authority of old regimes. New forms of wealth creation undermined the dominance of traditional elites. Dizzying technological advance altered ways of life, handed the West global dominance, spurred arms races, and enabled devastating warfare on a scale previously unimaginable. All these phenomena, whether beneficial or catastrophic, shook existing political attachments, ideological beliefs, moral values, and perceptions of reality.

Russia was one of the first non-Western nations to attempt to modernize. The impact of this effort, alongside the fight against tsarist oppression, preoccupied its radical intelligentsia. Although fully conversant with European thought, many of its members perceived the West as morally and spiritually inferior to Russia and articulated alternative ways of achieving a more perfect society. Their responses to Western-style development and the vision of the future they elaborated in its stead proved enticing to many intellectuals and leaders within other nations distressed by imperial authority, capitalism, and technological change.

Anxiously searching for alternatives to the rationalism, materialism, or hegemony of the West, a portion of humanity turned to
Russia for inspiration. Through its charismatic calls to justice, the
creative genius of its artists and writers, and its extremist and utopian rejection of the West, Russia helped to configure some of the
pivotal features of the modern era. Its thinkers bred a bewildering
array of political arrangements and cultural expressions, constructive and destructive, entertaining and vile, positive and negative.
All were manifestations of the antimodern rebellious mood that
was prevalent among large segments of the world's intelligentsias.
What Russian ideas offered them was a way of either rejecting the
contemporary world altogether or following a non-Western path
to modernity.

Many intellectuals interpreted Russian thought through the
lenses of their own national traditions and circumstances. Japanese
thinkers, for instance, understood Russian Nihilism in Buddhist
or Taoist terms. Gandhi fashioned a powerful national liberation
strategy by fusing elements of Tolstoyism and Hinduism. Middle
Eastern writers focusing attention on the Arab masses were attracted by the Populism of Dostoevsky and Tolstoy. Politically disturbed nations, such as Weimar Germany, took Russian rejectionism more to heart than did stable ones like Britain or America.

Underneath these national and regional differences, however,
there was a large degree of uniformity. For the world's intelligentsias originated as by-products of societies undergoing the broadly
analogous processes of modernization and experiencing the rise of
global communications. Whether Chinese or American, Egyptian
or French, Indian or Dutch, by the early twentieth century, the intellectuals and countercultures of the world were speaking the
same philosophical and political language. More often than not,
radicals everywhere responded to the Russians' programmatic critique of Western modernity in like fashion, with ambivalence, if
not revulsion, toward capitalism, imperialism, and liberal politics.

If contemporary Islamic radicalism, resurgent neo-Nazism, or
the militant anarchist wing of the antiglobalization movement are
indicative, the passions that generated reverence for Russian ideas
early in the twentieth century are as strong as ever. Desperate

yearnings for a new ideal order result from the traumas and transitions of recent world history. The West is suspect on account of its legacy of imperialism, its popular culture, its religious tolerance, its political and economic systems, or its foreign policies. Often, the West (now more frequently identified with America alone) is scapegoated for misfortunes whose causes are local and unrelated to it. And it is always identified with the ongoing and often painful challenges of modernization.

Whatever the reasons, ideological visions that conflict with Western political and developmental paradigms continue to be powerful and destabilizing forces as they have been for over a century. The discontentment that fostered worldwide fascination with Russian culture remains vigorous—all the more so since the collapse of the Soviet Union left those alienated from capitalism and Western dominance desperate to identify new alternatives to them. But Russia is no longer the icon of anti-Westernism, and nothing as vibrant, inventive, or capable of global appeal seems likely to replace it.

NOTES

Prologue

1. M. Buber, *Between Man and Man* (New York, 1965), 157.

Chapter 1. Organizing Revolution: The Russian Terrorists

1. The best introduction to the subject remains J. Joll, *The Anarchists* (New York, 1964). P. Marshall, *Demanding the Impossible* (London, 1992) is an essential reference, as are the works of P. Avrich.

2. See, for example, the title of the first chapter of R. Hunter, *Violence and the Labor Movement* (New York, 1914).

3. Quotation from A. Kelly, *Mikhail Bakunin* (New Haven, 1987), 151. My treatment of Bakunin draws heavily on this insightful biography, as well as on I. Berlin, *Russian Thinkers* (Harmondsworth, 1979), and J. Cahm, "Bakunin," in *Socialism and Nationalism*, ed. E. Cahm et al., vol. 1 (Nottingham, 1978), 33–49.

4. Quotation from Berlin, *Russian Thinkers*, 111.

5. Cited in Kelly, *Bakunin*, 131–132.

6. M. Bakunin, "Reaction in Germany," in *Russian Philosophy*, ed. J. Edie et al., vol. 1 (Knoxville, 1976), 388, 406.

7. Cited in R. Hare, *Portraits of Russian Personalities* (London, 1959), 58.

8. Besides Kelly, *Bakunin*, see M. Confino, *Violence dans la violence* (Paris, 1983), and A. Gleason, *Young Russia* (Chicago, 1983), chaps. 10–11.

9. Quotations from English translation of the text in B. Dmytryshyn, ed., *Imperial Russia: A Source Book, 1700–1917*, 2d ed. (Hinsdale, IL, 1974), 350–354.

10. All scholarship on the novel has been superseded by A. Drozd, *Chernyshevskii's What Is to Be Done?* (Evanston, 2001).

11. Cited in F. Venturi, *Roots of Revolution* (Chicago, 1960), 331.

12. Cited in I. Paperno, *Chernyshevsky and the Age of Realism* (Stanford, 1988), 17–18.

13. J. Frank, *Through the Russian Prism* (Princeton, 1990), 187.

14. S. Cassedy, "Chernyshevskii Goes West," *Russian History*, no. 1 (1994): 2 n. 3, 7–16.

15. R. Stites, "Women and Communist Revolutions," *Studies in Comparative Communism* (Summer/Autumn 1981): 106–122.

16. Cited in A. Ulam, *In the Name of the People* (New York, 1977), 326. See his chaps. 12–14 on the People's Will in general.

17. K. Fant, *Alfred Nobel* (New York, 1993), 32, 94, and passim; W. Laqueur, *Age of Terrorism* (Boston, 1987), 104–106, 112, 344 n. 46.

18. The quotation is from M. Pokrovsky, cited in A. von Borcke, "Violence and Terror in Russian Revolutionary Populism," in *Social Protest, Violence and Terror in Nineteenth- and Twentieth-Century Europe*, ed. W. Mommsen et al. (New York, 1982), 53.

19. A. von Borcke, *Die Ursprünge des Bolschewismus: die jakobinische Tradition in Russland* (Munich, 1977), 436–440.

20. A. Geifman, *Thou Shalt Kill: Revolutionary Terrorism in Russia* (Princeton, 1993); M. Hildermeier, "Terrorist Strategies of the Socialist-Revolutionary Party," and M. Perrie, "Political and Economic Terror in the Tactics of the Russian Socialist-Revolutionary Party," both in Mommsen, *Social Protest*.

21. P. Avrich, *Anarchist Portraits* (Princeton, 1988); G. Haupt, "Rôle de l'exil dans la diffusion de l'image de l'intelligentsia révolutionnaire," *Cahiers du monde russe et soviétique* (July–September 1978): 235–249.

22. G. Grigor'eva, G. Ivanova, I. Kozhevnikova, and T. Tsoktaeva articles in *100 let russkoi kul'tury v Iaponii*, ed. L. L. Gromkovskaia (Moscow, 1989).

23. Perrie, "Political and Economic."

24. Laqueur, *Age of Terrorism*, 50.

25. J. Maura, "Terrorism in Barcelona," *Past and Present*, no. 41 (1968): 137.

26. P. Zarrow, *Anarchism and Chinese Political Culture* (New York, 1990), 102.

27. P. Sinha, *Indian National Liberation Movement and Russia (1905–1917)* (New Delhi, 1975), 147–148, 170–172, 217 ff.

28. Haupt, "Rôle de l'exil," 236.

29. J. Hulse, *Revolutionists in London* (Oxford, 1970), chap. 2; E. Taratuta, *E. M. Stepniak-Kravchinskii* (Moscow, 1973).

30. J. Crump, *Origins of Socialist Thought in Japan* (London, 1983), 38–39; Gromkovskaia, *100 let*, 11–15, 61–70.

31. Cited in D. Price, *Russia and the Roots of the Chinese Revolution* (Cambridge, MA, 1974), 193; and see Mau-Sang Ng, *Russian Hero in Modern Chinese Fiction* (Hong Kong, 1988).

32. O. Lang, *Pa Chin and His Writings* (Cambridge, MA, 1967).

33. M.-A. Leblond, "L'Anarchiste dans le roman français," *La Revue socialiste* 37 (1903): 185–213.

34. Cited in D. Brewster, *East-West Passage: A Study in Literary Relationships* (London, 1954), 106–109.

35. Arthur Conan Doyle, *Complete Sherlock Holmes* (Garden City, NY, n.d.) 607–621.

36. D. Lerner, "Influence of Turgenev on Henry James," *Slavonic and East European Review* 20 (1941): 47–49.

37. N. Pernicone, *Italian Anarchism, 1864–1892* (Princeton, 1993); T. Ravindranathan, *Bakunin and the Italians* (Kingston, 1988).

38. W. Bernecker, "Strategies of Direct Action and Violence in Spanish Anarchism," in Mommsen, *Social Protest*, 88–111; T. Kaplan, *Anarchists of Andalusia, 1868–1903* (Princeton, 1977); R. Carr, *Spain, 1808–1975* (Oxford, 1972), 439–450.

39. P. Mazgaj, *Action Française and Revolutionary Syndicalism* (Chapel Hill, 1979); F. Ridley, *Revolutionary Syndicalism in France* (Cambridge, 1970); A. Varias, *Paris and the Anarchists* (New York, 1996), 95–99.

40. Avrich, *Anarchist Portraits*, chaps. 12 and 20; J. Hart, *Revolutionary Mexico* (Berkeley, 1987), passim; S. Simon, "Anarchism and Anarcho-Syndicalism in South America," *Hispanic American Historical Review* (February 1946): 38–59.

41. Laqueur, *Age of Terrorism*, 42–48. My treatment of the proliferation of the "Russian Method" draws throughout on this valuable work.

42. Cited in S. Neumann, *Permanent Revolution*, 2d ed. (London, 1965), 69.

43. F. Gross, *Violence in Politics: Terror and Political Assassination in Eastern Europe and Russia* (The Hague, 1972), 39–44, 61; Laqueur, *Age of Terrorism*, 88.

44. L. Nalbandian, *Armenian Revolutionary Movement* (Berkeley, 1963); Gross, *Violence*, 44–49; Laqueur, *Age of Terrorism*, 43.

45. S. Christowe, *Heroes and Assassins* (New York, 1935); Gross, *Violence*, 24, 54–57; M. MacDermott, *Freedom or Death: The Life of Gotsé Delchev* (London, 1978).

46. S. Fay, *Origins of the World War*, vol. 1 (New York, 1930), 403.

47. V. Dedijer, *Road to Sarajevo* (New York, 1966), chap. 10; M. Djilas, *Land without Justice* (New York, 1958), x; B. Jelavich, *Russia's Balkan Entanglements* (Cambridge, 1991), 235–265; D. MacKenzie, *Serbs and Russians* (Boulder, 1996), 346 ff., 360.

48. Gromkovskaia, *100 let*, 62–63; Laqueur, *Age of Terrorism*, 68–69; R. Storry, *Double Patriots: A Study of Japanese Nationalism* (Westport, CT, 1976 [1957]); O. Tanin et al., *Militarism and Fascism in Japan* (Westport, CT, 1973 [1934]), 102 ff.

49. Cited in Sinha, *Indian National Liberation*, 195. On India and Russian terrorist methods, see Sinha in general as well as E. Brown, *Har Dayal* (Tucson, 1975); and S. Ghose, *Western Impact on Indian Politics* (Bombay, 1967), chap. 5.

50. See Government of Bengal, Home (Political) Confidential File No. 390C of 1909, West Bengal State Archives, Calcutta, 17–19. My thanks to Michael Silvestri for the document.

51. On the Safransky connection, see P. Heehs, *The Bomb in Bengal* (Delhi, 1993), 90–91.

52. Cited in A. Samanta, ed., *Terrorism in Bengal: A Collection of Documents*, vol. 2 (Calcutta, 1995), 1068.

53. M. Green, *Tolstoy and Gandhi* (New York, 1983), 257.

54. K. Short, *Dynamite War: Irish-American Bombers in Victorian Britain* (Atlantic Highlands, NJ, 1979), 2–4, 116; C. Townshend, *Political Violence in Ireland* (Oxford, 1983), 158–160, 387–388.

55. A. Camus, *"The Just" and "The Possessed"*, trans. H. Jones and J. O'Brien (Harmondsworth, 1970), and *The Rebel*, trans. A. Bower (New York, 1991).

56. Along with Marcuse and Fanon, see P. Avrich, "Legacy of Bakunin," *Russian Review* (April 1970): 131 ff.; A. MacIntyre, *Herbert Marcuse* (New York, 1970), chap. 8; B. Perinbam, "Fanon and the Revolutionary Peasantry," *Journal of Modern African Studies* (September 1973): 427–445; J. Woddis, *New Theories of Revolution* (New York, 1972).

57. E. Abrahamian, *Iran between Two Revolutions* (Princeton, 1982), 464 ff.; N. Keddie, *Roots of Revolution: An Interpretive History of Modern Iran* (New Haven, 1981), 215 ff.

58. Cited in D. Hodges, *Legacy of Che Guevara* (London, 1977), 58, and see 181.

59. Along with Debray, see Avrich, "Legacy," 131 ff.; D. James, *Ché Guevara* (New York, 1969), 308, 314–316, 329; R. Rubinstein, *Alchemists of Revolution* (New York, 1987), 214–215.

60. Frank, *Prism*, 66; W. Mommsen, "Non-legal Violence and Terrorism," in Mommsen, *Social Protest*, 392–393.

61. R. Drake, "Red Brigades," in *Terrorism in Europe*, ed. Y. Alexander et al. (New York, 1982), 102–140.

62. E. Cleaver, *Soul on Ice* (New York, 1968), 12; Avrich, "Legacy," 131.

63. D. Agmon, "HAMAS: From Kindergartens to Suicide Attacks," *Ma'ariv*, February 28, 1996), 11, Internet transmission of Israel Information Service News Analysis, March 3, 1996.

64. *All Things Considered*, National Public Radio broadcast, October 27, 2001; *New Republic*, December 31, 2001, and January 7, 2002, 22.

65. S. Lunev, "Chechen Terrorists—Made in the USSR," *Jamestown Foundation Prism: A Bi-Weekly on the Post-Soviet States* (Internet), vol. 2, no. 2, pt. 3 (January 26, 1996): 2.

Chapter 2. Kropotkin's Anti-Darwinian Anarchism

1. Quotations from G. Woodcock et al., *Anarchist Prince: A Biographical Study of Peter Kropotkin* (London, 1950), 224–225, and J. Joll, *Anarchists* (New York, 1964), 161–162. For Kropotkin's biography, see also M. Miller, *Kropotkin*

(Chicago, 1976), and A. Kelly, "Lessons of Kropotkin," *New York Review of Books,* October 28, 1976.

2. On which see D. Todes, "Darwin's Malthusian Metaphor and Russian Evolutionary Thought," *Isis* (December 1987): 537–551, and A. Vucinich, *Social Thought in Tsarist Russia* (Chicago, 1976), 78–95.

3. Todes, "Darwin's."

4. P. Kropotkin, *Mutual Aid: A Factor of Evolution* (New York, 1972 [1914]), 49.

5. P. Kropotkin, *Fields, Factories and Workshops* (New Brunswick, NJ, 1993 [1893]).

6. Ibid., 361, 364.

7. Ibid., 408.

8. P. Kropotkin, *Conquest of Bread and Other Writings*, ed. M. Shatz (Cambridge, 1995) 33.

9. Cited in A. Walicki, *History of Russian Thought* (Stanford, 1979), 284.

10. P. Kropotkin, "On the Russian Revolution," in *Conquest of Bread*, 259.

11. Cited in Miller, *Kropotkin*, 173.

12. For Kropotkin on revolutionary violence, see C. Cahm, *Kropotkin and the Rise of Revolutionary Anarchism* (Cambridge, 1989); and M. Fleming, "Propaganda by the Deed: Terrorism and Anarchist Theory," in *Terrorism in Europe*, ed. Y. Alexander et al. (New York, 1982), 8–28.

13. Cited in H. Shpayer-Makov, "Reception of Peter Kropotkin in Britain," *Albion* (Fall 1987): 374.

14. Cited in Miller, *Kropotkin*, 164.

15. Cited in R. Sonn, *Anarchism and Cultural Politics in Fin-de-Siècle France* (Lincoln, NE, 1989), 215, 255.

16. Cited in A. Varias, *Paris and the Anarchists* (New York, 1996), 136.

17. For Kropotkin's place in the avant-garde's anarchism, see D. Egbert, *Social Radicalism and the Arts* (New York, 1970), 237–249 and passim; E. Herbert, *Artist and Social Reform: France and Belgium, 1885–1898* (New Haven, 1961); R. and E. Herbert, "Artists and Anarchism: Unpublished Letters of Pissarro, Signac, and Others," pt. 1, *Burlington Magazine*, November 1960, 472–482; pt. 2, December 1960, 517–522; B. Nicolson, "Anarchism of Camille Pissarro," *The Arts*, no. 2 (1946–1947): 43–51.

18. See P. Kropotkin, *Selected Writings on Anarchism and Revolution*, ed. M. Miller (Cambridge, MA, 1970), 292–293.

19. For the mutual intellectual stimulation of Morris and Kropotkin, see J. Hulse, *Revolutionists in London* (Oxford, 1970), chap. 4; E. P. Thompson, *William Morris* (New York, 1977), 772–773.

20. G. Stickley, *Craftsman Homes* (New York, 1979 [1909]), 1–5 and passim.

21. Cited in L. Bowman, *American Arts and Crafts: Virtue in Design* (Los Angeles, 1990), 35.

22. Kropotkin, *Fields*, 361, and *Mutual Aid*, 55. On the American Arts and Crafts movement, see E. Boris, *Art and Labor: Ruskin, Morris, and the Craftsman Ideal in America* (Philadelphia, 1986), 158–160, 236; T. J. Lears, *No Place of Grace: Antimodernism and the Transformation of American Culture* (New York, 1981), chap. 2; and L. Mumford, *Roots of Contemporary American Architecture* (New York, 1952), 431–432.

23. R. Fishman, *Urban Utopias in the Twentieth Century: Ebenezer Howard, Frank Lloyd Wright, and Le Corbusier* (Cambridge, MA, 1982), 7.

24. See R. Beevers, *Garden City Utopia: A Critical Biography of Ebenezer Howard* (New York, 1988); P. Kitchen, *A Most Unsettling Person: The Life and Ideas of Patrick Geddes* (n.p., 1975).

25. P. Hall, *Cities of Tomorrow* (Oxford, 1988), chaps. 4–5 and passim; F. Jackson, *Sir Raymond Unwin* (London, 1985), 17–18, 114, and passim.

26. See L. Mumford, *City in History* (New York, 1961), 515, and, *Culture of Cities* (New York, 1938); see also P. Marshall, *Demanding the Impossible* (London, 1992), 575–578.

27. On garden cities outside of Britain, see P. Conkin, *Tomorrow a New World* (Ithaca, NY, 1959), and Hall, *Cities*, 148–161.

28. Sources used in the discussion of China include A. Dirlik, *Anarchism in the Chinese Revolution* (Berkeley, 1991); G. Hoston, *State, Identity, and the National Question in China and Japan* (Princeton, 1994); M. Meisner, *Li Ta-chao and the Origins of Chinese Marxism* (Cambridge, MA, 1967), 13–14, 55–56, 141–144, 206, 275 n. 9, chaps. 4 and 9; P. Zarrow, *Anarchism and Chinese Political Culture* (New York, 1990).

29. I. F. Stone cited in P. Avrich, *Anarchist Portraits* (Princeton, 1988), 105.

30. See C. Ward, *Anarchy in Action* (London, 1973), esp. chaps. 6, 7, and 11. Also see Marshall, *Demanding*, 597–601; S. Osofsky, *Peter Kropotkin* (Boston, 1979), 157–159.

31. A. Bramwell, *Ecology in the Twentieth Century* (New Haven, 1989), 65, 67, 70, 122, 234, and passim; Osofsky, *Peter Kropotkin*, 159.

32. G. Mitman, *State of Nature: Ecology, Community, and American Social Thought, 1900–1950* (Chicago, 1992), 1–8, 54–55, 60–61, 65, 67–69, 71–73, 78, 84–85, 132, 184–185.

33. M. Nowak et al., "Arithmetics of Mutual Help," *Scientific American*, June 1995, 76.

34. U. Linse, *Ökopax und Anarchie: Eine Geschichte der ökologischen Bewegungen in Deutschland* (Munich, 1986), 74, 76, 79, 82, 91, 102, and passim; I. Whyte, "Berlin, 1870–1945," in *Divided Heritage*, ed. I. Rogoff (Cambridge, 1991), 228 ff.

35. K. Holmes, "Origins, Development, and Composition of the Green Movement, in *Greens of West Germany*, ed. R. Pfaltzgraf, Jr., et al. (Cambridge, MA, 1983), 18, 23–25, and passim; A. Dobson, *Green Political Thought* (London, 1990), 7, 9, 15–17, 25–26, 38–39.

36. M. Bookchin, *Ecology of Freedom* (Palo Alto, 1982), *Post-Scarcity Anarchism* (Berkeley, 1971), and *Defending the Earth* (Boston, 1991), 13, 59; Dobson, *Green Political Thought*, 40–41, 117–119, 123–124, 194–204; Marshall, *Demanding*, chap. 39; Osofsky, *Peter Kropotkin*, 151.

Chapter 3. Dostoevsky's Messianic Irrationalism

1. G. Steiner, *Tolstoy or Dostoevsky* (New York, 1959), 7, 18.

2. Quoting F. Hemmings, *Russian Novel in France, 1884–1914* (London, 1950), 1.

3. V. Rozanov cited in R. Jackson, *Dialogues with Dostoevsky* (Stanford, 1993), 1.

4. For introductions to Dostoevsky's life and work, see D. Fanger, *Dostoevsky and Romantic Realism* (Cambridge, MA, 1965); J. Frank, *Dostoevsky*, 5 vols. (Princeton, 1976–2002); R. Freeborn, "Nineteenth Century," in *Cambridge History of Russian Literature*, ed. C. Moser, rev. ed. (Cambridge, 1992); A. de Jonge, *Dostoevsky and the Age of Intensity* (New York, 1975); and K. Mochulsky, *Dostoevsky* (Princeton, 1967).

5. Cited in Mochulsky, *Dostoevsky*, 639.

6. Dostoevsky cited in S. Linnér, *Starets Zosima in "The Brothers Karamazov"* (Stockholm, 1975), 16.

7. Cited in J. Andrew, *Russian Writers and Society in the Second Half of the Nineteenth Century* (Atlantic Highlands, NJ, 1982), 57–58.

8. M. Bakhtin, *Problems of Dostoevsky's Poetics* (Minneapolis, 1984), 5, 6, and passim.

9. On this aspect of his philosophy, see W. Dowler, *Dostoevsky, Grigor'ev, and Native Soil Conservatism* (Toronto, 1982); and B. Ward, *Dostoevsky's Critique of the West* (Waterloo, Ont., 1986).

10. Dostoevsky, *Brothers Karamazov*, trans. C. Garnett (New York, 1980), 233.

11. M. Friedman, *Stream of Consciousness* (New Haven, 1955), 6, 64–69, 73.

12. Dostoevsky, *Notes from Underground*, trans. M. Katz, 2d ed. (New York, 2001), 18.

13. Ibid., 10.

14. Ibid., 19.

15. Quotation from V. Zenkovsky, *History of Russian Philosophy*, vol. 1 (New York, 1953), 424.

16. Dostoevsky, *Crime and Punishment*, trans. S. Monas (New York, 1968), 443, 527–528.

17. Ibid., 526.

18. Dostoevsky, *Notes from Underground*, 17.

19. Dostoevsky, *Brothers Karamazov*, 291.

20. Quotations respectively in Dowler, *Dostoevsky, Grigor'ev*, 80, and de Jonge, *Dostoevsky*, 213.

21. Words of R. Fülöp-Miller, *Fyodor Dostoevsky* (New York, 1950), 92.

22. E. de Vogüé, *Russian Novelists* (New York, 1974), 20–21, 141, 171.

23. First quotation in Hemmings, *Russian Novel*, 48; others in W. Edgerton, "Penetration of Nineteenth-Century Russian Literature into the Other Slavic Countries," in *American Contributions to the Fifth International Congress of Slavists*, vol. 2, *Literary Contributions* (The Hague, 1963), 69–70.

24. Cited in Hemmings, *Russian Novel*, 25.

25. Cited in R. Wellek, ed., *Dostoevsky: A Collection of Critical Essays* (Englewood Cliffs, NJ, 1962), 2. Wellek's introduction is an excellent overview of the European reception of Dostoevsky.

26. Cited in Hemmings, *Russian Novel*, 11–12.

27. Cited in G. Painter, *Proust: The Later Years* (Boston, 1965), 182.

28. Cited in Hemmings, *Russian Novel*, 109. Besides Hemmings, for the impact of Dostoevsky on French literature in this era, see M. Fayer, *Gide, Freedom, and Dostoevsky* (Burlington, VT, 1944); J. Onimus, ed., *Dostoïevski et les lettres françaises* (Nice, 1981); and H. Peyre, *French Novelists of Today* (New York, 1967), chap. 4.

29. Cited in I.-M. Frandon, "Dostoïevski et Barrès," in Onimus, *Dostoïevski et les lettres françaises*, 55.

30. Cited in H. Muchnic, *Dostoevsky's English Reputation (1881–1936)* (New York, 1969 [1938–1939]), 36.

31. Cited in E. Knowlton, "A Russian Influence on Stevenson," *Modern Philology* (December 1916): 450.

32. Cited in J. Stokes, "Wilde on Dostoevsky," *Notes and Queries* (June 1980): 216.

33. Cited in Wellek, *Dostoevsky*, 10, and Muchnic, *Dostoevsky's Reputation*, 73–76.

34. Fülöp-Miller, *Fyodor Dostoevsky*, chap. 6; Hemmings, *Russian Novel*, 85–86 n. 2; J. Romein, *Dostojewski in de Westersche Kritiek* (Haarlem, 1924), pt. 1, chap. 4.

35. S. Freud, "Dostoevsky and Parricide," in *Standard Edition of the Complete Psychological Works of Sigmund Freud*, ed. J. Strachey, vol. 21 (London, 1961), 177.

36. J. Frank, *Through the Russian Prism* (Princeton, 1990), chap. 9; J. Rice, *Dostoevsky and the Healing Art* (Ann Arbor, 1985), 210–225, and *Freud's Russia* (New Brunswick, NJ, 1993).

37. J. Murry, *Fyodor Dostoevsky* (London, 1916), ix, 21, 22, 26, 27, 37, 41, 263.

38. Cited in P. Kaye, *Dostoevsky and English Modernism* (Cambridge, 1999), 43.

39. Cited in W. Leatherbarrow, *Fedor Dostoevsky: A Reference Guide* (Boston, 1990), xxii–xxiii, and Wellek, *Dostoevsky*, 12.

40. *Essays of Virginia Woolf*, ed. A. McNeillie, vol. 2 (New York, 1987), 79.

41. Cited in B. Handley, "Virginia Woolf and Fyodor Dostoevsky," *Virginia Woolf Miscellany* (Fall 1988): n.p.

42. V. Woolf, *Common Reader*, first series (New York, 1948), 251, 253.

43. Cited in R. Bush, *T. S. Eliot* (New York, 1983), 51–52. On Eliot and Dostoevsky, see also J. Pope, "Prufrock and Raskolnikov," *American Literature* 17 (1945): 213–230, and "Prufrock and Raskolnikov Again," *American Literature* 18 (1947): 319–321; and S. Sultan, *Eliot, Joyce, and Company* (New York, 1987), 33, 74–75, 106–109.

44. G. Orwell, *An Age Like This*, vol. 1 of *Collected Essays* (New York, 1968), 508.

45. Quotations from Sultan, *Eliot, Joyce*, 82, 83. Kaye, *Dostoevsky*, overlooks the evidence of Dostoevsky's influence on Joyce.

46. S. Klessmann, *Deutsche und amerikanische Erfahrungsmuster von Welt: Eine interdisziplinäre, kulturvergleichende Analyse im Spiegel der Dostojewski-Rezeption zwischen 1900 und 1945* (Regensburg, 1990), 218.

47. The most thorough overviews of Dostoevsky's German reception are V. Dudkin et al., "Dostoevskii v Germanii (1846–1921)," *Literaturnoe nasledstvo* 86 (1973): 662–678, and Klessmann, *Erfahrungsmuster*. For important context on this subject and other aspects of the impact of Russian thought on Germany, see also R. Williams, *Culture in Exile: Russian Emigrés in Germany, 1881–1941* (Ithaca, NY, 1972).

48. F. Stern, *Politics of Cultural Despair* (Berkeley, 1974), 210.

49. Cited in W. Gesemann, "Nietzsches Verhältnis zu Dostoevskij," *Die Welt der Slaven*, no. 2 (1961): 147.

50. Both quotations from L. Lowenthal, "Reception of Dostoevski's Work in Germany, 1880–1920" in *Arts in Society*, ed. R. Wilson (Englewood Cliffs, NJ, 1964), 138.

51. Cited in ibid., 128.

52. Cited in Stern, *Politics*, 210.

53. Quotations in Lowenthal, "Reception," 131–132.

54. Moeller van den Bruck, introduction to F. Dostojewski, *Rodion Raskolnikoff*, vol. 1 (Munich, 1908), v, ix, x, xv.

55. Cited in Lowenthal, "Reception," 131–132.

56. W. Sokel, *The Writer in Extremis: Expressionism in Twentieth-Century German Literature* (Stanford, 1968), 151–155.

57. O. Spengler, *Decline of the West*, (New York, 1939), 1: 309; 2:194–196.

58. R. Kappen, *Die Idee des Volkes bei Dostojewski* (Würzburg, 1936).

59. H. Hesse, *My Belief* (New York, 1974), 71.

60. T. Mann, *Reflections of a Nonpolitical Man* (New York, 1918).

61. Quotations respectively from T. Mann, "Dostoevsky—within Limits," in *Thomas Mann Reader*, ed. J. Angell (New York, 1950), 448; T. Mann, *Story of a Novel* (New York, 1961), 125; and *Letters of Thomas Mann* (New York, 1971), 107.

62. L. Venohr, *Thomas Manns Verhältnis zur russischen Literatur* (Meisenheim am Glan, 1959).

63. Cited in D. Iehl, "Über einige Aspekte des Bewusstseins bei Kafka und Dostojevskij," in *Dostojevskij und die Literatur*, ed. H. Rothe (Cologne, 1983), 391.

64. W. Dodd, *Kafka and Dostoyevsky* (New York, 1992); R. Poggioli, "Kafka and Dostoyevsky," in *The Kafka Problem*, ed. A. Flores (New York, 1946), 97–107.

65. K. Jaspers, *Philosophy*, vol. 2 (Chicago, 1970), 101–102; Dudkin, "Dostoevskii v Germanii," 678.

66. C. Guignon, ed., *Cambridge Companion to Heidegger* (Cambridge, 1993), 28–29.

67. Fanger, *Dostoevsky and Romantic Realism*, 232–233.

68. J.-P. Sartre, *Essays in Existentialism* (New York, 1968), 40–41.

69. On Sartre and Dostoevsky, see Peyre, *French Novelists*, chap. 9.

70. On Camus and Dostoevsky, see J. Kellog, *Dark Prophets of Hope* (Chicago, 1975), and G. Strem, "Theme of Rebellion in the Works of Camus and Dostoievsky," *Revue de littérature comparée*, no. 2 (1966): 246–257.

71. A. Camus, *Myth of Sisyphus and Other Essays* (New York, 1961), 104–112 (with quotations at 111 and v respectively), and *The Rebel: An Essay on Man in Revolt* (New York, 1991), 3–11, 21–22, 55 ff., 252, 291–292, 302–306, and passim.

72. A. Camus, *The Fall*, trans. J. O'Brien (New York, 1961).

73. Cited in H. Peyre, *French Literary Imagination and Dostoevsky* (University, AL, 1975), 50.

74. Klessmann, *Erfahrungsmuster*, 212–262; J. Meyers, *Hemingway* (New York, 1985), 72, and *Scott Fitzgerald* (New York, 1994), 58.

75. A. and B. Gelb, *O'Neill* (New York, 1973), 79, 233.

76. Cited in E. Elliott, ed., *Columbia Literary History of the United States* (New York, 1988), 747.

77. Among other works, see J. Clayton, *Saul Bellow*, 2d ed. (Bloomington, 1979), 61–69, 79, 141–144; G. Cronin et al., eds., *Conversations with Saul Bellow* (Jackson, MS, 1994), 13, 21, 126, 208, 210, 212.

78. R. Alter, *After the Tradition: Essays on Modern Jewish Writing* (New York, 1969), 95.

79. M. Shechner, *After the Revolution: Studies in the Contemporary Jewish American Imagination* (Bloomington, 1987), 124.

80. A. Schlesinger, Jr., *Vital Center* (Boston, 1949), 39, 53, 85, 88–89.

81. Quotations from Klessmann, *Erfahrungsmuster*, 262, 263.

82. N. Mailer, *American Dream* (New York, 1965); Tom Wolfe, "Son of *Crime and Punishment*," in *Norman Mailer*, ed. R. Lucid (Boston, 1971), 151–161.

83. D. Fiene, "Vonnegut's Quotations from Dostoevsky," *Notes on Modern American Literature* 1 (1977): item 29.

84. C. McCullers, "Russian Realists and Southern Literature," in her *Mortgaged Heart* (Boston, 1971), 252–258, with quotation at 252.

85. Cited in F. Gwynn, "Faulkner's Raskolnikov," *Modern Fiction Studies* 4, no. 2 (1958): 169. See also J. Weisgerber, *Faulkner and Dostoevsky* (Athens, OH, 1974), 351–365.

86. L. Getz, *Flannery O'Connor* (New York, 1980), 48, 76, 78–79; B. Ragen, *Wreck on the Road to Damascus* (Chicago, 1989).

87. Quotations from L. Lawson et al., eds, *Conversations with Walker Percy* (Jackson, MS, 1985), 13, 15, and J. Tolson, *Pilgrim in the Ruins: A Life of Walker Percy* (New York, 1992), 183, 490.

88. D. Peterson, "Notes from the Underworld: Dostoevsky, Du Bois, and the Discovery of Ethnic Soul," *Massachusetts Review*, no. 2 (1994): 225–247.

89. L. Hughes, *The Big Sea* (New York, 1940), 228.

90. Cited in D. Peterson, "Justifying the Margin: The Construction of 'Soul' in Russian and African-American Texts," *Slavic Review*, no. 4 (1992): 749.

91. Cited in D. Nisula, "Dostoevski and Richard Wright," in *Dostoevski and the Human Condition*, ed. A. Ugrinsky et al. (Westport, 1986), 163.

92. Cited in D. Peterson, "Richard Wright's Long Journey from Gorky to Dostoevsky," *African American Review*, no. 3 (1994): 381 and 380.

93. Quotations from Frank, *Prism*, chap. 3.

94. O. Paz, *On Poets* (New York, 1986), 93–94; E. Anderson-Imbert, *Spanish-American Literature*, vol. 2 (Detroit, 1969), 552, 563, 579, 618, 676; E. R. Monegal, *Jorge Luis Borges* (New York, 1978), 287); B. Sarlo, *Jorge Luis Borges* (London, 1993), 51.

95. Cited in I. Iu. Kratchkovsky, *Among Arabic Manuscripts* (Leiden, 1953), 58. See also S. Hafez, *Genesis of Arabic Narrative Discourse* (London, 1993), 91–97, 172, 192, 199, 217, and M. Moosa, *Origins of Modern Arabic Fiction* (Washington, DC, 1983), 75–78.

96. Cited in M. Badawi, *Short History of Modern Arabic Literature* (Oxford, 1993), 112. See also A. Jad, *Form and Technique in the Egyptian Novel, 1912–1971* (London, 1983), 97–104.

97. M. Teimur [*sic*], "Arabskie pisateli o russkoi i sovetskoi literature," *Sovremennyi vostok*, September 1958, 65–66.

98. On Japan and Dostoevsky, see L. L. Gromkovskaia, *100 let russkoi kul'tury v Iaponii* (Moscow, 1989); L. Klein, ed., *Far Eastern Literatures in the Twentieth Century* (New York, 1986), 93–95, 127; K. Rekho, "Tvorchestvo Dostoevskogo i iaponskaia literatura," in *Russkaia klassika v stranakh vostoka*, ed. L. L. Gromkovskaia (Moscow, 1982), 150–162; J. T. Rimer, ed., *Hidden Fire: Russian and Japanese Cultural Encounters, 1868–1926* (Stanford, 1995), 17–48; Nobori

Shomu, "Russian Literature and Japanese Literature," in *Russian Impact on Japan*, ed. P. Berton et al. (Los Angeles, 1981), 42–51, 58.

99. D. Keene, *Dawn to the West: Japanese Literature of the Modern Era: Fiction* (New York, 1984), 224.

100. Cited in P. Anderer, "Kobayashi and Dostoevsky," in Rimer, *Hidden Fire*, 44, 43, 46, respectively.

101. Quotations from I. Iu. Gens, "Russkaia klassika na iaponskom ekrane," in Gromkovskaia, *100 let*, 312, 322. And see J. Goodwin, ed., *Perspectives on Akira Kurosawa* (New York, 1994), 7, 12, 20, 36–37, 56, 90–91, 133–134, 186, 247.

102. Cited in O. Lang, *Pa Chin and His Writings* (Cambridge, MA, 1967), 232.

103. E. Thompson, "Poetic Transformations of Scientific Facts in *Brat'ja Karamazovy*," and "Note on Non-Euclidean Geometry," both in *Dostoevsky Studies*, no. 8 (1987): 73–91.

104. T. Adorno, *Jargon of Authenticity* (Evanston, 1973).

Chapter 4. Tolstoy and the Nonviolent Imperative

1. Cited in H. Gifford, ed., *Leo Tolstoy: A Critical Anthology* (Harmondsworth, 1971), 21.

2. For introductions to Tolstoy's life and thought, see I. Berlin, "The Hedgehog and the Fox" and "Tolstoy and Enlightenment," both in his *Russian Thinkers* (Harmondsworth, 1978); B. Eikhenbaum, *Tolstoi in the Seventies* (Ann Arbor, 1982); R. Gustafson, *Leo Tolstoy: Resident and Stranger* (Princeton, 1986); and A. Maude, *Life of Tolstoy* (Oxford, 1987).

3. Tolstoy cited in Gustafson, *Leo Tolstoy*, 3.

4. Cited in J. Meyers, *Married to Genius* (New York, 1977), 23.

5. Tolstoy, *Anna Karenin (sic)*, trans. R. Edmonds (Harmondsworth, 1978), 510.

6. Tolstoy, "Law of Love and the Law of Violence," in *Confession and Other Religious Writings*, trans. J. Kentish (Harmondsworth, 1987), 182.

7. Cited in V. Zenkovsky, *Russian Thinkers and Europe* (Washington, DC, 1953), 126.

8. T. Bondareff, *Labor: The Divine Command. The Suppressed Book of the Peasant Bondareff* (New York, 1890), with introduction by Tolstoy; Tolstoy, *Anna Karenin*, 298, 344, 346–349, 359, 363, 367, 369, 689, and *Resurrection*, trans. L. Maude (Oxford, 1994), bk. 1, chap. 1, and bk. 2, passim.

9. Tolstoy, *Anna Karenin*, 850; and see his "What Is Religion and of What Does Its Essence Consist?," in *Confession*, 88–89, 119–120.

10. Tolstoy, "What Is Religion?," in *Confession*, 94 (quotation), 102; see also his *What I Believe*, in *Confession; The Gospel in Brief; and What I Believe*, trans. A. Maude (London, 1940), 325.

11. Cited in Gustafson, *Leo Tolstoy*, 10.

12. Cited in G. Spence, *Tolstoy the Ascetic* (Edinburgh, 1967), 25.

13. Cited in Gustafson, *Leo Tolstoy*, 10.

14. "Letter on Non-Resistance" to Ernest H. Crosby, in Tolstoy, *Essays and Letters*, trans. A. Maude (Freeport, NY, 1973 [1909]), 180.

15. Cited in Gustafson, *Leo Tolstoy*, 183–185, 188.

16. Tolstoy, "Law of Love and the Law of Violence" and "Letter on Non-Resistance."

17. See Tolstoy, *Anna Karenin*, pt. 8.

18. Tolstoy, *Resurrection*, 398–399, 400–403, 406–408, 426–431.

19. Cited in P. Marshall, *Demanding the Impossible: A History of Anarchism* (London, 1992), 370.

20. Cited in ibid., 377. See also Tolstoy, *Resurrection*, 433–436.

21. M. Holman, "Half a Life's Work: Aylmer Maude Brings Tolstoy to Britain," *Scottish Slavonic Review* (Spring 1985): 39–53.

22. W. Hammer, "German Tolstoy Translations," *Germanic Review* (January 1937): 49–61; E. Hanke, *Prophet des Unmodernen: Leo N. Tolstoi als Kulturkritiker in der deutschen Diskussion der Jahrhundertwende* (Tübingen, 1993), 215–217.

23. Cited in F. Hemmings, *Russian Novel in France* (London, 1950), 56–57.

24. W. Edgerton, "Artist Turned Prophet," in *American Contributions to the Sixth International Congress of Slavists*, vol. 2, *Literary Contributions*, ed. W. Harkins (The Hague, 1968), 79–81.

25. M. Hasan, "Some Aspects of Tolstoyana in India," in *Essays on Leo Tolstoy*, ed. T. Sharma (Meerut, 1989), 1–23.

26. P. Berton et al., eds., *Russian Impact on Japan* (Los Angeles, 1981), 37, 112 n. 3, 113; G. Lensen, "Russian Impact on Japan," in *Russia and Asia*, ed. W. Vucinich (Stanford, 1972), 365.

27. O. Hachtmann, "Türkische Übersetzungen aus europäischen Literatur," *Die Welt des Islams* 6 (1918): 16, 22–23; S. Hafez, *Genesis of Arabic Narrative Discourse* (London, 1993), 134, 192, 201; A. Shifman, *Lev Tolstoi i Vostok* (Moscow, 1960), 152 ff., 274 ff., 400, 431–465.

28. A. Tavis, *Rilke's Russia* (Evanston, 1994), 92–93.

29. Henry James's letter to H. Walpole, in Gifford, *Leo Tolstoy*, 105.

30. R. Freeborn, "Nineteenth Century," in *Cambridge History of Russian Literature*, ed. C. Moser (Cambridge, 1992), 249.

31. Cited in Gustafson, *Leo Tolstoy*, 292.

32. Quotation from V. Shklovsky, "Art as Technique," in *Russian Formalist Criticism*, ed. L. Lemon et al. (Lincoln, NE, 1965), 17.

33. Cited in R. Hughes, "Tolstoy, Stanislavski, and the Art of Acting," *Journal of Aesthetics and Art Criticism* (Winter 1993): 39.

34. Cited in D. Davie, ed., *Russian Literature and Modern English Fiction* (London, 1967), 49.

35. M. Proust, *On Art and Literature, 1896–1919* (n.p., 1958), 378–379.

36. T. Mann, *Story of a Novel* (New York, 1961), 125 (first quotation); J. Stern, "Theme of Consciousness: Thomas Mann," in *Modernism, 1890–1930*, ed. M. Bradbury et al. (London, 1991), 418 (other quotations).

37. Cited in S. Spurdle, "Tolstoy and Martin du Gard's *Les Thibault*," *Comparative Literature*, no. 4 (1971): 326.

38. Hemmings, *Russian Novel in France*; T. Lindstrom, *Tolstoï en France (1886–1910)* (Paris, 1952), 40, 44–51, chap. 8.

39. Cited in T. Motyleva, *O mirovom znachenii L. N. Tolstogo* (Moscow, 1957), 583.

40. *Letters of James Joyce*, vol. 2, ed. R. Ellmann (New York, 1966); see also vol. 1, ed. S. Gilbert (New York, 1966), 364; R. Ellman, *James Joyce* (New York, 1982), 247, 358, 661; J. Raleigh, "Joyce and Tolstoy," *Literary Theory and Criticism*, ed. J. Strelka (New York, 1984), 1137–1157 (quotation on 1137); F. Moretti, *Modern Epic* (London, 1996), 168–179.

41. V. Woolf, "Russian Point of View," in *Collected Essays*, vol. 1 (New York, 1967), 244–245.

42. M. Holquist, "Did Tolstoj Write Novels?," *American Contributions to the Eighth International Congress of Slavists*, ed. V. Terras, 272–279 (quotation on 274).

43. Cited in J. Meyers, *Hemingway* (New York, 1985), 133–134.

44. Cited in ibid., 134.

45. A. Leroy-Beaulieu, "Léon Tolstoï," *Revue des deux mondes* 60 (1910): 826–827.

46. P. Waddington, *From the Russian Fugitive to the Ballad of Bulgarie* (Oxford, 1994), 112–114.

47. E. Eigner, *Robert Louis Stevenson and the Romantic Tradition* (Princeton, 1966), 131–133.

48. R. Sonn, *Anarchism and Cultural Politics in Fin-de-Siècle France* (Lincoln, NE, 1989), 216–220.

49. R. Jans, *Tolstoj in Nederland* (Bussum, 1952), 24–25; *Complete Letters of Vincent van Gogh*, vol. 3 (Greenwich, CT, n.d.), 52, 54, 474.

50. R. Rolland, *Tolstoy* (New York, 1911), 5.

51. Ibid., 1.

52. E. de Vogüé, *Russian Novelists* (New York, 1974), 244, 268–269. See also A. Suarès, *Tolstoi vivant* (Paris, 1911), 23 and passim.

53. H. Ellis, *The New Spirit* (Washington, DC, 1935), 167 and passim.

54. G. Perris, *Life and Teaching of Leo Tolstoy* (London, 1904), 1.

55. D. Bodde, *Tolstoy and China* (Princeton, 1950); Shifman, *Lev Tolstoi i Vostok*, 17 ff., 46–172.

56. H. Hesse, *Gesammelte Werke*, vol. 12 (Frankfurt am Main, 1970), 347–350.

57. M. Carlson, *"No religion higher than truth"*: *A History of the Theosophical Movement in Russia* (Princeton, 1993), 161–162 and passim. On Blavatsky, see B. Campbell, *Ancient Wisdom Revived* (Berkeley, 1980), passim.

58. Inter alia, see Hanke, *Prophet des Unmodernen*, and Kh. Shtul'ts, "Tolstoi v Germanii," *Literaturnoe nasledstvo 75*, bk. 2 (1965): 361–460.

59. G. Stark, *Entrepreneurs of Ideology: Neoconservative Publishers in Germany, 1890–1933* (Chapel Hill, 1981), 4–9, 15–19, 58–111, 137, 141, 177–180.

60. M. Green, *Tolstoy and Gandhi* (New York, 1983), 68–69.

61. Quotation from P. Carter, *Spiritual Crisis of the Gilded Age* (DeKalb, IL, 1971), 106; and see W. G. Jones, ed., *Tolstoi and Britain* (Oxford, 1995), 1.

62. M. Hirschfeld, *Sexualpathologie: Ein Lehrbuch für Ärzte*, vol. 1 (Bonn, 1921), 151.

63. J. A. Symonds, *Essays Speculative and Suggestive*, vol. 2 (London, 1970 [1890]), 46–47.

64. Ellis, *New Spirit*, 173–174, 212, 214–216 ff., 271, 275, 277 ff., 286.

65. Quoting Henry Gifford in Gifford, *Leo Tolstoy*, 299.

66. G. Zytaruk, *D. H. Lawrence's Response to Russian Literature* (The Hague, 1971), chap. 3 and passim (quotations on 88 and 93).

67. Cited in M. Esslin, "Modernist Drama," in Bradbury et al., *Modernism*, 531.

68. *The Savour of Salt: A Henry Salt Anthology*, ed. G. Hendrick (Fontwell, Sussex, 1989), 47; H. Salt, *Animals' Rights* (Clark's Summit, PA, 1980), 26, and *Seventy Years among Savages* (New York, 1921), 79, 203–206. And see C. Spencer, *Heretic's Feast: A History of Vegetarianism* (Hanover, NH, 1995), 250, 252, 274–275, 282, 285–290, 293–294, 296.

69. A. Rose, "Some Influences on English Penal Reform," in Jones, *Tolstoi and Britain*, 257–277.

70. P. Brock, *Freedom from War: Nonsectarian Pacifism (1814–1914)* (Toronto, 1991), 294.

71. Ibid., chap. 15; H. Josephson, ed., *Biographical Dictionary of Modern Peace Leaders* (Westport, 1985), 415–416, 559–560; G. Jochheim, *Antimilitaristiche Akstionstheorie* (Frankfurt am Main, 1977), 97–109, 134–137, and passim.

72. W. Armytage, *Heavens Below: Utopian Experiments in England* (Toronto, 1961), 333–334 and chap. 5; M. Holman, "Purleigh Colony," in Jones, *Tolstoi and Britain*, 153–183; D. Hardy, *Alternative Communities in Nineteenth-Century England* (London, 1979), 172–181, 186–210.

73. A. Bramwell, *Ecology in the Twentieth Century* (New Haven, 1989), 99–100, 180, 189; W. Linse, *Ökopax und Anarchie: Eine Geschichte der ökologischen Bewegung in Deutschland* (Munich, 1986), 11, 75, 136, 174–175.

74. M. Green, *Mountain of Truth: The Counterculture Begins at Ascona, 1900–1920* (Hanover, NH, 1986); Hanke, *Prophet des Unmodernen*, pt. 2, chap. 2.

352

75. On the reception of Tolstoy in Japan, see N. Bamba et al., *Pacifism in Japan* (Vancouver, 1978); Berton et al., *Russian Impact on Japan*; C. Fischer, *Lev N. Tolstoj in Japan* (Wiesbaden, 1969); and Lensen, "Russian Impact on Japan."

76. Cited in C. Gluck, *Japan's Modern Myths: Ideology in the Late Meiji Period* (Princeton, 1985), 171.

77. Cited in Berton et al., *Russian Impact on Japan*, 38.

78. Cited in ibid., 39.

79. Cited in Gluck, *Japan's Modern Myths*, 217.

80. Cited in Shifman, *Lev Tolstoi i Vostok*, 464–465; and see passim, 373–465, on Tolstoy's reception in the Islamic nations.

81. L. L. Gromkovskaia et al., eds., *Russkaia klassika v stranakh vostoka* (Moscow, 1982), passim.

82. M. Yaseen, "Tolstoy and Premchand," in Sharma, *Essays on Leo Tolstoy*, 125–134.

83. On the Tolstoy-Gandhi relationship, see J. Brown, *Gandhi* (New Haven, 1989); D. Dalton, *Mahatma Gandhi* (New York, 1993); Green, *Tolstoy and Gandhi*; J. Hunt, *Gandhi in London* (New Delhi, 1978).

84. M. Gandhi, *Gandhi's Autobiography* (Washington, DC, 1948), 172.

85. Cited in M. Green, *Voice of a New Age Revolution* (New York, 1993), 168.

86. M. Gandhi, *Economic and Industrial Life and Relations*, vol. 1 (Ahmedabad, 1957), 104–105.

87. Quoted in Dalton, *Mahatma Gandhi*, 7–9.

88. Quotations respectively from M. Gandhi and L. Tolstoy, *Letters*, ed. B. Srinavasa Murthy (Long Beach, CA, 1987), 40; Gandhi, *Gandhi's Autobiography*, 198.

89. Gandhi, *Hind Swaraj* (Ahmedabad, 1989), 72. See Tolstoy's similar logic concerning India in his "Meaning of the Russian Revolution," in *Russian Intellectual History*, ed. M. Raeff (New York, 1966), 340.

90. Cited in Dalton, *Mahatma Gandhi*, 10–11.

91. Cited in G. Woodcock, *Mohandas Gandhi* (New York, 1971), 110.

92. A. Doctor, *Anarchist Thought in India* (Bombay, 1964), 53.

93. For instance, see J. Narayan, "Tolstoy and Gandhi," *France-Asie/Asia* (May–June 1961): 2031–2034.

94. R. Albertson, "Christian Commonwealth in Georgia," *Georgia Historical Quarterly* (September 1945): 125–142; J. Dombrowski, *Early Days of Christian Socialism in America* (New York, 1966), chap. 12.

95. L. Veysey, *The Communal Experience* (New York, 1973), 42–50, 112, 148, and passim.

96. Cited in A. Davis, *American Heroine: The Life and Legend of Jane Addams* (New York, 1973), 136.

97. Cited in J. Smith, "Tolstoy's Fiction in England and America" (Ph.D. diss., University of Illinois, 1939), 31.

98. W. D. Howells, *A Traveler from Altruria*, ed. D. Levy (Boston, 1996); C. Goldfarb, "From Complicity to Altruria: The Use of Tolstoy in Howells," *University Review—Kansas City* (June 1966): 311–317.

99. P. Frederick, *Knights of the Golden Rule: The Intellectual as Christian Social Reformer in the 1890s* (Lexington, KY, 1976).

100. Ibid., 14–19, 21–22, 24, chap. 7, and passim; Dombrowski, *Early Days*, 137.

101. J. Addams, *Twenty Years at Hull House* (New York, 1911), 194, 259–280, chap. 16; Davis, *American Heroine*, 42, 50 ff., 62–64, 102, 135–139, and passim; Maude, *Life of Tolstoy*, 2:364–367, 370.

102. Cited in E. Wagenknecht, *Seven Worlds of Theodore Roosevelt* (New York, 1958), 70–72.

103. First two quotations cited in Davie, *Russian Literature and Modern English Fiction*, 7; next two in "Mr. Roosevelt's Attack on Tolstoy," *Current Literature* (July 1909): 64.

104. C. Darrow, *Resist Not Evil* (Montclair, NJ, 1972 [1902]), introduction (by C. Chatfield) and 7–8; C. Darrow, *Story of My Life* (New York, 1932), 210; I. Stone, *Clarence Darrow: For the Defense* (Garden City, 1941), 27, 30, 31, 255, 275, 341.

105. On Bryan and Tolstoy, see P. Glad, *The Trumpet Soundeth: William Jennings Bryan and His Democracy* (Lincoln, NE, 1960), passim.

106. C. Lunardini, *ABC-CLIO Companion to the American Peace Movement* (Santa Barbara, 1994), 81–83; J. Nelson, *Peace Prophets: American Pacifist Thought, 1919–1941* (Chapel Hill, 1967), 37, 91–94.

107. Quotations in Dalton, *Mahatma Gandhi*, ix, 177, 181–182.

108. Telephone conversation of March 1997 with Clayborne Carson, editor of the King papers; cf. Eugene Genovese's undocumented assertion that King admired Tolstoy, in his "Martin Luther King, Jr.: Theology, Politics, Scholarship," *Reviews in American History* 23, no. 1 (1995): 9.

109. R. Luker, *Social Gospel in White and Black: American Racial Reform, 1885–1912* (Chapel Hill, 1991), 46, 242–243, 250–254; R. Hofstadter, *Social Darwinism in American Thought* (Philadelphia, 1944), 167; P. Gianakos, "Ernest Howard Crosby," in *Peace Movements in America*, ed. C. Chatfield (New York, 1973), 1–19.

110. *Literaturnoe nasledstvo* 75, bk. 1, 490–493.

111. W.E.B. Du Bois, "On Tolstoy," in *Writings by W.E.B. Du Bois in Periodicals Edited by Others*, ed. H. Aptheker (Millwood, NY, 1982), 2:295.

112. Frederick, *Knights*, chap. 5; Luker, *Social Gospel*, 314–323.

113. A. Davis, *Spearheads for Reform: The Social Settlements and the Progressive Movement* (New York, 1967), 99–100; L. Hughes, *Fight for Freedom: The Story of the NAACP* (New York, 1962), chap. 1; J. H. Holmes, *I Speak for Myself* (New York, 1959), 166; Josephson, *Biographical Dictionary*, 422–424; C. Kellog, *NAACP*, vol. 1, *1909–1920* (Baltimore, 1967), 10 ff.; Luker, *Social Gospel*, 323;

W. Walling, *Russia's Message* (New York, 1908), frontispiece, 414, 427 ff.; N. Weiss, *National Urban League, 1910–1940* (New York, 1974), chap. 4.

114. I. Bell, *CORE and the Strategy of Nonviolence* (New York, 1968), 7–15; V. Brittain, *Rebel Passion: A Short History of Some Pioneer Peace-makers* (London, 1964), 104–112; J. Farmer, *Freedom—When?* (New York, 1965), 55; Luker, *Social Gospel*, 322; A. Meier et al., *CORE: A Study in the Civil Rights Movement, 1942–1968* (New York, 1973), chap. 1.

115. G. Steinem, *Revolution from Within: A Book of Self-Esteem* (Boston, 1992), 44 ff.; Dalton, *Mahatma Gandhi*, 203–204 n. 21.

Chapter 5. Destroying the Agents of Modernity: Russian Anti-Semitism

1. Jews in central Poland suffered fewer restrictions than did residents of the Pale.

2. On pre-1881 Russian anti-Semitism, see J. Klier, *Imperial Russia's Jewish Question, 1855–1881* (Cambridge, 1995) and *Russia Gathers Her Jews* (DeKalb, IL, 1986).

3. S. Dudakov, *Istoriia odnogo mifa* (Moscow, 1993), chap. 3; D. El'iashevich, "Ideologiia antisemitizma v Rossii," in *Natsional'naia pravaia prezhde i teper'*, ed. R. Sh. Ganelin (St. Petersburg, 1992), 48–55, 67–69.

4. Cited in H.-D. Löwe, *Tsars and the Jews* (Chur, Switzerland, 1993), 81 n. 65.

5. See A. Goldenweiser, "Legal Status of Jews in Russia," in *Russian Jewry (1860–1917)*, ed. J. Frumkin et al. (New York, 1966), 85–119, and A. Kappeler, *Russland als Vielvölkerreich* (Munich, 1992), 220–224 and passim.

6. Statistics from Löwe, *Tsars and Jews*, 37–59, 86–88; A. Orbach, "Development of the Russian Jewish Community, 1881–1903," in *Pogroms*, ed. J. Klier et al. (Cambridge, 1992), 140–141; S. Zipperstein, "Russian Maskilim," in *Legacy of Jewish Migration*, ed. D. Berger (New York, 1983), 34, 38.

7. On Jewish wealth and poverty, see Löwe, *Tsars and Jews*, 88–92; C. Ruud et al., *Fontanka, 16* (Moscow, 1993), 280–281; and R. Weinberg, "Pogrom of 1905 in Odessa," in Klier, *Pogroms*, 251–254.

8. Cited in N. Shepherd, *A Price below Rubies: Jewish Women as Rebels and Radicals* (Cambridge, MA, 1993), 1–2.

9. E. Haberer, *Jews and Revolution in Nineteenth-Century Russia* (Cambridge, 1995); E. Mendelsohn, *Class Struggle in the Pale* (Cambridge, 1970).

10. Cited in L. Schapiro, *Russian Studies* (New York, 1988), 266.

11. Cited in S. Lambroza, "Pogroms of 1903–1906," in Klier, *Pogroms*, 221.

12. This is the theme of Löwe, *Tsars and Jews*.

13. Besides sources cited above, see C. Wynn, *Workers, Strikes, and Pogroms* (Princeton, 1992), 7–8, 261–263, and chap. 7.

14. Quotation from S. Ettinger, "Modern Period," in *History of the Jewish People*, ed. H. Ben-Sasson (Cambridge, MA, 1976), 881.

15. Cited in M. Vetter, "Die russische Emigration und ihre 'Judenfrage,' " in *Russische Emigration in Deutschland 1918 bis 1941*, ed. K. Schlögel (Berlin 1995), 108.

16. See Shepherd, *Price below Rubies*, chaps. 2 and 3 and epilogue.

17. See R. Sh. Ganelin, "Chernosotennye organizatsii," in Ganelin, *Natsional'-naia pravaia prezhde i teper'*, 77–94; H. Rogger, *Jewish Policies and Right-Wing Politics* (Berkeley, 1986), chap. 7, and "Russia," in *The European Right*, ed. H. Rogger and E. Weber (Berkeley, 1966); S. A. Stepanov, *Chernaia sotnia v Rossii (1905–1914 gg.)* (Moscow, 1992).

18. S. Witte, *Memoirs of Witte*, trans. S. Harcave (Armonk, NY, 1990), 405.

19. Cited in Rogger, *Jewish Policies*, 209–210.

20. Gosudarstvennaia Duma, *Stenograficheskie otchety*, tretii sozyv, sessiia V, chast' 1, col. 1056; tretii sozyv, sessiia V, chast' 1, col. 812; G. Iurskii, *Pravye v tret'ei Gosudarstvennoi Dume* (Kharkov, 1912), 35–40; Nikolaus Markow, *Der Kampf der dunklen Mächte* (Frankfurt am Main, 1944).

21. Gosudarstvennaia Duma, *Stenograficheskie otchety*, chetvertyi sozyv, sessiia II, chast' 3, cols. 697–698; chetvertyi sozyv, sessiia I, chast' 1, cols. 2092–2093.

22. Cited in C. Read, *Religion, Revolution, and the Russian Intelligentsia* (Totowa, NJ, 1979), 99.

23. Gosudarstvennaia Duma, *Stenograficheskie otchety*, tretii sozyv, sessiia I, chast' 1, col. 3083.

24. N. Cohn, *Warrant for Genocide: The Myth of the Jewish World Conspiracy and the "Protocols of the Elders of Zion"* (New York, 1967), 112.

25. The standard study on the *Protocols* was Cohn, *Warrant for Genocide*, but it has been superseded by C. De Michelis, "Les *Protocoles des sages de sion*: Philologie et histoire," *Cahiers du monde russe* 38, no. 3 (1997): 263–306, and the works of M. Hagemeister: "Die 'Protokolle der Weisen von Zion,' " in *Russland und Europa*, ed. E. Hexelschneider (Leipzig, 1995), 195–206; "Neuere Forschungen und Veröffentlichungen zu den 'Protokollen der Weisen von Zion,'" in N. Cohn, *"Die Protokolle der Weisen von Zion"* (Baden-Baden, 1998), 267–289; and "Der Mythos der 'Protokolle der Weisen von Zion,' " in *Verschwörungstheorien*, ed. U. Caumanns et al. (Osnabrück, 2001), 89–110.

26. From translation of *Protocols* in H. Bernstein, *Truth about the "Protocols of Zion"* (New York, 1971 [1935]), 324.

27. Ibid., 312.

28. Ibid., 311.

29. Ibid., 333.

30. Papus [G. Encausse], *Catholicisme, satanisme et occultisme* (Paris, 1897), 7–8 (first quotation); J. Webb, *Occult Establishment* (La Salle, IL, 1976), 214–217.

31. Dudakov, *Istoriia odnogo mifa*; Klier, *Imperial Russia's Jewish Question*, chaps. 12, 18; C. De Michelis, "Un professionalista dell'antisemitismo ottocentesco: Osman Bey," *La Rassegna mensile di Israel* 63, no. 2 (1997): 51–61.

32. The articles of M. Hagemeister supersede all previous biographical accounts: "Sergej Nilus und die 'Protokolle der Weisen von Zion,' " *Jahrbuch für Antisemitismusforschung* 5 (1996): 127–147; and "Wer war Sergej Nilus?," *Ostkirchliche Studien* 40, no. 1 (1991): 49–63.

33. The quotation is from Butmi, cited in H. Rollin, *L'Apocalypse de notre temps* (Paris, 1939), 337.

34. M. Vetter, *Antisemiten und Bolschewiki* (Berlin, 1995), 72.

35. Cited in S. Wilson, *Ideology and Experience: Anti-Semitism in France* (East Brunswick, NJ, 1982), 424.

36. So far as I know, there are no previous studies of this topic.

37. P. E. Shchegolev, *Okhranniki i avantiuristy* (Moscow, 1930), 55–56; W. Langer, *Franco-Russian Alliance, 1890–1894* (New York, 1967 [1929]), 214; Wilson, *Ideology*, 409–428, 556, and passim.

38. S. Morcos, *Juliette Adam* (Dar al-Maaref, Libya, 1962), 183–211 and passim; Rollin, *L'Apocalypse*, 290 and chap. 11.

39. On Cyon, see Cohn, *Warrant for Genocide*, 106; F. Fox, "*Protocols of the Elders of Zion* and the Shadowy World of Elie de Cyon," *East European Jewish Affairs* 26, no. 1 (1997): 3–22; and Rollin, *L'Apocalypse*, chaps. 11–13. Fox attempts to substantiate Rollin's argument that Cyon was the author of the *Protocols*, but does not provide evidence to link the two.

40. Rollin, *L'Apocalypse*, 17 ff., 279–281, 445–446.

41. Wilson, *Ideology*, 672, 676, 677.

42. P. Mazgaj, *Action Française and Revolutionary Syndicalism* (Chapel Hill, 1979), 39, 43–44, 53, and passim.

43. On the *Protocols* in France, see P.-A. Taguieff, ed., *Les Protocoles des sages de sion*, 2 vols. (Paris, 1992).

44. E. Jouin, *Le Péril judéo-maçonnique*, 3 vols. (Paris, 1920); P. Pierrard, *Juifs et catholiques français* (Paris, 1970), 153, 157–166, 235, 241–245, 254, and passim; De Michelis, "Protocoles," 270, 290 n. 18.

45. Cited in E. Weber, *Action Française* (Stanford, 1962), 200.

46. The standard work on the Russian right in Germany remains W. Laqueur, *Russia and Germany* (New Brunswick, NJ, 1990), chaps. 4–6.

47. The *Protocols* appeared in *Luch sveta*, no. 3 (1919); see Hagemeister, "Sergej Nilus," 136–137, 146 n. 81, and Rollin, *L'Apocalypse*, 175. On Vinberg see J. Burbank, *Intelligentsia and Revolution* (New York, 1986), 171–177, and Laqueur, *Russia and Germany*, 63n, 121–122, 126–130.

48. Hagemeister, "Sergej Nilus," 137; W. Meyer zu Uptrup, "Wann wurde Hitler zum Antisemiten?," *Zeitschrift für Geschichtswissenschaft* 43 (1995): 693; M. Sabrow, *Der Rathenaumord* (Munich, 1994), 48, 54–55, 78, 114.

49. The following account of pre-Versailles German anti-Semitism is based on W. Altgeld, "Die Ideologie des Nationalsozialismus und ihre Vorläufer," in *Faschismus und Nationalsozialismus*, ed. K. Bracher et al. (Berlin, 1991), 128–131; H. Berding, *Moderner Antisemitismus in Deutschland* (Frankfurt am Main, 1988), chaps. 1–3; W. Jochmann, "Die Ausbreitung des Antisemitismus," in *Deutsches Judentum in Krieg und Revolution 1916–1923*, ed. W. Mosse (Tübingen, 1971), 409–510; H. Strauss, ed., *Hostages of Modernization: Studies of Modern Antisemitism, 1870–1933/39*, vol. 1 (Berlin, 1993).

50. Cited in D. C. Large, *Where Ghosts Walked: Munich's Road to the Third Reich* (New York, 1997), xxii–xxiv.

51. Cited in J. Katz, *Jews and Freemasons in Europe, 1723–1939* (Cambridge, MA, 1970), 177.

52. B. Hamann, *Hitlers Wien* (Munich 1996); A. Joachimsthaler, *Korrektur einer Biographie: Adolf Hitler 1908–1920* (Munich, 1989), 40, 41, 44–45, 69, 97, 162, 174, 179–180, 184, 234; I. Kershaw, *Hitler, 1889–1936* (New York, 1999), 52, 58, and chap. 2.

53. "I Was Hitler's Boss," *Current History* 1 (November 1941): 193–199; H. Auerbach, "Hitlers politische Lehrjahre," *Vierteljahrshefte für Zeitgeschichte* 25, no. 1 (1977): 17–18; Meyer zu Uptrup, "Wann wurde Hitler," 687–697.

54. On Rosenberg, see R. Cecil, *Myth of the Master Race* (London, 1972), and Laqueur, *Russia and Germany*, 80–90.

55. On Eckart and his relationship with Rosenberg, see R. Engelman, "Dietrich Eckart and the Genesis of Nazism" (Ph.D. diss., Washington University, 1971), 113 ff. and passim; M. Plewnia, *Auf dem Weg zu Hitler* (Bremen, 1970), 36, 94 ff.; D. Rose, *Die Thule-Gesellschaft* (Tübingen, 1994), 108–128 and passim; H. Wilhelm, *Dichter, Denker, Fememörder* (Berlin, 1989), 58–59, 70, 72, 99–107.

56. Cited respectively in J. Fest, *Hitler* (New York, 1974), 132, and Meyer zu Uptrup, "Wann wurde Hitler," 692.

57. Dr. J. St., "Lügen der Antisemiten," *Allgemeine Zeitung des Judentums* 83 (August 29, 1919, and September 5, 1919). For their absence in earlier anti-Semitic literary representations of Jews, see R. Robertson, *The 'Jewish Question' in German Literature, 1749–1939* (Oxford, 1999).

58. A. Drexler, *Mein politisches Erwachen* (Munich, 1919); Cecil, *Myth*, 29; W. Horn, "Ein unbekannter Aufsatz Hitlers aus dem Frühjahr 1924," *Vierteljahrshefte für Zeitgeschichte* 16 (1968): 285; Meyer zu Uptrup, "Wann wurde Hitler," 693, 697; R. Phelps, "Anton Drexler," *Deutsche Rundschau* 87 (December 1961): 1136. Drexler's book could not have been written before his exposure to the *Protocols*: according to Auerbach, "Hitlers politische Lehrjahre," 7, the press that published his book was not founded until April 1, 1919.

59. Cited in Engelman, "Eckart," 248; see also Rose, *Thule*, 153–154. J. Lukacs, *Hitler of History* (New York, 1997), chap. 2, also dates Hitler's anti-Semitism to the Munich years but does not account for its origin and evolution.

60. Strauss, "Hostages of 'World Jewry,' " in *Hostages of Modernization*, ed. Strauss, 1:165–173.

61. D. Eckart, *Der Bolschewismus von Moses bis Lenin* (Munich, 1924), 49.

62. R. Breitling, *Die national-sozialistische Rassenlehre* (Meisenheim am Glan, 1971), 32–35; Meyer zu Uptrup, "Wann wurde Hitler," 691–692.

63. R. Phelps, "Hitlers Grundlegende Rede über den Antisemitismus," *Vierteljahrshefte für Zeitgeschichte* 16, no. 4 (1968): 390–420.

64. A. Hitler, *Sämtliche Aufzeichnungen 1905–1924*, ed. E. Jäckel (Stuttgart, 1980), 89–90 (quotation); Wilhelm, *Dichter*, 95.

65. As in Breitling, *Rassenlehre*, 43, and A. Stein, *Adolf Hitler: Schüler der "Weisen von Zion"* (Karlsbad, 1936).

66. A. Hitler, *Mein Kampf*, trans. R. Manheim (Boston, 1943), 661.

67. I. Kershaw, *Hitler* (London, 1991), 23–30.

68. Cited in Fest, *Hitler*, 137.

69. For this and the next paragraph, see, inter alia, R. Bytwerk, *Julius Streicher* (New York, 1983), 132, 138, 168, and fig. 7, and W. Meyer zu Uptrup, "Der Kampf gegen die 'jüdische Weltverschwörung,' " in *Vom Vorurteil zur Vernichtung?*, ed. E. Geldbach (Münster, 1995), 161–180.

70. Cited in L. Dawidowicz, *War against the Jews* (New York, 1975), 94–95.

71. Cited in A. Bullock, *Hitler and Stalin* (New York, 1992), 82.

72. Laqueur, *Russia and Germany*, 113 (first quotation), 134–137; R. Sh. Ganelin, "Das Leben des Gregor Schwarz-Bostunitsch, pt. I," in Schlögel, *Russische Emigration in Deutschland*, 201–208; M. Hagemeister, "Das Leben des Gregor Schwarz-Bostunitsch, pt. II," in ibid., 209–218 (with quotations at 212).

73. Rollin, *L'Apocalypse*, 510; J. Carlson, *Under Cover* (New York, 1943), passim; L. Bondy, *Racketeers of Hatred* (London, 1946), 66–105.

74. On these proposals, see D. Goldhagen, *Hitler's Willing Executioners* (New York, 1996), chap. 2; J. Schoeps, "From Anti-Judaism to Anti-Semitism," in *Resurgence of Right-Wing Radicalism in Germany*, ed. U. Wank (Atlantic Highlands, NJ, 1996), 6–9; and Strauss, "Hostages."

75. Cited in R. Wistrich, *Antisemitism* (New York, 1991), 118–119.

76. Cited in R. Singerman, "American Career of the *Protocols of the Elders of Zion*," *American Jewish History* (September 1981): 54. This is the major source on the Brasol-Ford relationship.

77. A. Lee, *Henry Ford and the Jews* (New York, 1980).

78. S. Polovinkin, ed., *Sergei Aleksandrovich Nilus* (Moscow, 1995), 204; M. Hagemeister, letter of April 10, 1998, to author.

79. H. Ford, *The International Jew* (Los Angeles, 1948), 163, 169, and passim.

80. N. Hapgood, "Henry Ford's Jew-Mania," *Hearst's International*, November 1922, 106, 108.

81. D. Pipes, *The Hidden Hand: Middle East Fears of Conspiracy* (New York, 1996), 311 and passim.

Chapter 6. Conveying Higher Truth Onstage: Ballet and Theater

1. On Diaghilev, see the secondary sources referenced throughout the chapter.

2. Cited in J. Bowlt, ed., *Russian Art of the Avant-Garde* (New York, 1976), 3.

3. K. Balmont, "Elementary Words on Symbolist Poetry," in *Silver Age of Russian Culture*, ed. C. Proffer et al. (Ann Arbor, 1975), 18.

4. J. Acocella, "Reception of Diaghilev's Ballets Russes by Artists and Intellectuals in Paris and London, 1909–1914" (Ph.D.. diss., Rutgers University, 1984), 245.

5. S. Diaghilev, "Slozhnye voprosy," *Mir iskusstva* 1 (1899): 2, 15.

6. Quoted in J. Kennedy, *"Mir iskusstva" Group* (New York, 1977), 83.

7. Dostoevsky cited in M. G. Nekliudova, *Traditsii i novatorstvo v russkom iskusstve kontsa XIX-nachala XX veka* (Moscow, 1991), 92.

8. W. Richardson, *Zolotoe Runo and Russian Modernism* (Ann Arbor, 1986), 59–60.

9. Cited in I. S. Zil'bershtein, *Sergei Diagilev i russkoe iskusstvo*, vol. 1 (Moscow, 1982), 12–13.

10. Respective Benois quotations from J. Bowlt, *Silver Age* (Newtonville, MA, 1982), 60, and B. Rosenthal, "Theatre as Church," *Russian History* 4, pt. 2 (1977): 123.

11. A. Kamensky et al., *World of Art Movement in Early Twentieth-Century Russia* (Leningrad, 1991), 12–13.

12. A. Benois, *Reminiscences of the Russian Ballet* (London, 1941), 285.

13. Cited in E. Bridgman, "Mir iskusstva," in *Art of Enchantment: Diaghilev's Ballets Russes*, ed. N. Van Norman Baer (New York, 1988), 32–33, 36.

14. Benois quotations in ibid., 34.

15. Cited in R. Taruskin, *Stravinsky and the Russian Traditions*, vol. 1 (Berkeley, 1996), 540–541, 550.

16. Cited in ibid., 2:1072–1073.

17. Cited in ibid., 1:445.

18. Bridgman, "Mir iskusstva," 38.

19. Cited in C. Spencer, *The World of Serge Diaghilev* (New York, 1979), 51.

20. Cited in M. Martin, "The Ballet *Parade*," *Art Quarterly* (Spring 1978): 87.

21. Fokine cited in L. Garafola, *Diaghilev's Ballets russes* (New York, 1989), 8.

22. Both quotations from ibid., 35–36.

23. Cited in A. Kisselgoff et al., "Balanchine," *TriQuarterly* (Fall 1973): 392.

24. Cited in Acocella, "Reception," 280.

25. Cited in J. Pasler, *Confronting Stravinsky* (Berkeley, 1986), 68–70.

26. Taruskin, *Defining Russia Musically* (Princeton, 1997), 362–363, 399–460, and *Stravinsky*, 1:445 (quotation), vol. 2, chaps. 15, 17–18, and passim.

27. J. Bowlt, *Khudozhniki russkogo teatra* (Moscow, 1991), 8–25, and "From Studio to Stage," in Baer, *Art of Enchantment*, 44, 48–49, 51–53; N. Van Norman Baer, "Design and Choreography," in ibid., 64.

28. Kamensky, *World of Art Movement*, 152.

29. Cited in Garafola, *Diaghilev's*, 367.

30. In general, see Acocella, "Reception," chap. 5, and Garafola, *Diaghilev's*, chap. 10.

31. V. Duke, *Passport to Paris* (Boston, 1955), 128–129.

32. K. Silver, *Esprit de Corps* (Princeton, 1989), 22, 174 ff.

33. A. Schaeffner, *Essais de musicologie* (Paris, 1980), chap. 8.

34. F. Aprahamian, "Ravel, Roussel, Satie, and Les Six," in *Heritage of Music*, ed. M. Raeburn et al., vol. 4 (Oxford, 1990), 60; Taruskin, *Stravinsky*, 2:991–1006 (with sauce quotation at 992).

35. M. Sert, *Two or Three Muses* (London, 1953), 84–85.

36. U. Berger, "Le Modèle idéal?," in *Spiegelungen: Die Ballets Russes und die Künste*, ed. C. Jeschke et al. (Berlin, 1997), 15–28; Acocella, "Reception," 308–309.

37. Cited in R. Labrusse, "Matisse's Second Visit to London and His Collaboration with the Ballets Russes," *Burlington Magazine*, September 1997, 594; and see J. Perl, "Setting the Stage," *New Republic*, January 5 and 12, 1998, 27.

38. *Apollinaire on Art*, ed. L. Breunig (New York, 1972), 394.

39. F. Swinnerton, *The Georgian Literary Scene* (London, 1969), 222.

40. In general see Acocella, "Reception," chap. 6; Garafola, *Diaghilev's*, chap. 11; L. Honigwachs, "Edwardian Discovery of Russia, 1900–1917" (Ph.D. diss., Columbia University, 1977), chap. 7.

41. Cited in F. Kermode, "Poet and Dancer before Diaghilev," *Salmagundi* 33–34 (1976): 23.

42. Cited in Honigwachs, "Edwardian," 277–279.

43. Martin Green, *Children of the Sun* (New York, 1976), xx, 4, 6, 27–28, 31, 35, 41, 81–82, 85–86, 141–142.

44. J. Fletcher, *Life Is My Song* (New York, 1937), 68.

45. See L. Gordon, *Eliot's Early Years* (Oxford, 1977), 107–108 (second quotation); H. Howarth, *Notes on Some Figures behind T. S. Eliot* (Boston, 1964), 235 (first quotation), 306–310; Kermode, "Poet and Dancer," 46.

46. S. Levy, "The Russians Are Coming: Russian Dancers in the United States, 1910–1933" (Ph.D. diss., New York University, 1990), chap. 1. See pp. 21–22 for the sword incident.

47. Cited in L. Garafola, "The Ballets Russes in America," in Baer, *Art of Enchantment*, 128.

48. Cited in N. MacDonald, ed., *Diaghilev Observed by Critics in England and the United States* (New York, 1975), 162. See also 134, 144, 146–147, 155.

49. Cited in H. Robinson, *Last Impresario: The Life, Times, and Legacy of Sol Hurok* (New York, 1994), 47.

50. Berger, "Modèle"; and B. Zeidler, "Die Ballets Russes in der Berliner Kunst," in Jeschke, *Spiegelungen*, 185–254.

51. C. Einstein, "Leon Bakst und die russische Ballett," in *Russen in Berlin, 1918–1933*, ed. F. Mierau (Weinheim, 1988), 362–373.

52. Cited in Acocella, "Reception," 323–324.

53. Cited in Honigwachs, "Edwardian," 269.

54. Cited in ibid., 268.

55. See D. Harris, "Diaghilev's Ballets Russes and the Vogue for Orientalism," in Baer, *Art of Enchantment*, 85–88; C. Mayer, "Impact of the Ballets Russes on Design," in *Avant-Garde Frontier*, ed. G. Roman et al. (Gainesville, FL, 1992), 15–44; Spencer, *World*, chap. 7.

56. Cited in Harris, "Diaghilev's," 87.

57. Cited in ibid., 84.

58. For clothing, see P. Poiret, *King of Fashion* (Philadelphia, 1931), 123–125, 182–183; P. Wollen, "Fashion/Orientalism/the Body," *New Formations* 1, no. 1 (Spring 1987): 5–33; G. Howell, *In Vogue* (London, 1991), 18–19, 21, 40; M. Battersby, *Decorative Twenties* (New York, 1988), 46, and *Art Deco Fashion* (New York, 1984), 62, 67–68; R. Lyman, *Paris Fashion* (London, 1972), 66, 80–81, 87–88; C. Probert, *Hats in Vogue* (New York, 1981), 8–21; E. Charles-Roux, *Chanel and Her World* (London, 1981), 141, 168–173, 192–199; Bowlt, *Khudozhniki*, 24–25.

59. Cited in Mayer, "Impact," 20.

60. A. Gold et al., *Misia* (New York, 1980), 288, 292; Taruskin, *Stravinsky*, 2:1516–1517.

61. W. Packer, *Art of Vogue Covers* (New York, 1980), 20, 80, and *Fashion Drawing in Vogue* (London, 1983), 58–59.

62. Cited in Honigwachs, "Edwardian," 265 n. 2.

63. Garafola, *Diaghilev's*, viii–ix; N. Criss, "Istanbul," in *Der Große Exodus*, ed. K. Schlögel (Munich 1994), 62–63.

64. M. Esipova and L. Grisheleva articles in *100 let russkoi kul'tury v Iaponii*, ed. L. L. Gromkovskaia (New York, 1989), 258–279 and 328–348.

65. Robinson, *Last Impresario*.

66. J. Robbins, "Evolution of the Modern Ballet," *World Theatre* (Winter 1959–1960): 315–320; J. Acocella, "After Diaghilev," *Art in America* (March 1991): 37–41; Kisselgoff, "Balanchine," 380–395; Spencer, *World*, chap. 6; N. Reynolds, "In His Image: Diaghilev and Lincoln Kirstein," in *Ballets Russes and Its World*, ed. L. Garafola et al. (New Haven, 1999), 291–311.

67. Levy, "Russians," chap. 6.

68. N. Perloff, *Art and the Everyday* (Oxford, 1991), 1–2, 4 (quotation); R. Shattuck, *The Banquet Years* (New York, 1968), 157–158, 155n; Taruskin, *Stravinsky*, 1:776–777.

69. S. Collier et al., *Tango!* (London, 1995), 69–70, 183–184 (with quotation at 69); J.-C. Baker et al., *Josephine* (New York, 1993), 134; Levy, "Russians," chap. 4; M. and J. Stearns, *Jazz Dance* (New York, 1994), chap. 31.

70. For the section on vaudeville that follows, see Levy, "Russians"; L. Billman, *Film Choreographers and Dance Directors* (Jefferson, NC, 1997), 20–22, 28; Garafola, *Diaghilev's*, 216 ff.; MacDonald, *Diaghilev*, 133, 210; M. Morris, *Madame Valentino* (New York, 1991), 45.

71. Cited in Levy, "Russians," 130–131.

72. On Kosloff in Hollywood, see ibid., chap. 3; Morris, *Madame*; L. Garafola, "Tanz, Film, und die Ballets Russes," in Jeschke, *Spiegelungen*, 164–184.

73. G. Studlar, "Douglas Fairbanks: Thief of the Ballets Russes," in *Bodies of the Text*, ed. E. Goellner et al. (New Brunswick, NJ, 1995), 107–124.

74. In general, see V. Nemirovitch-Dantchenko, *My Life in the Russian Theatre* (New York, 1968); N. Gorchakov, *Theater in Soviet Russia* (New York, 1957); D. Magarshack, *Stanislavsky: A Life* (London, 1950); M. Slonim, *Russian Theater from the Empire to the Soviets* (New York, 1962); K. Rudnitsky, *Russian and Soviet Theater, 1905–1932* (New York, 1988).

75. Cited in Slonim, *Russian Theater*, 114.

76. Cited in ibid., 115.

77. Cited in P. Miles, ed., *Chekhov on the British Stage* (Cambridge, 1993), 39.

78. See L. Senelick and N. Nillson articles in *Chekhov's Great Plays*, ed. J.-P. Barricelli (New York, 1981).

79. S. le Fleming, "Chekhov and Merezhkovsky," in *Russian Writers on Russian Writers*, ed. F. Wizgell (Oxford, 1994), 34–35.

80. Cited in M. Esslin, "Modern Theatre, 1890–1920," in *Oxford Illustrated History of Theatre*, ed. J. Brown (Oxford, 1995), 356.

81. Quotations common in all writings by and about Stanislavsky and Nemirovich-Danchenko.

82. R. Hughes, "Tolstoy, Stanislavski, and the Art of Acting," *Journal of Aesthetics and Art Criticism* (Winter 1993): 39–48; also see J. Clayton, "Search for Belief: Tolstoj and the Theatrical Sign," *Balagan*, no. 2 (1995): 32–48.

83. K. Stanislavsky, *Stanislavski's Legacy* (New York, 1968), 8, 27.

84. Cited in Gorchakov, *Theater*, 47–48. And see I. Soloviova, "Do You Have Relatives Living Abroad?," in L. Senelick, *Wandering Stars: Russian Emigré Theatre, 1905–1940* (Iowa City, 1992), 75–76.

85. Nemirovitch-Dantchenko, *My Life*, 346–349; and see pt. 5, passim.

86. Cited in Gorchakov, *Theater*, 33 ff., 43.

87. Cited in ibid., 44. Slonim, *Russian Theater*, 198, incorrectly attributes this statement to Meyerhold as proof of his divergence from Stanislavsky.

88. On Meyerhold, in addition to the sources listed above, see E. Braun, ed., *Meyerhold on Theatre* (New York, 1969); M. Hoover, *Meyerhold* (Amherst, 1974); A. Law et al., *Meyerhold, Eisenstein, and Biomechanics* (Jefferson, NC, 1996); R. Leach, *Vsevolod Meyerhold* (Cambridge, 1989); K. Rudnitsky, *Meyerhold the Director* (Ann Arbor, 1981); R. Williams, *Artists in Revolution* (Bloomington, 1977), chap. 4.

89. Cited in Williams, *Artists*, 90.

90. Meyerhold quoting Tolstoy in Braun, *Meyerhold on Theatre*, 27.

91. Cited in R. Bartlett, *Wagner and Russia* (Cambridge, 1995), 99.

92. Meyerhold quoting Andrei Bely in Braun, *Meyerhold on Theatre*, 137.

93. Cited in Leach, *Vsevolod Meyerhold*, 136.

94. The term is from Slonim, *Russian Theater*, 213.

95. Cited in Law et al., *Meyerhold, Eisenstein*, 23.

96. Cited in Bartlett, *Wagner*, 99.

97. Cited in Gorchakov, *Theater*, 202.

98. Cited in Rudnitsky, *Russian*, 93–94.

99. G. Abensour, *Vsévolod Meyerhold* (Paris, 1998).

100. Cited in Rudnitsky, *Meyerhold*, 76. He made this statement during the 1905 revolution, but it reflects his later attitude as well.

101. See A. Bartoshevich entry in Senelick, *Wandering*, 102–115; Honigwachs, "Edwardian," chap. 6; Miles, *Chekhov*, chaps. 3, 5–7.

102. Cited in R. Williams, *Russia Imagined* (New York, 1997), 63.

103. Cited in Slonim, *Russian Theater*, 225.

104. L. Senelick, *Chekhov Theatre* (Cambridge, 1997), 154–162.

105. See E. Munk, ed., *Stanislavski and America* (Greenwich, CT, 1967); Senelick, *Wandering*; and H. Wish, "Getting along with the Romanovs," *South Atlantic Quarterly* (July 1949): 356–357.

106. See P. Egri, *Chekhov and O'Neill* (Budapest, 1986).

107. J. Logan, *Josh* (New York, 1976), 24 (quotation), 48 ff., 310–311, 318, 322, and introduction to Nemirovitch-Dantchenko, *My Life*, x.

108. Senelick, *Wandering*, 6.

109. On Nazimova, in addition to the main sources listed for this section, see Morris, *Madame*, 65 ff.

110. Williams, *Russia Imagined*, 61.

111. Robinson, *Last Impresario*, 95.

112. According to Joshua Logan: see his introduction to Nemirovitch-Dantchenko, *My Life*, xiii.

113. Ibid., vi.

114. Cited in S. Carnicke entry in Senelick, *Wandering*, 118.

115. C. Innes, "Theatre after Two World Wars," in Brown, *Oxford Illustrated History of Theatre*, 414; also see L. Strasberg, *A Dream of Passion* (Boston, 1987); R. Shteir, "Sisters, Samovars, and Second Acts," *American Theatre* (April 1998): 27–31.

116. E. Kazan, *A Life* (New York, 1988), 85.

117. M. Banham, ed., *Cambridge Guide to Theatre* (Cambridge, 1995), 5.

118. J. Logan, *Movie Stars, Real People, and Me* (New York, 1978), 55–56.

119. See H.-J. Gerigk, *Die Russen in Amerika* (Stuttgart, 1995), 305–399, 468–470.

120. See, e.g., R. Brustein, "The Heritage of MXAT," *New Republic*, August 11, 1997, 29–32.

121. For this influence, see: N. G. Anarina, "Dve vstrechi," in Gromkovskaia, *100 let*, 280–303; J. Rimer, ed., *Hidden Fire* (Stanford, 1995), pt. 2; and S. Jones, "The Lower Depths: Gorky, Stanislavsky, and Kurosawa," in *Explorations*, ed. M. Ueda (Lanham, MD, 1986), 174–208.

122. Cited in Senelick, *Chekhov Theatre*, 104.

123. L. Fiedler, *Max Reinhardt in Selbstzeugnissen* (Reinbek bei Hamburg, 1975), 77; N. N. Sibiriakov, *Mirovoe znachenie Stanislavskogo* (Moscow, 1988), pt. 2, chaps. 1–2.

124. J. Willett, *Theatre of the Weimar Republic* (New York, 1988), 79.

125. Esslin, "Modern," 379.

126. See J. Fuegi, "Russian Epic Theatre Experiments and the American Stage," *Minnesota Review*, n.s., no. 1 (1973): 102–112, which argues that the Meyerhold influence was established well before that of Brecht, who is usually thought to be the originator of this branch of theater.

127. The evidence for this comes from the following sources: K. Eaton, "Brecht's Contacts with the Theater of Meyerhold," *Comparative Drama* (Spring 1977): 3–21, and *Theater of Meyerhold and Brecht* (Westport, CT, 1985); J. Fuegi, *Brecht and Company* (New York, 1994), 125–126, 156, 226, and passim, and letter to author (December 30, 2000); Hoover, *Meyerhold*, 258 ff.; W. Koljasin, "Theater und Revolution," in *Deutschland und die russische Revolution*, ed. G. Koenen et al. (Munich, 1998), 703–732; Law et al., *Meyerhold, Eisenstein*, 14, 63; Leach, *Vsevolod Meyerhold*, chap. 9; Mierau, *Russen in Berlin*, 531–551.

128. C. Innes, *Erwin Piscator's Political Theatre* (Cambridge, 1972), 185–187.

129. Cited in Fuegi, *Brecht and Company*, 155.

Chapter 7. Abstract Art and the Regeneration of Mankind

1. V. Kandinsky, *Concerning the Spiritual in Art* (New York, 1977 [1914]), 9.

2. The influence of Western painting in Russia is well researched; the reverse direction barely figures in the historiography.

3. Kandinsky, *Concerning*, 2.

4. Ibid., 55.

5. R. Williams, *Artists in Revolution* (Bloomington, 1977), 10.

6. See, e.g., A. G. Kostenevich, *Pol' Sezann i russkii avangard nachala XX veka* (St. Petersburg, 1998).

7. M. Tuchman, "Hidden Meanings in Abstract Art," in Los Angeles County Museum of Art, *The Spiritual in Art* (Los Angeles, 1986), 37.

8. Kandinsky, *Complete Writings on Art*, ed. K. Lindsay et al. (Boston, 1982), 1:410.

9. On Kandinsky, see M. Dmitrieva-Einhorn, "Zwischen Futurismus und Bauhaus," in *Deutschland und die russische Revolution*, ed. G. Koenen et al. (Munich, 1998), 742–743; W. Everdell, *First Moderns* (Chicago, 1997), chap. 20; Y. Heibel, "They Danced on Volcanoes: Kandinsky's Breakthrough to Abstraction," *Art History* (September 1989): 342–361; R.-C. Washton Long, *Kandinsky* (Oxford, 1980); M. Roskill, *Klee, Kandinsky, and the Thought of Their Time* (Urbana, 1992); P. Weiss, *Kandinsky and Old Russia* (New Haven, 1995).

10. Kandinsky, *Complete*, 1:377, 397, 409; 2:745.

11. Ibid., 1:476.

12. Roskill, *Klee*, 33.

13. Cited in B. Altshuler, *Avant-Garde in Exhibition* (New York, 1994), 45.

14. See N. Stangos, ed., *Concepts of Modern Art*, 3d ed. (London, 1994), 43, 108; and Roskill, *Klee*, 49.

15. Cited in R. Williams, *Russia Imagined* (New York, 1997), 55.

16. See P. Weiss, *Kandinsky in Munich* (Princeton, 1979).

17. Kandinsky, *Complete*, 1:382.

18. Ibid., 379–380n.

19. Cited in Roskill, *Klee*, 34.

20. Kandinsky, *Complete*, 1:387; B. Smith, *Modernism's History* (New Haven, 1998), 73 ff.

21. Kandinsky, *Complete*, 1:98–99 (quotation), and *Concerning*, passim.

22. Kandinsky, *Complete*, 1:364.

23. Kandinsky, *Concerning*, 24, 29.

24. Cited in Smith, *Modernism's*, 73.

25. Kandinsky, *Complete*, 2:740.

26. Ibid., 2:586 and passim.

27. Cited in R.-C. Washton Long, "Expressionism, Abstraction, and the Search for Utopia in Germany," in Los Angeles County, *Spiritual in Art*, 214–215.

28. Cited in Dmitrieva-Einhorn, "Zwischen," 745.

29. Kandinsky, *Complete*, 2:512.

30. M. Droste, *Bauhaus 1919–1933* (Berlin, 1990), 234; F. Karl, *Modern and Modernism* (New York, 1985), 38–39.

31. My treatment of Malevich relies throughout on the special issue of *Soviet Union* 5, pt. 2 (1978), and Armand Hammer Museum of Art, *Kazimir Malevich* (Los Angeles, 1990).

32. K. Malevich, *Essays on Art*, ed. T. Andersen, vol. 1 (Copenhagen, 1968), 27, 44.

33. Cited in M. Dabrowski, "Malevich and Mondrian," in *Avant-Garde Frontier*, ed. G. Roman et al. (Gainesville, FL, 1992), 150.

34. Cited in G. Roman, "Tatlin's Tower," in Roman, *Avant-Garde Frontier*, 51.

35. Malevich, *Essays*, 122.

36. Cited in W. Simmons, "The Step Beyond," in *Soviet Union*, Malevich issue, 156.

37. Cited in Williams, *Artists*, 123.

38. Respective quotations from B. Groys, *Total Art of Stalinism* (Princeton, 1992), 15; and Malevich, *Essays*, 104–105.

39. Malevich, *Essays*, 169.

40. My discussion of Constructivism relies on: J. Bowlt, "Aleksandr Rodchenko as Photographer," in *Avant-Garde in Russia*, ed. S. Barron et al. (Los Angeles, 1980), 52–58; M. Dabrowski et al., *Aleksandr Rodchenko* (New York, 1998); H. Gassner, "Constructivists," in Guggenheim Museum, *Great Utopia* (New York, 1992), 298–319; Groys, *Total*, chap. 1; *Art into Life: Russian Constructivism* (New York, 1990); C. Lodder, *Russian Constructivism* (New Haven, 1983); S. Lissitzky-Küppers, ed., *El Lissitzky* (Dresden, 1976).

41. Ya. Chernikhov cited in J. Bowlt, ed., *Russian Art of the Avant-Garde*, (New York, 1976), 260–261.

42. Lissitzky cited in C. Lodder, "Transition to Constructivism," in Guggenheim Museum, *Great Utopia*, 272.

43. A. Gan cited in Bowlt, *Russian Art of the Avant-Garde*, 221.

44. A. Rodchenko, "Program of the Productivist Group," in *The Tradition of Constructivism*, ed. S. Bann (New York, 1974), 20.

45. Cited in Roman, "Tatlin's," 51–52.

46. Rodchenko, "Program," 19.

47. Quotation from title of a book in Rodchenko's library, cited in A. Lavrent'ev, "On Priorities and Patents," in Dabrowski et al., *Aleksandr Rodchenko*, 55.

48. The quotation is from the title of a book by R. Stites (Oxford, 1989).

49. Cited in Lissitzky-Küppers, *El Lissitzky*, 345.

50. A. Gastev cited in W. Rakitin, "Vorwärts zur Rekonstruktion der Welt," in *Konstruktivistische Internationale Schöpferische Gemeinschaft*, ed. B. Finkeldey et al. (Düsseldorf, 1992), 69.

51. Lissitzky cited in V. Margolin, *Struggle for Utopia* (Chicago, 1997), 36.

52. On the Dada-Kandinsky link, see H. Segel, *Turn-of-the-Century Cabaret* (New York, 1987), chap. 7.

53. Cited in ibid., 353.

54. Cited in ibid., 350.

55. Cited in ibid., 342.

56. Cited in H. Düchting, *Wassily Kandinsky* (Cologne, 1991), 82–83.

57. Cited in R. Radford, *Dali* (London, 1997), 327.

58. J. Miró, *Selected Writings and Interviews* (New York, 1992), 273.

59. See J.-L. Cohen, "L'Architecture en France," in *Paris-Moscou 1900–1930* (Paris, 1979), 272–285, and *Le Corbusier and the Mystique of the USSR* (Princeton, 1992); A. Ozenfant, *Journey through Life* (New York, 1939).

60. For Holland, see G. Imanse, "Van *Sturm* tot *Branding*," in *Berlijn-Amsterdam* (Amsterdam, 1982), 251–264; F. Gribling, "Tussen De Stijl en het constructi-

visme," in ibid., 269, 273; C. Blotkamp, *De Stijl: The Formative Years* (Cambridge, MA, 1986), 4–5, 8; S. Ex, "De Stijl und Deutschland," in Finkeldey et al., *Konstruktivistische*, 73, 78; R. Stommer, "Von der neuen Ästhetik zur materiellen Verwirklichung," in ibid., 140–142; P. Overy, *De Stijl* (London, 1991), 32, 36, 71, 89.

61. Cited in Ex, "De Stijl," 78.

62. On the Russian Revolution and art in Weimar Germany, see *Dada-Constructivism* (London, 1984); Finkeldey et al., *Konstruktivistische*; W. Herzogenrath, "Die holländische und russische Avantgarde in Deutschland," in *Malewitsch-Mondrian und ihre Kreise* (Cologne, 1976), 40–50; A. Nakov, "Revelation of the Elementary," in *Dada and Constructivism* (Tokyo, 1988), 10 ff.; J. Weinstein, *End of Expressionism* (Chicago, 1990).

63. A point made by I. Golomstock, *Totalitarian Art* (New York, 1990), 13–14.

64. Cited in K. Hays, "Photomontage," in Roman, *Avant-Garde Frontier*, 170, 178.

65. Cited in T. Benson, *Raoul Hausmann and Berlin Dada* (Ann Arbor, 1987), 59–60.

66. Cohen, "L'Architecture"; M. Mudrak, "Environments of Propaganda," in Roman, *Avant-Garde Frontier*, 75 ff.; Rakitin, "Vorwärts," 69.

67. D. Pike, *German Writers in Soviet Exile* (Chapel Hill, 1982), chap. 2, with quotation at 23; also see E. Lersch, "Hungerhilfe und Osteuropakunde," in Koenen, *Deutschland und die russische Revolution*, 616–645.

68. Both cited in Dmitrieva-Einhorn, "Zwischen," 736–737.

69. Respective quotations from Smith, *Modernism's*, 174, and W. Grasskamp, "Historical Continuity of Disjunctions," in *Divided Heritage*, ed. I. Rogoff (Cambridge, 1991), 17.

70. The Bauhaus discussion builds on Dmitrieva-Einhorn, "Zwischen"; E. Forgacs, *Bauhaus Idea and Bauhaus Politics* (Budapest, 1995); Lodder, *Russian Constructivism*, chap. 8, and "VKhUTEMAS and the Bauhaus," in Roman, *Avant-Garde Frontier*, 196–240; C. Maier, "Between Taylorism and Technocracy," *Journal of Contemporary History*, no. 2 (1970): 27–61; Kh. Shedlikh, "Baukhauz i VKhUTEMAS," in *Vzaimosviazi russkogo i sovetskogo iskusstva i nemetskoi khudozhestvennoi kul'tury*, ed. Z. S. Pyshnovskaia (Moscow, 1980), 133–156. I contest the assertions of Stephen Bann, "Russian Constructivism and Its European Resonance," in *Art into Life*, 213–221; Lodder, *Russian Constructivism*, 229, and "VKhUTEMAS," 205–206; and Margolin, *Struggle*, who minimize the influence of Russian Constructivism on the Bauhaus. The fact that the Russian Constructivist aesthetic was somewhat reshaped in Germany is not an adequate reason for denying the initial impact, which was fundamental, even when German traditions and conditions are taken into account. Lodder, the leading scholar of the movement in Russia, overlooks the evidence when she asserts that German artists mistook Russian Constructivism for a machine-age or individualistic art form and

had no understanding of its communist goals. Even if they were not communists, they saw themselves as adopting these art forms in order to forge a radically new society.

71. Respective quotations from J. Hahl-Koch, "Kandinsky's Role in the Russian Avant-Garde," in Barron, *Avant-Garde in Russia*, 84; C. Haxthausen, "Der Künstler ohne Gemeinschaft," in Bauhaus Archiv, *Kandinsky: Russische Zeit und Bauhausjahre* (Berlin, 1984), 75; and F. Mierau, ed., *Russen in Berlin, 1918–1933* (Weinheim, 1988), 185.

72. See Kandinsky, *Complete*, vol. 2, passim.

73. On the Hungarian connection, aside from works by Lodder and Margolin, see J. Allen, *Romance of Commerce and Culture* (Chicago, 1983), 56–57; E. Hight, *Moholy-Nagy: Photography and Film in Weimar Germany* (Wellesley, 1985); W. Kemp, *Foto-Essay* (Munich, 1978), 58; R. Kostelanetz, *Moholy-Nagy* (New York, 1970), xv, 8; K. Passuth, "Ungarische Künstler," in Finkeldey et al., *Konstruktivistische*, 235–240; Rakitin, "Vorwärts," 68–69, 72 n. 3. Margolin's misinterpretation of Russian Constructivism as purely functionalist/utilitarian rather than as a branch of Russian formalism prevents him from recognizing Moholy's debt to it. According to E. Hight, *Picturing Modernism* (Cambridge, MA, 1995), it is difficult to untangle the Moholy-Rodchenko relationship in photography, but she shows clearly that Moholy's aesthetics had roots in Russian Constructivism and Russian formalism.

74. Quotations from Dmitrieva-Einhorn, "Zwischen," 752.

75. Stommer, "Von der neuen," 145–146; J.-L. Cohen, *Mies van der Rohe* (London, 1996), 29, 32–36, with quotation at 34.

76. Quoting J. Willett, *Art and Politics in the Weimar Period* (New York, 1978), 133.

77. Cited in W. Curtis, "Berthold Lubetkin and Tecton," *Architectural Association Quarterly*, no. 3 (1976): 35.

78. Cited in H. Chipp, ed., *Theories of Modern Art* (Berkeley, 1968), 316.

79. See Smith, *Modernism's*, 174 ff. and passim.

80. On Germany, see I. White, "Berlin 1870–1945," in Rogoff, *Divided Heritage*, 240–247, and "National Socialism and Modernism," in *Art and Power*, ed. D. Ades et al. (London, 1995), 262–263.

81. G. Mosse, *Masses and Man* (New York, 1980), 233.

82. Quotations cited in Forgacs, *Bauhaus*, 39.

83. W. Laqueur, *Weimar* (New York, 1974), 179.

84. B. Buchloh, "From Faktura to Factography," *October* (Fall 1984): 112.

85. On Italy, see V. Barnett, "Russian Presence in the Venice Biennale," in Guggenheim Museum, *Great Utopia*, 466–473; G. Berghaus, *Futurism and Politics* (Providence, 1996), 180 ff.; C. De Michelis, "Russia e Italia," in *Storia della civiltà letteraria russa*, vol. 2 (Turin, 1997), 702–703; A. Nakov, "Last Exhibition,"

in *First Russian Show* (London, 1983), 8, 11, 46; M. Stone, *Patron State* (Princeton, 1998).

86. See the catalog *Ausstellung der faschistichen Revolution* (Rome, 1933); Buchloh, "From Faktura," 112; and T. Schumacher, *Surface and Symbol: Giuseppe Terragni* (New York, 1991), 162.

87. On the International Style in America, I have used the following: P. Blake, *No Place Like Utopia* (New York, 1993); Smith, *Modernism's*, 191 ff., 216 ff., and passim; T. Smith, *Making the Modern* (Chicago, 1993); and C. Wiseman, *Shaping a Nation* (New York, 1998).

88. Cited in Smith, *Making*, 399–400.

89. See V. Marquardt, "Louis Lozowick," in Roman, *Avant-Garde Frontier*, 241–274; Z. Popkin, "Art: Three Aisles Over," *Outlook and Independent*, November 26, 1930, 502–503, 515–516; B. Zabel, "Louis Lozowick," *Archives of American Art Journal* 14 (1974): 17–21.

90. Cited in N. Harris, *Cultural Excursions* (Chicago, 1990), 359.

91. Cited in Willett, *Art and Politics*, 137.

92. Cited in Allen, *Romance*, 10–11.

93. J. Tschichold, *Die neue Typografie* (Berlin, 1987 [1928]), 11–14, 38–40, and passim. See also K. Broos, "From De Stijl to a New Typography," in *De Stijl*, ed. M. Friedman (Minneapolis, 1982), 163; "Commercial Art" in *Dictionary of Art*, ed. J. Turner (New York, 1996), 7:650–656; R. Marchand, *Advertising and the American Dream* (Berkeley, 1985), 140–153; Willett, *Art and Politics*, chaps. 14–15.

94. Cited in E. Doss, *Benton, Pollock, and the Politics of Modernism* (Chicago, 1991), 155.

95. Allen, *Romance*; G. Chanzit, *Herbert Bayer and Design in America* (Ann Arbor, 1987); L. Engelbrecht, "Association of Arts and Industries: Background and Origins of the Bauhaus Movement in Chicago," 2 vols. (Ph.D. diss., University of Chicago, 1973); Margolin, *Struggle*, 236–250; H. Wingler, *Bauhaus* (Cambridge, MA, 1978), 193, 196, 204, 207.

96. Quotation from J. B. Jackson, *Discovering the Vernacular Landscape* (New Haven, 1984), 119–123.

97. See, e.g., *Design in America: The Cranbrook Vision* (Detroit, 1983), 129–130, 133–143, 254–255, and passim; J. Lukach, *Hilla Rebay* (New York, 1983), 150, 154. And see Guggenheim Museum, *Great Utopia*, 470, 632, for exhibitions of Russian Suprematist porcelain abroad that helped to publicize the style independently of the Bauhaus.

98. T. Clark, "Jackson Pollock's Abstractionism," in *Reconstructing Modernism*, ed. S. Guilbaut (Cambridge, MA, 1990), 178, 239.

99. On the tie between Russian art and Abstract Expressionism, see G. Levin, "Miró, Kandinsky, and the Genesis of Abstract Expressionism," in *Abstract Expressionism: The Formative Years*, ed. R. Hobbs (New York, 1978), 27–40, and

"Wassily Kandinsky and the American Avant-Garde, 1912–1950" (Ph.D. diss., Rutgers University, 1976); D. Thistlewood, ed., *American Abstract Expressionism* (Liverpool, 1993); P. Wollen, *Raiding the Icebox* (Bloomington, 1993), chap. 3.

100. Cited in Levin, "Miró," 35–37.

101. Respective quotations from Levin, "Wassily Kandinsky," 35–36, and Altshuler, *Avant-Garde*, 69.

102. R. Crunden, *American Salons* (New York, 1993).

103. C. Eldredge, "Nature Symbolized," in Los Angeles County, *Spiritual in Art*, 113–129, with O'Keeffe quotation at 118; Tuchman, "Hidden," 42–43.

104. R. Herbert et al., eds., *Société Anonyme and the Dreier Bequest* (New Haven, 1984).

105. See Lukach, *Hilla Rebay*, with quotation at 96.

106. See M. Allentuck, introduction to *John Graham's System and Dialectics of Art* (Baltimore, 1971); W. Rushing, "Ritual and Myth," in Los Angeles County, *Spiritual in Art*, 276; S. Alexandrian, *Surrealist Art* (London, 1970), 175, 214 ff.; M. Sawin, *Surrealism in Exile* (Cambridge, MA, 1995), 95–96, 330–331, and passim.

107. J. Graham, *System and Dialectics of Art* (New York, 1937), 7, 15, 16, and passim.

108. The quotation is from Karl, *Modern*, 131.

109. Cited in J. de Hart Mathews, "Art and Politics in Cold War America," *American Historical Review* (October 1976): 772–773.

110. Cited in S. Guilbaut, *How New York Stole the Idea of Modern Art* (Chicago, 1983), 4.

111. See B. Buchloh, "Cold War Constructivism," in Guilbaut, *Reconstructing*, 85–112; Guilbaut, *How*; Guilbaut, "Postwar Painting Games," in his *Reconstructing*, 35; F. Rubenfeld, *Clement Greenberg* (New York, 1997); Smith, *Modernism's*, 241 ff.

112. L. Trotsky, *Art and Revolution*, ed. P. Siegel (New York, 1992), 104–121 (with quotation at 119); Karl, *Modern*, 358; Sawin, *Surrealism*, 22–23.

113. Smith, *Modernism's*, 188 ff., 222.

114. See *Canadian-American Slavic Studies*, Burliuk issue, no. 1–2 (1986); Mizusawa Tsutomu, "Japanese Dada and Constructivism," in *Dada and Constructivism* (Tokyo, 1988), 25–33 (with last quotation at 32); Omuka Toshiharu, "To Make All of Myself Boil Over," in ibid., 19–24 (with first two quotations at 22, 24), and "Varvara Bubnova," in *Hidden Fire*, ed. J. Rimer (Stanford, 1995), 101–113; Smith, *Modernism's*, 326–329.

115. See J. Franco, *Modern Culture of Latin America* (Harmondsworth, 1970); E. Lucie-Smith, *Latin American Art of the Twentieth Century* (London, 1993), 14–15, 52, 54; P. Marnham, *Dreaming with His Eyes Open* (New York, 1998), 97; A. Reed, *Mexican Muralists* (New York, 1960); Smith, *Modernism's*, 210 ff.; E. Sullivan, *Latin American Art in the Twentieth Century* (London, 1996), 266–67, 288; Wollen, *Raiding*, 191 ff.

Chapter 8. The Dream of Communism

1. On the creation of the one-party system, see O. Figes, *A People's Tragedy: A History of the Russian Revolution* (New York, 1996), chaps. 11–16; J. Keep, *Russian Revolution* (New York, 1976); and R. Pipes, *Russian Revolution* (New York, 1990), chap. 12.

2. See R. Stites, *Russian Popular Culture* (Cambridge, 1992); and S. Kotkin, *Magnetic Mountain: Stalinism as a Civilization* (Berkeley, 1995).

3. B. Madison, *Social Welfare in the Soviet Union* (Stanford, 1968).

4. S. Kotkin in "1991 and the Russian Revolution," *Journal of Modern History* (June 1998): 425, comes close to doing so. S. Plaggenborg offers important insights into the nature of Soviet repression: see his "Stalinismus als Gewaltgeschichte," in *Stalinismus: Neue Forschungen und Konzepte*, ed. Plaggenborg (Berlin, 1998), 71–112.

5. Respective quotations from A. Sinyavsky, *Soviet Civilization* (New York, 1990), 83, and Molotov, in F. Chuev, ed., *Molotov Remembers* (Chicago, 1993), 317.

6. On this issue, see A. Gleason, *Totalitarianism* (New York, 1995); also G. Boffa, *The Stalin Phenomenon* (Ithaca, NY, 1982).

7. This point is made by K. Jowitt, *New World Disorder: The Leninist Extinction* (Berkeley, 1992), 74.

8. Cited in Figes, *People's*, 742–743, and Kotkin, *Magnetic Mountain*, ix.

9. See Kotkin, *Magnetic Mountain*, and Sinyavsky, *Soviet Civilization*, chap. 4.

10. Cited in L. Heller, "A World of Prettiness," *South Atlantic Quarterly* (Summer 1995): 691.

11. The quotation is from N. Jasny, *Soviet Industrialization, 1928–1952* (Chicago, 1961), 73.

12. Cited in J. Hughes, *Stalinism in a Russian Province* (London, 1996), 14–15, 71.

13. Cited in T. Judt, "The Believer," *New Republic*, February 14, 2000, 42.

14. Contrary to the viewpoint of M. Malia, *Russia under Western Eyes* (New York, 1999).

15. Cited in P. Foner, *Mark Twain: Social Critic* (New York, 1958), 118.

16. J. Hulse, *Revolutionists in London* (Oxford, 1970), 43–47; B. Naarden, *Socialist Europe and Revolutionary Russia* (Cambridge, 1992), 160–162.

17. D. Caute, *Communism and the French Intellectuals* (New York, 1964), pt. 2, chap. 1; F. Furet, *Le Passé d'une illusion* (Paris, 1995), 134; T. Zeldin, *France, 1848–1945: Anxiety and Hypocrisy* (Oxford, 1981), 365 ff.

18. W. Z. Foster, *From Bryan to Stalin* (n.p., 1937), 63.

19. Cited in C. Lasch, *American Liberals and the Russian Revolution* (New York, 1962), 134.

20. A. Lindemann, *Red Years* (Berkeley, 1974), 34 ff., 56–63.

21. Cited in G. Michon, *Franco-Russian Alliance* (New York, 1969), 84.

22. Cited in D. Caute, *Fellow Travellers* (New York, 1973), 22.

23. Cited in V. W. Brooks, *Confident Years: 1885–1915* (New York, 1952), 483.

24. Cited in G. Koenen, "Indien in Nebel," in *Deutschland und die russische Revolution*, ed. Koenen (Munich, 1998), 584.

25. "Frida Kahlo," in *Dictionary of Art*, ed. J. Turner (New York, 1996), 17:721.

26. A. Gide, *Journals*, vol. 3 (New York, 1949), 232, 276.

27. Cited in P. Hollander, *Political Pilgrims* (New York, 1981), 122.

28. S. and B. Webb, *Soviet Communism: A New Civilisation?*, 2 vols. (New York, 1936).

29. Cited in S. Morcos, *Juliette Adam* (Dar al-Maaref, Libya, 1962), 43.

30. A. Suarès, *Tolstoi vivant* (Paris, 1911), 23.

31. V. Tissot, *Russes et allemands* (Paris, 1884), xiv.

32. Cited in N. Ia. Berkovskii, *O mirovom znachenii russkoi literatury* (Leningrad, 1975), 32.

33. A. Gide, *Dostoevsky* (London, 1949), 90.

34. On Rolland's wife, see S. Koch, *Double Lives* (New York, 1994), 21–22.

35. Cited in Koenen, "Indien in Nebel," 563–564.

36. Cited in Caute, *Fellow Travellers*, 78.

37. Cited in ibid., 5.

38. R. Rolland and M. Gandhi, *Correspondence* (New Delhi, 1976), 244.

39. See A. Gide, *Retour de l'U.R.S.S.* (Paris, 1936); P. Travers, *Moscow Excursion* (New York, 1934); and Caute, *Fellow Travellers*, 19.

40. See Caute, *Fellow Travellers*, and Hollander, *Political Pilgrims*, passim.

41. Cited in Caute, *Fellow Travellers*, 241.

42. The following account is based primarily on J. Diggins, *Rise and Fall of the American Left* (New York, 1992); Lasch, *American Liberals*; N. McInnes, "Labour Movement," in *Impact of the Russian Revolution, 1917–1967* (London, 1967), 32–133; Naarden, *Socialist Europe*; and Zeldin, *France*, 365 ff.

43. Quotation from R. Crossman, ed., *The God That Failed* (Washington, DC, 1991 [1949]).

44. J. Arch Getty, "The Future Did Not Work," *Atlantic Monthly*, March 2000, 115–116. A more extended study making similar, and equally unsustainable, arguments is E. H. Carr's *Soviet Impact on the Western World* (New York, 1947). P. Johnson, *Modern Times* (New York, 1992), 259–260, does the same to misrepresent the New Deal from the right.

45. P. Flora et al., "Zur Entwicklung der westeuropäischen Wohlfahrtsstaaten," *Politische Vierteljahresschrift* 18 (1977): 767; S. Koven et al., "Womanly Duties: Maternalist Politics and the Origins of Welfare States," *American Historical Review* (October 1990): 1086 n. 41; G. Nash, *Life of Herbert Hoover*, vol. 3 (New York, 1996), 80; A. Ogus, "Landesbericht Grossbritanien," in *Ein Jahr-*

hundert Sozialversicherung, ed. P. Köhler et al. (Berlin, 1981), 344–345; D. Rodgers, *Atlantic Crossings: Social Politics in a Progressive Age* (Cambridge, MA, 1998), 295, 305.

46. Al Smith cited in G. Wolfskill et al., *All But the People: Franklin D. Roosevelt and His Critics* (London, 1969), 166.

47. Cited in A. Schlesinger, Jr., *Age of Roosevelt* (Boston, 1960), 3:191.

48. Rodgers, *Atlantic Crossings*, 380–381, 420, 424, 479–480, 502–508; B. Sternsher, *Rexford Tugwell and the New Deal* (New Brunswick, NJ, 1964), 9.

49. Respective quotations from J. M. Keynes, *End of Laissez-Faire* (London, 1927), 34–35, and Carr, *Soviet Impact*, 33.

50. M. Frances, "Economics and Ethics: The Nature of Labour's Socialism, 1945–1951," *Twentieth Century British History*, no. 2 (1995): 220–243; R. Millward et al., eds., *Political Economy of Nationalisation in Britain, 1920–1950* (Cambridge, 1995), chaps. 2 and 14; P. Wiles, "Power without Influence," in *Impact of the Russian Revolution*, 206–273.

51. Cited in J. Weeks, *Sex, Politics, and Society* (London, 1981), 184.

52. Cited in M. Kazin, "Agony and Romance of the American Left," *American Historical Review* (December 1995): 1506.

53. W. Cooper, *Claude McKay* (Baton Rouge, 1987); T. Kornweibel, Jr., *"Seeing Red": Federal Campaigns against Black Militancy, 1919–1925* (Bloomington, 1998).

54. On France, see M. Miller, *Shanghai on the Métro: Spies, Intrigues, and the French between the Wars* (Berkeley, 1994), passim.

55. Cited in D. Fogelsong, *America's Secret War against Bolshevism* (Chapel Hill, 1995), 24–25.

56. Cited in J. Gaddis, *We Now Know: Rethinking Cold War History* (Oxford, 1997), 14.

57. Cited in E. May, *"Lessons" of the Past: The Use and Misuse of History in American Foreign Policy* (New York, 1973), 33.

58. Naarden, *Socialist Europe*, chap. 1; M. Poe, *A People Born to Slavery: Russia in Early Modern Ethnography* (Ithaca, NY, 2000).

59. Lasch, *American Liberals*, 12–29.

60. On France, see Miller, *Shanghai on the Métro*; on the United States, see S. Coben, "A Study in Nativism: The American Red Scare of 1919–20," *Political Science Quarterly*, no. 1 (1964): 52–75, and references in n. 74 below.

61. Cited in Fogelsong, *America's Secret War*, 24–25.

62. Cited by Kornweibel, *"Seeing Red"*.

63. Cited in P. Marshall, *Demanding the Impossible* (London, 1992), ix.

64. Cited in H. Shpayer-Makov, "Reception of Peter Kropotkin in Britain," *Albion* (Fall 1987): 373.

65. Cited in J.-J. Becker et al., *Histoire de l'anti-communisme* (Paris, 1987), 23–24.

66. A. Mitchell Palmer, "Case against the Reds," *Forum* (February 1920): 173–174, 180.

67. See, for example, S. Ross, *Working-Class Hollywood* (Princeton, 1998), passim.

68. Cited in R. Arnot, *Impact of the Russian Revolution in Britain* (London, 1967), 40.

69. Marquis de Custine, *Empire of the Czar* (New York, 1989), 155.

70. Naarden, *Socialist Europe*, 33–34.

71. Cited in T. Dennett, *Roosevelt and the Russo-Japanese War* (New York, 1925), 152; and see 119–120, 143–144.

72. Cited in Arnot, *Impact*, 103.

73. Cited in Miller, *Shanghai on the Métro*, 267 ff.

74. Cited respectively in R. Powers, *Not without Honor* (New York, 1995), 29, and J. Haynes, *Red Scare or Red Menace?* (Chicago, 1996), 45. Along with M. Heale, *American Anticommunism* (Baltimore, 1990), and S. Whitfield, *Culture of the Cold War*, 2d ed. (Baltimore, 1996), these are the major works on the history of U.S. anticommunism.

75. Cited in G. Salvemini, *Fascist Dictatorship in Italy* (New York, 1967 [1927]), 9.

76. Chamberlain and Daladier cited in J. Fest, *Hitler* (New York, 1975), 560–561.

77. Cited in E. Weber, "France," in *European Right*, ed. H. Rogger and E. Weber (Berkeley, 1966), 111.

Chapter 9. Communism and the New Forms of Dictatorship

1. For their differences, see R. Bessel, ed., *Fascist Italy and Nazi Germany* (Cambridge, 1996), and I. Kershaw and M. Lewin, eds., *Stalinism and Nazism* (Cambridge, 1997).

2. Cited in R. De Felice, *Mussolini il fascista* (Turin, 1968), 2:283 n. 2.

3. Italian communist leader Palmiro Togliatti cited in J. Schnapp, "Fascinating Fascism," *Journal of Contemporary History* (April 1996), 238.

4. Both W. Laqueur, "Russia under the Bolshevik Regime," *New Republic*, April 11, 1994, 35–40, and C. Maier, *Unmasterable Past: History, Holocaust, and German National Identity* (Cambridge, MA, 1988), passim, incorrectly argue that there were no such active borrowings. A. Bullock, *Hitler and Stalin* (New York, 1992), passim, and R. Pipes, *Russia under the Bolshevik Regime* (New York, 1993), chap. 5, suggest the lessons Hitler may have learned from Stalin, but the evidence they cite is limited. Two recent books comparing the Nazi and Soviet systems do not discuss the issue at all: D. Dahlmann and G. Hirschfeld, eds., *Lager, Zwangsarbeit, Vertreibung und Deportation: Dimensionen der Massenverbrechen in der Sowjetunion und in Deutschland, 1933 bis 1945* (Essen, 1999),

and Kershaw and Lewin, *Stalinism and Nazism*. Nor do any of the articles in
E. Jesse, ed., *Totalitarismus im 20. Jarhundert: Eine Bilanz der internationalen
Forschung* (Bonn, 1996), which includes Fascist Italy in the comparisons. In the
case of E. Nolte, *Der europäische Bürgerkrieg, 1917–1945: Nationalsozialismus
und Bolschewismus* (Frankfurt am Main, 1987), affinity between Nazi and Soviet
institutions and policies is often confused with direct imitation, and the differing
characteristics of the two systems are not made clear.

5. First quotation cited in G. Megaro, *Mussolini in the Making* (New York,
1967 [1938]), 102; second by fascist historian G. Volpe in A. Gregor, *Fascist Persuasion in Radical Politics* (Princeton, 1974), 16.

6. D. Mack Smith, *Mussolini* (New York, 1982), 41, 96.

7. Megaro, *Mussolini*, 102, 220–222.

8. Cited in E. Ludwig, *Talks with Mussolini* (Boston, 1933), 152.

9. B. Mussolini, *Opera omnia*, vol. 15 (Florence, 1954), 91–94, 123–125, 212
(quotation).

10. Ibid., vol. 11 (Florence, 1953), 231.

11. Cited in Gregor, *Fascist Persuasion*, 17.

12. Cited in Ludwig, *Talks*, 90.

13. Mussolini, *Opera omnia*, 15:92.

14. Cited in D. Settembrini, "Mussolini and the Legacy of Revolutionary Socialism," in *International Fascism*, ed. G. Mosse (London, 1979), 93–94.

15. Cited in Ludwig, *Talks*, 123, 150–151.

16. Cited in A. Lyttelton, *Seizure of Power: Fascism in Italy, 1919–1929*
(Princeton, 1987), 370.

17. Mack Smith, *Mussolini*, 178.

18. Cited in Ludwig, *Talks*, 212–213. See also I. Golomstock, *Totalitarian Art*
(New York, 1990), 52, 54; Mack Smith, *Mussolini*, 135; M. Stone, *Patron State*
(Princeton, 1998), 105.

19. M. Canali, *Il delitto Matteotti* (Bologna, 1997), chap. 8; G. Salvemini, *La
Terreur fasciste, 1922–1926* (Paris, 1930), 197 ff., 277–285.

20. L. Dupeux, *National bolchevisme*, 2 vols. (Paris, 1979).

21. Cited in R. Waite, *Vanguard of Nazism: The Free Corps Movement in Postwar Germany* (New York, 1952), 272.

22. I. Kershaw, *Hitler, 1889–1936* (New York, 1999), 202–203, 218.

23. A. Hitler, *Sämtliche Aufzeichnungen, 1905–1924*, ed. E. Jäckel (Stuttgart,
1980), 840–841. Speech of February 1923.

24. Cited in Waite, *Vanguard*, 273–274; and see P. Merkl, *Political Violence
under the Swastika* (Princeton, 1975), 586.

25. Kershaw, *Hitler, 1889–1936*, xxvii.

26. A. Hitler, *Reden, Schriften, Anordnungen. Februar 1925 bis Januar 1933*,
ed. B. Dusik (Munich, 1992), 228. Speech of April 2, 1927.

27. *Völkischer Beobachter*, April 8/9, 1923, p. 1.

28. Cited in D. C. Large, *Where Ghosts Walked: Munich's Road to the Third Reich* (New York, 1997), 203–204.

29. Hitler, *Sämtliche Aufzeichnungen*, 975. Interview of August 1923.

30. H. Rollin, *L'Apocalypse de notre temps* (Paris, 1939), 158.

31. A. Hitler, *Mein Kampf*, trans. R. Manheim (Boston, 1943), 475.

32. Ibid., 533, 534.

33. Hitler, *Sämtliche Aufzeichnungen*, 990. Speech of September 1923.

34. A. Hitler, *Im Kampf um die Macht: Hitlers Rede vor dem Hamburger Nationalklub*, ed. W. Jochmann (Frankfurt am Main, 1960), 103. Speech of February 1926.

35. B. Smith, *Heinrich Himmler* (Stanford, 1971), 92–93, 108, 139, 165–166; K. Heiden, *Der Fuehrer* (Boston, 1944), 308.

36. S. Aronson, *Beginnings of the Gestapo System* (Jerusalem, 1969), 26; W. Hoettl, *Secret Front* (New York, 1954), 58.

37. A. Hitler, *Monologe im Führerhauptquartier, 1941–1944*, ed. W. Jochmann (Hamburg, 1980), 366.

38. *Hitler's Secret Conversations, 1941–1944*, trans. N. Cameron et al. (New York, 1972 [1953]), 476, 534.

39. G. Reitlinger, *SS: Alibi of a Nation* (New York, 1968), 256.

40. Cited in K. Bracher, *German Dictatorship* (New York, 1970), 459.

41. Deutsches Historisches Museum, Berlin, online biography; R. Diels, *Lucifer ante portas: Es spricht der erste Chef des Gestapos* (Stuttgart, 1950), 295; R. Wistrich, *Who's Who in Nazi Germany* (New York, 1982), 80–81.

42. On which see A. Barkai, *Das Wirtschaftssystem des Nationalsozialismus* (Cologne, 1977); and R. Zitelmann, *Hitler: Selbstverständnis eines Revolutionärs* (Hamburg, 1987), chaps. 4–5.

43. A. Zoller, *Hitler Privat* (Düsseldorf, 1949), 158–159.

44. Cited in Zitelmann, *Hitler*, 233–234.

45. Hitler, *Monologe im Führerhauptquartier*, 366.

46. A. Hitler, "Denkschrift zum Vierjahresplan," in *Nazism: 1919–1945: A Documentary Reader*, ed. J. Noakes et al., vol. 2 (Exeter, 1994), 286. For Göring, see Bullock, *Hitler and Stalin*, 446.

47. Cited in E. Calic, ed., *Secret Conversations with Hitler* (New York, 1971), 32–33.

48. Cited in V. Reimann, *Goebbels* (Garden City, 1976), 46; and see 48 ff.

49. Cited in E. Leiser, *Nazi Cinema* (New York, 1975), 10.

50. As argued by P. Johnson, *Modern Times* (New York, 1992), 305.

51. See Nolte's articles in J. Knowlton, et al., trans., *Forever in the Shadow of Hitler? Original Documents of the Historikerstreit* (Atlantic Highlands, NJ, 1993), and Nolte, *Der europäische Bürgerkrieg*.

52. See, for instance, M. Heikal, *The Sphinx and the Commissar: The Rise and Fall of Soviet Influence in the Middle East* (New York, 1978), 55.

53. The essential work on the subject is A. Rubinstein, *Moscow's Third World Strategy* (Princeton, 1990).

54. Cited in P. Sinha, *Indian National Liberation Movement and Russia (1905–1917)* (New Delhi, 1975), 173.

55. I. Spector, *First Russian Revolution: Its Impact on Asia* (Englewood Cliffs, NJ, 1962); A. Banani, *Modernization of Iran* (Stanford, 1961), passim.

56. See the succinct analysis in L. Kolakowski, *Main Currents of Marxism*, vol. 2 (Oxford, 1978), 491–497.

57. Quotations from "Manifesto to the Peoples of the East," in *To See the Dawn: Baku 1920—First Congress of the Peoples of the East*, ed. J. Riddell (New York, 1993), 231–232.

58. A. Smith, *State and Nation in the Third World* (New York, 1983), 17 ff.

59. On this point, see A. Blakely, *Russia and the Negro* (Washington, DC, 1986), 135 ff.

60. Cited in A. Zolberg, "Dakar Colloquium," in *African Socialism*, ed. W. Friedland et al. (Stanford, 1964), 120.

61. Cited in P. Seale, *Struggle for Syria: A Study of Post-War Arab Politics, 1945–1958* (New Haven, 1987), 220.

62. F. Georgeon, *Aux origines du nationalisme turc* (Paris, 1980).

63. Cited in N. Criss, "Atatüruk's Movement at Its Start," *Atatürk Arastirma Merkezi dergisi* 6 (March 17, 1990): 361.

64. The section on Turkey is based on A. Kazancigil et al., eds., *Atatürk* (Hamden, CT, 1981), 95–96, 111, 117–118; R. Lowenthal, "Model of the Totalitarian State," in *Impact of the Russian Revolution, 1917–1967* (London, 1967), 292–300; A. Mango, *Atatürk* (London, 1999), 477 ff.; I. Spector, *Soviet Union and the Muslim World* (Seattle, 1959), 63–83; S. Vaner, "Turkey," in *Third World and the Soviet Union*, ed. Z. Laïdi (London, 1988), 57–75.

65. S. Hay, *Asian Ideas of East and West* (Cambridge, MA, 1970), 238. On the Chinese reception of Russian political ideas in general, see G. Hoston, *State, Identity, and the National Question in China and Japan* (Princeton, 1994).

66. Sun cited in R. A. Mirovitskaia, *Sovetskii soiuz v strategii Gomin'dana (20–30-e gody)* (Moscow, 1990), 48, 50. Also see R. North, *Moscow and Chinese Communists*, 2d ed. (Stanford, 1963), chap. 5.

67. Hua-yu Li, "Political Stalinization of China," *Journal of Cold War Studies* (Spring 2001): 28–47; M. Meisner, *Li Ta-chao and the Origins of Chinese Marxism* (Cambridge, MA, 1967); S. Schram, *Political Thought of Mao Tse-tung* (New York, 1969); B. Schwartz, *Chinese Communism and the Rise of Mao* (Cambridge, MA, 1951).

68. R. Faligot et al., *Chinese Secret Service* (New York, 1989).

69. D. Kaple, *Dream of a Red Factory* (New York, 1994).

70. Xudong Zhang, "Power of Rewriting: Postrevolutionary Discourse on Chinese Socialist Realism," *South Atlantic Quarterly* (Summer 1995): 915–946, and

"Memory of the Future: Soviet Culture and Its Chinese Reinvention" (paper presented at AAASS national convention, Washington, DC, October 27, 1995).

71. See W. Duiker, *Ho Chi Minh* (New York, 2000).

72. W. Laqueur, *Guerilla* (Boston, 1976), 176–177.

73. Cited in Hue-Tam Ho Tai, *Radicalism and the Origins of the Vietnamese Revolution* (Cambridge, MA, 1992), 225.

74. D. Nelkin, "Socialist Sources of Pan-African Ideology," in Friedland, *African Socialism*, 63–71; Blakely, *Russia and the Negro*, chap. 9.

75. Cited in Seale, *Struggle*, 101–102; and see Laïdi, *Third World*, 4.

76. My interpretation of the Russian model in Third World politics relies most heavily on the following: K. Jowitt, *New World Disorder: The Leninist Extinction* (Berkeley, 1992); Laïdi, *Third World*; Lowenthal, "Model"; S. MacFarlane, *Superpower Rivalry and Third World Radicalism* (Baltimore, 1985); J. Migdal, *Strong Societies and Weak States* (Princeton, 1988); C. Rosberg et al., eds., *Socialism in Sub-Saharan Africa* (Berkeley, 1979); R. Scalapino, *Politics of Development: Perspectives on Twentieth-Century Asia* (Berkeley, 1979); and Smith, *State and Nation*.

77. This dimension of postcolonial Third World politics is overlooked in C. Young, *The African Colonial State in Comparative Perspective* (New Haven, 1994).

78. Gregor, *Fascist Persuasion*, 137, 297.

79. T. Szulc, *Twilight of the Tyrants* (New York, 1959).

80. Heikal, *Sphinx*, 281.

81. Rosberg, *Socialism in Sub-Saharan Africa*, 198 ff.

82. H. Jackson, *FLN in Algeria* (Westport, 1977); W. Laqueur, *Communism and Nationalism in the Middle East*, 2d ed. (New York, 1957), 350–351.

83. W. Gutteridge, *Military Regimes in Africa* (London, 1975), 145 ff.; R. Jackson et al., *Personal Rule in Black Africa* (Berkeley, 1982), 8, 170 ff., 213 ff., 271.

84. P. Wiles, "Power without Influence," in *Impact of the Russian Revolution*, 246.

85. On Syria, see J. Devlin, *Syria* (Boulder, 1983), 46, 114; E. Picard, "USSR as Seen by the Ba'thists of Iraq and Syria," in Laïdi, *Third World*, 39–56; P. Seale, *Asad* (Berkeley, 1988) and *Struggle*, 148–150.

86. On Iraq, see M. Farouk-Sluglett et al., *Iraq since 1958* (London, 1990); Samir al-Khalil, *Republic of Fear: Inside Saddam's Iraq* (New York, 1989); Picard, "USSR."

87. Cited in M. Roberts, "A Socialist Looks at African Socialism," in Friedland, *African Socialism*, 92.

88. On economics, see P. Wiles, ed., *New Communist Third World* (New York, 1982), as well as other sources cited in n. 76 above.

89. T. Aluko, *Chief the Honourable Minister* (London, 1970), 41.

90. Cited in K. Grundy, "Mali: The Prospects of Planned Socialism," in Friedland, *African Socialism*, 176.

91. For these and other examples, see V. Lasky, *The Ugly Russian* (New York, 1965), passim.

92. J. Nehru, *Toward Freedom* (New York, 1941), 128.

93. B. Nayar, "Business Attitudes toward Economic Planning in India," *Asian Survey* (September 1971): 852, 864; S. Rudolph, "The Writ from Delhi," *Asian Survey* (October 1971): 962–963, 966–967; L. Veit, *India's Second Revolution: The Dimensions of Development* (New York, 1976), 21 ff.

94. R. Tignor, *Capitalism and Nationalism at the End of Empire: State and Business in Decolonizing Egypt, Nigeria, and Kenya* (Princeton, 1998), 180 ff.

95. Cited in A. Elon, "One Foot on the Moon," *New York Review of Books*, April 6, 1995, 34.

96. The following discussion is based largely on Rubinstein, *Moscow's Third World Strategy.*

INDEX